Studies
Economic Reform
and Social Justice

Two Views of Social Justice:
A Catholic/Georgist Dialogue

Edited by
Kenneth R. Lord

WILEY-
BLACKWELL

Studies in Economic Reform and Social Justice

Two Views of Social Justice: A Catholic/Georgist Dialogue

Edited by
Kenneth R. Lord

Registered Office
John Wiley & Sons Ltd, The Atrium, Southern Gate, Chichester, West Sussex, PO19 8SQ, United
Kingdom

Editorial Offices
350 Main Street, Malden, MA 02148-5020, USA
9600 Garsington Road, Oxford, OX4 2DQ, UK
The Atrium, Southern Gate, Chichester, West Sussex, PO19 8SQ, UK

For details of our global editorial offices, for customer services, and for information about how to
apply for permission to reuse the copyright material in this book, please see our website at www.
wiley.com/wiley-blackwell.

Library of Congress Cataloging-in-Publication Data

Two views of social justice : a Catholic/Georgist dialogue / edited by Kenneth R. Lord.
   p. cm.—(Studies in economic reform and social justice)
   "The American journal of economics and sociology, October 2012 Issue."
   ISBN 978-1-118-45004-8 (pbk. edition)—ISBN 978-1-118-45005-5 (casebound edition)
1. Social justice—Religious aspects—Catholic Church.   2. Social justice—Philosophy.
3. George, Henry, 1839–1897   I. Lord, Kenneth R.
   BX1795.S62T85 2012
   261.8—dc23

                                                                        2012030194

A catalogue record for this book is available from the Library of Congress.

Set in 10 on 13pt Garamond Light by Toppan Best-set Premedia Limited
Printed in Singapore by Markono Print Media Pte Ltd.

01—2012

Contents

Two Views of Social Justice: A Catholic/Georgist Dialogue

By Kenneth R. Lord*

ABSTRACT. Sixteen scholars have come together in this issue to examine eight social-justice themes from the perspectives of Catholic Social Thought and the philosophy of Henry George. The themes they address are natural law, human nature, the nature of work, the nineteenth-century papal encyclical *Rerum novarum*, causes of war, immigration, development, and wealth, and neighborhood revitalization. While they sometimes wrangle with each other, their common aspiration is the same as their nineteenth-century predecessors: to find solutions to the human suffering caused by injustice.

A Meeting of the Minds

When a Catholic archbishop from New York and a subordinate (although at the time it appears he considered him insubordinate) priest who was championing Henry George's platform for social and economic reform sparred publicly in the 1880s over their different views of the path to social justice, it is doubtful either would have envisioned a scholarly exchange of views on that topic under the joint auspices of a Jesuit university and two Georgist organizations some 120 years later. On July 22 to 27, 2007, 16 experts assembled at the University of Scranton to engage in a dialogue on the contributions of Catholic Social Thought (CST) and of Henry George to eight central tenets of social justice and economic reform that are as relevant in the twenty-first century as they were in the nineteenth. Their essays, subjected to lively response and rebuttal during that conference and rigorous review and updating thereafter, are the focus of this issue. The themes addressed are the following.

*Kenneth R. Lord is Associate Dean, Kania School of Management, and Professor, Management & Marketing Department, The University of Scranton. E-mail: kenneth. lord@scranton.edu

American Journal of Economics and Sociology, Vol. 71, No. 4 (October, 2012).

Natural Law

"Natural law" is a formative element in the contributions that both CST and Georgist economic theory bring to the troublesome political, economic, and social issues of this century. In its earliest known formulation (Aristotle's *Nichmachean Ethics*), natural-law theory pre-dates both the nineteenth-century writings of Henry George and the sixteenth-century classical canon that has been a mainstay of CST on the topic (*Summa theologiae* by St. Thomas Aquinas).

Professor Anthony J. Lisska walks us through the views of "traditional Thomists," "analytic Thomists," and "post-modernists" (the old English major in me remains confused about how anything other than prophesy about the future can be "post-modern," but I will leave that and such modern—or should I say "post-modern"—marvels as "fat-free sour cream" for another day and audience) in the analysis and contemporary application of St. Thomas' exposition of natural-law concepts. He observes that "moral theory rests upon the social nature of human persons together with the obligation of each human agent to act in such a way that one's natural, human ends are fulfilled," that "[a]ny law, which, all things being equal, hinders the development of a natural disposition in a human person, is inherently unjust," and that "the common good—the commonweal—of a society must be part of the enactment of every positive law based upon the natural law." However, while "an unjust law is no law at all, . . . [Aquinas] argued that conditions must be severe and exhibit rampant injustice before an unjust law ought to be overthrown and overturned."

From the Georgist perspective, Professor Francis K. Peddle reminds us that in George's view "[t]he distinction between human law and natural law is the first necessity in the study of political economy." Expressing the view that "the enactment of human laws in contravention of the natural law may obstruct and temporally displace the latter but can never permanently abolish it," he goes on to suggest that to "do anything economically to restrain unjustifiably human well-being or flourishing" is to act "against the strictures of normative economics." Most tax laws, he writes, "are contrary to the normal inclinations of human nature" (indeed, they are "market destroying and generative of spurious competition") and "morally unjustifiable taxing statutes such as income taxes and consumption taxes must generally be abolished and replaced by statutes that rely on land value taxation for the operations of the state."

Even in the differences between Georgist and Catholic views of natural law, both Professors Peddle and Lisska find some parallels and bases for agreement. Mr. Peddle observes that "George's view of the hierarchical structure of political economy, in terms of all its natural laws emanating from a single fundamental principle, the first law of political economy, is . . . foundational in a way that is analogous with the Thomistic position that the natural law participates in the eternal law." Proessor Lisska points to the following, which by now should be apparent from the above quotes from the two authors, as a presumed point of agreement: "[P]olitical and legal theory—and I submit, economic theory—must be attentive to 'human needs, human purposes, and the human good.' Henry George's treatise, it appears, would adopt this position also."

Human Nature

Dr. Joseph Koterski and Professor James Dawsey articulated the Catholic and Georgist positions, respectively, on human nature. Both build on the premise that humans were created in God's image, making them His "supreme product" (Dawsey) and imbuing them with "a dignity that sets humanity apart from the rest of creatures" (Koterski).

The Catholic position points to a "real but immaterial power of the soul—the will and its ability to make free choices"; hence moral virtue stems from "a well-honed disposition to have the right feelings as well as a readiness to act rightly" (Koterski). Similarly, "George visualized people as artisans, helpers of God, in improving the world." While Mr. George embraced Christianity, the Catholic and Georgist positions part on the question of the centrality of Jesus Christ in the ultimate expression and purpose of human nature. "[I]t is absolutely vital to emphasize here the need for imitating the life of Christ, that is, for modeling not just individual actions but our whole lives on the pattern of Christ's life," Professor Koterski writes. For Mr. George, on the other hand, Professor Dawsey suggests that "[r]edemption was not tied to Christ's death on the cross, but to human work."

While the Catholic finds heavenly inspiration for moral earthly behavior ("Once one recognizes that one's life is not for storing up earthly goods but heavenly ones . . . one can more easily gain a freedom in the spirit for the proper use of one's earthly goods"— Koterski), "George placed humans center-stage in changing the world," charting a "path to greater economic fairness . . . through right thinking, education, and political action" (Dawsey). What constitutes the correct focus and application of the human will? Reviewing papal encyclicals and the Second Vatican Council, Professor Koterski focuses on such objectives as "the development of underdeveloped peoples," "the protection of the unborn from abortion, of defective children from infanticide, of immigrants from racists, and of the senile and the comatose from deprivation of care," "the improvement of wages and working conditions, so as to ensure the stability of family life and the conditions needed for genuine human development, such as access to education, civic friendships, and rest," and "peace and disarmament." For Henry George, the aim, as expressed by Professor Dawsey, was "social progress . . . expressed in people's opportunity for a better, more bounteous life."

On the critical question of property that permeates much Georgist discussion, CST has long advocated the right to its private possession tied to the purpose of providing "individuals with a kind of independence that enhances their ability to do their duties to their dependence and that extends their freedom" (Koterski), while for Henry George "[t]o take away a person's God-given right to access nature's bounty in equal share to all others, or to charge a premium for what was God-ordained access, was tantamount to stealing part of that person's labor" (Dawsey).

Nature of Work

"Work is a fundamental reality of human existence" and "is at the center of issues related to morality and economic life," according to Mr. Brendan Hennigan and Professor Daniel K. Finn, respectively. In speaking to the topic of the nature of work from the perspective of CST, Professor Finn argues that "the worker as a person is the ultimate purpose of work and should never be subordinated to the objective output of the work done" and thus labor should have priority over capital. While "[a]ll the able-bodied [are] obliged to work, . . . the property claims of the well-to-do [are] not to exclude the poor from what they need"; indeed, the latter are obliged to share their surplus "because everything anyone owns is a gift from God." Any wage that falls short of providing the worker and his or her family with reasonable comfort "is an injustice even if the worker gives consent." Thus there is an "obligation of the owners of capital to ensure that their capital serves work"—"a stark challenge to U.S. corporate law, where boards of directors are legally restricted to serve only the interests of stockholders"—and the state has the "responsibility to specify in law the rights and responsibilities of labor and management."

According to Mr. Hennigan, George's "call for justice was based on respect for common and individual property rights, the independent nature of the laborer, cooperation, and equality of association in society." Justice and liberty are possible, he suggests, only "through equitable access of labor to the earth's resources, or what George calls the natural opportunities of nature." Giving George's ideas a decidedly twenty-first-century orientation, Mr. Hennigan gives his emphasis on "land" a broad interpretation: "land, in the economic sense, includes all the visible and invisible spatial-temporal resources, forces, and natural opportunities of nature, such as land, water, forests, minerals, electro-magnetic forces, and the broadband spectrum" and puts forward the suggestion that the "concentration of capital" in any of these sectors "leads to monopolies and oppression." Because "[w]ages will never rise to a natural level as long as the owners of land or capital take a greater share of the increase in wealth than is due to them," George adopted "the provocative view that landowners are not entitled to any share of the economic rent, because it is created by the community and not a product of one's labor." He predicted that "giving labor better access to land would increase wages, self-reliance, and an entrepreneurial spirit," would induce "greater cooperation between labor, commerce, and industry," would reduce "actual or hidden poverty," and would lead to "the actualization of individual potential, and an end to a misconceived class struggle between different economic classes or groups."

Mr. Hennigan gives credit to CST for its emphasis on "the dignity of the human person and the rights of workers" but calls it to task for not offering "any technical solution[s] to the question of land ownership and taxation." He calls upon Catholics and Georgists to build upon their common views—that "involuntary poverty is an evil," that "workers should not be exploited," that both private and common property rights should be upheld, and that "the universal destination of goods must be guided by what is just and right not only for the individual, but also for the community"—to "embrace a cooperative approach and work towards a new understanding on the nature of work and the distribution of wealth."

Rerum novarum

If the prior topics give the impression that adherents to the Catholic and Georgist positions share broad swaths of approaches to social issues while respectfully offering some unique perspectives, the reader in search of controversy will find more pointed differences in the (for the most part) gentlemanly sparring between Professors J. Brian Benestad and Mason Gaffney as they dissect the first of the modern social encyclicals, Pope Leo XIII's *Rerum novarum*, issued in 1891. That the discussion should assume more the form of a debate on the merits of that document is hardly a surprise, given that that it was published not long after (and some view it at least in part as a response to) a nineteenth-century conflict between Archbishop Michael Corrigan and Fr. Edward McGlynn alluded to earlier. Viewpoints differ as to who was picking a fight with whom, but their intellectual descendants are still duking it out more than a century later.

Professor Benestad characterizes "George's expectations from restrictions on land ownership, coupled with the unlimited right to accumulate all other kinds of wealth" as "utopian," arguing with Pope Leo XIII that "social reform . . . requires conversion to virtue, many kinds of public and private initiatives, and the continuous exercise of prudence by leaders in the various sectors of society." Professor Gaffney, on the other hand, views the broader array of solutions advocated in CST as "expound[ing] glittering generalities but resist[ing] getting down to brass tacks." Mr. George's contention that there is an "unlimited right to acquire wealth by one's labor," according to Professor Benestad, is something that "the Catholic Church could never accept" because "the Lockean view that one has a property in one's person" is contradictory to the "Catholic teaching that the human being is created in God's image, redeemed by Jesus Christ, and is a temple of the Holy Spirit" and the unrestrained pursuit of wealth "flies in the face of the biblical and Catholic teaching on the proper attitude toward money." In rebuttal, Professor Gaffney attributes such presumed evils as payroll taxes to "the idea that we do not own ourselves" and argued that "neither organized religion nor patriotism can substitute for individual wisdom and judgment and responsibility"; rather, "we own ourselves, even to the point of choosing when to serve God or the state." Rather than seeing an improper attitude toward money in Georgist economics, he charges that it is in adherence to the views propounded in *Rerum novarum* that "[p]eccadillos of the poor are magnified into menaces to civilization" while "mortal sins of the rich are overlooked." Professor Benestad takes the position that "George compromised his Christian beliefs by espousing a political philosophy that promised a solution to political and social problems without prior conversion to virtue," while Professor Gaffney castigates the Catholic Church for "Crusades, persecutions, inquisitions, Falangists, suppression of science, male chauvinism, tortures, burnings, stonings, massacres of Anabaptists and Cathars and Albigensians and witches, superstition, worship of relics and graven images" and points to *Rerum novarum* specifically as the substance on which "most of the fascist dictators of Europe" were weaned.

Between rounds the two professors seem to remember that Pope Leo XIII and Henry George had some things in common after all. Professor Benestad pens the following: "George desires to facilitate the access to the possession of land by all through a tax on land; Leo desires to assure access to all goods of the earth by teaching that charity requires Christians to share their wealth and talent." He adds that Pope Leo and George shared "respect for the Christian faith, love of virtue, and hatred of vice" and acknowledges that "[e]ven if George's land policy would not overcome scarcity, and eliminate vice and produce love of God, it might indeed contribute to bringing about a more just society." Professor Gaffney holds out hope for "future cooperation between at least some Georgists and some Catholics." He credits both Georgists and Catholics with giving "great weight to natural law and rights," viewing "much modern economic literature as pretentious trash" and denying "that population control is the panacea for apparent resource scarcity." Finally, he expresses optimism "that with goodwill on both sides we may find pathways through, over, around or under [our differences] to work together towards our common goals."

Causes of War

From any view of social justice, the waging of war is troubling—something acknowledged by both Professor Margaret Monahan Hogan (Catholic) and Ms. Alanna Hartzok (Georgist). The questions of whether and under what circumstances it may be justified represent points of departure for the two authors, however.

Drawing upon just-war theory, Professor Hogan argues that the direct cause of war is the sin of injustice and "war understood as rectification of injustice perpetrated . . . must be designated as good." To qualify for that designation, war must be waged for a just cause, with right intention, with probable success, in conformity with international law, and only as a last resort—but when those conditions arise, and particularly when the victimization of the defenseless offers no other remedy, war is not only justified by required: "If we have compelling evidence that innocent people who are in no position to protect themselves will be grievously harmed unless coercive force is used to stop an aggressor, then the moral principle of love of neighbor calls us to the use of force." And even as just war is waged, those in societies thus engaged should pray and strive for peace and work for justice.

To Henry George, "seeking gratification at the expense of others meant the private appropriation of land rent, the monopolization of industry, the subjugation of workers, odious public debt, the domination of women by men, and tariffs and other policies that limited the freedom to trade"—all yielding a "concentration of wealth and power" that leads "to ever greater degrees of organization of lethal force," according to Ms. Hartzok. Thus war is a product of but not a solution to injustice. Mr. George, she suggests, "would assuredly take offense to the very idea of a 'just war' and view anyone putting forth such reasoning as a propagandist for the elite-ruled status quo." Fast forwarding to this century, she concludes that events surrounding 9/11 became an elitist tool "to stir up war fever, thus manipulating the masses into a war on Iraq for the purpose of geopolitical control of Eurasia as a key to the neocon elite power drive for full-spectrum dominance." Her solution? "[D]ismantle the military-industrial-financial complex" and "focus progressive movements on the land problem."

Immigration

Rev. William O. O'Neill, S. J. and Professor John Beck bring scholarly treatment to a topic that tends to make the news in sound bites of presidential-campaign rhetoric—immigration. Father O'Neill points out that the Catholic Church "recognizes persons' right to change nationality for social and economic as well as political reasons." From the CST perspective, a "moral entitlement to *equal* respect or consideration, in concert with the ethical ideal of the common good" not only requires that immigrants be accorded human dignity but "justifies *preferential* treatment for those whose basic rights are most imperiled." Thus "states are morally bound to respect and promote the basic human rights of both citizen and resident alien, especially the most vulnerable—and of these, in particular, women and children." This recognition of migrant rights imposes such duties as provision, protection, redress, and, where necessary, rescue. Such a "distinctively Christian virtue of solidarity" implies "not merely taking the victim's side . . . but taking the victim's side *as* our own" in "coming to the aid of wounded humanity."

Professor Beck explores the views of Henry George on the emigration patterns of his time (a topic on which Mr. George wrote some 40 articles) and uses his broader social and economic prescriptions to arrive at policy recommendations for the present. Raising "concerns about cultural differences similar to arguments of conservative opponents of immigration today," Mr. George opposed the Chinese immigration taking place in his time on the grounds that it "would reduce wage rates . . . because the Chinese immigrants would accept a lower standard of living." It seems that "[i]n his later writings and speeches, George took a much more favorable view of European immigration than he had of immigration from Asia." He "attributed the negative effects of immigration to the monopoly power of privately owned land and argued that if his reforms of free trade and land value taxation were implemented the negative effects of immigration would be eliminated." This would occur because "by alleviating the downward pressure on wages, land-value taxation would reduce the incentive to emigrate from one's home country to find better economic opportunities elsewhere." Mr. George's land-value tax need not eliminate immigration in order to help address its adverse economic consequences, modern Georgists argue, noting "the potential for land-value taxation to raise revenues that could be redistributed to those harmed by immigration."

Development and Wealth

While issues of development and wealth are addressed robustly in both the Catholic and Georgist traditions, and both reject certain premises of neoclassical economics, from the perspective of one who is admittedly neither Catholic nor Georgist they seem to occupy very different places in the two paradigms. At the risk of simplifying (and perhaps misrepresenting) centuries of moral and economic reasoning, I offer the premise (I believe consistent with the articles by Professor Charles M. A. Clark and Dr. H. William Batt) that CST views economic development as but one part of "the broader framework of authentic human development" and one that must be guided by principles of charity and justice, whereas the Georgist view is that the equitable management of development and wealth (and the vehicle espoused for its realization—land-value taxation) are at the root of the positions taken on all of the other social-justice themes examined in this series of articles.

Professor Clark observes that CST "is not hostile to economic development, or even the materialistic aspects of economic development, but instead places economic development in its proper perspective"—a perspective that assumes that "economic activity is also social, political, cultural, and spiritual activity," that "market values do not supersede all other values," and that "the inherent dignity of each and every person needs to be the foundational value in understanding and evaluating economic and social actions." Neoclassical economic theory, he charges, "produces both bad ethical analysis and bad economic theory." In CST, wealth is "understood as a gift from God"; while humans participate in its creation, they must do so (and manage its distribution and use) in ways that are consistent with God's laws. That includes the "need to share wealth, especially with the poor." He identifies three problems with "consumerism": "the pursuit of more and more goods . . . becomes a false god," "the problem of seeking to have instead of seeking to be," and "the greed of the affluent promotes scarcity for the poor." In concert with Georgists, Professor Clark argues that "[t]he distribution of wealth and incomes cannot be left entirely to the market. He advises that "people of the poor countries" must be "at the center of their development drama" and that "[d]evelopment aid that continues and encourages further dependency will not help the authentic development of the poor."

The eminent Georgist Dr. H. William Batt notes that "[t]he world today faces challenges that Henry George never anticipated: skyrocketing population growth, environmental despoliation, blighted and degraded cities of tens of millions, and huge disparities in national wealth." He writes of "the transformation of nature into a commodity" that has been relied on "to generate wealth and for speculative gain." In this context, a redefinition of development is needed, he suggests, starting with the recognition that "the earth is finite," that the free-market theory "does not guarantee greater and more equal distribution of wealth," and that the discipline of economics "does not rest on the same epistemological premises as the natural sciences." He then applies Georgist philosophy to call for a reconfiguration of "the world's political and economic systems." Land-value taxation, he argues, "can . . . be collected for public service and be adequate for its total support at no loss to the general economy," "restores what is otherwise an imbalance between the public and the private realms of society," and "neutralizes and even reverses the centrifugal forces of sprawl development that have plagued many cities in the world." With added efficiency stemming from the taxation of "land" defined more broadly to include "any element and dimension of nature that had market value as a resource" (such as the electromagnetic spectrum, airport takeoff and landing timeslots, and cap-and-trade "pollution rights"), Dr. Batt sees the Georgist prescription offering "economic justice and clarity of vision, restoration of and protection for the commons," and "protection for the environment of the earth in a deft and gentle way that is within the capacity of governments to implement."

Neighborhood Revitalization

America's urban neighborhoods are the focus of calls for and proposed approaches to revitalization by Professor John A. Kromkoswki and Mr. John David Kromkowski representing the Catholic view and Mr. Joshua Vincent the Georgist. The "neighborhood movement of the 1970s grew out of and was greatly influenced by priests and organizers from urban parishes," the Kromkowskis write, and they trace the influence of Monsignor Geno Baroni and other Catholic activists to the emergence and evolution of neighborhood organizations in the decades that followed. Effective neighborhood organizations, they note, have mobilized and advocated for improved security, sanitation, family support, human-capital development, income production, property maintenance, and health and transportation services. The neighborhood and civil rights movements, they observe, share a common history and arose to address some common problems; they "should not be decoupled" but "mere racialism must broaden to include ethnicity and true pluralism." They find it "particularly important that sufficient capital flows to lower-income neighborhoods to permit home ownership, housing rehabilitation, development of new enterprises, and support of existing ones"—something that "should be facilitated through a combination of regulations assuring fair treatment of all neighborhoods and selective tax measures offering extra incentives to invest in neighborhoods with the greatest needs."

Mr. Vincent assails the "pernicious insistence on social rather than economic externalities as the cause of neighborhood decline." Thus the decline in population, jobs, community meeting places, and lending capital are symptoms, not causes, of decline. What, then, is to blame? "Taxes on capital, savings, and labor force those things to leave, in a matter of rational economic decision-making." He then traces the course of Clairton, Pennsylvania from a once-prosperous steel town, to a community decimated by urban blight with poverty levels well above state and national averages, and through an experiment with land-value taxation that reduced the tax burden on owner-occupied homes and multi-family dwellings and tripled the revenues from vacant parcels of land to "pay for the education of Clairton's children, and liberate working and middle-class families from the bonds of labor and capital taxation" and generate a significant uptick in building.

While Kromkowski and Kromkowski argue that George's land-tax remedy "lacks the breadth and scope of the neighborhood movement," Mr. Vincent, based on the views summarized above, sees that the issue (singular) "IS one of economics and justice, inextricably wed." The Kromkowskis question the evidence for the efficacy of a land-tax solution, observing that the "general failure of Georgists to get land-value taxation implemented, much less see the fruits, cannot be ignored," and note that "Fr. McGlynn did not close down the St. Stephen's Anti-Poverty Society that he founded while waiting for the Single Tax to be enacted." So where, given his advocacy of "selective tax measures," would a Georgist land tax fit into this picture? "If the land tax can actually be part ensuring that process, then the data must be prepared to show it so that citizens can support it and elected officials can enact it." Mr. Vincent's case study of the Clairton experience is a fitting follow-up to that challenge.

Widening the Web

The scholarly treatises on the eight social-justice themes find common ground and some significant differences between Catholic and Georgist scholars. While they sometimes wrangle with each other, their common aspiration is the same as their nineteenth-century predecessors: to find solutions to the human suffering caused by injustice.

Rev. David Hollenbach, S. J. (2009: 22) wrote as follows of social justice:

> *Social justice* addresses the economic and political structures and institutions through which our life together is organized. These structures and institutions should themselves be characterized by solidarity, i.e., they

should be marked by a reciprocal inclusiveness rather than by exclusion and inequality. This inclusive solidarity is demanded by the equal dignity of every person as created in the image of God and as having a capacity for freedom and reason.

Placing that "inclusive solidarity" into a global twenty-first-century context, Father Hollenbach (2009: 22) observes that while "markets and trade can be engines of improved well-being . . . many people, perhaps the majority in the poor countries of sub-Saharan Africa, lack all access to these markets and so do not benefit from them." As a result, "[e]xclusion and marginalization appear again as the markers of the injustice that causes poverty."

Speaking to the relevance of Henry George's philosophy today, Edward Lawrence (2007: 14) expressed the following:

> It is important to keep in mind that the primary concern of Henry George was the vast disparity in wealth between rich and poor. The single tax was not an end in and of itself, but rather a means to the end of securing greater fairness and equity, and allowing people to benefit from the fruits of their own labor.

Lawrence and his fellow Georgists hold out the hope that land-value taxation (with the definition of "land" broadened to include "not only the surface of the solid earth, but the water and minerals below the surface, the air space above the earth, and the lakes, rivers, and oceans") can bring about a remedy for the injustice that motivated Henry George to propose it.

One journal issue could not pretend to contain the richness of thought that has emerged through more than a century of the Georgist movement and the millennia over which CST has evolved. I believe as well that the distinguished scholars whose work is contained in these pages would join with me in asserting that their common purpose will be achieved only by engaging with and accommodating the diversity of views and the shared commitment of similarly motivated people from a broad spectrum of faith traditions, economic perspectives, political viewpoints, cultural identities and academic disciplines. To illustrate, we might consider the reflections of Elder D. Todd Christofferson (2009), an individual whose boundary-spanning legal and ecclesiastical roles (formerly legal counsel and senior vice president for two major banks and currently a member of the Quorum of the

Twelve Apostles of the Church of Jesus Christ of Latter-Day Saints) give him a singular perspective on the social-justice challenges and solutions of our time:

> The societies in which many of us live have for more than a generation failed to foster moral discipline. They have taught that truth is relative and that everyone decides for himself or herself what is right. Concepts such as sin and wrong have been condemned as "value judgments". . . . As a consequence, self-discipline has eroded and societies are left to try to maintain order and civility by compulsion. The lack of internal control by individuals breeds external control by governments. . . . In most of the world, we have been experiencing an extended and devastating economic recession. It was brought on by multiple causes, but one of the major causes was widespread dishonest and unethical conduct, particularly in the U.S. housing and financial markets. Reactions have focused on enacting more and stronger regulation. Perhaps that may dissuade some from unprincipled conduct, but others will simply get more creative in their circumvention. There could never be enough rules so finely crafted as to anticipate and cover every situation, and even if there were, enforcement would be impossibly expensive and burdensome. This approach leads to diminished freedom for everyone. . . . In the end, it is only an internal moral compass in each individual that can effectively deal with the root causes as well as the symptoms of societal decay. Societies will struggle in vain to establish the common good until sin is denounced as sin and moral discipline takes its place in the pantheon of civic virtues. . . . Each must be persuaded that service and sacrifice for the well-being and happiness of others are far superior to making one's own comfort and possessions the highest priority. . . . We cannot presume that the future will resemble the past—that things and patterns we have relied upon economically, politically, socially will remain as they have been. Perhaps our moral discipline, if we will cultivate it, will have an influence for good and inspire others to pursue the same course. We may thereby have an impact on future trends and events. At a minimum, moral discipline will be of immense help to us as we deal with whatever stresses and challenges may come in a disintegrating society.

The success of this dialogue will lie in those who are stimulated to enter the discussion, adding their own views, recommendations, and efforts to the quest for social justice.

Acknowledgments

When I arrived at the University of Scranton in the summer of 2006, the vision for the "Two Views of Social Justice" conference was already in place and solid work had begun to plan the conference and engage prominent scholars. The sponsoring organizations of that conference—the University of Scranton, the Robert Schalkenbach Foundation, and the Council of Georgist Organizations—contributed collectively and effectively to that task. The organization of any academic conference is incredibly time consuming, and the unique nature of this event, which brought together such a diverse array of organizations and participants, would not have happened without the solid commitment of a number of individuals, including Mr. Clifford W. Cobb, Dr. Hong V. Nguyen, Mr. Mark A. Sullivan, and Ms. Adele Wick of the Robert Schalkenbach Foundation (Dr. Nguyen is also on the Economics/Finance faculty at the University of Scranton), Mr. Ted Gwartney and Ms. Alanna Hartzok of the Council of Georgist Organizations, and Professor J. Brian Benestad, Dr. Edward M. Scahill, and Dean Michael O. Mensah of the University of Scranton.

Several outstanding reviewers spent many hours immersed in manuscripts (in some instances reviewing two or more) and providing constructive suggestions that helped shape this issue. I am indebted to Dr. Fred E. Foldvary, Dr. Daniel Haggerty, Mr. Matthew Harris, The Very Rev. Pedro Poloche STL, JCL, JV, Ms. Heather T. Remoff, Dr. Patrick Tully, and Ms. Adele Wick for their insights, attention to detail, and sharp focus on the purpose of this issue.

Finally, the path to publication was a convoluted one, as the publishing house that had originally intended to produce it as a volume ceased operation. I am deeply grateful to Mark Sullivan (administrative director), Cay Hehner (publications committee chair), Bill Batt, Gil Herman, and Damon Gross of the Robert Schalkenbach Foundation for their committed and timely efforts in connecting me with *The American Journal of Economics and Sociology*, and to Dr. Frederic S. Lee, the editor of that journal and professor of economics at the University of Missouri-Kansas City. This issue would not have materialized without his guidance and incomparable patience and the tireless labor, solid professionalism, and cheerful encouragement of Ms. Katherine A. Taylor, senior secretary in the Department of Economics at UMKC.

References

Christofferson, D. T. (2009). "Moral Discipline." *Ensign* 39(11): 105–108. http://www.lds.org/churchmagazines/ ENSN_2009_11_00_PDF_CompleteEnsign_04211_eng_000.pdf and http:// www.lds.org/general-conference/2009/10/moral-discipline?lang=eng.

Hollenbach, D. (2009). "The Catholic Intellectual Tradition, Social Justice, and the University." *Conversations* 36(Fall): 20–22.

Lawrence, E. (2007). "Henry George: The Relevance of His Philosophy Today." *Groundswell* 20(1): 2, 14–15.

Principal Concepts in Henry George's Theory of Natural Law: A Brief Commentary on *The Science of Political Economy*

By FRANCIS K. PEDDLE*

ABSTRACT. George sees the obstruction of the interaction between the active and passive factors of production, between the human and the natural, or anything that exacerbates the dualism between us and nature, as contrary to the functioning of political economy. His deliberations on the nature of action and desire lead to his formulation of the fundamental law of political economy. This essay elaborates on the guiding principles of that law, examines its basis in light of Ciceronian versus descriptive economics, considers its ramifications for socio-political institutions and economic reform, and addresses the question of social versus economic justice. The recognition of the power of economic rent in the distribution of income and wealth has once again made George's philosophy of economics a guide for reforms in public finance, the alleviation of poverty, and the long-term stewardship of the environment.

Introduction—Natural Law and Political Economy

In Henry George's last, unfinished work, *The Science of Political Economy*, there is little discussion of politics, societies, legal institutions, or what we now generally call public finance. Adam Smith devotes Book V of *The Wealth of Nations* to issues of public revenue and debt, and chapters 8 to 18 of David Ricardo's *Principles of Political Economy and Taxation* focus on the vicissitudes of what is commonly referred to today as tax incidence theory. John S. Mill's comments on direct and indirect taxation in his *Principles of Political*

*Francis K. Peddle is Vice-President (Academic) and Associate Professor of Philosophy, Dominican University College, Ottawa, Canada and President, Robert Schalkenbach Foundation, New York.

American Journal of Economics and Sociology, Vol. 71, No. 4 (October, 2012).

Economy formed the backbone of judicial decision-making on taxation well into the twentieth century. This is no oversight for George (1981: 27) declares early on in *The Science of Political Economy* that "the body economic, or "Greater Leviathan," always precedes and underlies "the body politic or Leviathan." Political economy is concerned with the body economic, not the body politic. Tax incidence theory and the field of public finance, for instance, sit atop the economic substructure.

The word "nature" and the phrase "law of nature" occur innumerable times in George's treatment of political economy. In the more philosophical and cosmological first chapters of Book I of *The Science of Political Economy*, which is concerned with the meaning of the phrase "political economy," nature, or the world, is distinguished into three elements or factors: (i) mind, soul or spirit; (ii) matter; and (iii) motion or force or energy. It is indisputable to him that priority must be given to the spiritual. Philosophy, for George (1981: 9), who had no technical training in the discipline, was simply the search for the nature and relation of things. Humanity is separated from the rest of nature in that humans are makers and producers. Humanity grows and advances by virtue of natural laws and the very constitution of things, not by virtue of any pact or covenant that may issue out of the body politic (1981: 23). The Greater Leviathan is thus a natural system and arrangement that may or may not be advanced by the all-too-human Leviathan. George's theory of the body economic is organic, not contractual, teleological, nor mechanistic. The state is thus an epiphenomenon of civilization. It is natural law that underlies all civilizations.

The "laws of nature" are dealt with explicitly by George in chapter VII of Book I of *The Science of Political Economy*. This section is the most illustrative in the Georgist corpus of his fundamental philosophical orientation. At the beginning of the chapter the epistemological divide between Kant and Hume is not cited directly. Whether knowledge arises from experience primarily or whether it intrinsically "belongs to our human nature as its original endowment" George (1981: 44) leaves alone as an insoluble philosophical problem. Unfortunately he states that the debate is "merely verbal" and unnecessary to join for purposes of political economy. This reflects and anticipates obliquely the general dismissal, in the late nineteenth and twentieth centuries, of metaphysical problems as mere verbiage and word games. George (1981: 208–209, 345–350) tends to blame this word-smithing primarily on the Germans and especially holds Kant and Hegel, and to a lesser extent Schopenhauer, up for rebuke. Kantian antinomies are not failures of thought for George but "confusion in the meaning of words" (1981: 348). Many of George's generation in the late nineteenth century sought solace in a more simplistic philosophy (Peddle 1993).

The idea that knowledge arises from human nature takes up the distinctions embedded in "ordinary perceptions" and "common speech." One immediately thinks of John Locke (1997: 468) in this context; for him "coexistence" is one of necessary relation. George appears to use the term initially as simply an underlying continuity or substratum. Later he sees it in the more Lockean sense of necessity or invariability (George 1981: 55). Succession and sequence deal with change, while coexistence represents the permanent. Lockean episte- mology is based simply on "the perception of the connexion and agreement, or disagreement and repugnancy of any of our ideas" (Locke 1997: 467). George thus appears to frame himself with the commonsense philosophers, but as we shall see, this categorization is itself too simplistic.

George's principal focus is on the nature of relations in observed phenomena. He notes that there are relations of coexistence and those of succession or sequence. One immediately thinks of John Locke in this context. "Coexistence" for Locke (1997: 468) is one of necessary relation. George appears to be using the term coexistence initially as simply an underlying continuity or substratum. Later he sees it in the more Lockean sense of necessity or invariability (George 1981: 55). Succession and sequence deal with change, while coexistence repre- sents the permanent. Lockean epistemology is based simply on "the perception of the connexion and agreement, or disagreement and repugnancy of any of our ideas" (Locke 1997: 467). Relations of sequence are merely temporal. They are successive juxtapositions and contingent positionings, but reveal no causal connection. George (1981: 45) then identifies another form of succession, that of consequence. This is a necessary relation of cause and effect. These sorts of relations are irreversible and invariable. For George, espying causal relations is the essence of human reason and the basis of what we call "science."

The simplest causal relation arises immediately out of self-consciousness and the exertion of the will. While George's discussion of consciousness in chapter VII of Book I is not sophisticated, it does indicate significantly that when he talks about the laws of nature he is not referring solely to physical laws but to spiritual and mental laws as well. This is a point for which George could be pilloried if it is not remembered that "spirit" or "mind" is one of the essential factors of the world and that political science is concerned with its own unique laws of nature. George states: "For natural law is not all comprehended in what we call physical law. Besides the laws of nature which relate to matter and energy, there are also laws of nature that relate to spirit, to thought and will" (1981: 437; see also Schwartzman 1991). An inquiry into the "how" of something is inevitably followed by one into the "why" of it, that is, purpose, motive, or intent. George (1981: 50–51) is prompted to cite Aristotelian teleology and the doctrine of final causes in this context. His comments on Aristotle and the "teleological argument" are prophetic and highly suggestive. He notes that teleological arguments are out of fashion in modern philosophy and viewed with suspicion if not contempt. The assault on ethical naturalism, scholastic philosophy, and classical discussions about the good lasted for almost a century after George's time. He knew nothing of G. E. Moore's (1966) naturalistic fallacy and the predominance of the Humean fact/value dualism. Final and beginning causes do, however, occur with great frequency in the common speech of ordinary people. It is out of such ordering principles that one comes to understand "Nature" as an all-comprehensive system. Nature is not to be confused with God. These are two distinct concepts for George. George (1981: 54) quotes Alexander Pope: "All are but parts of one stupendous whole, Whose body Nature is, and God the soul" (from the first Epistle of *An Essay on Man*, lines 267–268).

Rule-based systems of positive or human law are not the driving force of political economy, nor do they provide any of its content. George surmises that "law" originally meant something exclusively human, as it took the form of commands and rules of conduct. These are accompanied by sanctions and notions of right and wrong. The observation by us of invariable coexistences and sequences in phenomena led to the universalization of law. The human will was no longer seen as the law's sole originator. The idea of a "causative will" that transcends the human will became known as the "law of Nature." For George (1981: 56) laws of Nature (or the natural order) are nothing other than the invariable sequences that belong to the system of Nature. Detection of these invariable sequences, which are in fact consequences or causal relations, is a tendency that arises out of human mental necessity. Humans are not content until they come to the end of a causal sequence, no matter how many intermediate causes may have to be traversed. Science is the discovery of such laws of nature. Human laws, customs, and modes of thought originate in natural laws (George 1981: 59). The distinction between human law and natural law is the first necessity in the study of political economy (George 1981: 59, 61). George accuses "the accredited economic treatises" of wallowing in fundamental confusion about these two types of law.

What conclusions can be drawn from the aforementioned preliminary observations on George's view of the relation between natural law and political economy? Clearly, natural law must be understood as the key concept of the science of political economy. It is the concept that most sharply separates that science from jurisprudence, history, sociology, political science, anthropology, or economic soothsaying. Secondly, natural law deals with original human endowments and dispositions. There are traits inherent to human nature that cannot be taken away or, conversely, legislated into existence. These properties are objective and ineliminable. Thirdly, humans have an inherent motivation to seek the causes of things and to attribute a necessity to cause and effect relations. Fourthly, the identification of invariable causal relations also involves the pursuit of final causes, or the isolation of ultimate purposes. The teleological disposition, in its complex interpretations, is fundamental to the human endowment. Finally, the mental necessity of the human endowment leads to the identification of natural laws and to the world-view that Nature is an ordered system.

These philosophical views of Henry George are antithetical to the intellectual culture of most of the twentieth century. George seems out of tune even with his own time. Witness his attack on Herbert Spencer (George 1988) and the attack on him by Thomas Huxley (1890).

Furthermore, it is not easy to place George in any particular philosophical camp. Phrases such as "mental necessity" and "invariable causal relations," as well as his general sympathy with Enlightenment principles, seem to make him amenable to certain aspects of Kant's philosophy. On the other hand, he does not see such necessity as an *a priori* "mental construct" in either the strong Kantian sense of a pure category of the understanding or as an *a posteriori* form of subjective necessity in Hume's notion of custom, which prevails in his principle of causation. George thinks like a realist or what might loosely be called an "objectivist." (This, of course, brings to mind the philosophy of Ayn Rand; no direct affiliation is intended, however, although some of those familiar with George have canvassed the connections.) He is not, however, a scientist or an operational economist in the sense that prevails today, although he certainly does not eschew careful observation, experimentation, and induction. He is first and foremost a moralist. His major popular writings such as *Progress and Poverty*, *Social Problems*, and *Free Trade or Protection* are redolent with an overwhelming sense of the omnipresence of injustice and inhumanity. He seeks a soteriology in a positive-law type of economics and believes he has found it in the almost mystical vision of the "sovereign remedy" found in *Progress and Poverty*. Positive economics must be founded on and integrated with a normative economics, which is in turn only possible on the basis of natural law.

Political economy is not moral or ethical science (George 1971: 72–73). However, economics in George's view is nothing if it does not consider justice. But how can this discipline, political economy, which purports to concern itself with natural laws advance the human ethical project? How can "the science of the maintenance and nutriment of the body politic" contribute to the moral advancement of humanity?

Teleology, Normative Economics, and Modernity

The first question we may ask ourselves is whether George's view of natural law encapsulates and in some way advances the concepts long entrenched in the Western tradition of natural law theory with respect to the relation between ethics and economics. Natural law theory has its roots in classical antiquity, especially in Aristotle's *Nicomachean*

Ethics and other treatises. It was perhaps left, however, to a rhetorician like Cicero (1928: 33) more than a metaphysician to state succinctly the most often cited definition of natural law:

> True law is right reason in agreement with Nature; it is of universal application, unchanging and everlasting; it summons to duty by its commands, and averts from wrong-doing by its prohibitions. And it does not lay its commands or prohibitions upon good men in vain, though neither have any effect on the wicked. It is a sin to try to alter this law, nor is it allowable to attempt to repeal any part of it, and it is impossible to abolish it entirely. We cannot be freed from its obligations by Senate or People, and we need not look outside ourselves for an expounder or interpreter of it. And there will not be different laws at Rome and at Athens, or different laws now and in the future, but one eternal and unchangeable law will be valid for all nations and for all times, and there will be one master and one ruler, that is, God, over us all, for He is the author of this law, its promulgator, and its enforcing judge.

George's (1981: 60) description of natural laws is very Ciceronian. The Stoical influence on George is strong and under-examined in the Georgist literature. It is no accident that George quotes the late Stoic Roman Emperor, Marcus Aurelius, at the beginning of *Progress and Poverty*.

The confluence of reason, nature, and law, the characteristics of universality and unchangingness, and the status of cosmopolitan validity are all indicia of natural law in the many subsequent centuries of commentary and exposition. Most modern comments on natural law, especially in the philosophy of law in the United States, inquire no further back in the history of philosophy than St. Thomas Aquinas. In his "Treatise on Law" (1946: 993–1119), there is consideration of the various precepts of natural law as well as whether it is universal and unchangeable. A modern example would be Murphy and Coleman (1990: 67–108). There is a significant literature of interpretation and commentary on these passages in the *Summa Theologica* that stretches over many centuries and that has enjoyed a certain revival in recent decades after an extended eclipse in the twentieth century. An example of an important early development in this tradition is the Salamanca School (DeVitoria 1991). (For the contemporary revival of natural law doctrines, see Lisska 1996: 8–12, 15–48). Equally important is the recognition that natural law cannot be violated or avoided or expunged from the order of things. The obvious implication is that the enactment of human laws in contravention of the natural law may obstruct and temporally displace the latter but can never permanently abolish it. Many of the precepts of Georgist normative economics flow from an awareness of this principle.

Lest it be thought that there is no human factor whatsoever in George's view of political economy, that we are simply caught in a deterministic rat trap, from which no political will or social philosophy can disengage us, there arises in the discussion in Chapter X of *The Science of Political Economy* the idea of a "complex system" in which the human will, the active factor, is a principal actor. (It is the curious position of many current economists that there is a certain "natural" inevitability to the business cycle and the recurrence of recessions in the modern capitalist economy. Inscrutability seems to lead to the invocation of some mysterious natural force. George, of course, would never subscribe to such inscrutability. He thought the cause of industrial depressions was perfectly understandable, their frequency artificially induced, and their elimination possible through the comprehension of the natural laws of economics.) The human will is not fundamentally erratic, diabolical, mischievous, nihilistic, or world-negating. George does not give it, in its essence, any particular religious or moral coloring. The exertion of the human will on the material and forces of nature is inherently rooted in what might be called the economic teleology of the satisfaction of our material desires. As a system, political economy is concerned with human actions, not any actions, but those actions that have as their aim the satisfaction of human desires in the material sense (George 1981: 76). The three cosmological factors of the world identified at the beginning of *The Science of Political Economy*—spirit, matter, and energy—are now for the purposes of political economy re-articulated as human beings and nature, the active and passive factors of production embedded in the thought of Smith and Ricardo. Reason clearly distinguishes between human and natural agency, between a statue and a stone. Non-rational beings cannot do this. Political economy as a science deals with the relations brought about by a conscious will, which is the "primary motive power" behind the alteration of material forms with the objective of satisfying human material desires (George 1981: 80).

This exposition by George of the general character of political economy is easily rendered into the traditional language of Aristotelian-Thomistic views on teleology and natural law. The satisfaction of material desires is a necessary aspect of the development of human well-being. The well-being of individuals is an end in itself and this by definition is good. Material satisfactions are undoubtedly multiple and variable, but their limitation or abridgement, such as somehow curbing excessive greed or prioritizing among scarce resources, are not strictly speaking components of political economy. In this sense the multiple goods of material satisfaction are incommensurable and thus not to be strictly judged by the principles of political economy. The human disposition is developmental, that is, it must be understood as advancing from its potential to its actual nature. Hence, the Aristotelian distinction between potency ($\delta \acute{v} \nu \alpha \mu \iota \varsigma$) and act ($\nu \acute{\varepsilon} \rho \gamma \varepsilon \iota \alpha$) has a place in political economy and the institutional and political evaluations of positive economics, that is, economic policies, economically conse-quential legislation, and the determination of economic intelligence by normative economics. The economic obstruction of the human devel-opmental process, or the obstruction of the development of the human disposition from potency to actuality, necessarily undermines human well-being because it undermines the natural process whereby a human being attains self-actualization or complete human beingness. Frustrat-ing the possibility of attaining human well-being, or what today we normally subsume under the vague concept of equality of economic opportunity, is to make it difficult if not impossible to function as a human being. Negating human functionality, denying the possibility of individual self-actualization, in effect, truncating human nature, are all contrary to the fundamental principles of "eudaimonistic" ethics. (The phrases "happy economics," "civil happiness," and "human flourishing" have to some degree found their way into modern economic par-lance—see Bruni 2006. This is one of a number of different media for re-introducing Georgist economics and natural law theory into main-stream economics.) If you do anything economically to restrain unjus-tifiably human well-being or flourishing, you are acting against the strictures of normative economics.

George sees the obstruction of the interaction between the active and passive factors of production, between the human and the natural, or anything that exacerbates the dualism between us and nature, that restrains or negates the relation between the two, as in principle contrary to the functioning of political economy. And anything that is contrary to the functioning of the body economic is in principle contrary to individual well-being. (I am using the phrase "in principle" here because there are obviously instances where you may want to restrain such a relation for non-economic reasons, such as protection of ornamental gardens, parklands, or more broadly the environment. Such protections can be easily incorporated into the notion of the advancement of human well-being, on aesthetic or ecological grounds.) Furthermore, anything so contrary to individual well-being hinders social development and cooperation. Access to nature is therefore fundamental to the system of political economy simply because no economic activity can take place without the interaction of the active and passive factors of production. These are some of the teleological principles that undergird natural law and normative economics.

From the standpoint of the ethical naturalism of the Aristotelian-Thomistic tradition the developmental disposition of human nature towards the satisfaction of material desire, towards the attainment of the necessaries and luxuries (at least to some degree) of material life, is also the *nisus* that grounds the "oughts" of normative economics. Political economy, it can be said, is descriptive of natural processes of production and distribution. It is, however, in the discernment of the precise and unalterable structure of these natural processes that the "oughts" and "obligations" of positive-law economics are immersed. The Humean fact/value divide is overcome. One now has an evaluative dimension in normative economics that allows for ethical decision-making at the infinitely diverse levels of economic policy formulation. For example, laws that bestow special privileges in the form of licenses and exclusive rights with respect to access to broadcast spectrum (that is, entry monopolies) are not only in principle contrary to the productive laws of political economy but also must be sanctioned by normative economics on the ground that one ought not to restrict arbitrarily access to that which is created by God or that which is pre-given in nature. Of course, society in the interests of the efficiency goals of positive economics can put conditions on the bestowal of such privileges in recognition of the moral principle and thus reconcile the "ought" of normative economics with the goal of effectively developing the broadcast spectrum through the economic interests of a given group of individuals with a given skill set. If the conditions are properly calibrated, then the equity objectives of advancing human well-being are melded with the efficiency goals of the science of the economical production of goods and services.

"Oughts" and "obligations" are principally looked upon today as sets of rules and codes that determine the "normative" irrespective of the actual. In a sense the actual must conform to the rule whether or not it is in its nature to do so. Most tax laws in our society, for instance, are contrary to the normal inclinations of human nature and sound business practices. Adam Smith (1937: 779) captured these absurdities well when he said that: "The law, contrary to all the ordinary principles of justice, first creates the temptation, and then punishes those who yield to it; and it commonly enhances the punishment too in proportion to the very circumstance which ought certainly to alleviate it, the temptation to commit crime."

Georgist economics is a normative discipline, but it should not be conceptualized as normative in the sense of rule-imposing, even if those rules are a coherent system. Laws for George are laws because they are elicited out of the nature or order of things, material or mental, natural or spiritual. This runs against the modern current of positive law or human-made law as an end in itself or as a system of jurisprudence and a system of economic activity completely disengaged from natural law or the natural economy. In modern economics, for instance, the "underground economy" is viewed as an aberration or anomaly to be eradicated, absorbed, or co-opted somehow. That the underground economy may be a natural economy (apart from its criminal elements) is not entertained because that would then highlight the fact that the above-ground economy is the one that is artificial and non-natural. (For some discussion, see De Soto 2000; De Soto's position ignores the fundamental role of economic rent in the collateralization of legally formalized assets, especially real estate.)

George was sensitive to modern suspicions about traditional metaphysics and the grounding of political economy in speculative theology. He is of the view that a scientific approach to natural law, utilizing the hypothetico-deductive method, that is, a combination of principally deductive but nonetheless inductive reasoning, is sufficient. Unfortunately, these resonances with modernity were not enough to countervail the post-Georgist dismissal of his approach as archaic and riddled with supra-economic assumptions, speculations, and inferences (see Anderson 2003; Samuels 2003).

The Fundamental Natural Law of Political Economy

George neutrally defines "desire" in the widest of senses as that which generically prompts human action at the beginning of Chapter XI of the First Book of *The Science of Political Economy*. One should simply understand desire as a given or a condition precedent that is necessarily connected with human action. Desire and action are integral to the human disposition and necessary to its self-actualization. Human desires and their corresponding satisfactions are subjective, relative to the individual, and objective, relative to the external world. Some desires are immaterial, such as thought and feeling, some are material, relating to matter and energy (George 1981: 83). George does not, however, see a radical distinction between the different modalities of desire.

The deliberations on the nature of action and desire lead to George's formulation of the fundamental law of political economy in Chapter XII of the First Book. The principle of political economy, which is the foremost invariable sequence denominated as the law of nature, is that there is an inherent disposition in human beings "to seek the satisfaction of their desires with the minimum of exertion" (George 1981: 87). From this first natural law of political economy we can elaborate a number of guiding principles for the science of political economy:

(1) The fundamental law of political economy is not a principle of human selfishness. The assumption of selfish motives is just as irrelevant for the science of political economy as the assumption of its great correlate—sympathy, or conversely perhaps as pernicious as assuming benevolent human motives for efficient economic production. (It is commonly viewed that Adam

Smith encompassed the full universe of human motives and intentions with his two masterpieces *The Theory of Moral Sentiments* and *The Wealth of Nations*, which focuses on self-interest. The latter should not be equated with selfishness. This is often done by commentators, who have labeled it the "Adam Smith Problem," or the contradiction between "selfishness" of *The Wealth of Nations* and the "sympathy" and "benevolence" of *The Theory of Moral Sentiments*. For a brief discussion, see Grabill (2006). Self-interest is the operational mechanism for the exercise of economic judgment. Prudence with regard to the pursuit of one's economic interests gives rise to infinitely variegated cultural and historical socio-economic structures.)

(2) This law is a self-evident fact.

(3) It is a law of action.

(4) It is a law of development and economic cooperation.

(5) It is a law of order—without it there are only unintelligible conjunctions of fact and information. In this sense it is a law that involves both efficient and final causation, primary, intermediate, and proximate causes.

(6) It is the law that makes possible political economy. In other words there can be no economic production without its assumption.

(7) It is that from which all other deductions and explanations in political economy derive.

(8) It has the same unifying force in political economy that gravity once had for physics (or at least did have until the nineteenth century).

(9) It is "synderetic" (to be defined in relation to the Aristotelian-Thomistic tradition).

(10) The law expresses the literal meaning of the word "economic" or what is the most economical way of getting from point A to point B in the sense of requiring fewer resources or costing less money.

George sees the first law of political economy as universal and unfailing. It meets the precepts of natural law. It is also in the nature of a habit (ξις) in some senses, sometimes called a state of character, that is in a certain state or permanent condition (Aristotle 1915: 1105; Aquinas 1946: 1008). The dispositions towards living, such as the desire to exist or to survive and to seek nutrition and growth, are permanent conditions of being human and are thus at the core of virtue in Aristotelian ethics. (One may be tempted to see George's view of political economy and the material satisfaction of human desire as limited to the dispositions towards living. That would be to unduly restrict what George conceives of as human desire, which would include the widest possible range of spiritual and rational dispositions as well—Lisska (1996: 102).) The first law of political economy internally regulates these dispositions. The endangerment of control over the preservation of one's life, such as someone else having a proprietary interest in your body, obviously runs counter to this disposition. But what of the dispositions to rational formation and skill development? Does society, for instance, have an obligation to provide free university education to anyone who wants it? Is the educational system a commons that ought not to be enclosed? Economists tell us that education increases labor productivity and promotes higher wages. Few, however, advocate completely socialized education. (How Georgist economics might advance greater equality of educational opportunity is a largely uncultivated field of research and reflection.)

Another important aspect of the Georgist conception of the fundamental law of political economy is its characterization as an organizing principle. In this respect it has features of the classical Aristotelian-Thomistic "metaphysics of finality" and "synderesis." The former is a complex theory that interrelates the classical doctrine of essence with natural law theory. George does not contribute directly to that debate, but he does intuitively incorporate some of its features in his political economy. George is concerned with the "normality of functioning" of the human being (a phrase from Maritain 1951: 87). Outliers and exceptions to the rule do not, and cannot, defeat the natural law of political economy. If some people are uneconomical, spendthrifts, or debt addicts, then so be it. We are not concerned in political economy with individual aberrations or even with individual conformance to the natural physical and mental symmetries. Clearly, there are inherent in human nature universals and necessities, which reason recognizes.

This is its "realist ontology" to use the traditional phrase. Human nature is also inherently purposive, for George. The fundamental law of political economy is the guiding hand of that purposiveness in the sphere of economics. Again, it is not always individually or socially the case that such economic purposiveness will be transparent in either the Leviathan or the Greater Leviathan.

The other important aspect of the metaphysics of finality is the notion of the common good. Young (1996: 8–15) makes this the principal concept of the economic order. It is interesting to note that the "economic common good" thought of as an "abundance of goods and services" has a trans-economic goal, which is leisure or "freedom from economic activity." As Aristotle points out in Book I of the *Nicomachean Ethics* all inquiries aim at some good. Ethics and political science aim at human well-being, of faring well and living well. The moral virtues have a finality as well in that they culminate in justice in both its distributive and rectificatory aspects. Book V on justice and Books VIII and IX on friendship in the *Nicomachean Ethics* are the closest Aristotle comes in that text to what we might call today communal relations or issues surrounding equality, equity, and socio-political organization. Political economy, for George, is not about individual ethics, but he was sensitive to the fact that the proper functioning of the social whole has an effect on individual behavior and thus on a society's economic performance. The effect George's reforms may have on individual virtue-ethics and reciprocally the ontological assumptions about human nature that George gathered up into his political economy, and agenda for economic justice, are very fruitful domains of philosophical and economic inquiry.

As for "synderesis," this is also an organizing principle, which may be viewed as the process whereby secondary, tertiary, and perhaps even quaternary principles are elaborated or translated out of the first principle. For St. Thomas "synderesis" (deriving from $\sigma \upsilon \nu$ $\tau \eta \rho \acute{\epsilon} \omega$ and $\tau \acute{\eta} \rho \eta \sigma \iota \varsigma$—to give heed to, to watch over, to be vigilant) is not a power but a "habitus" or $\xi \iota \varsigma$, that is the bestowal on us by nature of practical principles (Aquinas 1946: 407). It is a "special nature habit." "Synderesis" incites to the good. It has to do with those things that are "naturally known without any investigation from reason." (For a thorough discussion of "synderesis" as a philosophical term of art, see

Lottin 1948: 101–349.) It is clear that for Aquinas "synderesis" is the key concept behind practical reasoning. It is a habit that contains "the precepts of natural law, which are the first principles of human action" (Aquinas 1946: 1008).

It is one of the theses of this essay that it is to the Scholastic notion of "synderesis" that one must look for a key area of confluence between the ethical naturalism of the Aristotelian-Thomistic tradition and the naturalistic economics of Henry George. The scholastics viewed "synderesis" as a "law of the mind," a phrase amenable to George (1987: 507–515; here he uses the phrase "law of mental development"). The laws of production and distribution, of value-in-production and value-in-obligation, of economic rent and wages, of property and of human progress are all derivable from the fundamental law of political economy. The human *nisus* towards the natural actions of integration, cooperation, association, and the harmonious interaction of whole and part are all crucial concepts for George (1987: 508) in the advancement of civilization and the interrelation of the moral law and political economy. The scholastic notion of "synderesis" is also isomorphic with George's view of the growth and development of society as organic. This is not surprising since the concepts of purpose, completion, perfection, and end, all deeply buried in teleological metaphysics since Aristotle's "metaphysical biology," are frequently associated with an organic perspective. (Philosophical theories of vitalism were quite pervasive in late nineteenth-century thought—for example, Eucken (1912).) The collective power, for George, is clearly distinguishable from the sum of individual powers, just as a surplus value, which has no economic value, is discernible in economic rent and is distinguishable from the return to wages and capital.

Political economy, organized by its first principle, which then investigates a multitude of natural laws, has a relation to the community or the state (George 1981: 66). It refers to a social whole rather than to individuals. It does not, however, refer to the political divisions of this social whole. Furthermore, political economy deals with the distribution of the results of "socially conjoined effort." (George 1981: 70). It is focused on human actions that aim at material satisfactions in the aggregate. The human element is the initiative or active factor, the natural element, the passive factor. The condition precedent to the active factor is access to the materials and forces of the natural element. This access brings about the relations that are the focus of political economy.

Ciceronian Ethics Versus Descriptive Economics

Aristotle (1915: 1107) defines moral, as opposed to intellectual, virtue as "a state of character concerned with choice, lying in a mean, i.e. the mean relative to us, this being determined by a rational principle, and by that principle by which the man of practical wisdom would determine it" (see also Aquinas 1964: 107–110). "Phronesis" (φρόνησις) practical wisdom or intelligence (or one could say "prudent"—a weaker term—or wise in human affairs) allows us to avoid the excess and the defect outside the mean. Aristotle, like George, sees a fixity in human nature from the standpoint of its essence. (George (1987: 504) states: "That the differences between the people of communities in different places and at different times, which we call differences of civilization, are not differences which inhere to the individuals, but differences which inhere in the society.") There are variances but they always to revert to the mean. George (1987: 503) calls this a "natural symmetry of mind," towards which all deviations tend to return. This general fixity or "common standard" with respect to human mental power does not, on the other hand, mean that civilization is static. On the contrary, George couples this generally static view of individual essence (although developmental within the confines of that essence) with a very dynamic approach to civilization and the advancement and deterioration of human collectives.

How these characterizations of human nature, moral virtue, law, and collective life get carried into political economy and even further into the Georgist program for economic justice and reform is one of the principal controversies in philosophical economics, which inquires into the mutually illuminating and reinforcing relationships between ethics and economics. Descriptive economics, or neoclassical economics, is primarily model-driven and algebraic. Its circumscribed scientific aspirations are, however, cosmopolitan in intent, even if it takes its conclusions as tentative and intrinsically alterable. This surface cosmopolitanism derives principally from its aura of scientific neutrality. This is why modern economists are able to serve ably in any institution in any culture. They are ubiquitous precisely because their deliberations for the most part have no conscious distributional consequences. Modern descriptive economics, teleologically-adverse and bereft of any first principles rooted in natural law or ethics, is easily assimilated to a broad range of political pathologies and has assumed, in its popular forms at least, a largely ceremonial role in contemporary discourse.

From another perspective philosophical economics may be characterized as a Ciceronian ethics of natural law confronting a mathematized, supposedly value-free, marginalist, and descriptive economics of efficiency. Solow (2006: 45) captures this dilemma well when he states: "Students of economics are indeed taught to make a clear distinction between positive statements (this is how this piece of the world works) and normative statements (some states of the world are better than others). They are taught that no 'ought' follows from an 'is,' except with the addition of a clearly defined ethical criterion." In modern economics this is viewed as an inevitable trade-off between equity, or those decisions that have distributional consequences, and the subscribers to free markets, efficiency, gains and losses, and issues under the rubric of what Aristotle called rectificatory or corrective justice. Foley (2006) declares that the issue is not to choose between equity and efficiency, precisely the Humean proposition put to most economics students in our marginalist or neo-classical educational system, but to analyze where the applications have gone wrong. The Scholastic tradition calls the divide between equity and efficiency the difference between distributive and commutative justice. Equity and distributional theory must ultimately revert in some sense to the Ciceronian definition of natural law as "true law is right reason in agreement with Nature." In this sense the insertion of Ciceronian-like ethical criteria into economics will be inevitably seen by the marginalists as supra-economic in much the same manner that legal positivists view "the natural necessities" (H. L. A. Hart) or "rights" (R. Dworkin) as something fundamentally extra-legal.

Natural law theorists do not see equity and efficiency as juxtapositional or co-lateral. Rather, their paradigm is foundational. The efficiency model, the precise analysis of gains and losses, the science of exchanges, depends upon a prior distribution. It is not just prior as a conceptual assumption, but prior in actuality. Of course, Aristotelians know that actuality precedes potentiality; therefore, the conceptual and actual dependency of efficiency on equity is ultimately based in the classical tradition. George's view of the hierarchical structure of political economy, in terms of all its natural laws emanating from a single fundamental principle, the first law of political economy, is thus foundational in a way that is analogous with the Thomistic position that the natural law participates in the eternal law. Such a hierarchy is deeply unpalatable to the descriptive economist and to the modern consciousness. Descriptivist economics is only oriented towards provisional and relative or comparative universals or low level generalizations from a given set of data. Likewise, there are powerful currents in modern philosophy that are only willing to make modest claims about keeping the conversation going, about the dialogical, the discursive, and the contextual.

On the other hand, the counter-modern, natural law economist works deductively from a given totality of law-like principles and relations between these principles. These relations have their particular determinations in various applications and guises, such as how the law of rent has a tendency to reduce wages, which can further be determined by the empirical data. Inductive results, however, in and of themselves cannot change the Ciceronian edict that the law of rent and its ineluctably negative effect on wages cannot be legislated away by positive law. The structural subsets of George's first law of political economy follow deductively. Human exchange, or the "propensity to truck, barter and exchange one thing for another," to use a celebrated phrase of Adam Smith's (1937: 13), is simply an exertion-reducing presupposition of any collective economic effort. Emma Rothschild and Amartya Sen describe the universal disposition to exchange as "a sort of oratory" and that this "general propensity to discursiveness gives rise to the division of labour, and thereby to universal opulence" (Haakonssen 2006: 322).

How does George elaborate the concept of "economic value" out of the first principle of political economy? The key is the inseparable notions of plus-exertion and minus-exertion. Value, generally, is "worth in exchange" and "the value of a thing in any time and place is the largest amount of exertion that any one will render in exchange for it; or to make the estimate from the other side, that it is the smallest amount of exertion for which any one will part with it in exchange" (George 1981: 350–251). The absence in many estimates of value of "making the estimate from the other side" frequently skews economic debates. The concept of "wealth effect" in rising real estate markets is one example. There is an ineliminable subjective element in value. It is not something that is intrinsic to things. On the other hand, value is not exclusively subjective, i.e., simply a function of the intensity of desire, but rather value is something that flows from how much one is willing to give for something. In effect this is an objective check on the intensity of desire. This is the economic concept of effective demand, or as George (1981: 253) states, "the desire to possess, accompanied by the ability and willingness to give in return." This objective check is competition, or the higgling of the market. Any attempt to eliminate competition is thus contrary to natural law and fundamentally counter-economic. George's concept of value is not exclusively labor based, like Ricardo's. Although his philosophy of economics is fundamentally producerist, it is not the quantity of labor that is exerted in production that determines value, but the amount of labor that is rendered in exchange for it. Value, determined through competition, is a "point of equation," or a measurable compromise between desire and satisfaction, demand and supply, tends to "the present cost of producing a similar thing" (George 1981: 254). (George's remarks on value, as a reconciliation of the subjective and the objective, of demand and supply, through competitive markets—a phrase that is a pleonasm since markets are by definition competitive—should put to rest any notion that he is a socialist or a Marxist.)

Land generally, or nature as such, cannot have any value since it is not produced, but created. However, land as a particular quality, or a certain locality, has no objective delimitor because it cannot be checked by the possibility of production, and thus is not subject to the competitive forces of the marketplace. The value of land that is monopolized, or that has an entry price, is therefore not in the nature of an exchange of service, but one of an "obligation to render service"

(George 1981: 255–256). This leads us to the all important distinction in George's philosophy of economics between "value from production" and "value from obligation."

George (1981: 259, 261) defines value from production as an addition to the socially conjoined effort or to the "common stock" of a community. This is wealth in the strictly politico-economic sense. Value from obligation "consists merely of the power of one individual to demand exertion from another individual." This form of value causes a new distribution of what already exists—it re-distributes the common stock, but it cannot be characterized, according to George, as wealth in the politico-economic sense.

In George's view the single most pernicious and pervasive error in the history of political economy has been its failure to define wealth because it has not recognized the fundamental distinction between the two kinds of value. And because it has not made this distinction systematically and forcefully it degenerated into the common idea that the wealth of a community is the sum of the wealth of individuals. Increases in value from obligation that impose obstacles to the satisfaction of desire, or that are exertion-plus, are regressive in the politico-economic sense, while value from production that saves future exertion, or that is exertion-minus, is progressive (George 1981: 260). (Critiquing and removing the institutional, legal and political obstacles created by the "commercial or mercantile system" of political economy is, of course, the great project of Book IV of Smith's *The Wealth of Nations.*) A progressive and reformist philosophy of economics is therefore both descriptive with respect to the identification of the negative effect of value from obligation on value from production, for example, deadweight losses from income and sale taxes, and normative with respect to its recommendations to remove or reduce monopolistic values from obligation. George likes to use the word "obligation" in this context because it expresses everything that may require the rendering of exertion without the return of exertion. Values from obligation are therefore market destroying and generative of spurious competition, or "effort-imposing activity through domination" (Young 1996: 22). The true, or absolute, value of anything is "the difficulty or ease of acquiring it" (George 1981: 267). High value usually results from scarcity.

The natural economic philosophy of George (1981: 276, 289) views wealth as a "service embodied in material form." Such notions as immaterial wealth, natural wealth, or natural capital are, in terms of political economy, oxymorons. Production from wealth is not the only purpose of human effort. It is, however, the exclusive focus of a science of political economy. George's treatment of capital has been generally criticized. In terms of the first law of political economy it is not difficult, however, to understand how capital, by increasing the sum of satisfactions, is exertion-minus. Capital suspends the time in which a given exertion shall be utilized. Capital changes the timing of the exercise of exertion that is utilized in the satisfaction of desire. This enhances efficiency and minimizes exertion. It is the calling of past exertion to present exertion.

In a well known statement, George (1981: 295) declares that "all capital is wealth, but not all wealth is capital." It is very difficult in our capital intensive culture to imagine the creation of wealth without capital. There are three key concepts in George's view of the relationship between wealth and capital: power, permanence, and utility. In a summary passage George (1981: 296, 301, 406, 413–415), who principally conceptualizes wealth as a "storehouse" or "halting-place," states:

> Wealth, in short, is labor, which is raised to a higher or second power, by being stored in concrete forms which give it a certain measure of permanence, and thus permit of its utilization to satisfy desire in other times or other places. Capital is stored labor raised to a still higher or third power by being used to aid labor in the production of fresh wealth or of larger direct satisfactions of desire.

All three concepts are linked to the basic idea of economization in wealth-production. The storage of labor in certain concrete forms has an inherent labor-saving power. The second power or capacity for satisfying desire is not capital *per se*. Rather, it is a concrete form that can be used at a later time or different place in the direct satisfaction of desire. Capital is stored labor raised to a third power because it is used in the production of more wealth and not in direct satisfaction. Capital is then a form of investment in the wealth-creation process. In the final analysis, capital is resolvable into labor. It is what generally makes the process of production continuous. Capital, in the economic sense, must therefore be involved in the creation of value from production, that is, in the changing of matter in place, form, or condition in aid of further production or in the satisfaction of desire.

Value from production is an economizing process of the more efficient utilization of capital in terms of its inherent power, permanence, and ease of utilization. As the Greater Leviathan progresses such values are constantly diminishing. As more wealth is produced through technological innovation and the replacement of labor by capital, there is a diminution of the value of articles associated with economic production. On the other hand, the values associated with obligation tend to increase as society advances. There is thus an inverse relation between wealth and the two forms of value. As wealth increases, value from production decreases and at the same time value from obligation increases (George 1981: 311). This paradox of true wealth leading to the destruction of value and spurious or relative wealth augmenting a pseudo-value is the direct cause of the tremendous maldistributions of wealth in modernity. And it is these maldistributions that cause the great social and political upheavals that plague modern civilization.

Socio-Political Institutions and Economic Reform

To consciously or unconsciously design socio-political and economic institutions that run counter to the natural law is, for George (1981b), the main cause of the many ills that plague economic life and society. (The effect of institutions on prosperity and poverty is the focus of "neo-institutional economics," whose main spokesperson is 1993 Swedish Bank Prize winner Douglass North.) That which impedes and perverts these the relations between the active and passive factors of production undermines economic justice and contradicts the natural laws that permeate the inner structure of political economy. The principal economic malaise of modernity, in George's view, is not that we have incompetently managed our economies, or collected insufficient data on wages and capital formation, or paid slight attention to the poor and unemployed, but that we have failed to come to grips intellectually with the conflict between the structure of our socio-political institutions and the natural laws of economics.

There is a fundamental distinction in *The Science of Political Economy* between the laws of production, which are physical laws, and the laws of distribution, which are moral laws (George 1981: 440–453). George declares that, hitherto, political economy viewed production as in accordance with natural laws and distribution a function of human laws. The truth of the matter, in his view, is that both sets of laws are laws of nature. The "is" of economic production and the generation of wealth and the "ought" of the distribution of that wealth are therefore to be found in the same source, i.e., the natural law. But the "ought," or right or justice, has only to do with that category of the world that we call "spirit," while the "is" of economic production obviously is concerned with matter and energy. Nonetheless the laws of distribution are just as immutable as the laws of production.

The natural law of political economy is advanced principally through two forms of cooperation, the one directed or conscious, the other spontaneous (George 1981: 391–393). There is both a combination and separation of effort in cooperation. Cooperation itself is elaborated out of the principle of exchange, which is the third of the three modes of production after adapting and growing (George 1981: 332). George's two kinds of cooperation are a naturally logical division of the methods of action, union, and initiative with respect to the development of the economy of labor. Directed or conscious cooperation proceeds from without and is guided by a controlling will. Spontaneous or unconscious cooperation proceeds from within and is a correlation of the actions of independent wills (George 1981: 383).

George's (1981: 391, 412) discussion of cooperation in *The Science of Political Economy* makes clear that intelligence cannot be aggregated and that thought is the originating element of all production. (The utilization of research teams in scientific research is a necessary division of labor given the extreme specialization in today's empirical sciences, but one has to be very cautious with regard to how this limits individual intellectual initiative. This caution is even more pronounced in the social sciences and humanities.) Directed cooperation necessarily results in the non-utilization, or the diminution to some degree, of mental power. The subordination of one human will to another in order to secure certain unities of action and productive initiative will result in the loss of productive power where a constant application of intelligence is required. Market exchanges by definition are operations that require foresight, calculation, and judgment. Exchange, in George's view, properly belongs to production, not distribution.

Inequalities in the distribution of wealth do not arise from competition (George 1981: 402–403). Competition arises naturally from the first principle of political economy and is non-severable from exchange and cooperation. Competition has the effect of diminishing value, but not wealth. Monopolistic practices that reduce competition therefore reduce cooperation and the reduction of cooperation retards the advancement of civilization.

Distribution, and distributive justice, ultimately deal with how we assign ownership. Ownership is the determination of property, or proprietary interest, in that which is produced (George 1981: 455). For George, the law of distribution and the law of property are different expressions of the same fundamental law. Expediency, utility, institutions, legislation, and human law are not the source of property rights, although expediency and human law are often the justification for such rights. George (1886: 123–133; 1981: 455–459) severely criticizes John Stuart Mill for basing the institution of property on human law. This is not to say that property and the assignment of ownership and various bundles of rights associated with property are not existing systems of laws or historically developed social and political institutions. Legal possession must be clearly distinguished from possession by virtue of the natural law.

George's (1981: 460) fundamental dictum of natural law, that is, the natural laws of distribution, is that there can be no recognition of the ownership of land. Put another way, this is the natural law that gives the product to the producer. Civilization and human development have gone through some extraordinary twists and turns to find the origin of property in human law. Since property in land (nature) is contrary to the natural law, there can be no ethical justification for it. Any attempt to do so is sophistry and a confusion of terms.

All the factors of production have a return, that is, a distribution. There are relations of cause and effect between all the factors of production. There are necessary relations between land, labor, and capital. It is only when these relations are fettered in such a manner as to return to the privileged holder of some portion of pre-given nature, at the expense of the producers, the results of the "socially conjoined effort" that a conflict arises between human law and the natural law. On the basis of natural law there cannot be any morally justifiable reason for the retention of economic rent by an entity that claims a putative title in positive law. The natural law, for George, has the status not only of origination with respect to institutional law but it is the alembic through which all positive law is to be judged and evaluated.

Social institutions can be in harmony with the natural laws of political economy or they can distort such laws through a complex of dysfunctionalities. This has been very much the case historically. Economic reform is not therefore simply an incremental process of adjustment, but a radical restructuring of hundreds of years of embedded conventions, rules, prohibitions, and obscurities. The definition of "land" in dozens of legal statutes in many countries as that which includes both land and the improvements to the land is an obvious jurisprudential example of systematic obfuscation of definition when it comes to the human law. Such a lack of clarity in the natural law is not possible. Interest-based politics has historically dominated economic institutions. A recognition of natural law, and its ultimate inviolability, would reverse this dominance.

Social Versus Economic Justice?

In a general sense both social and economic justice focus on the social whole. Social justice tends towards the amelioration and equalization of individual capacities. It has been since the late nineteenth century more amenable to interaction with the Austrian subjective theory of value, marginal utility and re-distributive *in personam* forms of taxation, subsidization, and the overall program of welfare economics. Justice as fairness, as procedural, as remedial, and as corrective has not achieved the concrete levels of proximate equality, freedom of opportunity, and security of economic outcomes that many theoreticians of cosmopolitan human rights and progressive international development had envisaged (Jupp 2000: 92–109).

Georgist reformist economics is more radical because it examines civilization from the standpoint of the natural laws that inform all human institutions and customs and that are sourced in the human will and its external manifestations. Its theory of value is objective in nature, oriented towards the interrelational capacity of human effort and natural materials and forces. It focuses, for example, on *in rem* forms of taxation that would render nugatory the requirement for a re-distribution of wealth and income because it would ameliorate significant inequalities *ab initio*.

George's philosophy, although conservative in respect of open markets, free exchanges, and individual freedoms, radically critiques human institutions so as to bring them into conformance with the natural law. For example, morally unjustifiable taxing statutes such as income taxes and consumption taxes must generally be abolished and replaced by statutes that rely on land value taxation for the operations of the state. Economic justice for George is therefore one of unfettering natural law so that the potential and opportunities of everyone in the community can be self-actualized and not hindered in that self-actualization by unjust positive laws. It is a philosophy that seeks to harmonize natural and positive law.

Social justice is generally seen as not being dependent on the recognition of the natural law. It focuses not only on equality of economic opportunity but even more on equality of economic outcomes. Ben S. Bernanke (2007), the Chairman of the U.S. Federal Reserve Board, stated that the three bedrock principles to which most Americans subscribe are "equality of economic opportunity," "no guarantee of equality of economic outcomes," and "the placement of some limits on the downside risks to individuals affected by economic change." These are the key foundations of the American "market-based" economy.

The attainment of greater equality of economic outcomes is seen as principally a matter of *re-distributive*, not distributive, justice. A status quo is accepted in terms of the production of wealth and some morally justifiable re-distributive decisions are made in terms of apportioning that wealth more equally among the various members and classes of society. Concepts of equality of opportunity, of fairness (perhaps in the Rawlsian sense), and of social utility are often invoked to substantiate such re-distributive policies. Social justice is therefore primarily retrospective and adjustive, not prospective and preventative, as in George's concept of economic justice based on the natural law. A system of social justice is based solely on positive law with a certain number of utility and rights principles marshaled as the organizing directives for policy formation.

Economic justice, with a reform agenda based on natural law, has reconciliation and harmonization with the inherent structures of production and distribution as its primary characteristic. The reformist agenda of social justice activists tends to assume that there are ineradicable conflicts between the various factors of production and distribution, between economic classes, that equity and efficiency are mutually exclusive, that re-distribution invariably requires trade-offs, and that the best one can hope for is a modicum of the distribution of wealth such that no one absolutely falls below a subsistence level of existence. The achievement of social justice is therefore always a balancing act between the market-based forces of economic efficiency and reward, and the restraints of economic fairness (commutative justice) and of the reasonably equitable distribution of wealth in society. The recognition of the role of natural law in economic thinking and justice is a radical shift away from welfare economics and the regulation of economic behavior by legislative fiat.

Conclusion—Crosscurrents in Social Economics, Natural Law, and Post-Neoclassical Economics

The *Science of Political Economy* is rooted in and in some senses is the culmination of the tradition of classical political economy. The marginalist revolution of Alfred Marshall, Stanley Jevons, Carl Menger, and Leon Walras (for a good discussion of the "marginalist revolution," see Médaille 2007: 63–71) was already inaugurated in the first half of the 1870s even before the publication of George's *Progress and Poverty* in 1879. George was also competing against a powerful subjectivist theory of value that originated in the Austrian school of Eugen Böhm-Bawerk, Friedrich von Wieser, and many others. He thought of most of his contemporaries in the marginalist, Austrian, and historical schools as unscientific and incoherent. It was these schools that prevailed in the twentieth century.

Natural law has always been invoked by a panoply of writers in economics and philosophy to underwrite a particular set of indisputable claims or chain of such claims. In the Enlightenment natural law was often associated with scientific naturalism and the shedding of metaphysical and theological first principles. By reverting to marginal utility as a first principle, economics in the second half in the nineteenth century was able to treat the three distinct factors of economics, and the returns to those factors, as uniform and homogenous. Nevertheless, the distribution of income in society, according to John Bates Clark ([1899] 1965: v), a leading figure in the neo-classical school of economics, was "controlled" by a natural law. (For an excellent analysis of the neoclassical treatment of George's philosophy of economics, see Gaffney (1993).)

Every agent of production is an owner of an input who gets a justifiable return in the production function. This return or the receipt of "the amount of wealth that each agent creates" is a factor payment. Factor payments consume all the values of the total output and thus there is no such thing as "surplus value" or anything that is over and above the inputs of the agents of production. There is no economic rent, no wages, and no profit. Clark's controlling natural law was a soulless, mechanistic, and mathematized system of market pricing based on utility-maximizing self-interest.

George's retention of the qualitative differences between the factors of production and his single-minded identification of economic rent as a non-economic surplus value that must be appropriated for society on moral grounds was utterly out of step with the abolition of such moral distinctions in the marginalist revolution. George's philosophy depended on a very strong evaluation of the qualitative uniqueness of economic rent in both the ethical sense as well as in the sense of it being a peculiarly unavoidable aspect of functional distribution. This distribution had to precede the science of exchanges and their associated systems of corrective justice, according to natural law, as Aristotle had established in the *Nicomachean Ethics*. The marginalist revolution inverted the classical statement of justice. The consequence for political economy was that social justice now became merely a matter of doing something to ameliorate the human condition after all the agents of production receive the amount of wealth they create.

Georgist reforms contribute to social economics by concentrating on economic justice in the Greater Leviathan. The post-neoclassical revolution is taking many forms. George's theory of the recapture of economic rent for social purposes is an inescapable part of that revolution. After more than a hundred years of marginalist and neo-classical hegemony the science of economics is returning to its ethical and classical roots. The land issue, nature, and the environment generally are no longer understood as simply a factor input. Equally, the recognition of the power of economic rent, especially urban ground rents, in the distribution of income and wealth has once again made George's philosophy of economics a guide for reforms in public finance, the alleviation of poverty, and long-term stewardship of the environment.

References

Anderson, R. (2003). *Critics of Henry George.* Oxford: Blackwell.

Aquinas, T. (1946). *Summa Theologica.* Trans. Fathers of the English Dominican Province. New York: Benziger Brothers.

———. (1964). *Commentary on Aristotle's Nicomachean Ethics.* Trans. C. I. Litzinger. Notre Dame: Dumb Ox Books.

Aristotle (1915). *The Complete Works of Aristotle.* Trans. W. D. Ross. Oxford: Oxford University Press.

Bernanke, B. S. (2007). "The Level and Distribution of Economic Well-Being." Remarks to Greater Omaha Chamber of Commerce, February 6.

Bruni, L. (2006). *Civil Happniess, Economics and Human Flourishing in Historical Perspective.* New York: Routledge.

Cicero, M. T. (1928). *De Re Publica.* Trans. C. W. Keyes. Cambridge, MA: Loeb Classic Library, The Harvard University Press.

Clark, J. B. ([1899] 1965). *The Distribution of Wealth: A Theory of Wages, Interest and Profit.* New York: August Kelly.

De Soto, Hernando. (2000). *The Mystery of Capitalism.* New York: Basic Books.

DeVitoria, F. (1991). *Political Writings.* Eds. A. Pagden and J. Lawrence. Cambridge: Cambridge University Press.

Eucken, R. (1912). *Life's Basis and Life's Ideal.* Trans. A. G. Widgery. London: Black.

Foley, D. (2006). *Adam's Fallacy: A Guide to Economic Theology.* Cambridge, MA: Harvard University Press.

Gaffney, M. (1993). *The Corruption of Economics.* London: Shepheard-Walwyn.

George, H. (1886). *The Principles of Political Economy.* London: Longmans.

———. (1981). *The Science of Political Economy.* New York: Robert Schalkenbach Foundation.

———. (1981b). *Social Problems.* New York: Robert Schalkenbach Foundation.

———. (1988). *A Perplexed Philosopher.* New York: Robert Schalkenbach Foundation.

Grabill, S. J. (2006). "The Fallacy of Adam's Fallacy." *Journal of Markets & Morality* 9(2).

Haakonssen, K. (2006). *The Cambridge Companion to Adam Smith.* New York: Cambridge University Press.

Huxley, T. (1890). *Collected Essays.*

Jupp, K. (2000). "Justice & Natural Law." *Geophilos* (1): 92–109.

Lisska, A. (1996). *Aquinas' Theory of Natural Law.* Oxford: Oxford University Press.

Locke, J. (1997). *An Essay Concerning Human Understanding,* Ed. R. Woolhouse. New York: Penguin.

Lottin, D. O. (1948). *Psychologie et Morale aux XII*[e] *et XIII*[e] *Siecles.* Louvain: Abbaye du Mont Cesar.

Maritain, J. (1951). *Man and the State.* Chicago: University of Chicago Press.

Médaille, J. (2007). *The Vocation of Business: Social Justice in the Marketplace.* New York: Continuum.

Moore, G. E. (1966). *Principia Ethica.* Cambridge: Cambridge University Press.

Murphy, J., and J. Coleman. (1990). *Philosophy of Law.* Boulder: Westview Press.

Peddle, F. K. (1993). "Henry George and Albert Schweitzer: Economic Justice and Reverence for Life." *Good Government* October.

Samuels, W. (2003). "Why the Georgist Movement Has Not Succeeded: A Speculative Memorandum." *American Journal of Economics and Scoiology* 62(3): 583–592.

Schwartzman, J. (1991). "Henry George and the Concept of Natural Law," Lafayette College Conference on Henry George, June 13–14.

Smith, A. (1937). *The Wealth of Nations.* New York: Modern Library.

Solow, R. (2006). "How to Understand the Economy." *New York Review of Books* 53(18): November 16.

Young, J. (1996). *The Natural Economy.* London: Shepheard-Walwyn.

Natural Law and the Roman Catholic Tradition: The Importance of Philosophical Realism

By Anthony J. Lisska*

Abstract. The intellectual tradition of Roman Catholicism considers natural-law theory as providing the philosophical machinery for articulating concepts central to thinking about moral theory, legal theory, and the social order. The thrust of this essay is to explicate the positions rooted in the writings of Aquinas on natural-law theory, a theory with which a Georgist might find some stimulating similarities. Conditions necessary for natural-law moral and legal theory are considered through an analysis of the central metaphysical concepts together with their historical development and contemporary significance.

Introduction

This essay addresses the wellspring of recent work in natural-law theory rooted in the texts of Thomas Aquinas, especially as illustrated by contemporary English-speaking philosophers. A central theme is the elucidation of the connections of natural-law theory with philosophical accounts associated with Roman Catholicism. The goal is to address those questions that focus attention on the realist and not the post-modernist foundation—in other words, a real order found in nature—for moral, political, and legal theory. Emphasis on analysis and interpretation will be directed towards what might be called the analytic tradition of contemporary Anglo-American philosophy rather than the traditional philosophical school known as Neo-Thomism. What is interesting conceptually is that much recent philosophical analysis in natural-law moral and legal theory extends beyond Neo-Thomism. For example, the late British philosopher,

*Anthony J. Lisska is the Maria Theresa Barney Professor of Philosophy at Denison University.

American Journal of Economics and Sociology, Vol. 71, No. 4 (October, 2012).

Philippa Foot, once endorsed the moral theory of Aquinas with the following words (1978: 2): "It is my opinion that the *Summa Theologiae* is one of the best sources we have for moral philosophy." The intellectual tradition of Roman Catholicism, however, considers natural-law theory as providing the philosophical machinery for articulating concepts central to thinking about moral theory, legal theory, and the social order. The tradition of natural law has focused attention on the role of human nature and the human person in moral theory. This is in contrast to the two major moral theories that dominated contemporary philosophy in most of the twentieth century: the utilitarianism rooted in John Stuart Mill and the formalism found in Immanuel Kant. Issues derived from natural-law theory include but are not limited to the following: just war theory, crimes against humanity, human natural rights, positive and negative human rights, and self-actualization moral theories. Moreover, these issues are central to the ethical naturalism found in Aristotle's *Nicomachean Ethics* and brought forward in the Roman Catholic tradition through Thomas Aquinas in his *Summa Theologiae, Prima Secundae,* Questions 90–97 (1946)—which is the classical cannon on natural law—and in Aquinas's *Commentary on Aristotle's Nicomachean Ethics* (1964: 2). Aquinas's ethical theory of natural law is grounded on the "order of nature" found in the human person and based upon a realist account of human nature.

The Donnybrook Between Henry George and Archbishop Michael Corrigan

In an essay written principally for an audience familiar with the writings of Henry George, a brief excursion into the ecclesiastical skirmish between the Georgists and several Roman Catholic prelates seems appropriate. This intellectual disagreement notwithstanding, an analysis of natural-law theory can be useful and enlightening for contemporary students of Henry George's writings. George did adhere to a form of natural-law and natural-right theory. In *Progress and Poverty*, George (2006: 186) wrote that "the use of the land" is "a right that is natural and inalienable." George provided, however, little analysis or justification for his theory of natural rights other than that they are God-given. This would be what contemporary philosophers would refer to as a theory of "Divine Prescriptivism" or "Theological Definism."

The late nineteenth-century annals of the Roman Catholic Church in the United States are replete with the struggles and eventual rancor that developed between Henry George together with Father Edward McGlynn and McGlynn's immediate ecclesiastical superior, Archbishop of New York Michael Corrigan. That a serious battle of social ideas emerged is not to be denied. Contemporary Georgists, it appears, know much about the nineteenth-century disagreement but little about the historical events leading up to this skirmish over revolutionary social ideas. Corrigan was a staunch member of the conservative wing of late nineteenth-century American Bishops; his nemesis was the liberal leaning Archbishop John Ireland of St. Paul. The conservative ecclesiastical leaders often appeared to be ultramontane (strongly emphasizing Papal authority) while the liberals wanted the Roman Church to be more responsive to the social policies not only of modern philosophical and theological writings, but also more conscious of the human enhancement central to the American experience of democracy. These two ecclesiastical wings clashed often over policy matters; two leading issues were the expected Papal condemnation of the Knights of Labor and the establishment of the Catholic University of America in Washington under the direct auspices of the American Bishops. The earlier debates over the role of Papal Infallibility centering on the First Vatican Council in 1869 began fueling these fires. Many American Bishops were opposed to defining this dogma, but Pius IX, who convened Vatican-I, wanted this item to be passed by the assembled prelates in Rome. Pius IX won this round, but not without causing deep alienation and serious consternation among members of his church, especially in parts of Germany, England, and the United States.

An historical query that one might pose judiciously is that had Henry George been running for Mayor in another major or minor American city—possibly St. Paul with Archbishop John Ireland as the reigning Roman Catholic ecclesiastical person in the area, Baltimore under James Cardinal Gibbons, or Peoria with Bishop John Lancaster Spalding in charge—this intellectual and social theory skirmish between George and the American Roman Catholic Church might not have occurred or at least would have been more modulated. In fact, it was Cardinal Gibbons who, despite the strong urging of Corrigan to the contrary, interceded with the Roman authorities not to condemn officially the writings of Henry George. In many ways, it was an historical accident that this rumbling event occurred in New York City. Personalities did enter into this fray. McGlynn and Corrigan had an intense dislike for one another going back to their mid-century student days in Rome (Morris 1997: 93).

Pius IX was followed by Leo XIII, a forward thinking and judicious successor to St. Peter in Rome. His 1891 Encyclical, *Rerum Novarum*, attempted to straddle the line between capitalism and socialism and to address the social issues of marginalization following from the industrial revolution. A decade earlier, Leo, in one of his first pontifical acts, wrote his famous encyclical, *Aeterni Patris*, in which he called for a renewed interest in the writings of Thomas Aquinas, the significant thirteenth-century medieval philosopher and theologian. From the impetus of this encyclical emerged the philosophical movement often referred to as Neo-Thomism; an important part of this philosophical network was to address the then contemporary social, economic, and political issues regnant in the western world. This follows directly from the philosophical commentaries of Thomas Aquinas on Aristotle's *Nicomachean Ethics* and the *Politics*, in which moral theory is closely related as a foundational inquiry for both economic theory and politics. Leo, however, probably did enunciate a more stringent theory of private property rights than one finds in the texts of Thomas. Nonetheless, it is in considering this close relationship between a moral theory rooted in a theory of the human person from which would develop both an economic theory and a political theory that a contemporary Georgist might consider with some interest the foundational moral principles articulated in natural-law moral and political theory. The thrust of this essay is to explicate in the contemporary idiom the positions rooted in the writings of Aquinas on natural-law theory, a theory with which a Georgist might find some stimulating similarities. Various contemporary articulations of natural-law theory will also be discussed along with differing interpretations.

Contemporary Work on Aquinas: The Connections with Roman Catholicism

At the beginning of an essay on Thomas Aquinas and natural-law theory, one must realize that there is no one singular interpretation of Aquinas's philosophical theories now accepted by most philosophers. For example, the contemporary state of scholarship delving into the philosophical work of St. Thomas illustrates fairly distinct and differing approaches to Aquinas's set of philosophical texts. Recent work falls generically into three categories. First, there are the more traditional Thomists, mostly Roman Catholic philosophers, who assume that significant philosophical insights are found in the metaphysical and moral realism of Aquinas and that these insights need to be explicated and considered afresh by contemporary students of natural-law theory. For the most part, these Thomist philosophers received their academic training in the important schools of neo-scholasticism both in North America and in Western Europe. Most of these philosophers undertook their formative work rooted in classical scholasticism as this philosophical school developed through the first two thirds of the twentieth century. In this group would be Etienne Gilson, Jacques Maritain, Anton Pegis, Joseph Owens, Ralph McInerny, John Wippel, Mary Clark, Benedict Ashley, William Wallace, and the legion of students trained in both North American and European institutes of traditional scholasticism. Most philosophers who identify themselves as "Neo-Thomists" would fit into this category. A sub-set under this generic rubric would be those philosophers following the insights of the Louvain Jesuit, Joseph Marechal, known as "Transcendental Thomists." These Transcendental Thomists attempt to reconcile the philosophical theories of Kant and Aquinas.

A second group are those philosophers called "Analytic Thomists," whose philosophical training and general perspective are rooted in English-speaking Angelo-American analytic philosophy. Recently, John Haldane from the University of St. Andrews in Scotland coined the term "Analytical Thomism." (Philosophers in this group, in addition to Haldane, would be Peter Geach, Elizabeth Anscombe, Anthony Kenny, Norman Kretzmann, James Ross, Brian Davies, Scott MacDonald, John Finnis, Eleonore Stump, John Peterson, and Christopher

Martin, among others. These philosophers can be grouped both generationally and in terms of American or British ancestry and identity.) In contrast to the more traditional Neo-Thomists, this group of philosophers, for the most part, discovered the philosophical texts and the corresponding insights of St. Thomas after studying analytic philosophy, principally within the confines of secular philosophy departments both in England and in the United States and Canada. Not all philosophers in this second group are Roman Catholics, although many are.

Thirdly, there is an emerging group of Cambridge University post-modernists associated with the work of John Milbank and Catherine Pickstock whose work is directed more towards theological issues. Advocates of what they call "Radical Orthodoxy," these theologians propose a re-evaluation of the concept of rationality and of truth in Thomas, which they consider compatible with several post-modernist themes. Milbank and Pickstock's (2001) *Truth in Aquinas* argues for this position. Some recent theological ethics, moreover, exemplifies this post-modernist thrust.

Hence, in English-speaking philosophy, three somewhat distinct groups of contemporary philosophers work seriously with the natural-law texts of St. Thomas: (1) the classical Neo-Thomists (with the Transcendental Thomists as a sub-set); (2) the Analytic Thomists; and (3) the post-modernist students of Aquinas linked to the Radical Orthodoxy movement.

Aquinas as a Philosopher

This essay considers Thomas Aquinas as a philosopher. One discovers significant discussions of philosophical issues connected with more than several issues central to major themes in analytic philosophy. Riding on the coattails of John Wippel's (2000) *magum opus* on Aquinas's metaphysics, it is clear that one can articulate a substantive philosophical approach in Aquinas that is independent conceptually from his theological concerns. Hence, this essay questions the revisionist Aquinian studies position, whose seeds are found in the major writings of the twentieth century Neo-Thomist, Etienne Gilson, suggesting that approaching Aquinas simply as a philosopher separated from theological matters is misguided conceptually (McInerny 2006). In addition, this essay argues against the Pickstock and Milbank claim that Aquinas's philosophical account of truth is reducible to a theological analysis. Aquinas can be read as a philosopher seeking tough-minded responses to significant philosophical issues. This analysis borrows heavily from what the late Henry Veatch (1971: 4) called "the structural history of philosophy," which attempts to lay bare the presuppositions with which every great philosopher works. In the contemporary dialectic going on in moral and legal theory in analytic philosophy, Aquinas's insights have much to offer. As this essay unfolds, Aquinas will be seen as a significant player in contemporary analytic philosophy's discussions of natural law. Nonetheless, several Neo-Thomist developments in natural law theory will not be neglected.

Aeterni Patris and the Renewal of Natural-Law Thinking in Roman Catholicism

Of principal interest to Georgists will be the principal role that Pope Leo XIII played in the late nineteenth-century resurgence of studies in Thomas Aquinas. Mason Gaffney (2000), for one, considers Leo XIII's social encyclical, *Rerum Novarum*, as particularly directed against the economic positions, especially private property, held by Henry George. Sociologist C. Joseph Nuesse (1985), however, argues that there is little evidence that Leo's encyclical was directed even remotely against the work of George. (See also Benestad 1986.) Accordingly, any discussion of natural-law theory in contemporary Roman Catholicism requires a brief account of the rise of Neo-Thomism in the last quarter of the nineteenth century. On August 4, 1879, Joachim Pecci, who recently had become Pope Leo XIII, published his influential encyclical, *Aeterni Patris*, calling for a re-examination and a restructuring—indeed a restoration—of what he considered to be classical Thomistic thought. Contemporary historians of philosophy realize that medieval philosophy is a broader, more complicated, and more sophisticated category in intellectual inquiry than the freshly elected Pope Leo XIII considered possible. Moreover, Pope John Paul II's 1998 encyclical, *Fides et Ratio*, substantively emphasized the arguments for philosophical realism first articulated by Leo XIII. That is the telling point in these issues—the importance of philosophical realism, especially in moral theory. It is important, therefore, to consider briefly the background out of which Leo XIII drafted *Aeterni Patris* (Boyle 1981).

Understanding the structure and content of *Aeterni Patris* requires coming to terms with the state of nineteenth-century Western European philosophy, when the shadow of Immanuel Kant hovered heavily over the philosophical enterprise. While Kantian theories were, of course, being undertaken within the context of the then recent work of Hegel, nonetheless the transcendental theory of Kant serves as the theoretical backdrop from which one needs to understand the rise of Neo-Thomism. With Kant, what Veatch called "the transcendental turn" is dominant. In using "the transcendental turn," Veatch brought to the forefront of philosophical discussion the radical nature of conceptual dependency that characterizes Kantian philosophy. In other words, the Kantian theory rendered the approach to philosophy dependent on the epistemological categories that structure the human mind. As a result, it was impossible to obtain a philosophical foothold in the nature of external reality. This conceptual dependency marked by the transcendental turn, therefore, entails a denial of both metaphysical and moral realism and depicts a foundationalism common to much modern and contemporary philosophy. One consequence of the transcendental turn is the abandonment of what we might call philosophical realism, which is understanding in some way the nature of external reality. *A fortiori*, this abandonment entails that natural-law theory rooted in any "order of nature" is suspect philosophically. This explains the almost absence of serious work in and entrenched philosophical opposition to natural-law theory in the predominant secular writers in western philosophy during the first three quarters of the twentieth century.

Part of the drive for the renewed interest in the philosophy of Thomas Aquinas in the last part of the twentieth century and now in the early years of the twenty-first rests in philosophical worries—what Aristotle referred to as "*aporia*"—similar to those that Joachim Pecci confronted in the 1870s. There are at least three factors contributing to this renewed interest in Aquinas's philosophy. All three, moreover, are conjoined with the burgeoning field of contemporary Aristotelian studies. First, there is the general rejection of the foundationalist heritage common to modern philosophy, with its roots in Descartes's *Meditations* and clearly articulated in Kant's two *Critiques*. Foundationalism accepts the Cartesian method found in the *Meditations* where the first philosophical query is an epistemological question— "How do I know that I know?" Secondly, the last third of the twentieth century witnessed the rejection of non-cognitivist positions commonly held earlier in the century. Non-cognitivist theories entailed the denial of any moral objectivity; natural-law theory fell under this critical umbrella. Thirdly, philosophical criticism in analytic philosophy has developed about the rise and entrenchment of post-modernism, with its dismissal of philosophical realism. The challenge of post-modernism to classical natural-law theory is neither an arcane nor idle philosophical question. Writing in the English Dominican monthly, *New Blackfriars*, Pickstock (2000) asked the following question: "How should one respond to the death of realism, the death of the idea that thoughts in our minds can represent to us the way things actually are in the world? For such a death seems to be widely proclaimed by contemporary philosophers." Natural-law theory requires a lively realism contrary to Pickstock's claims.

In *Truth in Aquinas*, Pickstock and Milbank's analysis of Aquinas's concept of truth is an attempt to place St. Thomas in the post-modernist camp. More than several Aquinas scholars raised serious questions about this particular anti-realist interpretation. Oxford philosopher and Aquinas scholar Anthony Kenny (2001: 14) indicated his intellectual concerns with this post-modernist analysis of Aquinas. "Since I have never myself been cast into the abyss of postmodernism, however, it may be churlish of me to sniff at any crumb of comfort that may be offered to those who have suffered that misfortune. But one thing I do know: *Truth in Aquinas* is far from being the truth on Aquinas."

The philosophical maxims that Milbank and Pickstock utilize together with the subjectivity of non-cognitivist moral theories are similar structurally to the transcendental turn that bothered Joachim Pecci in the nineteenth century. This is the denial of philosophical realism required by a study of human nature, which is central to natural-law theory. These philosophical positions dismiss conceptually any possibility for an ontological discussion of an "order of nature."

Recently, philosophers in the Anglo-American tradition have been attracted to the philosophical realism of Aquinas. A cluster of issues exerted a profound influence on the activity of philosophy in the last part of the twentieth century within which arose significant interest in the moral realism of Aquinas. What has been called "ordinary language philosophy," which was prevalent in the middle part of the twentieth century as developed in the writings and lectures of three prominent British analytic philosophers (Ludwig Wittgenstein, John Austin, and Gilbert Ryle), articulated a set of philosophical positions that challenged the prevailing themes of conceptual foundationalism common to modern and contemporary philosophy. This anti-foundationalism expressed by several mid-century philosophers rendered the philosophical ground, as it were, ripe for a reconsideration of the writings of Thomas Aquinas. Roman Catholic analytic philosophers Peter Geach and Elizabeth Anscombe, who were both students of Wittgenstein at Cambridge, initiated this work. John Haldane (2000a: 38) has expressed this changed direction in philosophy in the following passage: "Our knowledge of the external world is the starting point for philosophical reflection, the task of which is not to *justify* this knowledge but to *explain* it; to give an account of the scope of cognition, its genesis and its operations." In other words, the role of realism was beginning to replace the transcendental nature of contemporary philosophy. This replacement paved the way for a new appreciation of the realist thrust of Aquinas's natural-law philosophy.

In his analytic effort to understand the philosophy of Aquinas, Scott MacDonald (1993: 160) articulated much the same realist theme: "Aquinas does not build his philosophical system around a theory of knowledge. In fact, the reverse is true: he builds his epistemology on the basis provided by other parts of his system, in particular, his metaphysics and psychology." In other words, a realist theory of reality must precede any efforts at epistemology. Put more philosophically, Aquinas adopts both an ontological realism—reality has structured categories—and an epistemological realism—these categories are knowable.

This philosophical order is applicable directly to elucidating Aquinas's theory of natural law based upon some form of an order of nature. In other words, Aquinas accepts as philosophically sound the possibility of understanding reality. Moral theory, then, is a second-order activity based on the metaphysical foundation of the human person, which is the essence or natural kind—the order of nature—of human nature. Haldane argues against any traditionally Kantian foundationalist dimension in Aquinas's epistemology. One notices immediately the differences with Kant. Aquinas rejects what Veatch called "the transcendental turn," which is central to Kantian moral theory and independent of any realist order of nature. Moreover, most metaphysicians in the Roman Catholic tradition have been philosophical realists.

The anti-realism of post-modernism, the non-cognitivist denial of moral objectivity common to emotivism reducing moral judgments to expressions of deeply held emotions, and the transcendental turn characteristic of Cartesian and Kantian foundationalism are coextensive with the set of issues that Leo XIII challenged in 1879. Once *Aeterni Patris* was promulgated, Neo-Thomism developed rapidly as a major force in Roman Catholic philosophy. (The interested reader might consult McCool 1994.) In many ways, Neo-Thomism in its beginnings was a fruitful attempt undertaking serious philosophical analysis. That Neo-Thomism was perceived as somewhat fossilized in the middle part of the last century is a sad story that goes beyond the limits of this inquiry. Following the Second Vatican Council, the growth and development in Roman Catholic philosophical circles of various forms of continental philosophy had the consequence of rendering classical Neo-Thomist work marginal at best and obsolete at worst. Paradoxically, it was the analytic Thomists who helped restore vitality to the philosophy of Thomas Aquinas. It is with these philosophers, moreover, where one finds some of the best new creative work in natural-law moral and legal theory.

Neo-Scholasticism and Natural Law

A mainstay of scholastic work in natural-law theory in the United States in the first half of the twentieth century was the Catholic

University of America. The faculty took as its mission to apply the realist philosophy of Aquinas to the pressing social and political issues of the day, especially as these were being played out in the United States. Ignatius Smith, the Dominican Dean of the School of Philosophy, supported this philosophical dimension of the faculty with enthusiasm. John A. Ryan was a vibrant philosophical voice in this arena for Roman Catholic social and political discussions. Gaffney (2000: 5) notes that some commentators on Ryan judged that he expressed positive leanings towards several of George's positions.

In France, and later in the United States, Jacques Maritain was an advocate of using the philosophical insights of Aquinas in developing a theory of natural law. Maritain exerted efforts at the elucidation of a theory of natural human rights compatible with modern political theory. His *Man and the State* (1951) prompted serious work in natural-law discussions on rights theory. Yves Simon (1965: 7–8) undertook an explanatory role similar to Maritain and offered one of the more thorough accounts in the mid twentieth century of classical natural-law theory. His arguments in *The Tradition of Natural Law* articulate well that philosophical realism is a necessary condition for a consistent theory of natural law. The works of Maritain and Simon brought natural-law theory into secular discussions on major political and legal issues, especially natural-rights theory. Maritain was involved with the United Nations Declaration of Human Rights.

Secular Theories of Natural Law: Hart, Fuller, and MacIntyre

In discussing the renewal of natural-law theory in the mid twentieth century, one must begin with the natural-law writings of H. L. A. Hart (1961) and Lon Fuller (1964). Hart and Fuller contributed substantively to the revival of natural-law jurisprudence by focusing discussions on the Nuremberg trials with the corresponding criminal charges of "Crimes Against Humanity." Central to this revival are Hart's "core of good sense" in natural-law theory and Fuller's account of "procedural natural law." The contributions of Hart and Fuller to the contemporary revival of secular natural-law theory were significant and substantive.

Twenty years later, analytic philosophy and moral theory in English-speaking philosophy charted a new course with the publication in

1981 of Alasdair MacIntyre's remarkable treatise, *After Virtue*. The roots of much of MacIntyre's work lie in Aristotle and Aquinas. Nonetheless, Elizabeth Anscombe's (1958) important article "Modern Moral Philosophy" served as an earlier wake-up call to analytic philosophers. Anscombe indicated what she took to be the theoretical and practical bankruptcy of much analytic moral theory at the time, which was based either on emotivism or utilitarianism. Furthermore, she called for a re-working of philosophical psychology, a re-interpretation of practical reason, and a return to some sense of moral virtue. These three themes, Anscombe argued, were necessary conditions for a constructive renewal of ethical theory in analytic moral philosophy. MacIntyre's philosophical writing followed this general schema. Anscombe and MacIntyre are sympathetic with Mortimer Adler's (1990: 254) bold claim: "Aristotle's *Nicomachean Ethics* is the only sound, practical and undogmatic moral philosophy in the whole Western tradition." Leo XIII and John Paul II—and *a fortiori* Thomas Aquinas—would accept the spirit of Adler's judgment.

MacIntyre exerted significant influence in the resurgence of interest in the moral philosophy of both Aristotle and St. Thomas with *After Virtue* (1981), *Whose Justice, Which Rationality* (1988), *Three Rival Versions of Moral Enquiry* (1990), and *Dependent Rational Animals* (1999). Each monograph is a clarion call for renewed work in Aristotelian ethical theory. What natural law philosopher Russell Hittinger (1989: 449) proposed more than 20 years ago has proven to be accurate:

> MacIntyre has been a pioneer figure in what I have elsewhere referred to as the "recoverist" movement: those who wish to retrieve . . . the common morality of the West. If nothing else, MacIntyre has made this recoverist project professionally respectable. Less than a decade [now over two decades] has passed since its publication, yet many are already prepared to admit that *After Virtue* represents something pivotal.

MacIntyre argues, furthermore, that Aquinas was a premier commentator on Aristotle. MacIntyre's *After Virtue* produced a cottage industry centering on the discussions of virtue ethics. Anscombe and MacIntyre, among others, have argued against placing the virtue ethics of Aristotle and Aquinas into the theoretical dustbin with those theories of ethical naturalism rejected during most of the twentieth century.

The Role of the Human Person in a Teleological Context: Rational Nature, Affective Nature, Social Being

Given the renaissance of natural law in contemporary philosophy (those interested in this recent revival of natural-law theory might consult the author's (Lisska 2007) review essay on eight recent natural-law books), one needs to consider how the moral theory of Aquinas relates to the recent work in contemporary moral philosophy rooted in a theory of natural kinds. A natural kind would be an essence that defines the members of a certain class. Many historians of philosophy argue that the classical canon of natural-law theory is the set of passages in Questions 90–97 from the *Prima Secundae* of Aquinas's *Summa Theologiae*. Four principal points need addressing in order to render meaningful Aquinas's account of ethical naturalism rooted in the works of Aristotle:

1. The foundation of a theory of the human person.
2. The requirement of reason (knowing) as opposed to voluntarism (willing).
3. A theory of obligation.
4. The role of God in natural-law theory.

The concept of a sophisticated teleology rooted in a theory of the human person based on dispositional properties is central to an explication of Aquinas's position. Teleology, from the Greek work "*telos*" meaning "end," refers to the moral actions rooted in human nature. This is the ontological foundation for natural law in the human person, or human nature.

Foundation in the Human Person

Aquinas bases his moral theory, and *a fortiori* his theory of society and of human or positive law and a derivative but not an explicit theory of human rights, on the foundation of the human person as an instance of a natural kind. Aquinas argues that a human person is, by definition, a substantial unity grounding a set of potentialities, capacities, or dispositions. (In his metaphysics, the substantial form is the ontological ground for this set of dispositional properties.) Aquinas divides these capacities into three generic headings, which serve as the basis of this theory of a natural kind for human persons. This is Aquinas's account of human nature—the human natural kind and "order of nature"—which is based upon the insights of Aristotle's *Nicomachean Ethics* and his *De Anima*.

1. The set of Living Dispositions (what humans share with plants).
2. The set of Sensitive Dispositions (what humans share with animals).
3. The set of Rational Dispositions (what renders humans unique in the material realm).

Thomas's ethical naturalism provides for the moral protection that prevents, in principle, the hindering of the development of the basic human dispositions. Considered schematically, a living disposition is the capacity or drive all living beings possess in order to continue in existence. In human persons, this capacity is to be protected. (While Finnis and Veatch, among others, have developed a theory of human rights from the writings of Aquinas, there is not developed explicitly in Aquinas a theory of rights. The work of Brian Tierney (1997) might be consulted on these issues. However, a right is determined on the foundation of protecting the basic human dispositional properties.) Had humans been created or evolved differently (for example, Aquinas appears to have accepted evolution through the *rationes seminales* of Augustine), a different set of proscriptions would hold. A protection is what it is because human nature is what it is. This analysis is similar structurally to what Hart (1961: 194) in his discussion of the "natural necessities" called the human right to the protection against violence.

In a similar fashion, one of the rational dispositions Aquinas considered is the drive human beings have to know—our innate curiosity to know and to understand. Aquinas suggests that this disposition is only developed when human persons know propositions that are true. Hence, human persons have a "moral claim" to the truth. Again, these basic claims protect what human persons are as human beings. Oxford philosopher John Finnis once argued, for instance, that college faculty have an obligation not to teach that which is known to be false because this fractures the right to true propositions, which right students as human persons possess intrinsically. Finnis offered the same principle for political, academic, and religious leaders. This is based, Finnis (1998: 160) argues, upon the classic position of "a conception of human dignity and worth, precisely as it bears on the interpersonal act of communication." The moral claim would also hold for political leaders, especially in determining methods for governing society. In this regard, natural-law theory, in principle, responds to political queries about the social order. Aquinas also argues that this disposition is the basis for what he, following Aristotle, referred to as the social nature of human persons. Aquinas rejected the atomistic view of human nature exemplified, for instance, in Hobbes's egoistic account of human nature or indicated in the human isolation of Sartre's existentialism. What is central in Aquinas's theory of natural law, accordingly, is that moral theory rests upon the social nature of human persons together with the obligation of each human agent to act in such a way that one's natural, human ends are fulfilled. This, of course, leads to the attainment of *eudaimonia* or "functioning well" as a human person. Moreover, the necessity of reason as opposed to will is emphasized continually in the writings of Thomas. Throughout his discussion of law-making and moral theory, Aquinas argues that reason, both speculative and practical, is to be employed with vigor. Law is, as Aquinas emphatically states, "an ordinance of reason." A purely voluntarist account, which reduces moral justification to "an act of willing" or "undertaking an action," is, according to Aquinas, incorrect. (In contemporary jurisprudence, both Fuller and Golding defend versions of reason and are opposed to a voluntarist account.) Teleology counts for the development of these dispositional properties that determine the nature of a human person. This is similar to what the twentieth-century psychologist, Carl Rogers (1964: 160–167), referred to as "self-actualization."

The English Dominican, Columba Ryan (1965: 28), once wrote that these three general aspects of human nature are "the good of the individual survival, biological good, and the good of human communication." In his *The Morality of Law*, Fuller (1964: 184–186) argued for communication as a necessary condition for what he called a substantive theory of natural law. The American philosopher of law, Martin Golding (1974: 242–243), referred to the living dispositions as the "basic requirements of human life," the sensitive dispositions as the "basic requirements for the furtherance of the human species," and the rational dispositions as "the basic requirements for the promotion of [a human person's] good as a rational and social being." In his *Aquinas*, Finnis (1998: 81) writes as follows: "The order Aquinas has in mind is a metaphysical stratification: [1] what we have in common with all substances, [2] what, more specifically, we have in common with other animals, and [3] what is peculiar to us as human beings."

Martha Nussbaum (1993: 263–264) of the University of Chicago, in elucidating themes in Aristotelian moral theory, articulated eight fundamental properties analogous to the Aristotelian analysis: "we can nonetheless identify certain features of our common humanity, closely related to Aristotle's original list." Nussbaum's eight characteristics are mortality, the body, pleasure and pain, cognitive capability, practical reason, early infant development, affiliation or a sense of fellowship with other human beings, and humor. Like MacIntyre, Nussbaum is much concerned that English-speaking moral theory has been caught up in what she takes to be an overly Kantian direction. Rather than posing the "obligation question" first—which is a common Kantian approach—Nussbaum suggests that moral philosophers need to ask the Aristotelian question first: "What kind of lives should we live?" Nussbaum argues that Aristotelian moral theory—and Aquinas's ethical naturalism would fit here also—can provide a necessary corrective to the strict deontological or Kantian approaches to moral theory on the one hand and to utilitarian approaches on the other. Both of these moral theories, until recently, dominated contemporary analytic moral philosophy. Through most of the twentieth century, ethical naturalism as found in Aristotle and Aquinas was not a vibrant component of significant moral discussions in analytic philosophy. But the philosophical landscape has changed.

In his *Natural Law and Natural Rights*, Finnis (1982: 85–92) put forward what he took to be a list of basic human goods: life, knowledge, play, aesthetic experience, friendship, practical reasonableness, and religion. Finnis, however, argues that this set of basic goods is known by practical reason and is not grounded in a philosophical anthropology (Finnis 1983). The point here is that these theories of ethical naturalism, for the most part, depend upon the concepts of the human person and practical reason and require the "functioning well" of that person—all of which are rooted in Aristotle's concept of *eudaimonia* or "happiness." Furthermore, for each of these philosophers, with the exception of Finnis, *eudaimonia* is rooted in the natural kind of the human person, which is the metaphysical foundation necessary for moral theory in natural law theory.

Alasdair MacIntyre and Philippa Foot

In his first major discussion of Aristotelian moral theory, *After Virtue*, MacIntyre was chary about committing his theory to any one particular ontological foundation. In *Dependent Rational Animals*, however, MacIntyre reconsidered and defended his return to the metaphysical biology that he rejected in *After Virtue*. Haldane (2000b: 154) wrote about MacIntyre and the metaphysical underpinnings of natural-law theory in the following way:

> There is a further reason to view MacIntyre apart from the other figures mentioned, for until quite recently he has argued that moral philosophy can and should be conducted without reliance upon a general account of human nature of the sort provided by the Aristotelian-Thomistic tradition, and which has within that tradition generally been thought to be essential for ethics. In his most widely discussed book, *After Virtue*, MacIntyre goes so far as to disparage the very idea of what he there terms "metaphysical biology," but in his most recent work, *Dependent Rational Animals*, published almost twenty years later, he retracts this criticism and argues that an idea of the good for an agent cannot be formed independently of having a conception of the kind of being it is.

Haldane focused attention on this metaphysical turn now found in MacIntyre's later works. MacIntyre (1999: x) himself explained this significant change in his position:

> In *After Virtue* I had attempted to give an account of the place of the virtues, understood as Aristotle had understood them, within social prac- tices, the lives of individuals and the lives of communities, while making that account independent of what I called Aristotle's "metaphysical biology." Although there is indeed good reason to repudiate important elements in Aristotle's biology, I now judge that I was in error in supposing an ethics independent of biology to be possible. . . . No account of the goods, rules and virtues that are definitive of our moral life can be adequate that does not explain—or at least point us towards an

explanation—how that form of life is possible for beings who are biologically constituted as we are, by providing us with an account of our development towards and into that form of life.

MacIntyre is not alone in recommending a return to Aristotelian moral and legal theory. An earlier passage noted Philippa Foot's judgment about the importance of Aquinas's moral theory; in addition, she wrote the following about the significance of the Aristotelian tradition in moral theory (2000: 123):

> What then is to be said about the relation between fact and value? My thesis . . . is that the grounding of a moral argument is ultimately facts about human life—facts of the kind that Anscombe mentioned in talking about the good that hangs on the institution of promising, and of the kind that I spoke of in saying why it was a part of rationality for human beings to take special care each for his or her own future. In my view, therefore, a moral evaluation does not stand over against the statement of a matter of fact, but rather has to do with facts about a particular subject matter, as do evaluations of such things as sight and hearing in animals, and other aspects of their behaviour. . . . Similarly, it is obvious that there are objective, factual evaluations of such things as human sight, hearing, memory, and concentration, based on the life form of our own species. [Likewise] the evaluation of the human will should be determined by facts about the nature of human beings and the life of our own species. . . . [Thus] moral action is rational action, and . . . human beings are creatures with the reason to recognise reasons for action and to act on them.

Twenty years earlier in a passage previously noted, Foot wrote that she considered Aquinas's moral theory important even for secular theories of morality. Haldane (2000b: 152) once noted the importance of Foot's analysis: "Yet it was Foot, an atheist, who most fulsomely acknowledged the value of Thomas's writings for anyone working in moral philosophy." In her introductory remarks written a quarter century ago in *Virtues and Vices*, Foot (1978: 1–2) defended her position on Aristotle and Aquinas in the following way:

> It is certain in any case that the most systematic account [of the virtues] is found in Aristotle, and in the blending of Aristotle and Christian philosophy found in St. Thomas. By and large Aquinas followed Aristotle—sometimes even heroically—where Aristotle gave an opinion, and where St. Thomas is on his own, as in developing the doctrine of the theological virtues of faith, hope and charity. . . . [In addition] in his theocentric doctrine of happiness, he still uses an Aristotelian framework where he can . . . for

instance in speaking of happiness as man's last end. However, there are different emphases and new elements in Aquinas's ethics: often he works things out in far greater detail than Aristotle did, and it is possible to learn a great deal from Aquinas that one could not have got from Aristotle. It is my opinion that the *Summa Theologiae* is one of the best sources we have for moral philosophy, and moreover that St. Thomas's ethical writings are as useful to the atheist as to the Catholic or other Christian believer.

MacIntyre's and Foot's remarks are important in the contemporary discussions of the renewal of natural-law theory based on the writings of Aristotle and Aquinas. Both suggest the importance of a metaphysically grounded theory of an "order of nature" found in the human person. This position is a necessary condition for explicating a consistent view of natural-law moral and legal theory in Thomas Aquinas.

A Possible Account for a Theory of Obligation

In providing a theory of obligation, one might interpret Aquinas as adopting a "metaphysics of finality." Veatch (1990: 116) uses this concept (which is gleaned from the insights of R. A. Gauthier, the French Dominican commentator on Aristotle and Aquinas, who first addressed the issues of the metaphysics of finality) in several of his works. The ends to be attained are determined by the content of the natural kind of the human person; this differs radically from ordinary teleological theories like utilitarianism. Therefore, the dispositional view of human nature enables Aquinas's version of natural-law theory to provide a justification for a theory of obligation. In other words, these ends ought to be obtained because of the very dispositional structure of human nature. The ends are not arbitrary but are determined by the natural kind of human nature itself. Obligation is rooted in the ends themselves. This is an important claim necessary to explicate conceptually Aquinas's account of teleology. This teleology grounded in the concept of a natural kind comprised of dispositional properties provides an alternative account of teleology to that found in modern utilitarianism.

An important jurisprudential corollary follows from this analysis. The role that this theory of ethical naturalism contributes to successful law-making should be apparent. Any law, which, all things being equal, hinders the development of a natural disposition in a human person, is inherently unjust. Aquinas provides a set of criteria by means of which a theory of natural rights could be developed, and from that, a justified theory of law.

Human Nature and the Existence of God

In the texts on law in the *Summa Theologiae*, Aquinas does speak of eternal law and divine law. A requisite part of this analysis is to discuss how these concepts fit into the scheme of interpretation put forward in this essay. Briefly put, divine law is revelation or biblical propositions; as such, this theological concept does not apply to a philosophical analysis. Eternal law, on the other hand, is reducible to the divine archetypes in the mind of God. The above analysis suggests that what Aquinas needs for a consistent account of natural law is a metaphysical theory of natural kinds. This is the first question Aquinas must answer in his ontology if he is to develop a theory of natural law. Once he has justified his theory of natural kinds, then a second ontological question arises: Is the individual instance of a natural kind itself ontologically self-explanatory and totally independent, or is it a dependent being? In other words, are Peter, Paul and Mary independent beings in their ontological foundations, or are they existentially dependent beings? Aquinas argues for dependency, but he regards this question of ontological dependency emphatically as a second-order metaphysical question.

It is only at this juncture in Aquinas's metaphysical scheme that God enters. God, as necessary being, provides the answer to this second-order metaphysical question about the dependent character of individuals of natural kinds. However, one could construct a theory of natural law on the basis only of a natural-kind ontology composed of dispositional properties. What Aquinas provides additionally is an explanation in terms of ontological dependency. A naturalist account, so Aquinas would suggest, is not a false moral theory but rather an incomplete metaphysical theory. He can develop a theory of ethical naturalism from his account of a human essence as a natural kind. It is only when one asks about ontological dependency, however, that God as a Source of Existence becomes significant philosophically. Aquinas adopts a consistent metaphysics of natural kinds without an appeal to a divine being. This alone can serve as the ontological ground for natural law in Aquinas. On a related note, if one asks about an interpretation of scripture passages about human beings made in the image and likeness of God, Aquinas uses the exemplar language manifested in the eternal law that he adopted from Augustine and, *a fortiori*, from Plato. This exemplar language explains the eternal law.

To put this important matter a bit differently, natural-kind theory in Aquinas is based upon the empirical principles he discovered and adopted in the Aristotelian texts, both those that came to Paris from the Islamic translating institute at Toledo and especially those texts that his Dominican confrere, William of Moerbeke, provided for him from the Middle East. This empiricism requires that *"Nihil est in intellectu quod non prius fuerit in sensu"* (nothing is in the intellect that was not first in the senses). This epistemological maxim asserts that human knowers become aware of the content—the concepts—of natural kinds through the empirical process worked out in Aristotle's *De Anima* and in Book Two of the *Posterior Analytics*, which are texts in the philosophy of mind in Aristotle that Aquinas appropriated almost *in toto*. Since moral theory is a second-order activity for Aquinas, as it was for Aristotle, the concept of a human essence first must be determined. Aquinas does not argue that a human knower needs Divine knowledge in order to be aware of essences. Aquinas rejected the theory of Divine Illumination proposed by Augustine and adopted by earlier medieval philosophers.

It is possible, therefore, to defend the theoretical possibility for reconstructing the texts of Aquinas so that a version of natural law makes good philosophical sense without requiring as a necessary condition a position of Theological Definism. Aquinas was, of course, a theologian and a philosopher. The argument proposed in this analysis, however, articulates the "logic" of his argument suggesting that the role of God in natural-law theory is a final ontological question. Aquinas's hylomorphic metaphysics can account for the content of a human essence—the natural kind—without an appeal to the eternal law. There is no need, therefore, to appeal to a divine being in order to understand the content of a human essence. The foundation of natural law depends upon natural kinds, which is a metaphysical issue resolved in terms of Aquinas's metaphysics, not his theology.

Natural Law and the Common Good

One relevant aspect of natural-law theory to contemporary political thought concerns the common good and the role of community in moral and political theory. Aquinas argues that the common good—the commonweal—of a society must be part of the enactment of every positive law based upon the natural law. Finnis renders the common good into English as "the public good." A law is never justified for the private interest of one or a few citizens. Furthermore, the common good or the commonweal of a society must not be neglected arbitrarily through the enactment of a law. Like Aristotle before him, Aquinas believed that a human person, as a social person, achieved her development through the auspices of a society. Donne's claim that "No man is an island" would ring true to Aquinas. The recent work of Michael Sandel (1984: 15–17) and Charles Taylor (1989) on the importance of community hearkens back to Aquinas on the common good. The common good, while based on the concept of human nature, nonetheless is more than the collection of individual goods. It is that set of goods necessary to maintain the fabric of a just society. The rules for governing society are rooted in the development of the human person and contribute to the functioning well of the commonweal of the society. Finnis argues that the elements of the common good are "justice and peace." Finnis (1998: 226–227) elaborates on this concept by suggesting that "peace," "concord—the tranquility of order," and "a sufficiency of at least the necessities of life" are necessary conditions for the common good. Of course, each of these is more than the acquisition of an individual virtue or a specific individual good.

In her political writings based on Aristotelian insights, Nussbaum actively promotes the concept of the social or public good. This is a significant influence of natural law on contemporary political theory. Nussbaum once wrote the following about the importance of Aristotelian insights on the role of government and politics (Magee 1998: 53):

> I think there are a lot of good things [in Aristotle's political theory], and among the good things is an account of the proper function of government or politics as the provision to each citizen of all the necessary conditions for the living of a rich good human life. This view seems to me well worth

examining today, as an alternative to views that see the job of government in connection with the maximization of utility.

Aquinas adopted these Aristotelian insights on the nature of society and the role of good government. In a different text, Nussbaum (1993: 265) continues her reflections on this theme:

> I discuss an Aristotelian conception of the proper function of government, according to which its task is to make available to each and every member of the community the basic necessary conditions of the capability to choose and live a fully good human life, with respect to each of the major human functions included in that fully good life. I examine sympathetically Aristotle's argument that . . . that task of government cannot be well performed, or its aim well understood, without an understanding of these functionings—[i.e.], the major human functions included in that fully good life.

This second passage is taken from *The Quality of Life*, an anthology Nussbaum jointly edited with the Swedish Bank Prize economist, Amartya Sen. Nussbaum's texts mirror the natural-law suggestions of one scholar (Golding 1975: 31) who asserted that political and legal theory—and I submit, economic theory—must be attentive to "human needs, human purposes, and the human good." Henry George's treatise, it appears, would adopt this position also. Nussbaum's work is similar structurally with several important themes long associated with natural-law moral and political theory. Paul Sigmund (1993: 117) of Princeton University once wrote that Aquinas's ". . . integrated and logically coherent theory of natural law . . . continues to be an important source of legal, political and moral norms," and that Aquinas's "accomplishments have become part of the intellectual patrimony of the west, and have inspired political and legal philosophers . . . down to the present day." Nussbaum, Finnis, and Sigmund address the conceptual importance of considering the role of the common or public good in any attempt to work out a constructive and consistent social and political theory. This is consistent with traditional Roman Catholic social theory. The shadows of Aristotle and Aquinas hover significantly over the philosophical remarks on the nature of society and the rule of law articulated by these contemporary philosophical realists. A Georgist would find several of these positions intellectually compatible.

The Response of Contemporary Jurisprudence to Thomas Aquinas

In natural-law jurisprudence, philosophers in the analytic tradition offer evidence of significant work with the texts of Aquinas. Finnis is probably the most influential contemporary Aquinas scholar writing on natural-law theory. His *Natural Law and Natural Rights* developed a contemporary reconstruction of classical natural-law theory, where he noted (1982: 398): "Most persons who study jurisprudence or political philosophy are invited at some stage to read Thomas Aquinas's Treatise on Law." Finnis appropriated the early insights of the American Neo-Thomist, Germain Grisez. Grisez's (1965) seminal article on practical reason, which appeared in the old *Natural Law Forum*, is an important hallmark in what is called "the new natural law theory." More than any other analytic philosopher, Finnis's work is almost singularly important in bringing Aquinas's treatise on natural law into mainstream twentieth-century jurisprudence. Finnis's *Natural Law and Natural Rights*, conjoined with his *Fundamentals of Ethics* (1983) and his treatise on Aquinas's political theory, *Aquinas: Moral, Political and Legal Theory* (1998), articulate and defend this "new natural law theory." Robert George has published profusely defending Finnis's account of natural law. His *Making Men Moral* (1993) proposes to reconcile natural-law theory with human-rights theories in the American Liberal tradition. George attempts to engage in a philosophical dialectic with the work of Ronald Dworkin, Robert Nozick, and John Rawls, all of whom are among the foremost philosophers of human-rights theory in recent American political philosophy. George suggests that natural-law political theory can assist in developing a more substantive and a less formalist moral and political theory.

In offering a critique of Finnis's theory of natural law, which rejects a philosophical anthropology as a necessary condition, Veatch and McInerny argue that Finnis's account of Aquinas removes the metaphysical foundation for natural law (Lisska 1991). Finnis's theory is reducible to the claim of "Natural law without nature." It appears that the shadow of Kant hovers more heavily on this so-called new theory of natural law than Grisez, Finnis, or George are wont to admit.

Veatch is another non-Thomist twentieth-century philosopher who worked vigorously with the natural-law theory of Aquinas and who addressed the importance of natural law in developing an adequate account of human rights. His last books were *Human Rights: Fact or Fancy?* (1986) and *Swimming Against the Current in Contemporary Philosophy* (1990). Acknowledging the importance of Thomas Aquinas on his own philosophical work, Veatch (1990: 13) once wrote the following: "May I simply say that my own program ought perhaps to be regarded as amounting to little more than exercises in dialectic, and in a dialectic directed to the overall purpose of trying to rehabilitate Aristotle and Aquinas as contemporary philosophers." This development of rights theory in natural law is an important and significant contribution to contemporary political theory.

Other persons doing important work in this area are two University of Notre Dame faculty, Jean Porter on natural-law theory and David Solomon on virtue ethics. Porter's (1999) *Natural and Divine Law* and *Nature as Reason: A Thomistic Theory of the Natural Law* (2005) provide a historical analysis of the origins of medieval natural-law theory together with suggestions for renewed interest in Aquinas for what she calls Christian Ethics. Christina Trainia (1999) of Northwestern University published *Feminist Ethics and Natural Law*, which proposes an interconnectedness between contemporary feminist ethical theory and natural-law foundations. (Trainia and her Northwestern University colleagues sponsored a cross-disciplinary 1997 conference, "The Character, Influence, and Recovery of Thomist Moral Reasoning," dedicated explicitly to the renewed interest in Aquinas's moral theory.) Eleonore Stump, now of St. Louis University, and Cornell's Scott MacDonald (1999) edited a *Festschrift* for their mentor, Norman Kretzmann, entitled *Aquinas's Moral Theory.* David Braybrooke (2001) from the University of Texas has attempted to understand insights from the natural-law tradition in his re-working of modern political philosophy. These examples illustrate the serious work undertaken of late in natural-law moral theory and jurisprudence by both Roman Catholic and non-Roman Catholic philosophers and indicate that more has occurred recently than one finds during the first three quarters of the twentieth century—Hart and Fuller notwithstanding, both of whom had a deep respect for natural-law jurisprudence in St. Thomas.

While natural-law theory, with particular reference to Aquinas's texts, is often considered a theoretical source for natural rights,

Aquinas does not consider explicitly the concept of natural right. Contemporary philosophers like Veatch, Finnis, and Henrik Syse, however, argue that a philosophical derivation of rights from Aquinas's moral theory is possible. The recent work of Brian Tierney (1997) on the history of rights theory is a significant analysis into this thicket of jurisprudential issues. According to Veatch, one determines a concept of "duty" based on the set of human dispositional properties. Next, a natural right becomes the "protection" of the duties derived from the natural kind of the human person. This proposed derivation, so Veatch suggests in *Human Rights: Fact or Fancy*, limits the present debate on the nature and scope of rights and offers a response to L. W. Sumner's (1986: 20) claim that "the rhetoric of rights is out of control." Veatch argues, however, only for the possibility of "negative rights," which are protections; he is less certain about the derivation in natural-law theory of "positive rights" or "entitlements." A negative right as a protection would be exemplified in the rights to property, life, and liberty. These are, Veatch argues, the "rights not to be interfered with." Positive rights as entitlements, on the other hand, would be exemplified in the rights to education, health care, retirement benefits, and so forth. One might respond to Veatch's position on the issue that natural-law theory only justifies negative rights by arguing that Aquinas's account based on the fundamental dispositions of the human person could justify a limited set of positive human rights. Nussbaum's capabilities theory offers a justification of positive rights. In fact, Nussbaum (2007: 15) uses this approach in her critique of several judgments recently offered by the Roberts's United States Supreme Court. Space constraints, however, limit the explication of this argument here. Nonetheless, it is important to note that in opposition to most modern and contemporary liberal theories of right, in Aquinas's mind the concept of right cannot be separated from the concept of the good. (For a contemporary discussion of a general Thomistic theory of human rights, one might consult Syse 2007.)

While Aquinas in the *Summa Theologiae* (1946: IIa—IIae, Q. 57) discussed *jus naturale* as contrasted with *jus positivum*, any indication of a natural right in the modern sense is either absent from his thought or muddled at best. Aquinas's use of *jus*, nonetheless, is often translated as "right." This discussion immediately precedes the general analysis of justice or "*justitia.*" Aquinas discussed the concept of justice in the following way: "It is proper to justice, in comparison with the other virtues, to direct human persons in their relations with others; this is appropriate because justice denotes a kind of equality." The term "*jus*" derived from "*justitia*" is more properly rendered into English as "the just thing" or "the just state of affairs." Hence, a "*jus*" is a "right thing" that occurs among persons or between persons and things; in other words, it is the "right thing" that takes place in various human situations. In light of this account of justice, Aquinas considers a *jus* that is natural and a *jus* that is positive. A natural *jus* comes about by the very nature of the case while a positive *jus* arises only with common consent, either between individual persons or between the community and its citizens.

In Aquinas's view, accordingly, a *jus* refers to a relational state of affairs that either holds or does not hold. This *objective* sense of *jus* is different conceptually from the *subjective* account of a human right as articulated by later medieval and Renaissance philosophers. For these later philosophers, right evolves into a *subjective* claim that one is due something or one needs to be protected from some action, which corresponds to the modern account of a human right. The sixteenth-century Jesuit, Francisco Suarez, elucidated this concept of individual natural right. He defined a *jus*, which is a right, as "a certain moral power that every human person has, either over her own property or with respect to what is due to her" (Suarez 1612). This "moral power" is a subjective natural right. (Recent scholarship indicates that the concept of a subjective natural right may have developed as early as the fourteenth century in the writings of the Franciscan philosophers and theologians.) Suarez articulated in addition a list of individual natural rights for human agents, which is more rights theory than one discovers in the texts of Aquinas. For Aquinas, on the other hand, *jus* is an *objective*, relational state of affairs; this is fundamentally different from what later philosophers call a "*jus*," which is subjective. Simply put, *jus* in Aquinas is an *objective* relational state; *jus* in later medieval and modern philosophers is a *subjective* claim referring to some quality or action. This distinction indicates significant differences found in the concepts of *objective* and *subjective* rights.

While Aquinas does not articulate a theory of natural rights, none-theless the contemporary philosopher might propose a derivative theory in which a right might be that which protects the development of the dispositional properties. An example might go like the following: Aquinas argued that a principal living disposition, what Columba Ryan called the "biological good," is the foundation for a sense of continuing in existence. This living disposition is the meta-ethical grounding, so Aquinas argued, for the moral claim that it is immoral to engage in arbitrary killing. Human life, therefore, is to be protected. It follows that killing is an immoral action, not because it violates a divine commandment, but rather because killing frustrates or hinders the continual development of the natural dispositional property to continue in existence—the biological good. This argument reminds one of Hart's (1961: 190–195) concept of "survival" as a natural necessity." Natural-law theory entails that what comprises evil is the repression or destruction of a natural dispositional property. The same natural-law argument applies to the development of sensitive and rational dispositional properties and their opposing repressions or destructions. A human person has, therefore, a *subjective* power or right that protects the possibility of the development of the disposi-tional properties, which in turn grounds the *objective* right. (For a more thorough discussion of these issues, see Lisska 1996, 2001: ch. 9.)

Aquinas (1946: IIa–IIae, Q. 58, a. 1), like Aristotle, wrote that justice "is a habit whereby a human person renders to each one what is due by a constant and perpetual will." It follows that justice, by its very name and function, implies the concept of equality. Justice, therefore, entails a relation to another; this follows because no entity is ever equal to itself but always to another. Justice is twofold. First, legal or general justice directs human agents towards fulfilling the common good or the public interest of the community or *civitas.* The second category of justice directs the human agent in matters relating to particular goods and specific persons. These two categories of justice are what Aquinas refers to as "commutative justice" and "distributive justice." Commutative justice is concerned with the mutual dealings between two persons, while distributive justice, on the other hand, is concerned with the relations between the community itself—the *civitas*—and the citizens in the community. In effect, distributive justice is concerned with the distribution of the common goods of the *civitas* proportionately and fairly to the citizens of the *civitas*. Commenting on the virtue of justice as elucidated by Aquinas, the English Dominican Thomas Gilby (1975: xv) once wrote: "Justice is an analogical value pitched at various levels according as it renders what is due for the common good of the political community (*justitia generalis*), to one private person from another (*justitia commutativa*), and to one person from the political group (*justitia distributiva*)."

Aquinas's account of justice is dependent upon the Aristotelian analysis. Aquinas, it would appear, has some *prima facie* structural links to the contemporary "justice as fairness" doctrine pronounced by John Rawls; Rawls (1972: 85–86) suggested that fundamentally the concept of justice is the "fair dealings" of the citizens in a society with one another and the "fair dealing" of the society itself with the citizens of the society. It would appear that Aquinas was ahead of his time in his Aristotelian analysis of justice as fairness. A Georgist might find the preceding analysis of human rights theory useful theoretically and practically.

Human or Positive Law in the Natural-Law Tradition

For Aquinas, the structure of positive or human law is a straightforward extrapolation from the concepts central to a justified theory of natural law. Positive law is the articulation and promulgation of statutes that provide for the smooth working of a community. Aquinas, following Aristotle, argued for the common good, which is best accomplished through a workable system of law. The purpose of positive law is to establish and enhance the general conditions that make the common good possible. In his *Commentary on the Nicomachean Ethics*, Aquinas (1964: Book V, Lecture 2) wrote: "Laws are passed to ensure the smooth running of the commonwealth." In his short monograph, *On Kingship*, Aquinas discussed the function of positive law: "If by nature, human persons are to live together, then the community they form needs to be ruled. . . . Any organism would disintegrate were there no unifying force working for the common good of all the members" (*De Regimine Principium*, I).

Positive law, for Aquinas, is the set of prescriptions enacted, articulated, and promulgated by the person or persons in charge of the community in order to provide for the smooth functioning of the common good. Golding (1975: 31) once suggested the following insights, noted earlier, about the intrinsic value of considering positive or human law from the natural-law perspective: "The lesson of the natural law tradition is that both [legal effectiveness and legal obligation] involve attention to human needs, human purposes and the human good. Whatever the problems of this tradition, we cannot ignore its lesson in trying to understand the law that is."

Golding articulated the following five principles as necessary conditions for natural law jurisprudence:

1. Laws possess directive power.
2. This directive power is based on reason.
3. The will is subservient to reason; this is in opposition to the voluntarism of the legal positivists.
4. Reason ultimately directs laws for the purpose of the common good and for the good of the individual (this is in opposition to the jurisprudential theory known as legal realism).
5. There is a necessary connection between law and morality.

The influence of Fuller's procedural natural law hovers over Golding's principles. Golding is interested in determining the rules of procedure necessary for a legal justification of working towards an end in the process of law-making. This is the "purposiveness" of law, a theme to which Golding holds as a necessary condition for a theory of natural-law jurisprudence.

In matters concerning the extent and pervasiveness of the legal system, Aquinas, it would appear, might be regarded as a "legal conservative." Sigmund (1993: 220) once noted that "Lord Acton described Aquinas as 'the First Whig' or believer in the limitation of governmental power." In quoting Isidore, Aquinas (1946: Ia–IIae, Q. 95, a. 1, *sed contra*) articulated his own position that the primary purpose of law is to protect the innocent:

> We remember what Isidore once wrote: "Human laws have been made so that human audacity might be held in check by their threat, and also so that the innocent might be protected from those exerting evil; and among those

capable of doing evil, the dread of punishment might prevent them from undertaking harm." It should be noted, however, that these matters are most important and necessary for human beings. Therefore it is necessary that human laws should be made.

From these texts, it would appear that Aquinas would not accept a legal system that entailed a primary function of law to foster social change or any more modern conceptions of the legal enterprise. In addition, it would seem that Aquinas's interest principally rests in what contemporary jurisprudence would refer to as criminal law and is less concerned about procedural law. Aquinas appears to have no concept of what Hart referred to as secondary rules of law, which provide for the procedures that render law-making possible.

Aquinas undertook most of his philosophical writing on legal matters within the Aristotelian framework, which argued emphatically that all humans are by nature social beings. It follows that, while the promotion of the common good or the public interest is an integral part of the legal system, nonetheless this promotion is, so it seems, always implemented with a legal conservative leaning. Contemporary readers may be surprised in knowing that Aquinas (1946: Ia–IIae, Q. 96, a. 2) argued that any constitutive authority should be careful and cautious about undertaking radical changes in the law or promulgating restrictive laws. "Human law does not forbid all vices, from which virtuous persons keep themselves, but only the more serious vices, which the majority can avoid, and principally those that harm others, and which must be prohibited in order for human society to survive." Later in the *Summa Theologiae* (IIa–IIae, Q. 77, a. 1, ad 1), he wrote that "human law cannot forbid all and everything that is against virtue; it is sufficient that it forbids actions that go against community life." These passages suggest, furthermore, that Aquinas would reject any position entailing excessive moral perfectionism or any semblance of Puritanism in the legal system. The following passage indicates this set of claims: "So also in human government, it is right for those who are in authority to tolerate some evil actions so as not to hinder other goods or to prevent some worse evil from occurring. As Augustine writes in *On Ordination* (II, 4): 'If one suppresses all prostitution, then the world will be torn apart by lust' " (Aquinas 1946: IIa–IIae, Q. 10, a. 11).

In discussing legal matters, Aquinas often referred to the insights found in the writings of Augustine. Aquinas again followed Augustine in arguing that an "unjust law is no law at all." In the *Summa Theologiae*, Aquinas (1946: Ia–IIae, Q. 96, a. 4) articulated this important philosophical maxim central to contemporary jurisprudence:

> A law is unjust when it is contrary to the human good and contrary to the things we have discussed above: either from the end as when a person presiding imposes a law with undue burdens or prescribes a law which does not pertain to the commonweal of the society but rather to his own proper desires and glories. Or even on the part of the author, as when someone makes a law beyond the power commissioned to him. Or also from the very form, for example, as when burdens are dispensed unequally upon members for the community, even if they are ordained to the common good. Cases like this are more like acts of violence than laws, because, as Augustine writes, "A law that is not seen as just is no law at all." Hence, such laws do not oblige in the matter of conscience except perhaps in order to avoid scandal or a disturbance.

Martin Luther King (1963) referred to these passages with such fervor in his *A Letter from a Birmingham Jail*. What Aquinas suggests is that any human law that hinders the development of human flourishing fundamentally is unjust. An unjust law does not meet the criteria for legal justification as developed within the context of the natural-law theory. It follows, therefore, that in Aquinas's mind, neither procedural consistency nor legal precedent is a sufficient condition for a just law.

On the other hand, while Aquinas did argue emphatically that an unjust law is no law at all, given the overall conservative bent of his jurisprudence, he argued that conditions must be severe and exhibit rampant injustice before an unjust law ought to be overthrown and overturned. In *On Kingship* (Nos. 43–44), he enunciated the conditions under which a tyrant might be overthrown:

> Finally, provision must be made for facing the situation should the king stray into tyranny. Indeed, if there is not an excess of tyranny, it is more expedient to tolerate the milder tyranny for a bit rather than by acting in revolt against the tyrant, to become involved in many perils more grievous than the tyranny itself. . . . This is wont to happen in tyranny, namely, that the second event becomes more grievous than the preceding event, inasmuch as, without abandoning the previous oppressions, the tyrant himself thinks up fresh ones from the malice of his heart.

In these discussions, Aquinas resonates clearly with more than several philosophical arguments central to contemporary political theory and jurisprudence.

Renaissance Scholasticism and Natural-Law Theory

Natural-law theory in the Roman Catholic tradition, as applied to a general theory of international law as well as to specific human-rights theory, developed theoretically in the sixteenth century. Renaissance scholastic philosophers, especially the Dominicans Francisco de Vitoria (1492–1546), Domingo de Soto (1494–1560), Bartolemo Las Casas (1474–1566), Domingo Banez (1528–1640), and the Jesuit Francisco Suarez (1548–1617), all developed specific accounts of natural-law moral and legal theory. These Renaissance scholastic philosophers and theologians, mostly followers of the teachings of Aquinas, were important in the development of human-rights theory. All were part of the intellectual brain trust at the School of Salamanca in Spain and participated in a movement often referred to as the "Second Scholasticism." In sixteenth-century Europe, the University of Salamanca became the leading center of the study of Aquinas's works. It is in de Vitoria and Suarez where one finds what has become the modern concept of human-rights theory spelled out in some detail. Suarez's *De Legibus* is an important treatise for the development of human-rights theory. Less well known is the work of Bartolemo Las Casas, the Spanish Dominican friar who, at the time of the Spanish conquests, argued assiduously both in his writings and before the Spanish courts for the justification of fundamental natural rights for the native peoples in the Americas.

The Dominicans of the Salamanca School were concerned, among other pressing philosophical inquiries, to limit the abuses endemic to the emerging colonial movements, especially when Spanish colonization escapades entailed the enslavement of both Africans and Native Americans. The thrust of the Dominican theory limited the circumstances under which other human persons might be enslaved. In effect, these theories could, as Richard Tuck (1979: 49) once argued, "help to undermine the slave trade." Tuck claimed that the welfare of the human person rather than a radical theory of human liberty characterized the Dominican School at Salamanca. These Dominican Friars articulated the issues central to the Aristotelian concepts of distributive justice and not the set of issues connected with absolute liberty. (This analysis, in turn, placed limits on the concept of human freedom. In essence, this limit follows from an Aquinian rather than a Scotus/Ockham view of free will and its corresponding theory of human action. This once again suggests that the theoretical importance of the intellectualist/voluntarist differences should not be dismissed too easily.)

Prior to the advent of the Salamanca School, Dominican followers of Aquinas, especially Thomas Di Vio Cajetan (1469–1534) and Konrad Kollin (d. 1536), developed a theory of natural law in accord with classical Aristotelian-based Thomism and what they took to be a humanist Aristotelianism developed in the late fifteenth century (Brett 1997: 116). Cajetan wrote an extensive commentary on the complete *Summa Theologiae* of Thomas Aquinas. (So important and influential is Cajetan's commentary on Aquinas's *Summa Theologiae* that the critical Leonine edition of Aquinas's *omina opera* contains Cajetan's commentary published along with the texts of the *Summa Theologiae*.) The jurisprudential contributions of de Vitoria and his successors, most scholars argue, focused on a modern theory of subjective human rights. De Vitoria, who first studied in Paris, was well trained in the classical Thomism then common in Spanish universities. Recent scholarship suggests that the importance of the Second Scholasticism School at Salamanca is not easily placed into either the category of subjective or objective rights. Legal historian Annabel Brett (1997: 124) noted: "[The] doctrine of rights . . . [and] . . . the achievements within political theory in general of the School of Salamanca cannot be fully understood without an appreciation of the complexity of the late medieval heritage of *jus.*"

The Influence of Aquinas's Theory of Natural Law

It is difficult to elucidate clearly and evenly the exact contributions that Aquinas's theory of law—especially his account of natural law—have made in the development of western legal and political theory. That Aquinas's theory of law had an effect on the later development of a theory of international law is generally accepted as correct historically. The Dominican friar, de Vitoria, is often regarded as one of the pioneer thinkers responsible for a theory of international law. De Vitoria's work, *De Indis*, a series of lectures first given at Salamanca in 1532, serves as the harbinger of later discussions on international law. The University of Cambridge's Quentin Skinner argued that de Vitoria, accepting the Aristotelian concept of a "perfect society" acquired from his reading of Aquinas, developed "a courageous and thoroughgoing defense of the Indians in a long essay entitled *De Indis recenter inventis*" (Skinner 1990: 407). De Soto published several of de Vitoria's philosophical lectures on rights theory. Grotius refers to de Vitoria in the *Prolegomena* to his *De jure belli et pacis* and in his *Mare Liberum*; Grotius was also influenced by the writings of Suarez. Suarez's contribution to the analysis of what eventually became the modern concept of individual human right as subjective, it must be remembered, is dependent on the earlier though conceptually different account of *jus* as objective found in the texts of Aquinas's *Summa Theologiae*.

The general influence of medieval natural-law theory on the development of the United States Constitution, especially the "Bill of Rights," is often suggested but difficult to establish. The American jurist, Henry Sumner Maine, once wrote that Thomas Jefferson was influenced by the French philosophers, who in turn had written about human rights in the context of natural law. The English Dominican, Vincent McNabb (1929: 1065) suggested that the especially French concept that "all men are born equal" was coupled with the more familiar English concept that "all men are born free" in the first lines of the Declaration of Independence. In his *The Philosophy of the American Revolution*, Morton White (1978: 23) once argued that Locke, in considering the nature of self-evident principles necessary for his account of natural law, was ". . . indebted—directly or indirectly—to Aquinas for some of the views to be found in the English philosopher's *Essays on the Law of Nature.*" Sigmund (1993: 228) suggests that the line of influence of Aquinas on Locke, for instance, was at best indirect and most probably came through the writings of Richard Hooker. Hooker's work, so American historian of moral theory Vernon Bourke (1968: 107) has maintained, is an "excellent summary of Thomistic ethics." Bourke also notes that Hooker is sometimes referred to as "the Anglican Aquinas."

Thin Versus Thick Theories of Human Nature: A Response to Rawls, Dworkin, and Nozick

This natural-law account based on a metaphysics of natural kinds articulated in this essay suggests a moral and a jurisprudential limit for contemporary-rights philosophers like Ronald Dworkin, Robert Nozick, and John Rawls. All three adopt what might be called a "thin theory" of the human good. Hence, their theories lack any substantive content based on the foundational principles of human nature, which is a theoretical problem with most theories of liberal jurisprudence. Liberalism in jurisprudence, by its very definition, denies any role for substantive content to the fabric of law-making. Without the content that a theory of human person provides, jurisprudence is limited in its attempt at achieving a substantive theory of human rights. Rawls's person who has a passion for counting blades of grass in city squares or Dworkin's beer-drinking TV addict both may be leading a good life—one of "integral human fulfillment," to use a Finnis term—provided they have chosen these ends after mature reflection. A thick theory of human nature espoused by the ethical naturalism in the Aristotelian/Aquinian scheme put forward in this essay requires more than what Rawls, Nozick, and Dworkin's thin theories permit. Henry George, it would appear, would side with Thomas in opposition to the adoption of a "thin" theory of the human good found in contemporary liberal rights theorists.

This natural-law schema provides a set of properties that determine the content of the human good to be attained. Without this content, one falls quickly into the vacuum of formalism. Such formalism is, in many ways, the hallmark of Kantian moral theory, most "good reasons" moral theories, all legal positivism, much legal realism, and most liberal jurisprudence. One might ask what justifies a morally right action for Kant or a set of human rights for Dworkin, Nozick, or Rawls? In the end, it is the exercise of reason itself—what contemporary moral philosophers often refer to as a "good reasons approach" to moral reasoning. What the natural-law position offers, if only in a broad and general way, is a set of human properties or qualities—human nature—without which a justification of a moral theory or a legal system—including a set of human rights—is sought in vain. Since human nature or essence depends upon the foundational structure of a natural kind, a set of metaphysical claims is a necessary condition towards explicating natural-law theory. In commenting on Rawls's theory of moral justification, Nussbaum (1986: 311) once noted: "Aristotle's view of *phronesis* (i.e., practical reason) cannot avail itself of this strategy . . . [of] value neutral abilities such as imagination, empathy, factual knowledge." Hence, the person of practical reason utilizes more reasoning abilities than "an enumeration of intellectual abilities," which is the paradigm for a "good reasons" theory of moral justification.

Summary Observations

This concludes the discussion of classical and contemporary ontology necessary for understanding a moral theory based on the order found in nature and its connection with the necessary conditions for natural-law theory. The historical accounts of natural law are important aspects of this narrative. This analysis, however, is in accord with classical Roman Catholic philosophy where religious faith and reason are conceptually different yet non-contradictory inquiries. Roman Catholic theology, moreover, has never accepted the theoretical chasm between faith and reason. Hence, this conceptual framework is radically different from much Reformation theology. Furthermore, this essay explains how a concept of teleology might be incorporated into contemporary natural-law theory.

The heritage of ethical naturalism in Roman Catholicism, with its emphasis on natural-law theory as found in Thomas Aquinas, has been re-discovered by contemporary analytic moral philosophers and philosophers of law. Several important issues formulated in the analytic tradition of moral and legal philosophy have their roots structurally aligned with the questions posed so vigorously by Thomas Aquinas in the central tradition of natural-law theory. These metaphysical and moral queries reflect a tradition of moral realism that is important for normative ethical and political theory and for jurisprudence. Natural-law theory at its best has a realist foundation based on human persons actually living in the twenty-first century. This moral theory has rationality articulated as a necessary condition and is cognizant thoroughly of the common good or the public interest. This theory, central to the tradition of Roman Catholicism but now witnessing a wider intellectual appeal, is well worth the attention of contemporary philosophers, theoretical political scientists, legal scholars, and philosophers of economic thought. Natural-law theory, once thought to be part of the dustbin of antiquated theories on the nature of law, now provides vibrant excitement in writings found in contemporary moral theory, social and political theory, and jurisprudence. However, ethical naturalism, in order to be grounded in an order of nature, demands a realist ontology of natural kinds. This essay has attempted to spell out the set of conditions necessary for natural-law moral and legal theory through an analysis of the central metaphysical concepts together with their historical development and contemporary significance. Finally, the students of Henry George should be in general agreement with this realist moral theory.

References

Adler, M. (1990). "A Sound Moral Philosophy." In *Reforming Education*. New York: Collier Books, Macmillan Publishing Co.

Anscombe, E. (1958). "Modern Moral Philosophy." *Philosophy* 33(124): 1–19.

Aquinas, T. (1946). *Summa Theologica*, tr. Fathers of the English Dominican Province. New York: Benziger Brothers.

——. (1964). *Commentary on Aristotle's Nicomachean Ethics*. Trans. C. I. Litzinger. Notre Dame: Dumb Ox Books.

Benestad, J. B. (1986). "Henry George and the Catholic Views of Morality and the Common Good, II: George's Proposals in the Context of Perennial Philosophy." *American Journal of Economics and Sociology* 45(1): 115–123.

Bourke, V. (1968). *History of Ethics*. Garden City, NY: Doubleday.

Boyle, L. (1981). "A Remembrance of Pope Leo XIII: the Encyclical *Aeterni Patris*." In *One Hundred Years of Thomism*. Ed. V. B. Brezik, pp. 7–23. Houston, TX: Thomistic Institute.

Braybrooke, D. (2001). *Natural Law Modernized*. Toronto: University of Toronto Press.

Brett, A. (1997). *Liberty, Right, and Nature: Individual Rights in Later Scholastic Thought*. Cambridge: Cambridge University Press.

Finnis, J. (1982). *Natural Law and Natural Rights.* Oxford: Clarendon Press.

——. (1983). *Fundamentals of Ethics.* Oxford: Oxford University Press.

——. (1998). *Aquinas: Moral, Political and Legal Theory.* Oxford: Oxford University Press.

Foot, P. (1978). *Virtues and Vices and Other Essays in Moral Philosophy.* Oxford: Blackwell.

——. (2000). "Does Moral Subjectivism Rest on a Mistake?" In *Logic, Cause and Action.* Ed. R. Teichmann. Cambridge: Cambridge University Press.

Fuller, L. (1964). *The Morality of Law.* New Haven, CT: Yale University Press.

Gaffney, M. (2000). *Henry George, Dr. Edward McGlynn, & Pope Leo XIII.* New York: Robert Schalkenbach Foundation.

George, H. (2006). *Progress and Poverty.* New York: Robert Schalkenbach Foundation.

George, R. (1993). *Making Men Moral.* Oxford: Oxford University Press.

Gilby, T. (1975). "Introduction." In *Summa Theologiae.* New Blackfriars Edition, Vol. 37: "Justice." New York: McGraw-Hill Book Company.

Golding, M. (1974). "Aquinas and Some Contemporary Natural Law Theories." *Proceedings of the American Catholic Philosophical Association:* 242–243.

——. (1975). *The Philosophy of Law.* Englewood Cliffs, NJ: Prentice-Hall.

Grisez, G. (1965). "The First Principle of Practical Reason." *Natural Law Forum* 10: 168–196.

Haldane, J. (2000a). "Insight, Inference and Intellection." In *Proceedings of the American Catholic Philosophical Association: Insight and Inference,* 75, p. 38. Bronx, NY.

——. (2000b). "Thomistic Ethics in America." *Logos* 3(4).

Hart, H. L. A. (1961). *The Concept of Law.* Oxford: Oxford University Press.

Hittinger, R. (1989). "After MacIntyre: Natural Law Theory, Virtue Ethics and *Eudaimonia.*" *International Philosophical Quarterly* (December).

Kenny, A. (2001). "Aquinas and the Appearances of Bread" (a review of *Truth in Aquinas*). *Times Literary Supplement* October 5: 14.

King, M. L. (1963). "Letter from a Birmingham Jail." *Christian Century* 80(June 12): 767–773.

Lisska, A. J. (1991). "Finnis and Veatch on Natural Law in Aristotle and Aquinas." *American Journal of Jurisprudence* 36: 55–71.

——. (1996, 2001). *Aquinas's Theory of Natural Law: An Analytic Reconstruction.* Oxford: The Clarendon Press.

——. (2007). "On the Revival of Natural Law: Several Books from the Last Half-Decade." *American Catholic Philosophical Quarterly* 81(4): 613–638.

MacDonald, S. (1993). "Theory of Knowledge." In *The Cambridge Companion to Aquinas.* Eds. N. Kretzmann and E. Stump. Cambridge: Cambridge University Press.

MacIntyre, A. (1981). *After Virtue.* South Bend, IN: University of Notre Dame Press.

——. (1988). *Whose Justice, Which Rationality.* South Bend, IN: University of Notre Dame Press.

——. (1990). *Three Rival Versions of Moral Enquiry.* South Bend, IN: University of Notre Dame Press.

——. (1999). *Dependent Rational Animals: Why Human Beings Need the Virtues.* Chicago: Open Court Press.

Magee, B. (1998). *The Great Philosophers.* Oxford: Oxford University Press.

Maritain, J. (1951). *Man and the State.* Chicago: University of Chicago Press.

McCool, G. (1994). *The Neo-Thomists.* Milwaukee: Marquette University Press.

McInerny, R. (2006). *Praeambula Fidei.* Washington, DC: Catholic University of America Press.

McNabb, V. (1929). "St. Thomas Aquinas and Law." *Blackfriars* 10(May): 1047–1067.

Milbank, J., and C. Pickstock. (2001). *Truth in Aquinas.* London: Routledge.

Morris, C. R. (1997). *American Catholic.* New York: Random House.

Nuesse, C. J. (1985). "Henry George and 'Rerum Novarum': Evidence is Scant that the American Economist Was a Target of Leo XIII's Classic Encyclical." *American Journal of Economics and Sociology* 44(2): 241–254.

Nussbaum, M. (1986). *The Fragility of Goodness.* Cambridge: Cambridge University Press.

——. (1993). "Non-Relative Virtues." In *The Quality of Life.* Eds. M. Nussbaum and A. Sen. Oxford: Clarendon Press.

——. (2007). "Constitutions and Capabilities: 'Perception' Against Lofty Formalism." *Harvard Law Review* 121(1): 5–97.

Pickstock, C. (2000). "Imitating God: The Truth of Things According to Thomas Aquinas." *New Blackfriars* 81(953/954): 308.

Porter, J. (1999). *Natural and Divine Law.* Grand Rapids: Wm. B. Eerdmans Publishing Co.

——. (2005). *Nature as Reason: A Thomistic Theory of the Natural Law.* Grand Rapids: Wm. B. Eerdmans Publishing Co.

Rawls, J. (1972). *A Theory of Justice.* Oxford: Oxford University Press.

Rogers, C. (1964). "The Valuing Process in the Mature Person." *Journal of Abnormal and Social Psychology* 68(2): 160–167.

Ryan, C. (1965). "The Traditional Concept of Natural Law: An Interpretation." In *Light on the Natural Law.* Ed. I. Evans. Baltimore: Helicon Press, Inc.

Sandel, M. (1984). "Morality and the Liberal Ideal." *New Republic* May 7: 15–17.

Sigmund, P. (1993). "Law and Politics." In *The Cambridge Companion to Aquinas.* Eds. N. Kretzmann and E. Stump. Cambridge: Cambridge University Press.

Simon, Y. (1965). *The Tradition of Natural Law*. Ed. V. Kuic. New York: Fordham University Press.

Skinner, Q. (1990). "Political Philosophy." In *The Cambridge History of Renaissance Philosophy*. Eds. C. B. Schmitt and Q. Skinner. Cambridge: Cambridge University Press.

Stump, E., and S. MacDonald. (1999). *Aquinas's Moral Theory: Essays in Honors of Norman Kretzmann*. Ithaca, NY: Cornell University Press.

Suarez, F. (1612). *De Legibus*, Bk. I, 2.

Sumner, L. W. (1986). "Rights Denaturalized." In *Utility and Rights*. Ed. R. G. Frey, p. 20. Oxford: Basil Blackwell.

Syse, H. (2007). *Natural Law Religion and Rights*. South Bend, IN: St. Augustine's Press.

Taylor, C. (1989). *Sources of the Self*. Cambridge, MA: Harvard University Press.

Tierney, B. (1997). *The Idea of Natural Right*. Atlanta: Scholars Press.

Trainia, C. (1999). *Feminist Ethics and Natural Law*. Washington, DC: Georgetown University Press.

Tuck, R. (1979). *Natural Rights Theories: Their Origin and Development*. Cambridge: Cambridge University Press.

Veatch, H. B. (1971). *For an Ontology of Morals*. Evanston, IL: Northwestern University Press.

——. (1986). *Human Rights: Fact or Fancy?* Baton Rouge, LA: Louisiana State University Press.

——. (1990). *Swimming Against the Current in Contemporary Philosophy*. Washington, DC: Catholic University of America Press.

White, M. (1978). *The Philosophy of the American Revolution*. New York: Oxford University Press.

Wippel, J. F. (2000). *The Metaphysical Thought of Thomas Aquinas: From Finite Being to Uncreated Being*. Monographs of the Society for Medieval and Renaissance Philosophy; Washington, DC: Catholic University of America Press.

Human Nature from a Georgist Perspective

By JAMES DAWSEY*

ABSTRACT. George's view of human nature was also deeply rooted in the Judeo-Christian tradition. Since God's creation was good, so too were humans intended for good—not evil. Through creation, each person was accorded dignity by God and equal status with all other humans, regardless of the accidents of birth. God established people as stewards rather than owners of the world; they were entrusted with the special labor of enacting just and eternal laws that would perpetuate creation itself and dispense God's bounty for all. He intended them to be rational beings, seekers of justice, communitarian and free. By allowing, participating in, and often benefitting from unjust structures regarding land ownership, Christians engaged in theft. It was thus up to George and others in "the movement" to build consensus, to persuade, to become politically involved, and ultimately to inaugurate, practice, and enforce land laws allowing equal opportunity to all.

The Prophet from San Francisco

In a letter so personal that it was only released after Henry George's death, George disclosed to the Rev. Thomas Dawson what drove him to write *Progress and Poverty* (George 1981: 311–312):

> Because you are not only my friend, but a priest and a religious, I shall say something that I don't like to speak of—that I never before have told to any one. Once, in daylight, and in a city street, there came to me a thought, a vision, a call—give it what name you please. But every nerve quivered. And there and then I made a vow. Through evil and through good, whatever I have done and whatever I have left undone, to that I have been true. It was that that impelled me to write *Progress and Poverty* and that sustained me when else I should have failed. And when I had finished the

*James Dawsey is Wolfe Chair and Professor of Religious Studies, Religion Department, Emory & Henry College.

American Journal of Economics and Sociology, Vol. 71, No. 4 (October, 2012).

last page, in the dead of the night, when I was entirely alone, I flung myself on my knees and wept like a child. The rest was in the Master's hands. That is a feeling that has never left me; that is constantly with me. And it has led me up and up. It has made me a better and a purer man. It has been to me a religion, strong and deep.

If of another time, a different place, we might think of Henry George principally as a religious figure rather than political economist or social philosopher.

An opponent to George, once trying to make light of his ideas, satirized him as the "Prophet of San Francisco" (the Duke of Argyll's essay "The Prophet of San Francisco" originally appeared in the *Nineteenth Century* for April, 1884; it is most accessible today as included in its entirety with rebuttal in George 1965). But as if from Balaam's mouth, this attempt to demean and curse captured a remarkable truth: Henry George shared much indeed with the biblical personages of yore. George's childhood was suffused with pious instruction; his homelife in his 30s and 40s was marked by prayer, hymns, and private devotion. As a mature man, his faith in Providence grew to the extent that he fully trusted the continuity of this life into an eternal after. And George's greatest wish for this world was simply that God's plan for justice become concrete. Was George a prophet? In many ways, yes. George's comments to the Rev. Dawson reveal a calling every bit as focused as Isaiah's (Isaiah 6: 1–13), as personal as Jeremiah's (Jeremiah 1: 4–10), as mystifying as Ezekiel's (Ezekiel 1–2), and, in its own way, as compelling as Moses' (Exodus 3–4). "I have observed the misery of my people," God said to Moses, "I have heard their cry on account of their taskmasters. Indeed I know their sufferings" (Exodus 3: 7). Was not the aforesaid vision that George related to his friend, the Rev. Dawson, of the same type?

George (1942: 9–10) penned the following sentiments at the beginning of *Progress and Poverty*: "It is as though an immense wedge were being forced, not underneath society, but through society. Those who are above the point of separation are elevated, but those who are below are crushed down. . . . In the United States it is clear that squalor and misery, and the vices and crimes that spring from them, everywhere increase. . . . It is in the older and richer sections of the

Union that pauperism and distress among the working classes are becoming most painfully apparent.... This association of poverty with progress is the great enigma of our times." And 500 pages later, George's (1942: 549–552) conclusion was again like Moses', just for a different time and different place:

> Though it may take the language of prayer, it is blasphemy that attributes to the inscrutable decrees of Providence the suffering and brutishness that come of poverty; that turns with folded hands to the All-Father and lays on Him the responsibility for the want and crime of our great cities.... We slander the just one.... It is not the Almighty, but we who are responsible for the vice and misery that fester amid our civilization. The Creator showers upon us his gifts—more than enough for all.
>
> Can it be that the gifts of the Creator may be thus misappropriated with impunity?... Turn to history, and on every page may be read the lesson that such wrong never goes unpunished.... May we even say, "After us the deluge!"... The struggle that must either revivify, or convulse in ruin, is near at hand, if it be not already begun.
>
> But if, while there is yet time, we turn to Justice and obey her, if we trust Liberty and follow her, the dangers that now threaten must disappear .... With want destroyed; with greed changed to noble passions; with the fraternity that is born of equality taking the place of jealousy and fear that now array men against each other; with mental power loosed by conditions that give to the humblest comfort and leisure; who shall measure the heights to which our civilization may soar? Words fail the thought! It is the Golden Age.... It is the culmination of Christianity—the city of God on earth.... It is the reign of the Prince of Peace!

Humans as Creatures Created by God

Given George's affinity for Moses and the prophets, it is no surprise that his view of human nature was also deeply rooted in the Judeo-Christian tradition. "The earth is the Lord's and all that is in it, the world, and those who live in it," the Psalmist wrote (Psalms 24: 1), and that was George's belief. The conviction that God made the world was the cornerstone of one of his most famous addresses, "Thou Shalt Not Steal" (delivered at the Second Public Meeting of the Anti-Poverty Society, in the Academy of Music, New York, May 8, 1887). God created the world and intended its natural bounty for all, was George's point. To appropriate for a few what God had intended for the benefit of all was nothing less than stealing.

Like everything in nature, people were the works of a powerful creator. Although finite and fallible to be sure, humans were more than simply another element of creation; they were God's supreme product, created in His image. Men and women were children of God, the very apex of God's creation. Thus, to enslave people, to impoverish them, was to deny God's will and to corrupt into mere beasts what God intended as highest in creation (George 1942: 309–310). And as for evolutionary forces? Civilizations, he argued, did not evolve forward because a process of natural selection improved and elevated certain human powers of knowledge and skill, but advanced as men and women comported themselves to the eternal plan for justice laid down by the creator God (George 1942: 475–552).

George's view of how humans fit into the scheme of creation was grounded in three concepts strongly voiced in Judaism and Christianity. The first concept is simply that since God's creation was good, so too were humans intended for good—not evil. The second affirms the special standing of people in God's creation. Through creation, each person was accorded dignity by God and equal status with all other humans, regardless of the accidents of birth. People, in fact, superseded all other elements of creation. And the third speaks to human responsibility. The high status of humans brought great responsibility, for God established people as stewards rather than owners of the world. God made the world and owned it. People benefitted from it and were entrusted with the special labor of enacting those just and eternal laws that would perpetuate creation itself and dispense God's bounty for all.

A Good Creation

Did George think humans good? Certainly, he considered creation good. Genesis begins with a story in which God Himself affirms after each moment of creation that what He had created was good (Genesis 1:4, 10, 12, 18, 21, 25, 31) and the story culminates with a special blessing for humankind. After creating people in His own image, God entrusted them with all else that He created (Genesis 1: 29–30):

> See, I have given you every plant yielding seed that is upon the face of all the earth, and every tree with seed in its fruit; you shall have them for food.

And to every beast of the earth, and to every bird of the air, and to everything that creeps on the earth, everything that has the breath of life, I have given every green plant for food.

And while many in the Christian tradition have grabbed on to the use of the word "dominion" in the King James Version (and like-minded translations) and somewhat twisted the biblical passage to emphasize God's gift of power to people, George rightly emphasized the goodness of creation. That is, George affirmed everywhere in his writings that God created a good world, intended as a storehouse to benefit all humankind. This was the very starting point of his political economy. Through nature, God provided abundant resources for all, including the animals, in Genesis.

This affirmation of God's handiwork applied to humans too. Male and female, in the biblical passage, were created in the image of God. They were created on the last day of creation as the culmination of God's work. And afterwards, God looked upon them and everything else that He had made and said "indeed, it was very good" (Genesis 1: 31).

George emphasized the positive side of human nature. This is illustrated by a wonderful passage in *Progress and Poverty* where George (1970: 178–179) reminds us of what occurs when well-bred men and women joined at a feast. All are anxious that the neighbor savor the occasion; none are greedy; all are generous. And so, the repast provides enjoyment for the whole community. The natural condition for people is not selfishness; not acquisitiveness. Those are corruptions of human nature. Rather, harmony is God's design for humans—and social harmony is what marks human nature when justice abounds.

This is not to say, however, that George did not see humans as fallen creatures. He did. And it was exactly their fallen state that allowed for the misery that one encounters in the world—but more about that fallen state shortly.

Created in the Image and Likeness of God

As mentioned, George affirmed the great dignity of human beings. But what did it mean to him that people were created in the image and likeness of God?

In the early Church, being created in the image of God connoted humans' abilities to love and to reason. The Christian Fathers held that human love, though imperfect, was a characteristic that came from God. So, too, was rationality: Since created in God's image, the human mind could think like God thought. If thinking correctly, humans reasoned as God reasoned. Understanding God and God's designs were true possibilities. As for the likeness of God, the Church Fathers tended to emphasize people's abilities to develop, learn, prosper. Especially growing in love and growing in wisdom were indications of the likeness of God (Ramsey 1985: ch. 4).

George (1970: 177–178) recaptured the insight of the Fathers perfectly when he discussed how men were inspired.

> It is not selfishness that enriches the annals of every people with heroes and saints. . . . Call it religion, patriotism, sympathy, the enthusiasm for humanity, or the love of God—give it what name you will; there is yet a force that overcomes and drives out selfishness; a force that is the electricity of the moral universe; a force beside which all others are weak. . . . He who has not seen it has walked with shut eyes. He who looks may see, as says Plutarch, that "the soul has a principle of kindness in itself, and is born to love, as well as to perceive, think, or remember."

But George (1970: 180) on his own added important caveats to the old Patristic views. First, George stressed how important psychologically it was for people to work. Humans want to labor. As God was a creator, humans too are artisans who enjoy molding the stuff of God's creation into useful sustenance. Fulfillment comes from work. In *Pacem in Terris* (*Proclaiming Justice and Peace* 1991: 130, paragraphs 18–20), John XXIII acknowledged the human need to work, so expanding traditional human rights to include "the right to work." Man was not only to be given the right to work, but "also to be allowed the exercise of personal initiative in the work he does." Second, George emphasized human curiosity. He saw the mind as a wondrous instrument for multiplying the bounty of nature. In that sense, he wrote (George 1970: 180): "Man is the unsatisfied animal. . . . Each step that he takes opens new vistas and kindles new desires. He is the constructive animal; he builds, he improves, he invents. . . . Whatever be the intelligence that breathes through nature, it is in that likeness that man is made." So, through their backs and minds people provided continuity to God's activity of creation. And third, again we see the significance George gave to social harmony. Peaceful association allowed people to free up mental power. That the planting and harvesting of some could feed many permitted social improvement of the whole group. Personal and social progress were made possible through cooperation (George 1970: 197).

Eighty-five years after George penned these ideas, we notice this same mixture—(1) that humans were created by God in such a way as to find fulfillment through work and (2) that human work is by nature social and finds its greatest fulfillment in a harmonious society—in the encyclical *Pacem in Terris* where Pope John XXIII established the conditions of work as corollary to human rights. After expanding the commonly accepted notion of human rights to include the right to dignity (or respect) and broadening the concept of liberty to include such as the means necessary for the proper development of life, the ability to choose and pursue professions, and the ability of sharing in the benefits of culture, Pope John XXIII (*Proclaiming Justice and Peace* 1991: 130, paragraph 20) reaffirmed Pope Pius XII's dictum: "Nature imposes work upon man as a duty, and man has the corresponding natural right to demand that the work he does shall provide him with the means of livelihood for himself and his children." But then Pope John XXIII continued (paragraph 21):

> As a further consequence of man's nature, he has the right to the private ownership of property, including that of productive goods. This . . . is a right which constitutes so efficacious a means of asserting one's personality and exercising responsibility in every field, and an element of solidity and security for family life, and of greater peace and prosperity for the state.

Similar to George, we see tremendous emphasis on the right of humans to own the fruit of their own labor. And the Pope added a final caveat (paragraph 22): "Finally, it is opportune to point out that the right to own private property entails a social obligation as well." At the end of the section, John XXIII referenced further what he had meant by pointing to an earlier encyclical, *Mater et Magistra* (*Proclaiming Justice and Peace* 1991: 112–113, paragraph 189), that explained that "the resources which God and his goodness and wisdom has implanted in nature are well-nigh inexhaustible, and has at the same time given man the intelligence to discover ways and means of exploiting these resources for his own advantage and his own livelihood." This statement could have just as easily come from the mouth of George.

According to George, God created a bounteous world. In several writings, he described the world as "a great banquet." Nature provided, in great abundance, more than enough to satisfy all. Even the then much accepted Malthusian doctrine that population would naturally increase until it outstripped subsistence, only to be controlled by sickness and famine, he argued, was not inevitably true. For the argument understated the vastness of God's storehouse and the human ability to multiply that bounty through mental and physical labor (George 1970: ch. 6).

But most problematic, George thought, Malthus' argument hid the fact that the true root of poverty rested with injustice, not with God's creation. "Has the first comer at a banquet," he asked, "the right to turn back all the chairs and claim that none of the other guests shall partake of the food provided, except as they make terms with him?" (George 1970: 161). One person's rights were to be bounded everywhere by the rights of others to participate in God's feast.

There was a tremendous balance to the created order, George believed. God created a storehouse and created humans in such a way that they found fulfillment in labor. Labor increased the produce of the storehouse. Instead of greedy consumers, George visualized people as artisans, helpers of God, in improving the world.

As mentioned, George's thought recaptured for his time Hebrew Scripture's emphasis on man the steward of creation, rather than man the owner of creation. Although for a different century and society, George's view that the land does not belong in perpetuity to the latest one who holds deed to it but to society as a whole echoes the message of the Jubilee laws in Leviticus, the prophet Hosea's attack on Baal worship, and Psalm 24. The world and all of its fruits were created for the benefit of all.

So what are man's and woman's roles to be in God's creation? George agreed with the ancient Hebrews that people should enjoy the world's yield. As the Psalmist wrote,

So God brought his people out with joy,
    his chosen ones with singing.
He gave them the lands of the nations,
    and they took possession of the wealth of the peoples,
that they might keep his statutes
    and observe his laws. (Psalm 105: 43–45)

Enjoying the world, of course, is also a modern sentiment. But George emphasized also a second ingredient determinative among the Hebrews: Enjoyment cannot, should not, be separated from the responsibility to safeguard creation for others in society, present and future generations. As the quoted Psalm makes clear for the Hebrews, the human role includes keeping Justice. And, for George, keeping Justice meant promulgating and following the divine plan that allowed everyone in society fair opportunity to the earth's storehouse. All should be allowed access to the fields where they could labor. Establishing and protecting that opportunity was paramount. To be a steward of creation meant to fight for justice.

How God Intended Humans to Be

So Henry George affirmed that God created a good world, intended for the benefit of all; and that humans were the pinnacle of God's creation. By nature (that is, as God intended) people were not greedy, mean-spirited, selfish creatures. Rather, as George (1970: 178–179) portrayed with his example of a group of well-bred diners: "There is no struggling for food, no attempt on the part of anyone to get more than his neighbour; no attempt to gorge or to carry off. On the contrary, each one is anxious to help his neighbour before he partakes himself; to offer to others the best rather than pick it out for himself." What causes greed, is not human nature, but rather the sinful condition of the world.

How are people the pinnacle of creation? People are different from the lower animals, George (1970: 185) argued, because humans alone exhibit "the capacity to supplement what nature has done" through their own work. He, in fact, called man "the unsatisfied animal" who "has only begun to explore" (George 1970: 180). People are curious beings. Men and women are constructive; they build; they improve;

they invent. Their inclination, their love, is to seek out the mysteries of the universe and produce.

Intended to be Rational Beings

George wrote (1970: 180): "Whatever be the intelligence that breathes through nature, it is in that likeness that man is made." It is fair to say that George considered the human mind extraordinary. The mind was the instrument by which civilization advances. And it was through unleashing the power of the mind, imagination, where lay hope for a better society (George 1970: 182–183).

Henry George was a great believer in education, but he was an even greater believer in common sense. His clear argumentation and abundant use of everyday illustrations bespeak a person who believed that humans were rational creatures. What could be more down-to-earth than his argument against slavery? Slavery, of course, counteracted God's will for human freedom and dignity. But slavery also flew in the face of common sense. "Not only is slave labour less productive than free labour," he wrote, "but the power of masters is likewise wasted in holding and watching their slaves, and is called away from directions in which real improvement lies. . . . In a slave-holding community the upper classes may become luxurious and polished; but never inventive" (George 1970: 199). His argument: slavery not only denied God's intention of natural equality between people, but it undermined God's design for progress. His larger point: progress increases or decreases in proportion to the ability of societies to foster cooperation and liberty. What clear argumentation! People's minds paralleled the mind of their creator. When people thought rationally, they were thinking like God. Thus, rational thought led, with George, to discerning lasting, eternal verities.

Intended to be Seekers of Justice

George held that to be human was to long for justice. To the Hebrew prophets, in particular, justice or *tsedaqah* was that right relationship between the people and God, which only occurs when people are in right relationship with each other (and all of creation). Thus, for example, Amos chastised those who worshiped with offerings and songs but oppressed the poor. And Hosea claimed that God would prevent the very land from producing its fruits until the people repaired their broken relations with God and each other. There is a sense in which justice equals balance in God's world—that is, creation as intended. A well-known example can be found in Isaiah 11: 4–6, 9:

> With righteousness God shall judge the poor,
>   and decide with equity for the meek of the earth;
> he shall strike the earth with the rod of his mouth,
>   and with the breath of his lips he shall kill the wicked.
> Righteousness shall be the belt around his waist,
>   and faithfulness the belt around his loins.
> The wolf shall live with the lamb,
>   the leopard shall lie down with the kid,
> the calf and the lion and the fatling together,
>   and a little child shall lead them. . . .
> The nursing child shall play over the hole of the asp,
>   and the weaned child shall put its hand on the adder's den.
>
> They will not hurt or destroy on all my holy mountain;
>   for the earth will be full of the knowledge of the Lord
>   as the waters cover the sea.

Henry George tended more to associate justice with a particular type of equality. *To love God means to do justice,* a Hebrew prophet might say. George would have phrased it this way: *To love justice is to seek equality of opportunity to the bounty of nature.* Ultimately to him, justice meant "equal right to the land" (George 1970: 208). Of course, similar to Isaiah and other ancient followers of the Torah, George was convinced that good laws would promote such equal opportunity and were foundational for right relationships. Good laws would promote and restore balance in society and in the environment—that is as much the promise of Leviticus and the Prophets as it is of Henry George. And God gave laws, both natural and revealed, because people needed them. That too was the view of the prophets and of Henry George.

Intended to be Communitarian

Henry George held that people by nature were social. "[Man] does not require to be caught and tamed in order to induce him to live with his fellows," George (1970: 197) wrote. "The utter helplessness with which he enters the world, and the long period required for the maturity of his powers, necessitate the family relation. . . . The first societies are families, expanding into tribes, still holding a mutual blood relationship even when they have become great nations claiming a common descent."

Here we again see George's strong approbation of the Hebrew scripture, for example, in its accounts of the Creator's commands to Adam and Eve to "be fruitful and multiply" (Genesis 1: 28) and to cleave to each other "becoming one flesh" (Genesis 2: 24). George's affirmation of society echoes God's favor on the formation of cities, the nation of Israel, and the Christian Church.

Of course, in many ways Christianity is like a large river uniting many currents between not-always-fixed banks. There are approximately 2.2 billion Christians in the world gathered in more than 30,000 different denominations. And a large number of Christians idealize those saints of yesterday and today who have devoted themselves to a solitary existence of prayer and devotion. The *Life of St. Anthony* describing the great desert monk's private spiritual battle to deny himself the temptations of this world, for example, inspired many of the Christians of the fourth and fifth centuries, including St. Athanasius, St. Jerome, and St. Augustine of Hippo. Even though completely involved in the daily affairs of their day, these great personages longed "to find rest in God" (Augustine 1992: Book 1, chapter 1, paragraph 1). They tended to view the ideal Christian as an alien passing through this world on pilgrimage to an eternal habitation, heaven. To them, the Church provided a foretaste of Heaven. It existed as a fortress amidst a world of sin and chaos.

Needless to say, George's views had little in common with the anchorite ideal of desert monks or even the cenobite ideal of monasteries. His affinities were with the Social Gospel. George showed himself much more interested in God's Kingdom coming to earth than in the Christian getting to heaven. To George, community in fact provided the impetus that allowed humans to maximize their humanity. It was society that liberated mental powers. Human minds developed in proportion to peaceful and free association in communities. And in turn, the liberation of the intellect allowed for social progress (George 1970: 196–197). George considered people to be most human when interacting in community.

And prayer? Obviously the focus of George's prayer life was not escape from this world. One of his famous orations was actually a sermon delivered in the City Hall of Glasgow, Scotland, on Sunday, April 28, 1889. The topic of the sermon was the Lord's Prayer, especially that phrase petitioning "Thy kingdom come!" For George, prayer grew out of and led to involvement in society and commitment to bringing justice to the community in which one lived.

Intended to be Free

Like the Hebrews of antiquity, George held to a linear rather than cyclical view of history. He was no fatalist. And, he did not consider people puppets. In fact, people were endowed with tremendous liberty. He believed that people were created, as the Psalmist writes, "only a little lower than angels" (Psalms 8: 5) and as such retained immense potential to improve, to change for the better, and to set the course of their own future. George believed in progress for his time and in the possibility of even greater progress for a greater number of people in the future.

Three types of freedom found particularly strong affirmation in George's writings. Two have already been mentioned: to most fully become as intended by their Creator, humans required the freedoms to use their minds to full capabilities unhindered from tyranny and to associate themselves in peaceful communities that affirmed the equality of all people (George 1970: 196–197). At stake in these two freedoms lay a third: the unimpeded right to work for sustenance and for those higher enjoyments of body and spirit that actually distinguish human life from mere bestial existence.

What most acutely obstructs man and woman from obtaining the higher enjoyments of life are "the unjust and unequal distribution of wealth," George (1970: 207) argued. The dehumanizing evils were not consequences of progress; neither were they the consequences of natural laws. Rather, the dehumanizing evils came from the unjust restriction of people's desire, ability to do constructive work by the "monopolization of the natural opportunities that nature freely offers to all."

So the freedom to work was at the heart of George's thought. He began his study of the causes of misery in the midst of plenty in *Progress and Poverty* naturally enough with a discussion of wages. Wages result from labor, George pointed out. But before something is produced, before labor can even take place, the worker must have access to raw materials. As the laborer works and the raw materials are transformed, their value is increased. So labor does not produce of itself, from nothing; it starts with God's bounty and increases the value of that bounty. But what happens if people are denied access to God's storehouse? Then, they cannot produce (George 1970: 108). Poverty and its accompanying evils increase, George concluded, as workers are denied opportunity to access the gifts of nature intended for all.

With great insight, the editor A. W. Madsen entitled the last chapter (before the conclusion) of his abridged version of *Progress and Poverty* (George 1970) "The Call of Liberty." For sure enough, George concluded his great work with a paean to an open society where all would be offered fair access to the bounty of God's storehouse. In such a society there would be no slavery, no legalized theft of a worker's labor through landlordism. Labor would not "be robbed of its earnings while greed rolls in wealth" (George 1970: 212). Instead, such a free society would be "the culmination of Christianity—The City of God on earth, with its walls of jasper and its gates of pearl! It [would be] the reign of the Prince of Peace!" (George 1970: 213).

The Human Condition

According to traditional Christianity—that is, to theologians and ethicists as diverse as St. Augustine of Hippo (Augustine 1993) and Reinhold Niebuhr (1996) and to the confessional statements of established denominations (Catechism of the Catholic Church 1994: article 1, paragraph 7, section 2: 392; Westminster Confession of Faith 1646)—God's gift of free choice has allowed also for mistakes, miscues, and rebellion: sin. One of George's great accomplishments lay in identifying, describing, and offering a solution to a societal consequence of sin. How to explain the enigma that poverty increases as material progress takes place, he wanted to know? What a seeming contradiction! The greater the magnificence of society, the greater the misery; or, expressed more precisely, the greater the magnificence of some in society, the greater the misery of others—a host of others! (George 1970: 1–8). And then, what to do about that injustice that robbed people of their God-given right to benefit from nature's storehouse in proportion to their labor? The puzzle he addressed (and his solution, we would submit) not only addressed his times, but to a large extent addresses our own situation—that of a contemporary Western-styled society.

Misery Results from Sin

The Hebrew prophets affirmed that there was a societal price to human wickedness. And typically, Christian theologians too have explained many of society's miseries in terms of people's separation from God, a so-called Fall. (There has perhaps been a greater tendency in Christianity to emphasize the individual rather than that corporate character of sin encountered with Amos, Hosea, Isaiah, and Jeremiah, but Jews and Christians have agreed on the larger point: when humans disobey God unhappiness and suffering follow.) Although created good, the argument goes, humans have fallen away from their own created natures. While sometimes, as with Christian neo-Platonists, the Fall has been understood mostly as ignorance or an almost-innocent distancing, more often the Fall is explained by willful rebellion. All agree that the Fall took place immediately, either with the primordial angels or with the first humans. Usually, the story of Adam and Eve's desire to eat of the fruit of the tree of knowledge features in the explanations. And of course, there has been much discussion in Christianity over the cause of Adam and Eve's rebellion, the true significance of eating the fruit, the method by which the contagion of sin has been passed down to all successive generations.

Now it must be said that while George recognized greed and selfishness as human vices and affirmed the need for external controls on personal impulses, he did not concentrate attention on the corrupt nature of the human heart. Did he hold as the Apostle Paul in Romans 3:23 that "all have sinned and fall short of the glory of God"? Probably, but one could not attest so from his writings. Certainly, Henry George was no later-day Calvinist out to convert "Sinners in the Hands of an Angry God" (Jonathan Edwards' most famous sermon, preached in Enfield Connecticut, July 8, 1741 at the height of the Great Awakening), and personal sinfulness stood miles from the center of his thought.

Most forcefully, in fact, Henry George seems to have held that sinful acts actually arise from the desperate situation in which society places humans. He himself once gave the following example: as a young man, about the time his second child was born, George's personal situation had become so dire that he despaired. His family was starving. In George's words (George Jr. 1981: 149):

> I walked along the street and made up my mind to get money from the first man whose appearance might indicate that he had it to give. I stopped a man—a stranger—and told him I wanted $5. He asked what I wanted it for. I told him that my wife was confined and that I had nothing to give her to eat. He gave me the money. If he had not, I think I was desperate enough to have killed him.

The emphasis is clear: with George, it was more as if injustice creates vice than that vice creates injustice. Even the anarchists he held to be principally responding to social conditions ("Open Letter to Pope Leo XIII" in George 1965: 56). What might he have said in private about mass murderers like Idi Amin or Jeffrey Dahmer? Or thieves? Or sadists? Or pedophiles? To what extent would he have explained such sins as socially rooted?

From a theologian's point of view, we miss the deeper nuances of an Augustine or a Niebuhr that have marked so much of Christian thought about sin and evil. But we should not fault George for what he never set out to do. George purposed not to discuss theology, but to offer insight into and help with the rampant inequalities of contemporary society. His focus was firmly on society, not on what is interior to the hearts of individuals. Surely George realized that many injustices were not the consequences of immediate despair—that vicious acts often follow from men and women born in the best situations. He knew well that mental disorders and buried impulses from deep within the psyche can transform humans into ravenous beasts. And as a confessing Christian, he no doubt would have been concerned about such feelings as enmity, jealousy, anger, and envy that pop up occasionally from the hidden corners of every human's mind (Galatians 5: 13–26).

Structural Sin

But in spite of George's virtual silence regarding the origins and workings of personal sins, it is clear that he distanced himself from the naive optimism voiced by many in the Social Gospel movement of the late nineteenth century. He saw clearly that such proposals as improved work ethics and habits, better and more universal education, the formation of labor unions, and even the redistribution of land, while desired, provided no final solution to the maldistribution of wealth (George 1970: 116–127). Though he campaigned for public office, George held no illusions, as did the great Adolf von Harnack and other nineteenth-century liberal theologians, that more government, or even greater efficiency in it, might solve the evils of society. So also democracy, which he strongly affirmed, he saw as no panacea. Democracy increased, to be sure, the possibilities for rational discourse and the opportunities for people to exist in peaceful association, so one could expect improvement in democracies over despotic societies (George 1970: 196–197). But justice, he believed, would be possible only when the eternal laws designed by the Creator were effectuated in society.

While on the one hand Henry George had little to add to the theological discussion of personal wrongdoing he, on the other, broke new ground in discussing the structural nature of sin. Injustice did not so much result from dark actions of individuals, as from that human web of laws and customs that subverted God's eternal plan for how all should benefit from nature's storehouse. Good people, intending to do good, mistakenly acted sinfully, he thought, when they subscribed to common views of private ownership of land. "In permitting the monopolization of the natural opportunities that nature freely offers to all," he wrote, "we have ignored the fundamental law of justice" (George 1970: 207). Even Pope Leo XIII had fallen victim to wrong-headed arguments about the private ownership of land. Land (the bounty of nature) properly belonged to God and was intended for the benefit of all. A social structure, George insisted, that allowed what God had intended for all to be usurped by a few could not be just. In theological terms, in fact, it was demonic ("Open Letter to Pope Leo XIII" in George 1965).

Here, George's understanding of sin was actually quite sophisticated and anticipated much of the thrust of the Liberation Theology that arose a hundred years later in Latin America (Gutiérrez 1973). George (1970: 211) saw clearly the limitations of charity. Charity and works of mercy, while not to be disparaged, also did not bring justice. It was not enough to press for more just wages for laborers. And it was naive to think, as apparently did Pope Leo XIII, that these higher wages might be brought forth if workers were simply urged to unite in harmonious associations and if Christian employers and landowners were persuaded to be more charitable in their dealings with those they hired. (The most significant encyclicals of labor have been: *Rerum Novarum*—Pope Leo XIII, 1891; *Quadragesimo Anno*—Pope Pius XI, 1931; *Mater et Magistra*—Pope John XXIII, 1961; *Populorum Progressio*—Pope Paul VI, 1967; *Laborem Exercens*—Pope John Paul II, 1981; and *Centesimus Annus*—Pope John Paul II, 1991.) George's assessment was stern: In defending the accepted views of private ownership of property, Pope Leo XIII himself unwittingly undermined God's plan for justice in society.

With George then, sin appeared in more devious guise than as garbed in lists of vices. Good people could be sinful. All were sinful, to some extent. For by allowing, participating in, and often benefitting from unjust structures regarding land ownership, Christians engaged in theft. To take away a person's God-given right to access nature's bounty in equal share to all others, or to charge a premium for what was God-ordained access, was tantamount to stealing part of that person's labor ("Thou Shalt Not Steal," delivered at the Second Public Meeting of the Anti-Poverty Society, in the Academy of Music, New York, May 8, 1887).

Certainly, many people knowingly rebelled against God's plan for justice. These were the greedy, corrupt people—deformed, thought George (1970: 46–51), by the fear of want. But these spiritually twisted robber chiefs concerned George much less than did the vast majority of men and women whom he saw as simply misguided. By not being fully aware of the hidden consequences of society's innocent-looking structures, even the best-intentioned could be misled into terrible consequences. The misguided were not only victims of structural sin; they at the same time were unaware agents of oppression.

Thus, George's need to share the Truth! Knowing the cause by which men and women both innocently suffered misery while at the same time unwittingly authoring it, George could do no other than speak. In this, George acted very much like a later-day Jeremiah or Isaiah.

> Then I heard the voice of the Lord saying, "Whom shall I send, and who will go for us?" And I said, "Here am I; send me!" (Isaiah 6: 8)

After George experienced his initial vision of the great evil that fostered the maldistribution of nature's bounty, he worked tirelessly in writing *Progress and Poverty*. Then for the rest of his life, he labored unfalteringly through countless speaking engagements, writings, and campaigns in spreading the good news that the world could be put right if only society would adopt God's eternal laws giving all equal right to nature's bounty ("Open Letter to Pope Leo XIII" in George 1965). And today, that same work is carried forward determinedly through institutions like the Robert Schalkenbach Foundation and the Henry George Schools devoted to disseminating Georgist education.

Artisans for a New Tomorrow

George was no determinist. He lived in hope. But different from the Apostle Paul of I Corinthians 15, he emphasized not the future life of the resurrection, but this life. In a manner that certainly would have made the earliest Christians uncomfortable, George (1970: 207–213) stressed the human responsibility of bringing forth the Kingdom of God. One could not claim that Jesus was central to his theology. Redemption was not tied to Christ's death on the cross, but to human work.

George was an optimist when it came to the possibility of bringing about a better world. He looked upon himself and those others of like mind as artisans for a new tomorrow. In the mid-1970s, Juan Luis Segundo (1974) produced *A Theology for Artisans of a New Humanity*.

The title suggests both the similarities and differences between Henry George and the Latin American liberationists. Among the similarities, both shared a concern with economic and social structures and both shared a certain optimism that people can use their abilities to bring about a new society. The Latin American liberationists, however, very differently from George, worked within the structures of the Christian church. Their works tend properly to include traditional theological categories such as Christology and to be based on the scriptures and church tradition. George directed the concept of human progress toward economics. He paralleled economic health with spiritual well-being in a way, we must admit, that broke step with Jesus' recognition of the spiritual peril posed by wealth (Mark 10: 17–31). He lessened the necessity of God's grace, of Jesus' redemptive death. As a theologian, on these points George would not have found favor with such champions of orthodoxy as Paul, Augustine, and Karl Barth.

George placed humans center-stage in changing the world. In spite of the great misery experienced by many, George was convinced that social progress was possible, even inevitable—if, that is, we only would do our part in re-establishing those divine, eternal laws God had put in place when creating the universe. If we would do our part, then future generations would enjoy justice as expressed in people's opportunity for a better, more bounteous life. Humans could learn from past mistakes. Society could improve. The path to greater economic fairness, George held, was through right thinking, education, and political action.

What does it mean to be a responsible Christian? George linked Christianity together with citizenship. To be an artisan for a new tomorrow meant to work within those legislative and educational structures already part of democratic societies.

George was no relativist. Absolute truth could be found in the eternal laws established by the Creator that all have fair opportunity to nature's bounty. Social justice would result from understanding, establishing, and following God's design (George 1970: 214–220). Once seeing God's intention, men and women became themselves responsible for building a more just society. People, George might have said, became God's instruments for spreading and effectuating the new reality. It was up to George and others in "the movement" to build consensus, to persuade, to become politically involved, and ultimately to inaugurate, practice, and enforce land laws allowing equal opportunity to all.

The result would be, George believed, greater justice for his day and the preservation of nature's bounty for future generations. It is not surprising to see Georgists' goals intertwining with those of environmentalists. Although pre-dating the conservationist movement, George's ideas are at their core oriented toward ecology and the fight to create a sustainable planet. Humans were stewards of God's creation, he believed. People were partners with God in restoring the world and caring for the neighbor. George reminds us that God intended His land to provide bounty for all people including those yet unborn.

Humans' Sense of the Religious

Did Henry George consider people to be religious by nature? Not if one means by religious, going to church. And although a person of prayer, neither was meditation essential to who George was. Religion wasn't for him some irreducible feeling (Otto 1950) or sense of absolute submission (Schleiermacher 1996). Neither could religion be boiled down to some holiness code of *don'ts*: "no to gambling," "no to drinking." George was moral, but one does not need to be religious to be moral. He believed in God.

Henry George espoused the religion of the prophets. Perhaps George's most famous lecture was the one he entitled "Moses" (first delivered in San Francisco in June, 1878 and repeated many times in different places). In the speech, George presented Moses as one who initiated a new history. Moses led his people to freedom. Moses was one who understood that the possession of the land by a few, when all must use it, was the real cause of the people's enslavement. Moses saw clearly that land was a gift of the creator for all and that no single individual had the right to monopolize it. And Moses set up the jubilee laws that made land monopoly impossible and labor laws that allowed a day of rest.

Humans are most religious, George thought, when like Moses they are consumed with helping humanity attain a more just existence. Like Moses, religious people should be doers of the Word, not hearers only.

Was Henry George similar to Moses? In many ways, yes!

Again, are people by nature religious? All of us, George thought, long for a better reality. And although hesitant to assume that part of our nature, all of us, like Moses, are also called to be shapers of history. In the image and likeness of God, we are artisans for a new tomorrow.

References

Augustine (1992). *Confessions.* http://www.stoa.org/hippo.

———. (1993). *On Free Choice of the Will,* trans. T. Williams. Indianapolis: Hackett Publishing Company.

Catechism of the Catholic Church (CCC) (1994). English translation. United States Catholic Conference, Inc.—Libreria Editrice Vaticana.

George, H. (1942). *Progress and Poverty* (Fiftieth Anniversary Edition). New York: Robert Schalkenbach Foundation.

———. (1965). *The Land Question.* New York: Robert Schalkenbach Foundation.

———. (1970). *Progress and Poverty* (Abridged Edition), ed. A. W. Madsen. New York: Robert Schalkenbach Foundation.

George, H. Jr. (1981). *Henry George.* New York and London: Chelsea House.

Gutiérrez, G. (1973). *A Theology of Liberation: History, Politics, and Salvation,* trans. and eds. C. Inda and J. Eagleson. Maryknoll, NY: Orbis Books.

Niebuhr, Reinhold (1996). *The Nature and Destiny of Man: A Christian Interpretation: Human Nature.* Louisville: Library of Theological Ethics, Westminster John Knox Press.

Otto, R. (1950). *The Idea of Holy,* trans. J. W. Harvey. London: Oxford University Press.

Proclaiming Justice and Peace: Papal Documents from Rerum Novarum Through Centesimus Annus (1991), eds. M. Walsh and B. Daview. Mystic, CT: Twenty-Third Publications.

Ramsey, B. (1985). *Beginning to Read the Fathers.* Mahwah, NJ: Paulist Press.

Schleiermacher, F. (1996). *On Religion: Speeches to its Cultured Despisers,* trans. and ed. R. Crouter. Cambridge: Cambridge Texts in the History of Philosophy, Cambridge University Press.

Segundo, Juan Luis. (1973–1974). *Theology for Artisans of a New Humanity,* five vols. Maryknoll, NY: Orbis Books.

Westminster Confession (1646). http://www.reformed.org/documents/index. html?mainframe=http://www.reformed.org/documents/westminster_ conf_of_faith.html

Human Nature from a Catholic Perspective

By Joseph Koterski, S.J.[*]

ABSTRACT. Catholic views on personhood and human nature include emphasis on the dignity of each person, from womb to tomb. The claims made for this inviolable dignity invariably stem from the recognition that all human beings, regardless of their state of dependency, are made in the image of God and are thus the bearers of certain moral rights. But in our fallen state that image is wounded and needs to be repaired. Hence, Christians need to learn to recapitulate the life of Christ in their own lives by growing through the stages of human life according to the model that He presents to us. There are not only individual but corporate aspects to this growth. Catholic Social Teaching offers insights on the corporate and social condition in which we find ourselves. It has a healthy respect for the economic laws of the market and for the technical intricacies of efficient decision-making processes in local, national, and world economies, but out of respect for human nature there are moral norms that need to be respected and that may never be violated. On the topic of property and private ownership, considerable attention is given to the very purpose of private property (namely, to provide individuals with a kind of independence that enhances their ability to do their duties to their dependence and that extends their freedom). But always correlated with this defense of private property is a sense of the social demands on private property that come from the common good and the communal purpose of all earthly goods.

Introduction

Catholic views on personhood and human nature take shape from revelation and reason. When I speak of revelation, I mean not only the record of revelation that is to be found in the sacred scriptures that constitute the Bible, but the entire tradition of God's self-disclosure that began with creation and that culminates in the person of Jesus

*Rev. Joseph Koterski is Associate Professor of Philosophy, Fordham University.

American Journal of Economics and Sociology, Vol. 71, No. 4 (October, 2012).

Christ and the on-going mission of the Holy Spirit. When I speak of reason, I refer not only to the record of theological and philosophical reflection that the Church has long embraced, but also to the creative uses to which the human mind has been put in art and poetry, in history and the social sciences, and the manifold uses of human reason that the Church has long promoted in the course of her history.

For such a vast subject, it will be necessary to choose a small number of points for greater elaboration, while sketching out the rest of the subject in only a very general way. For this reason, I will try to lay out what I take to be the general lines of Christian anthropology as that subject tends to be understood within the Catholic Church, by making generous use of philosophical insights in the first section and then turning in the second section toward more specifically theological perspectives, first, the notion of recapitulation in Christ and, second, the Church's body of social teachings. Needless to say, the literature is vast. My immediate source for many of the claims here will be the *Catechism of the Catholic Church* (CCC 1994).

A General Sketch

The human being is a creature of God. Like everything else in the entire universe, human beings owe their existence and nature to the divine plan for creation, a plan now recognized to have been operating for millions of years before human beings came upon the scene. By virtue of its commitment to reason and revelation as reliable sources of knowledge, Catholicism can readily acknowledge the work of contemporary science to have traced the emergence of the cosmos back at least as far as the "Big Bang" and at the same time can hold that the entire universe is God's creation. The Catholic understanding here is not some Deist picture of a God who designed the natural laws of the universe and then stepped back to watch it all unfold, but rather the picture of a creator who actively sustains the universe at every moment of its being, who not only designed the laws of nature but is present to every part of the universe at once and is exercising providential care for what he loves.

The human being is not only a creature of God, but that particularly important kind of creature that was made in God's image and likeness, a dignity that sets humanity apart from the rest of creatures. Among the creatures that are animals, what separates human beings apart from the rest is the possession of the powers of intellect and will, that is, the power of understanding (conceived broadly so as to include the many ways in which thinking and knowing take place), and the power to make free choices and to love (once again, conceived broadly so as to include the various dimensions of deliberation, consent, affection, and so on, as well as to register the various and changing degrees of freedom that we may experience in the course of our lives and to note the factors that may constrain our freedom, to the point of diminishing or even eliminating our responsibility in some cases). There is much more to say about the topic of image and likeness—particularly about the shattering of the image and likeness at the time of fall (original sin) and about its restoration in Christ—and I will return to this material in the section on recapitulation in Christ.

Let me also offer some broad observations on such questions as human development in time, the relation of intellect and will to the emotions and the flesh, and the question of providing proper definitions and demarcations. In the course of commenting on questions like this, it will be possible to comment on many of the important issues that should be part of any systematic treatment of the Catholic understanding of personhood and human nature.

There have been Catholic thinkers in the course of history who were inclined to treat the subject using philosophical dualism in the general tradition of Plato and who have held that the person is really the soul that needs to use a body in this life. Most Christian theologians in the first millennium were, in effect, Christian Platonists, but this does not say enough. The question in a given case is whether the thinker was a committed Platonist who also wanted to be Christian, or (more commonly) a Christian who saw in Platonism a philosophy helpful to articulating the faith. It also seems clear that Aquinas and many others who embraced Aristotelianism after the recovery of Aristotle's texts in the 13th century generally saw themselves primarily as Christians but that the new Aristotelian categories, especially in his philosophy of nature, could be more useful for articulating and defending tenets of the faith than was the traditional Platonism. There were, of course, some who seem to have seen themselves primarily as

Aristotelians, such as Siger of Brabant and others who make up the school known now as the Radical Aristotelians.

The mainstream Catholic position is that the human person is truly a unity of body and soul and that God has promised the eventual resurrection of the body. Without trying to settle all the disputes among medieval scholastics or contemporary bioethicists on this question, it is relatively easy to see why the Thomistic version of Aristotelian hylomorphism has had so many adherents within Catholicism. Aristotle's vision of individual beings as substances, each one of which is a unified composite of matter and form, and his definition of human being as "rational animal," were easily taken up by Aquinas and accepted by many others after him as reliable philosophical insights that could be put into the service of the faith. (For a rigorous and insightful use of the basic Aristotelian-Thomistic paradigm, updated in terms of recent embryology, see Irving 2012).

Human life takes places in time. By virtue of having a bodily life that arises at a certain moment in time from the gametes provided by one's parents and that needs to develop over the course of long years, human beings tend to experience both growth and retardation of their powers of intellect and will over the course of time. A Platonist might think of these powers as always fully developed in the soul but prevented from being fully deployed by inadequate bodily development or by some injury to the body that the soul inhabits (the Socratic image, of course, would involve speaking of the body as the jail where the soul is imprisoned). While there have been Christian Platonists, Catholicism has generally come to find as more helpful a philosophy that takes its start from the Aristotelian position, once that position has been suitably modified. In that general approach, the powers of the mind are regarded as truly spiritual (that is, immaterial) powers of the soul, which is regarded as the animating principle of the material body. By virtue of their genuine dependence on various bodily organs, these spiritual powers themselves grow in the course of time, and their operations can be hampered or curtailed over the course of time by injury, disease, and senility. The chief modification in the basic Aristotelian position mentioned above is the development of a position on the immortality of the soul that is stronger than anything that can be found in any text of Aristotle that is extant today. For

Aquinas, the rational soul of a human being is capable of separate existence after death and serves as the bearer of personal subjectivity and selfhood, even though the separated soul in this state is incomplete by lack of a body to animate. For Catholics, the resurrection of Christ and the promise of the resurrection of the dead that are essential parts of the Christian faith speak to this question by assuring us of eventual re-embodiment in glorified bodies as part of the new heavens and new earth.

The necessity of development for our human powers and the inescapability of their being subject to the vicissitudes of injury, disease, senility, and death show the intrinsic importance of discussing this matter in terms of time and maturation. The genetic endowments of individuals, the prenatal environment of our gestation, the families that nurture us, the education we receive, and any other factors of nature and nurture—all of these contribute to the process by which the powers of any individual person's intellect and will develop. And yet for all of the material and social factors that condition their emergence and experience, these powers remain spiritual powers, immaterial in their very nature, and irreducible to any physicalist explanation, notwithstanding the dependence of these spiritual powers on various material factors for their operation. This position is the heart of hylomorphic philosophy, and it is the basis for the Thomistic development of that position. I do not at all mean to suggest that all Catholic thinkers are Thomists, but simply that Thomism has long been recognized as a particularly helpful theological and philosophical approach for articulating and defending any number of important positions within the Catholic faith. There is a long history to this recommendation of Thomism, most recently expressed in Pope John Paul II's encyclical *Fides et ratio* (Faith and Reason).

Without trying to provide the argument for the immaterial or spiritual character of intellect and will in its fullness here, it may be helpful to sketch the basic position briefly. Even though only individual beings and not their kinds (that is, species) have independent existence within the world of our earthly experience, the intellect grasps things by recognizing their kinds (that is, by noting the differences that are common to individuals of any one group but that differentiate the members of this smaller group from the rest of the individuals in some larger group). In short, the intellect grasps things by noticing what things are and what they are like. Utterly dependent on a physical brain, an animal organ, the intellect nevertheless does things that are not just physical actions. Its abilities include the capacity to grasp kinds, to make connections and assertions, to make distinctions and negations, and all the other activities of this sort, whether one is thinking about immaterial beings like God or angels, whether thinking about abstractions like numbers or theories, or whether thinking about things that are entirely material, like pipes and plumbing. Even when we are thinking about material things and have thoroughly material images as crucial parts of our thoughts, we are nonetheless making use of immaterial concepts and judgments and patterns of reasoning that transcend the material. We know by grasping "kinds" even though the "kinds" do not as such have material existence, but only the individuals that together make up the kind. (At issue here, of course, is the famous problem of universals. My point in raising it here is not to insist on a particular solution to the philosophical problem of universals, but merely to suggest that what-ever solution one advances to this problem requires that the knower be recognized to be using an immaterial or spiritual power and thus to have an immaterial or spiritual dimension.) It is possible to know timelessly true propositions (in mathematics, for instance) even though our statements and our thinking up of those statements will always take place in time. Even though human persons necessarily exist in time, our mental powers let us transcend time just as our power of will lets us rise above the patterns of material determination to self-determination.

Our will's power of free choice is something that transcends mate-riality, for we can choose against even the strongest desire that rises up in us, as anyone knows who has ever tried to lose weight, quit smoking, deal with sexual arousal, or conquer fear. If we were entirely material beings, then all of the instances of apparently free choice would turn out to be operations of our bodies that were fully determined by various material causes acting in or upon them; these actions would only appear to be free because we did not know in advance what these various causal lines would produce. It is not even clear what "to know" would mean in this case if it did not entail that the knower had at least a relative independence of those causes and thus the possibility of acting for or against those causal lines. But even if we were to overlook that point for the sake of argument, the need for assuming the reality of freedom in the sense of self-determination is indispensable in our account of our selves and the responsibility that we bear for our actions. Life in society would be impossible without this assumption.

The point is not that we are always perfectly free, but that free choice is something quite real in us, something that we can gain or lose, and something that can be measured by degree—we can be more or less free in various respects. In the language of the Church, there comes a time when we reach the age of reason, and what that claim means is that we can arrive at the point when we can be quite conscious and aware of what we are doing. We are then considered responsible for what we choose to do or not do. But developing virtuous habits, avoiding (or, more likely, trying to eradicate) bad ones, and growing in will-power are a life-long task, never complete, and always challenging—all this speaks to the reality of freedom in our choices. But freedom of choice cannot mean merely the absence of a cause; if so, our freedom would only amount to randomness or be as fickle as the breeze. Freedom in the sense required here has to mean self-determination—that is, the power of the self to control one's actions and even to control the direction of one's thinking. Metaphysically, this entails the position that there is some real but immaterial power of the soul—the will and its ability to make free choices. In a sense, this pair of powers (intellect and will) is at the deep core of the person, but it is crucial always to bear in mind that the authentic Catholic sense of these powers insists that the person is a whole, a unity of body and soul, and that our bodily actions are the expression of the person.

As easy as it is to grow very abstract about these topics, the Catholic position also tries to remain attentive to the fleshly realities of human existence—to such facts as our embodiment, the life of feeling and emotions, and the relations of family and society as important constituents in our account of personhood and human nature (we will need to say more about the social dimensions of the Church's understanding of the human person in the third part of this essay). In saying, for instance, that it is by virtue of having an intellect and a will that we bear a special resemblance to God, we need to add that intellect and will must always be thought about in relation to our embodiment. Our way of sensing with our eyes, for example, or hearing with our ears is like—but also decisively unlike—the way in which any other seeing creature sees or the way in which any other hearing creature hears. The reason for saying this is that the power of understanding permeates the operation of our sense organs, and so we see in a way that is correlated with our understanding—for us it is not just a matter of reacting to a stimulus but of constantly asking ourselves what we are seeing. Likewise, our way of feeling fear or boldness, hunger or thirst, pleasure or pain is, in some respects, like that of any other sentient creature, but it is also unlike the experience of any other such creature because of the way that intellect and will pervade all these other operations of our nature as well.

Since any effect shows forth something of its cause, all creatures may claim some likeness to God, but our possession of these is distinctly different. I think that this is true and crucially important simply for the proper description of our experience of emotion, feeling, appetite, and countless other features of conscious and embodied existence, let alone for the elaboration of a suitable notion of morality—that is, the prescriptive account of what we minimally may or may not do, and more broadly, what we should or should not do in order to be virtuous, to live in a way that is truly praiseworthy and more likely to bring happiness. As a short example for this point, we might consider the way in which Catholic moralists have regularly understood moral virtues as dispositions by which a person chooses the mean between the extremes of excess and deficiency in regard to action and feeling, in accord with right reason. Catholic moralists have regularly distinguished the *supernatural virtues* of faith, hope, and charity (sometimes called the *theological virtues*) that can only come about by the gift of divine grace from the various *moral virtues* (such as justice, temperance, or fortitude) that can arise by virtue of our own efforts (and are then called the *natural virtues*) or can be given to us by divine grace (and are then called *infused virtues*). In this understanding, a virtue such as courage or fortitude involves our becoming accustomed not only to act appropriately but also to feel the degree of boldness or fear that is proportionate to the danger of the situation, to the good to be accomplished, and to the resources at our disposal. Without entering into all the details of the debates here, the point is simply that Catholic moral theorists have tended to see moral virtue in terms of a well-honed disposition to have the right feelings as well as a readiness to act rightly. In this respect they differ from, say, Kantian moralists who tend to be suspicious of inclination and prefer to regard the person who acts against inclination as more genuinely virtuous.

It is my conviction that anyone's theory of morality will be directly correlated with one's vision of the human person, and that this in turn is directly correlated with one's metaphysics or theory of being. A strictly materialist metaphysics entails that the human person must be regarded as entirely material and without any spiritual dimension, and the corresponding theory of ethics will need to take this into account by holding for some form of utilitarian calculation of values in terms of pleasure and pain (however sophisticated one's description), with the faculty of human reason described in instrumental terms. Metaphysical dualism in any form will likewise have implications for one's view of the person and for what will make sense in ethics. Hylomorphic metaphysics has various direct correlations with the picture of the human person as well as for the view of ethics. My position is not that Catholicism conforms its view of the person to philosophical hylomorphism, but rather that Catholicism's respect for the truths about the human person that God has chosen to reveal and its experience of actual human beings provide a number of reasons why Catholic theorists have tended to prefer a hylomorphic philosophy.

In light of certain moral questions of perennial importance and of contemporary concern, let me conclude this first portion of the essay with some remarks about the definition of the term person and the proper demarcation of the set of human persons. It is crucial to identify the purposes for which a definition is offered. A definition that is designed, for instance, to differentiate one species from another will do well to focus on features that are distinctive of one group and lacking in another, but this approach will need to take mature healthy individuals of the species in question for the comparison. Precisely because it takes as its focus the mature healthy member of the species, this definition abstracts from the process of development and is not well suited to describing genuine members of this species in the earlier stages of their development. Other approaches to definition can do a better job at, say, the task of demarcating a species in ways that will be helpful to indicate which beings are and which beings are not members of the species by pointing to things like parentage or genetic make-up, but they do not put much as much emphasis on the typical traits of mature individuals within the species as on specific tests designed to help make judgment calls at the borders.

The problem of definition, in a way, is like the problem of map-making. Should we use a globe or a flat map? Should we distort the size of certain areas of the earth (near the poles, for instance) for the sake of allowing the map-user to figure out more easily the proper direction for travel, or should we make figuring out direction more difficult but determining area much easier? So long as one knows the type of distortion that is being allowed on the map for the sake of some other real feature of the world, we can use the map well, but only if the map did conform to the reality that we are trying to capture in this mode of representation.

With regard to our choices in regard to definitions and demarcation lines, the application is similar. When comparing one species of animal to another and trying to articulate what is distinctive about human beings, Aristotle's famous definition ("rational animal") does fine work. Its utility diminishes, however, if it were used as a demarcation-tool for trying to determine whether the unborn, the mentally retarded, the emotionally disturbed, the senile afflicted with dementia, or those damaged by serious disease, accident, or injury are still human. For the work of demarcating the group that is the human species, what one needs is the identification of non-arbitrary criteria of group membership. One needs to look to things like parentage and the chromosome patterns of our genetic make-up.

One can see the relevance of a distinction like this on some of the highly controversial questions of the present day. Catholic abhorrence for induced abortion, for infanticide, for euthanasia, for physician-assisted suicide, and so on comes from a sense that all human beings are persons, regardless of the stage of their development or the state of this independence or dependence. The presumption here is that the relevant definition of the human being is "a person made in the image and likeness of God." Likewise, Catholic social teaching (on the rights and duties of parents to educate their own children, the importance of a family wage, the duty of a society to respect human rights and to promote human development as well as to work for a system of ordered liberty and economic prosperity) flows from the importance of persons and the need to understand human persons as requiring appropriate conditions for their conception within a family, for their education and maturation and growth within appropriate circumstances, and for the use of their abilities and talents within a setting that makes it possible for them to profit from their labors and to be held responsible for their decisions.

Some of the most interesting and most disputed questions of our time arise in terms of our definitions and demarcation points. The considerable range of questions about animal rights, for instance, involves the use of functional definitions and the attempt to compare members of various animal species at the highest levels of their potentiality with very young or even disabled members of the human species. Questions about euthanasia, to take another case, are often framed in terms of the inability of some individuals to function at certain levels, but this approach also tends to misuse a definition designed for distinguishing one species as a whole from another as if that definition also warranted dismissing individuals from the rights of species-membership when they slip below a certain threshold of functionality. It is a use for which the definition is not well designed.

The point here is not to urge that one needs to be a Catholic in order to answer the question of animal rights or to know what to think about euthanasia, but rather to urge that the Catholic position on personhood and human nature has regularly made use of certain philosophical models in order to understand and present the Church's positions on disputed as well as on merely descriptive questions. Catholicism has used such philosophical models because of their philosophical realism and their epistemic reliability. These insights and these models have become deeply engrained in Catholic culture, and so it is no surprise to see that Catholicism as a social institution within American society has communicated not only the fact of its moral positions (for example, opposition to abortion and euthanasia, support for immigrant groups, the concept of a family-wage within economic policy) but also some of the philosophical argumentation that supports these positions (for example, the continuity argument that tries to make the case for opposition to abortion by showing the continuity in being of the child after birth with the unborn child all the way back to the moment of conception, or the use of the principles of distributive justice and of solidarity in the effort to resolve various problems about tax structures).

To summarize, Catholic views on personhood and human nature invariably include emphasis on the dignity of each human person, from womb to tomb. The claims made for this inviolable dignity invariably stem from the recognition that all human beings, regardless of their state of dependency, are made in the image of God and are thus the bearers of certain moral rights. The philosophical accounts used to articulate human nature and to defend human dignity are various, but many theorists have a decided preference for some form of hylomorphism of a generally Aristotelian sort, primarily because of the ways in which this approach seems favorable to a deep appreciation of human embodiment and of bodily and psychological development while at the same time allowing for an appreciation of the spiritual and immaterial aspects of the person associated with intellect and will. Finally, there tends to be great respect in Catholic views on personhood and human nature for stressing the intrinsically social character of human life. This dimension includes both the familial character of human origins and development and the variety of voluntary associations into which individuals will find it helpful to enter, ranging from marriage and friendship through politics and economics. But rather than continue these largely philosophical reflections, let us turn, albeit briefly, to two of the most important theological aspects of the Catholic understanding of these matters.

Recapitulation in Christ

The human being is made in the image and likeness of God. Sometimes people like to say "we are all children of God." While the sentiment here is clear enough, this is not an accurate reflection of Catholic understanding on this point. Strictly speaking, only the eternal Word is the Son of God—in the words of the Nicene Creed, "begotten, not made." We can become the children of God by adoption, and this adoption is effected by Christian baptism. With this act we are made the brothers and sisters of Jesus, with all the duties as well as the benefits of entering into the family. To say this is still to affirm philosophically that all human beings are members of the human species, and by this fact endowed with whatever natural rights are inherent in human nature, such as the right to life, and obligated by whatever duties fall to us by the natural law and by our state, such as the universal negative duty never to murder or the positive duties that may arise from our circumstances, such as to care for our dependents. But to say this is also to make the stronger claim that not all human beings are the children of God in the strict sense. What Catholics believe that baptism does is to begin the restoration of God's image and likeness in us by the gift of sanctifying grace—God's own life—within us. This gift of grace makes us the adopted children of God and thus makes us members of the Church. It brings forgiveness of any actual sins committed up to that point, and it begins the process of regeneration (being born "again"—"from above"—in the language of the story about Jesus's conversation with Nicodemus in the Gospel of John) that needs to continue all our lives, both by participation in the sacraments and by imitating Christ in all our choices and actions.

A crucial dimension of the Catholic understanding of the human person is the doctrine of original sin and the correlative doctrine of sanctification in Christ. For present purposes, let me presume a familiarity with the scriptural origins of the doctrine of the fall in Genesis, and let me pass over the history of the development of the doctrine by such theologians as Augustine (including the contested questions about how to understand the transmission of original sin from one generation to the next). Instead I would like to present a sense of the way in which we might understand how original sin affects us and how we believe divine grace to be at work to heal us. This requires us to consider the following points: all human beings are made in the image of God (whom we understand to be a Trinity of Divine Persons in One God), but the fall damaged our resemblance to the triune God by bringing about certain defects and wounds in us; our sanctification must include the reparation of these wounds.

We cannot claim to understand all the mysteries of God's divine life, but reflection on the ways of God's self-disclosure has made clear that God is both One and Three. In the language of the ecumenical councils of the Church, there are three Persons in the One God: the Father, the Son, and the Holy Spirit. Their very names are relational: the Father is the Father who has from all eternity begotten the Son; the Son is from all eternity the Son of the Father; the Spirit is the Love between them who from all eternity proceeds forth from the Father and the Son. (Let me acknowledge, without here entering into further discussion, of the important question of the *Filioque* that still divides the Roman Catholic Church from the Orthodox Churches.) While they are always one and always act in unison, it is possible to identify a type of love that is specially characteristic of each of the persons of the Trinity. The love especially associated with the Father is the love of gift and generosity, for He gives all of Himself (except the relation of Fatherhood) to the Son, and does so freely and without condition or reserve. The Son is particularly characterized by the love of receptivity and gratitude, for with the same freedom He receives what the Father bestows without condition or reserve, from all eternity. The love of the Holy Spirit is often designated in terms of joy and glory—that is, delight at the communion of perfect giving and the perfect receiving. (For the deeper understanding of these points, and detailed documentation, see Quay 1995, especially chapter 3).

As the one type of being that is made in God's own image and likeness, human beings also have a triadic structure, and concomitantly, a tri-partite pattern of loves. But human nature as we know it is invariably fallen nature, not some pure nature that is still unaffected by the fall. (Here too there is an enormous literature on the vexing problem of how to think about "pure nature." Was there ever actually such a state as Bonaventure held, or is this idea to be considered more in the fashion of a helpful hypothesis as Aquinas held, or is it an unhelpful notion that we should no longer employ as various figures within twentieth-century neo-scholasticism have maintained? I will not enter into this problem here.) One traditional way of describing the effects of the fall has been to say that our minds are darkened, our wills weakened, and our desires disordered. The advantages of this way of speaking are considerable. But for present purposes let me put the matter in terms of the damage to the types of love that ought to characterize human beings considered precisely as made in the image and likeness of the Trinity and the characteristic loves of each member of the Trinity.

Where there ought to be a love of generosity within us that is like that of the Father, human beings in their fallen state tend by nature only to love what strikes them as good and thus loveable. At any given time, or over the course of time, there can often be many apparent goods before us, and hence we need to choose among them. As noted earlier in this essay, our freedom in choice can be increased by growing in the power to discern true and genuine goods from among the apparent goods. As such, the tendency within our nature is to seek and pursue what appears to us as good, and especially those things that pass our tests for being genuinely good. But, curiously, our inclination to love what strikes us as good and thus in some way loveworthy is not the fullness of generosity, for we do not tend to give our love to what does not strike us as loveworthy. Growth in virtue can help us to become generous more often and more deeply, but the development of such a trait takes time and training. Secular under-standings of generosity and even altruism in this regard are historically dependent on Christian understandings of the virtue of charity—that is, learning how to love as God loves, for God loves not just what is already loveworthy but with an abundance of generosity that can be readily seen in the two greatest acts of divine charity: (1) creation—in which God brought the universe into being from nothing, and (2) redemption—in which God the Father sent His Son to redeem a world of sinners. In neither case is it a matter of God being attracted to what already seems good, but rather a matter of rendering good what was not good, either because it did not even exist or because it was sinful and disordered.

Second, while there ought to be a likeness between our own form of receptivity and the receptivity of the Son, the fall has also damaged this resemblance. There seems to be a kind of psychic inversion that takes place in us that is correlative to the defect in our love of generosity. If spontaneously and by nature we only tend to give our love to what strikes us as loveworthy, we fear that we will not receive love unless we appear loveworthy. So, instead of trusting with confidence that we will be loved and thereby receiving what is given freely and without condition, there is a tendency to manipulate our situations and to make ourselves appear more loveworthy, so that we will be the object of the love of others. In my understanding, this defect in us is quite likely that aspect of original sin that is especially responsible for being the source of much actual sin in our lives.

Thirdly, there ought to be within us a love of joy and delight in being witnesses to giving and receiving as our analog to the love of glory that is the characteristic love of the Holy Spirit. But, given the defects already noticed in us as the result of the fall, we find ourselves afflicted by damage in this third aspect of our likeness to God as well; that is, we easily become envious and jealous of love given and love received when we are not ourselves the subject or object of this love (Quay 1995). The point is not that any of these defects are yet actual sins, for "actual sin" according to the Catholic understanding of this matter requires that there be deliberate choice of something that is wrong—that is, one would have to know right from wrong, one would have to choose to do what one knew to be wrong, and the relative gravity of the sin would also depend on how serious the nature of the wrong was. Rather, the point here is to take note of the difference between any actual sins that anyone may commit and the fallen condition in which we find ourselves, that is, the fact of various defects in our inclinations with respect to love.

This account of the matter, to be sure, is only a brief outline of what needs much amplification. But perhaps by sketching out even this much it will be possible for us to see the Catholic understanding of our need for Christ, for redemption, and for sanctification. Catholic understanding has rightly focused on the person of Christ as the Incarnate Word in terms of the mission received by the Son as the Second Person of the Trinity from the Father to take on a human nature and to sacrifice Himself for us. Within this mystery the Church has rightly emphasized both redemption and sanctification. Redemption refers to the act by which God Himself generously paid the debt that we human beings have incurred by sin and thus the act by which God has saved us. Sanctification refers to the process by which the shattered image and likeness of God in us is restored and by which we are healed, that is, by which we are made to be like God again, made holy, or (to use the terminology emphasized here), made to love once again according to the pattern of loves that God intends that we freely choose for our actions and our loves.

The process of sanctification in the Catholic understanding has two main components: the life of the sacraments and the life of morality. For Catholics, Baptism is the sacrament by which sanctifying grace and thus the very life of God returns to us. The other sacraments that we may come to receive in the course of our lives continue the work of God in us. The sacrament of Reconciliation (penance) is a way to receive forgiveness for our sins and to be restored to friendship with God. The sacrament of the Eucharist (holy communion) is a way to receive the body and blood of Christ within us and thus to be nourished for our daily lives with His divine life. The sacrament of Confirmation seals us with the gifts of the Holy Spirit that first came to us in Baptism and strengthens the presence of those gifts within us for the duration of our lives. The sacrament of Anointing provides a medicine for body and for soul, not just in immediate preparation for death but at various times of sickness. The sacraments of Matrimony and Holy Orders provide divine graces needed for particular forms of life, that is, for marriage and for priestly life. Without God's grace, we cannot be healed. Without these sacraments, we would be left on our own, to do as best we can, perhaps with the aid of our human culture, and we would simply be at the mercy of God with respect to our salvation. (Here too there are various important questions that will not be entered into—about why Christians often still live so badly despite these gifts as well as about the possibility of salvation outside the Church and the sacraments; see CCC 1994: §846–848.) The Church understands the sacraments that Christ gave to the Church as the great gift of God by which His image and likeness are restored and strengthened within us.

The other important aspect in the process of sanctification concerns the moral life, that is, our response to God's initiative to restore us to Himself by the proper use of our powers of understanding and free choice. Many aspects of the moral life are accessible to every human person and every culture. The Church's understanding of the possibilities of achieving various degrees of understanding about the moral life even by the use of reason apart from revelation or faith goes hand in hand with the philosophical approach discussed earlier. When thinkers in the Thomistic tradition, for instance, say that grace builds on nature, they are affirming not only our need for grace to do something that we cannot do by nature, but also a certain basic goodness that remains in nature even after the fall. The Thomist view of nature does not think of our nature as utterly helpless or without recourse, but as genuinely wounded and suffering from some defects that can only be restored by grace.

But it is absolutely vital to emphasize here the need for imitating the life of Christ, that is, for modeling not just individual actions but our whole lives on the pattern of Christ's life. We understand the Son of God to have become incarnate in Christ, that is, to have taken upon Himself the fullness of our nature, from the moment of his conception in the womb of Mary by the power of the Holy Spirit. In His human life He shows us what our human lives and loves should be. Notwithstanding so many aspects of this mystery that we might want to consider here, let me concentrate for present purposes on just one: the stages of His life and the order of His loves present to us a pattern for our own. Christians need to learn to recapitulate the life of Christ in our own lives by growing through the stages of human life according to the model that He presents to us, for in His own life He has perfected what was imperfect, He has completed what was incomplete, and He was sanctified what was sinful (Quay 1995). A more complete account of this process and its challenges is beyond the scope of this essay. It would involve meditation on the life of Christ as recounted in the Gospel, to grasp both how the life of Christ recapitulates the life of Israel that is narrated throughout the whole of the Old Testament and how we need to recapitulate the life of Christ in our lives and families and cultures. Understanding this matter is absolutely crucial for grasping the Catholic understanding of the human person. For purposes of this essay in light of the present dialogue, however, we also need to turn briefly to a third consideration, the Church's social teaching.

The Church's Social Teaching

It is precisely by reason of expertise about human nature that the Church, in light of what has been revealed by Christ, claims to be justified in speaking authoritatively about social questions (CCC 1994: §2419–2425; Pius XI 1931: §41; Vatican Council II 1965: §4, 22; Paul VI 1967: §13; John Paul II 1987: §7; John Paul II 1991: §53–58). The ethical principles relevant for social morality transcend utilitarian calculations of a technical nature, and it is in the articulation and defense of these fundamental moral principles that theology and philosophy have an indispensable role to play.

The distinctly theological dimensions of Catholic Social Teaching (CST) include the vision of the human being as made in the image of God (Genesis: 1:26). They also argue against the claims that religion is oppressive to human freedom and self-realization and that only atheism guarantees authentic human freedom, as seen in Leo XIII 1891: §42; Pius XI 1931: §120, 130–135; John XXIII 1961: §205–211; Vatican Council II 1965: §19–21; John Paul II 1991: §13–14. Catholic Social Teaching makes clear that there are special obligations in charity incumbent on Christians to act as the brothers and sisters of Christ that they have become by baptism (CCC 1994: §1889; 1997; John Paul II 1981: §26), and the need to love one's neighbor as oneself, according to the understanding of neighbor made clear by the parable of the Good Samaritan (Luke 10: 29–37; CCC 1994: §2196). Once one recognizes that one's life is not for storing up earthly goods but heavenly ones (Luke 12:13–21; Leo XIII 1891: §18), one can more easily gain a freedom in the spirit for the proper use of one's earthly goods (CCC 1994: §1741–1742; Paul VI 1967: §12–20). It was in this spirit that the Second Vatican Council and the encyclicals of Pope Paul VI so firmly asserted the connection between working for development of underdeveloped peoples and credibility in evangelization (Vatican Council II 1965: §44).

Not everyone with whom we speak about questions of social justice and social order are likely to share our religious, biblical, or ecclesial commitments. Hence, although our deepest reasons are theological, there will frequently be need to make arguments for sound social policies on the basis of principles that do not require a specific religious faith to be compelling in practical matters. It will be enough for the sake of action in common if these principles will be recognized as true by people of good will on the basis of our common humanity. And even in dealings with our co-religionists, there will be areas where the social applications of revelation or tradition may not yet be as clear as we might like or where there may not yet be consensus about how best to proceed. Catholic moral theology in general, and not just in the area of social thought, has long insisted that philosophical reason is a reliable and crucial partner in the enterprise. Although faith comes first in the pairing of faith and reason (it is not merely rhetorical custom but a sound instinct that tends to place faith before reason, as in John Paul II 1998), there is a great role for philosophical reasoning to play. The ethical principles that are fundamental for good social order are rational in nature, and in the public square it may be helpful to articulate and defend them on philosophical grounds, even if one's deepest reason for holding them is religious in character.

Human Dignity

The foundation-stone of all the more specific principles of CST is respect for human dignity (John XXIII 1961: §82–83; Vatican Council II 1965: §12–22; John Paul II 1981: §4–10). The treatment given to this subject in all the major documents exemplifies the stereophonic approach to philosophy and theology that is typical of Catholic thought. When one asks how best to make the case for a social order that respects the dignity of each human person, the strongest reason may well be that each human being is made in the image of God, and so human beings, taken individually and socially, ought to be respected out of reverence for the God in whose image we are made and who has commanded this respect. But the need to respect the dignity of each human being is also accessible philosophically, and it may be helpful to use a more philosophical approach, especially in discussion with those who are hostile to or suspicious of organized religion, or even with certain Christians—students, for instance, who may be cynical about their religion, just testing it, or overly enamored with views they have heard from secular teachers or acquired from their culture.

To appreciate the meaning of human dignity and its ethical implications philosophically may require considerable patience in making a sustained rational argument for the human person as different in kind from any other animal, as irreducible to our biochemical constituents or our biologically based psychological drives and impulses, and as something more important than an anonymous element within mass culture. In the division of labors within a philosophy curriculum, this is the province of a sound course on the philosophy of the human person—one that explores the distinctive features of human life that simply cannot be explained away by facile reductionism. It is necessary to meet the challenges and objections raised by those who regard the claim that human beings are different in kind and wholly distinct in value as if this were merely special pleading. The possible approaches are many. Human language, for instance, is not just different in degree of sophistication from even the most complicated forms of animal communication, but different in kind. The specifically human forms of commitment and promise-keeping that are indispensable to any social order are not merely instinctive or emotional bonds but the results of free choices and thus matters of moral responsibility (Mansini 2005). Unlike the animal world, human sexuality is not merely a matter of estrus and biochemical stimulation; it involves persons, and the sexual relations of persons need to be mediated by words if the persons are to mean what the actions by their very natures are saying and if the actions are sincerely to say what the persons involved really mean. What these and many other areas of human life exhibit upon philosophical reflection is the genuine distinctiveness of personhood from all other types of being. It will also be important for presentations of CST to draw upon insights from other disciplines: for instance, epistemology, by considering the objectivity of truth and the criteria for assessing truth claims in the practical order; general ethics, by considering the norms of justice and the responsibility that flows from free choice; political philosophy, by noting the distinction between authority and the power at its disposal as well as the procedures for the detection of ideological efforts to reduce questions of principle to questions of mere power by the deconstructive techniques of such masters of suspicion as Freud, Marx, and Nietzsche.

The Main Principles of Catholic Social Thought

The series of papal and conciliar statements of the past century, from *Rerum Novarum* by Pope Leo XIII in 1891 through Pope John Paul II's

1991 *Centesimus Annus*, has articulated a number of such principles, including the right to private property (Leo XIII 1891: §4–8; Pius XI 1931: §44–52; John XXIII 1961: §109–112; John Paul 1991: §4–11, 30), and concomitantly, the universal destination of the goods of this world (Leo XIII 1891: §19; John XXIII 1961: §119–122; Paul VI 1967: §22–24; Vatican Council II 1965: §69; John Paul II 1961: §30–43); the duty of obedience to legitimate authority, and with it, the double-edged principle of subsidiarity (Pius XI 1931: §80; John XXIII 1963: §140; John Paul II 1991: §15); the duty of governments to work for the common good (Leo XIII 1891: §28–29; Pius XI 1931: §49; John XXIII 1961: §20; John XXIII 1963: §53–74), and correlatively the principle of solidarity (John XXIII 1963: §98ff; Paul VI 1967: §43ff; John Paul II 1981: §8, John Paul II 1987); and the right to authentic human development (Paul VI 1967: §12–21; John Paul II 1987: §27–34).

As its chief philosophical pillars, CST has relied especially upon natural-law theory and, to an important but lesser extent, personalism. The tradition of natural-law morality has its roots in ancient Stoicism and Roman law and has seen contemporary applications in the civil rights movement and the Nuremberg Trials, but its most prominent exposition comes from Thomas Aquinas, whose thought has been an indispensable support for the modern articulation of Catholic social thought (Leo XIII 1891: §6–8; John XXIII 1963: §8–38; John Paul II 1981: §14). Personalism is the name for a movement in contemporary philosophy that Popes Paul VI and John Paul II (John Paul II 1981: §15; 1991: §13) have used extensively in their contributions to Catholic thought about the great social questions. (Pope Paul VI had enormous esteem for the personalism of Jacques Maritain 1947, 1955.) By its focus on the human person, this approach offers the benefit of arguments that may have more immediate appeal than do natural-law arguments, if only because one appears to carry less metaphysical baggage (such as detailed investigation of teleology and natural function). Especially when one is working in the realm of international law, or operating politically in a pluralistic society where there is little patience for metaphysics, it may prove fruitful to make one's arguments about distributive justice and the social order on the tenet that all persons are moral subjects, each with certain inalienable rights. But despite the apparent rhetorical advantages of this approach, the popes have chosen not to let their case rest on personalism alone but to develop it in tandem with natural-law considerations. It is easy to see the reason for this when one considers the problem of precisely how one should properly define "person." On a wide range of social issues, including the protection of the unborn from abortion, of defective children from infanticide, of immigrants from racists, and of the senile and the comatose from deprivation of care, there are often virtually interminable debates about how to define personhood, particularly when one party or another finds it advantageous to rule some individuals whose existence is inconvenient out of the protected class of persons in the effort to solve some "social problem." The resolution of these questions about personhood invariably requires a return to considerations about human nature. In learning how to make these arguments, it will be crucial for students to appreciate that reliance on the functional definitions for personhood in terms of rationality or self-consciousness that are useful in helping to differentiate healthy mature adults of the human species from healthy mature adults of any other species do not suffice as non-arbitrary demarcation criteria for ruling individuals in or out of the species.

The Importance of Natural Law Theory for Social Principles

Natural-law argumentation is prominent in all the documents of the tradition from *Rerum Novarum* on. It may have been a desire to have Thomistic natural law's robust appeal to reason as discovering moral norms within human nature that led Pope Leo to call for the renewal of Thomism in his 1879 encyclical *Aeterni Patris*. Confronted by the rise of socialism and communism, Popes Leo XIII and Pius XI mounted a defense of the right of property, not by treating it in Locke's manner as an abstract right of individuals to do what they like with what they have appropriated and made more valuable by their labor, but with a strong sense of the demands of morality for its proper use. They follow the Thomistic reasoning that rights flow from duties. Because all human beings have by nature a duty to care not only for their own lives but for their families and dependents, they must have the right to acquire property sufficient to be able to carry out their duties. The correlative principle of solidarity makes it possible for them also to argue for the legitimacy of unions, and even of labor strikes under some conditions (Leo XIII 1891: §31–38; John Paul II 1981: §20), not on the Marxist logic that class warfare is inevitable, but on the natural-law grounds that justice requires the payment of fair wages. Given the intrinsically social dimensions of human nature, they urge that voluntary associations formed for the pursuit of the common good such as labor unions are indispensable for securing the conditions in which laborers can provide for themselves and their families. Throughout this tradition, CST documents invariably make the case that family life is the foundation for society (Leo XIII 1891: §9–10; Vatican Council II 1965: §47–52; John Paul II 1991: §39). Pope Pius XI, for instance, conjoins these points when he extends the notion of a "just wage" to the idea of a "family wage" (Pius XI 1931: §67–75; see also Leo XIII 1891: §3;, John XXIII 1961: §68–81, 185–189) out of recognition that CST must think of human beings not as mere individuals in the *laissez faire* marketplace of labor as subject to the interplay of supply and demand (Pius XI 1931: §53; Leo XIII 1891: §15; John Paul II 1981: §11–15; 1991: §42), but as intrinsically social, first by reason of membership in families and by extension as participants in various orders of society. The virtue of justice requires that governments promote the common good, including the improvement of wages and working conditions, so as to ensure the stability of family life and the conditions needed for genuine human development, such as access to education, civic friendships, and rest.

Correlative with the papal defense of the right of private property is the doctrine of the universal destination of goods. The documents make special use of Aquinas's view that God created the goods of this world for common human benefit (for example, *Rerum Novarum* §19 quotes Thomas Aquinas, *Summa theologiae* II-II: qq. 65–66). While individuals are justified in acquiring property and enhancing the value of what they cultivate, divine providence has made the goods of this world for the needs of all people. Hence, a person in genuine need may have a more fundamental claim than a person whose needs are already satisfied. By the careful attention paid to the genuine demands of distributive justice, the documents avoid both an abstract commitment to the unrestrained right to amass private property, as if one's use of the goods of this earth were indifferent to genuine human needs, and a disregard for the right to acquire the private property that one needs to take care of one's duties.

Further, and interconnected with the above two points, this tradition champions the principles of authentic human development and of subsidiarity. Authentic human development must include but cannot be limited to material development. The Catholic sense of development includes the person's physical, emotional, and intellectual growth, the maturation of a sense of moral responsibility, growth in the virtues and the ability to give and receive love, to make a life commitment that will enable the formation of families, and above all to grow in knowledge and love of God.

The principles of subsidiarity, first articulated explicitly by Pius XI in *Quadragesimo Anno*, serve to guide thinking about the appropriate level of decision-making. It is based on an understanding of the human being as an irreducibly unique person and as intrinsically ordered to family life and to society. In a sense, the principle of subsidiarity is a two-edged sword. Decisions that can be better made at a lower level of organization should not be reserved to higher levels of authority, but, on the other hand, higher levels of authority should recognize and honor the need to act for the common good where lower levels of organization cannot be as effective. The goal of this carefully balanced principle is thus to enhance both the common good, by ensuring that decision-making happens at effective levels, and the legitimate freedom for decision-making that tends to ennoble the individual person and social groups, whose legitimate freedom for self-determination it protects. It is, of course, a part of human nature that one tends to be more responsible for the decisions that one makes, and that one takes greater care of what is one's own (one's property, one's reputation, one's family, one's community).

The four chapters that constitute the first part of *Gaudium et Spes* from the Second Vatican Council are an importance presentation of the Catholic vision of the moral life. The five chapters that together make up its second part address a number of current moral problems under the headings of marriage and the family, the proper development of culture, socioeconomic life, political life, and questions of peace and disarmament. There are many passages that are primarily theological and scriptural, for example, the rightly famous passage in

§22 that Pope John Paul II so often quoted (for example in *Veritatis Splendor* §2): "It is only in the mystery of the Word incarnate that light is shed on the mystery of man . . . It is Christ, the last Adam, who fully discloses man to himself and unfolds his noble calling by revealing the mystery of the Father and the Father's love." It is passages like this that give this entire document its strongly Christological focus.

The elaborate anthropological and sociological analysis found in the first part of the document provides something like what any good natural-law theorist would ideally want to present as the vision of human life, human nature, and human personhood that is indispensable for ethics. That is, just as philosophical anthropology depends on metaphysics, so any ethics depends in important respects on anthropology (not to mention the primacy of ethics over *laissez-faire* economics). While the document certainly does have recurrent references to theological anthropology, it also quite clearly is engaged in philosophical anthropology by virtue of its effort to address those people of good will and open mind who may not share our religious presuppositions but who can be counted on to join the Council in its effort to read "the signs of the times." These signs of the times include the vast number of changes (both deep-seated and more superficial) in the social order, in public morals, in culture and attitudes, in religious practice, in technology and economic life, in communications and the media, and so on.

It is significant that the adversary that the Conciliar text is addressing here is the position that human nature itself changes and has changed, and that for this reason there can be no unchanging or objective morality and certainly no absolute or exceptionless moral norms. Historicity, in short, seems to imply the relativity of moral truth, and it is for precisely this reason that the Council apparently felt the need to address the many ways in which the world has been changing, so as to affirm that human nature has not changed. Not only does the Council bring to bear the theological and revealed notion that Christ, "the perfect man, reveals to human persons what human nature can and should be" (Vatican Council II 1965: §22, 29, 41, 45) but also that there is an abiding human nature—the very claim that scholastic natural-law theory has perennially made. Sin and grace, as it were, have quite a history, but the human constitution that is the battleground for sin and grace has an abiding character on which the Council can ask the readers of this document, whatever their own commitments, to reflect, so as to see the permanent moral demands of the natural law for how human beings ought to choose their actions and how they ought to form and reform their societies so as to ensure the protection of human persons, their marriages and families, their social associations, and their rights. For the Council, the vast amount of change that can be catalogued testifies not to a change in human nature, but to certain changes in how we understand the abiding needs of human nature and especially to a deep awareness of the changing social challenges that need to be met in order to respect human nature and human dignity.

There is considerable philosophical sophistication in the document's treatment of human nature. Not only does the document review and affirm the unity of matter and spirit, body and soul in each person, but it takes up the gauntlet of inadequate anthropologies by criticizing materialist reductions of the human person and the perversity of anthropological dualists (those who would try to distinguish between human *being* and human *personhood*—see Vatican Council II 1965 §25). The text of *Gaudium et Spes* at several points (for example, §13, 16, 37–39) takes up the disputed question of human freedom—the nature and proper description of freedom, genuine and faulty notions of autonomy, the legitimate and proper goals of free choice. In many ways this document seems to me to anticipate some of the great themes of the second chapter of John Paul II's (1993) *Veritatis Splendor*. In this section (§29) also we find the Council Fathers affirming the intrinsically social character of human nature (a point that is, as we have seen, absolutely crucial to CST), for the human person "achieves integral fulfillment only in the family, social life, and the political community." And these insights in turn justify the conclusion that society is not, as it tends to be for many political theorists, only a necessary evil or some artificial construct by virtue of a social contract (see §25, and also §75, which takes note of the fact that political community and public authority are "founded on human nature"). Likewise, there are important sections devoted to the differences between male and female and their indispensable complementarity—points that become crucial for the normative comments in the second part about the morality of marriage, family, and society.

In a very direct appropriation of Thomistic natural-law theory, the Council has an important section (§16) on conscience in general and on the need for human beings to follow certain fundamental moral principles of divine origin that come to be known through conscience. Not only does *Gaudium et Spes* teach that "the more a correct conscience prevails, the more do persons and groups turn aside from blind choice and try to be guided by objective standards of moral conduct," but it also makes considerable use of this notion in its later discussion of sexual ethics and marriage in §51, where it states that decisions about sexual activity and the regulation of the number and spacing of births depends not just on "a sincere intention and consideration of motives" but also on "objective criteria" that in turn need to be based on the "nature of the human person and his acts" as well as on the eternal life that each human person is called to share. (The Latin text of §51 reads: "*objectiva criteria ex personae eiusdemque actuum natura desumpta.*")

Likewise, within the chapter on human community (§24–31), the Council employs any number of other concepts and theses that are typical and distinctive of the natural-law tradition, including the correlation of duties and rights, inviolable human dignity, shared humanity, and the demands of the common good. Similarly, the third chapter of the second part on socioeconomic life is deeply in harmony with the previous tradition of CST, not only in its general claim that the inviolable dignity of the human person must be honored in the economic realm (§63), but in its rather technical analyses of topics like productivity, labor, property ownership, and distributive justice. There is, for instance, a vigorous case made that theories that obstruct economic and social reform in the name of a false liberty and a view of *laissez faire* economics as if moral principles were irrelevant should be treated as erroneous, as should theories that subordinate the basic needs of individuals to the collective organization of production. There is a healthy respect for the economic laws of the market and for the technical intricacies of efficient decision-making processes in local, national, and world economies, but as is very typical of CST, the document repeatedly insists that there are moral norms that need to be respected and that may never be violated. On the topic of property and private ownership, for instance, there is considerable attention given (very much in the natural-law tradition of moral argumentation) to the very purpose of private property (namely, to provide individuals with a kind of independence that enhances their ability to do their duties to their dependence and that extends their freedom). But always correlated with this defense of private property this document joins in adding a sense of the social demands on private property that come from the common good and the communal purpose of all earthly goods (§70–71).

Conclusion

The Catholic understanding of the human person and of human nature needs to be presented in a way that respects its roots in revelation and especially in our understanding of Christ and His mission. But, given the Church's profound and sustained use of philosophical principles, any such presentation also needs to make use of those forms of philosophy that the Church has called upon over the centuries as compatible and useful for explaining and defending certain aspects of her teaching on this subject. This usage of philosophy and theology is especially evident throughout the documentary tradition of CST that runs from *Rerum Novarum* through *Gaudium et Spes* to *Centesimus Annus* and *Caritas in Veritate* (Benedict XVI 2009). It is by the careful employment of philosophical concepts and the sorts of argument that are typical of the natural-law tradition and of personalism that there can be adequate explanation and defense of the various claims that are important to CST, not only by an appeal to the authority of the Church but also in terms that are readily intelligible for broader audiences and that can be made cogent and compelling to those of open mind and good will. These applications to questions of social order and to the moral life are intended to reflect the philosophically realist understanding of human nature that the Church has received and expanded, especially from the Aristotelian tradition. Deepest of all is the understanding of the human person and of human nature that comes from divine revelation, both as recorded on the pages of the Scriptures and as illumined by the life of Christ. Stated most succinctly, the central point is that human beings have a unique dignity and a special form of responsibility because they have been made in the image and likeness of God and because God has sent His own Son to save us and to restore us to that likeness to Himself after His image in us was shattered by sin. Only God was sufficient to redeem us, but He insists that the process of our sanctification include our own free cooperation with His grace.

References

Benedict XVI (2009). *Caritas in Veritate: Encyclical Letter Charity in Truth.* http://www.vatican.va/holy_father/benedict_xvi/encyclicals/documents/hf_ben-xvi_enc_20090629_caritas-in-veritate_en.html

Catechism of the Catholic Church (CCC) (1994). English translation. United States Catholic Conference, Inc.—Libreria Editrice Vaticana.

Irving, D. N. (2012). *Scientific and Philosophical Expertise: An Evaluation of the Arguments on "Personhood."* http://www.catholicculture.org/culture/library/view.cfm?recnum=6015

John XXIII (1961). *Mater et Magistra: Encyclical of Pope John XXII on Christianity and Social Progress.* http://www.vatican.va/holy_father/john_xxiii/encyclicals/documents/hf_j-xxiii_enc_15051961_mater_en.html

———. (1963), *Pacem in Terris: Encyclical of Pope John XXIII on Establishing Universal Peace in Truth, Justice, Charity, and Liberty.* http://www.vatican.va/holy_father/john_xxiii/encyclicals/documents/hf_j-xxiii_enc_11041963_pacem_en.html

John Paul II (Karol Wojtyla) [1961] (1981). *Love and Responsibility,* revised edition. Trans. by H. T. Willets. New York: Farrar, Straus, Giroux.

John Paul II (1981). *Laborem Exercens.* http://www.vatican.va/holy_father/john_paul_ii/encyclicals/documents/hf_jp-ii_enc_14091981_laborem-exercens_en.html

———. (1987). *Sollicitudo Rei Socialis.* http://www.vatican.va/holy_father/john_paul_ii/encyclicals/documents/hf_jp-ii_enc_30121987_sollicitudo-rei-socialis_en.html

———. (1991). *Centesimus Annus.* http://www.vatican.va/holy_father/john_paul_ii/encyclicals/documents/hf_jp-ii_enc_01051991_centesimus-annus_en.html

———. (1993). *Veritatis Splendor.* http://www.vatican.va/holy_father/john_paul_ii/encyclicals/documents/hf_jp-ii_enc_06081993_veritatis-splendor_en.html

———. (1998). *Faith and Reason: Encyclical Letter Fides et Ratio of the Supreme Pontiff John Paul II on the Relationship Between Faith and Reason.* http://www.vatican.va/holy_father/john_paul_ii/encyclicals/documents/hf_jp-ii_enc_15101998_fides-et-ratio_en.html

Leo XIII (1879). *Aeterni Patris: Encyclical of Pope Leo XIII on the Restoration of Christian Philosophy*. http://www.vatican.va/holy_father/leo_xiii/encyclicals/documents/hf_l-xiii_enc_04081879_aeterni-patris_en.html

———. (1891). *Rerum Novarum: Encyclical of Leo XIII on Capital and Labor*. http://www.vatican.va/holy_father/leo_xiii/encyclicals/documents/hf_l-xiii_enc_15051891_rerum-novarum_en.html

Mansini, G. (2005). *Promising and the Good*. Ann Arbor: Sapientia Press of Ave Maria University.

Maritain, J. (1947, 1955). *The Person and the Common Good*. New York: C. Scribner's Sons.

Paul VI (1967). *Populorum Progressio: Encyclical of Pope Paul VI on the Development of Peoples*. http://www.vatican.va/holy_father/paul_vi/encyclicals/documents/hf_p-vi_enc_26031967_populorum_en.html

Pius XI (1931). *Quadragesimo Anno: Encyclical of Pope Pius XI on Reconstruction of the Social Order*. http://www.vatican.va/holy_father/pius_xi/encyclicals/documents/hf_p-xi_enc_19310515_quadragesimo-anno_en.html

Quay, P. M. (1995). *The Mystery Hidden for Ages in God*. New York: Peter Lang.

Vatican Council II (1965), *Pastoral Constitution of the Church in the Modern World: Gaudium et Spes, Promulgated by His Holiness, Pope Paul VI*. http://www.vatican.va/archive/hist_councils/ii_vatican_council/documents/vat-ii_cons_19651207_gaudium-et-spes_en.html

Just Reward: The Nature of Work and Its Remuneration in the Economics and Ethics of Henry George

By Brendan Hennigan*

Abstract. Work is a fundamental reality of human existence. This essay examines in general terms the idea of work and labor, briefly explains the biblical foundation of George's perspective on work, and presents George's analysis on unemployment, technological change, and true competition. Finally, it discusses how access to the natural opportunities land provides liberates labor and advances the just distribution of wealth, connects these insights to Catholic Social Teachings (CST), and calls for more cooperation between these natural allies.

Introduction

I said to a Yorkshire sailor on my first voyage, "I wish I was home, to get a piece of pie." I recall his expression and tone, for they shamed me, as he quietly said, "Are you sure you will find a piece of pie there?"
—Henry George (1992: 353)

Work is a fundamental reality of human existence. From ancient to modern times workers have satisfied their needs and wants by impressing their labor on the earth's natural resources. Whether it involves a farmer ploughing his field, a shipwright building a boat, or an information technologist developing a new computer software program, work is one of the means by which humans satisfy their numerous and infinitely diverse needs, wants, and desires.

It is mostly through work that individuals acquire material goods and services for their own sustenance and well-being. One of the central themes that runs through the writings of Henry George is the

*Brendan Hennigan is Research Director of the Canadian Research Committee on Taxation.

American Journal of Economics and Sociology, Vol. 71, No. 4 (October, 2012).

natural right of all men and women to have equal access to land. He saw the laws of nature as underpinning the principles that govern the laws of production and distribution, economic and natural justice, and social progress. By inquiring into the nature of work one may better understand the fracture that occurred between man and nature with industrial and technological advancement.

This essay explores several themes relating to the nature of work. It examines in general terms the idea of work and labor, briefly explains the biblical foundation of George's perspective on work, and presents George's analysis on unemployment, technological change, and true competition. Finally, it discusses how access to the natural opportunities land provides liberates labor and advances the just distribution of wealth, connects these insights to Catholic Social Teachings (CST), and calls for more cooperation between these natural allies.

George's primary purpose was to discover why poverty could coexist with the increased capacity of nations to create wealth and then to use these findings to eliminate poverty. He wanted to refute the theory that wages are drawn from the advance of capital, and to show that there is no conflict between labor and capital. By examining and adapting the theories of Adam Smith and David Ricardo, he correlated the laws of production and distribution and harmonized the economic laws of rent, wages, and interest. In relation to CST, this essay shows that (1) labor does have priority over capital and (2) there is no real conflict between labor and capital in Georgist economics. The reconciliation of George's theories with CST succeeds or fails on these two points.

George, unlike Marx, did not believe that the cause of poverty was an inherent conflict between capital and labor. He did not lay the blame at the feet of employers. His advocacy (George 1992: 353) was against a "false and wrongful system," which deprived working people of the "natural opportunities of employment." His call for justice was based on respect for common and individual property rights, the independent nature of the laborer, cooperation, and equality of association in society. The thrust of George's argument (George 2003: 310) for the elimination of the economic and social evils associated with poverty was that it be accomplished by the "restoration to all men of their natural and unalienable right to the use, upon equal terms, of the elements on which and from which all men must live—the land."

While for George, equitable access to land was the solution for the problem of progress and poverty, the Catholic Church stresses other economic and ethical principles. CST increasingly emphasizes the personal and the cooperative nature of work in helping promote social justice and the common good among peoples and nations (John Paul II 1981: 22–24). The focus of a discussion on the rights of workers and the fair distribution of wealth should be on the intrinsic dignity of the human person and the valuable contribution of all types of labor to the development of society. Further, any real solution to the social problems caused by unemployment, underemployment, industrial pollution, over-consumption, globalization, labor alienation, workers' exploitation, and poverty must be sought through sound economic and ethical principles, addressing the problem of land monopolization and George's remedy. The implementation of George's great social reforms cannot alone be "accomplished by 'intelligent self-interest', and can be carried out by nothing less than the religious conscience" (George 1891: 22). (The meaning of "religious conscience" and its practical application is discussed later.) The tripartite dialogue between governments, religious groups, and trade unions relates directly to the subject of work and how communities may better respond to the economic and ethical character of the work (Peccoud 2004).

What needs to be developed is a philosophy of labor that incorporates the economic-ethical principles of Henry George with the Christian Gospel teachings on work, justice, community, and the common good. Political and environmental concerns regarding sustainable economic development, workers' rights, and natural resource use are a global issue. Ethical considerations and the responsibilities associated with property rights, stewardship of the earth's natural resource, land use, and economic development have particularly shaped the perspectives of sections of the Georgist movement and the Catholic Church on work and labor. (Taxation policy may be added to the Georgist position.) Questions raised are inevitably linked to the idea of natural rights, fair labor practices, distribution of wealth, and social development. Today, these issues are indirectly but rapidly gaining worldwide media attention and affecting public opinion and international politics, due mainly to grave concerns about the debasement of the earth's environment, global warming, and unsustainable economic development. Georgists would argue that these and other problems are rooted in the monopolization of the world's natural resources and the unjust distribution of wealth.

Respectful dialogue and cooperation among different nations, religions, and groups to find a true and lasting remedy to the problems of poverty and the unfair distribution of wealth are of paramount importance to worldwide peace and prosperity. An important component of this debate is understanding the nature of work, its personal and social dimension, the paradox of labor and freedom, and the riddle of wealth and want. Henry George's proposition was that these matters are not only social questions, but at their core religious ones (George 1891: 67).

Looking for Definitions of Work and Labor

Henry George proclaimed loudly and passionately that those willing and able to work should have work. For this to occur he believed all men and women must have equal access to the natural opportunities contained in the physical universe. It is through work that men and women provide the material means to live and prosper. Work is not an end in itself; it is only a means by which one satisfies one's desires (George 1992b: 130). Human work in all its various forms is intrinsically personal and social. It is through work that one provides for the needs of oneself, one's family, and society. It is important to the concept of the nature of work to make a distinction between the meaning of work and labor. In common language their usage seems to be interchangeable. In George's political economy the terms are not synonymous. This becomes important when we start to distinguish between the economic, moral, ethical, and even recreational motivation for bodily exertion.

In *Social Problems,* George (1992b: 129–138) addressed the issue of unemployment. He held the view that anyone who is willing to work should have access to the natural opportunities land provides. Work as a means, rather than an end in itself, is closely associated with the higher values often associated with work: self-respect, knowledge, and happiness. There is a necessary connection between individual desire, human exertion, and the satisfaction of those desires through physical or mental exertion. Work for work's sake, therefore, for George, deprives the individual of freedom. This type of work is akin to the forced labor of the sweatshop, the monotony of the assembly line, or the prisoner condemned to breaking rocks.

Two simple distinctions may help clarify George's position. Work is a general term used to describe human exertion: the toil and trouble involved in the expenditure of physical or mental resources. The economic term for exertion that aims to satisfy one's desires is "labor" (George 1992: 411–412). George was careful to distinguish between the power and act of laboring associated with physical or mental exertion, and the results of labor whose value is exchangeable (1992: 243–244). The initial factor in the production of wealth is always labor. Labor, in the economic sense, is the active or human factor of production and is thus "the producer of all wealth, the creator of all value" (George 1992: 411–412, 1992b: 130–131). George saw neither work as a curse nor labor as having its root in human selfishness. The nature of work is in accordance with the natural law of production and distribution. George believed that humans and society by not following natural law cause maladjustments in the social order. Throughout *Progress and Poverty*, George (2001) kept restating that *freedom* not slavery is the right of man. Therefore, poverty is a denial of justice when it limits the advancement of the individual within society.

Philosophers closer to the present day echo and further develop these themes. In her book *The Human Condition*, Hannah Arendt (1958: 70–174) proposed a distinction between labor and work. Her contention is that the necessity of the biological process of physical exertion and the products of work have been incorporated into the concept of labor. "The human condition of labor is life itself," while "[w]ork provides the 'artificial' world of things, distinctly different from all natural surroundings" (Arendt 1958: 7). The major aim of labor is not production as such, but the act of laboring. A situation has been created where the natural separation of labor and work has ceased to be a reality. This has had a dramatic and negative effect on mankind. Whether it be the exploitation of the workers by the capitalist or the glorification of the worker in Marxist ideology, the result is a compression and combining of the personal aspect of work (labor) with the necessary aspect of work (the act of producing some external thing). Thus, the personal condition of work is forfeited. Humans are treated as machines; they are dominated by factors of production and their ability to produce a product. The worker becomes a commodity. The person no longer controls or has a personal stake in her or his work life.

In his book *Philosophy of Labor*, Remy C. Kwant (1960: 1–27) sees a paradox in labor, a tension between freedom and restraint. Modern labor has liberated man from the restraints of the natural world, but there is a price to be paid for this freedom. The paradox of labor is that "modern labor improves the condition of man, but at the same time it threatens certain values" (Kwant 1960: 17). Furthermore, our working lives get increasingly monotonous through the standardization of our cultural landscape. In the end, he says, the nature of labor is very difficult to define. There is always an economic component to labor, but labor is a "social category." "The labor system provides for the common needs, and many common needs are beyond the realm of economics . . . (for example) the education system [not to mention spiritual, cultural or aesthetic needs] cannot be reduced to economics" (Kwant 1960: 122). George emphasized this point when speaking of the purpose of political economy and the values associated with human development. Political economy has an ethical component that cannot be disregarded when considering the fair distribution of wealth.

According to the Dominican friar M. D. Chenu (1963), it was not until the late 1950s that the term "theology of work" first appeared. The expression "morality of work" had been in use since the nineteenth century. Chenu wanted to make people aware and to encourage thoughtful Christians to "look beyond the abstract morality" of how one makes a living and see "the study of work as a subject in its own right, to its economic function and its historical role" (Chenu 1963: 2–3):

> We must understand the nature of work and its human and material orientation, in order to appreciate its internal laws and its spiritual needs from a Christian standpoint. If the "civilization of work" demands its own ethic, which up to the present no one has yet evolved, Christians can only

collaborate in this evolution by considering and understanding, in the first place, what work means to the people of the twentieth century.

Chenu's thoughts foreshadow later social encyclicals on the subject of human work.

E. F. Schumacher (1979: 3–4) in his book *Good Work* identifies the three main purposes of human work as follows:

1. First, to provide necessary and useful goods and services.
2. Second, to enable every one of us to use and thereby perfect our gifts like good stewards.
3. Third, to do so in service to, and in cooperation with others, so as to liberate ourselves from our inborn egocentricity.

Schumacher thought it was impossible to conceive of life at a truly human level without human work. Life is a "school of becoming and a school of self-development"; it cannot be conceived of without the idea of "personal freedom and personal responsibility" (Schumacher 1979: 32).

Economic Terms

In *Progress and Poverty*, George (2001) defined the terms "land," "labor," and "capital" and made clear distinctions between them. (George thought it was important to remove ambiguities from such terms used in political economy. They must have only one meaning and it is the job of the political economist to define them and then stick to the definitions.) Together these concepts make a coherent system in the production of all wealth. The two primary factors of production, George said, are land and labor. Land is everything in the material universe exclusive of man and his products. Labor is "all human exertion in the production of wealth" (George 2001: 31). Capital is derived from a union of the two. Everything must be excluded from capital that is included in land and labor. Land, labor, and capital all have an appropriate mode of return proper to their function. In the laws of distribution, for land the return is rent, for labor it is wages, and for capital it is interest.

George defines "work" as including all human exertion; in this sense work is subjective (see George 1992: 243–244, 2001: 32–33 for definition of different modes of labor). Land, labor, and capital are the factors of general production. All production comes from the union of land and labor. Capital is a form of wealth and is used to aid labor in supplementing the various modes of production by the process of adapting, growing, and exchanging natural products (George 1992: 414). Without going into great detail on George's exposé of the meaning of wealth it is sufficient to say that wealth includes "natural substances or products which have been adapted by human labor to human use or gratification, their value depending on the amount of labor which upon the average would be required to produce things of like kind" (2001: 42). In Georgist economic terminology labor is always used to describe "all human exertion in the production of wealth, whatever its mode" (1992: 411–412):

> Labor in fact is only physical in external form. In its origin it is mental or on strict analysis spiritual. It is indeed the point at which, or the means by which, the spiritual elements which is in man, the Ego, or essential, begins to exert its control on matter and motion, and to modify the world to its desires.
>
> As land is the natural or passive factor in all production, so labor is the human or active factor. As such it is the initiatory factor. All production results from the action of labor on land, and hence it is truly said that labor is the producer of all wealth.

It is labor that uses capital to produce more material goods such as tools, cars, houses, skyscrapers, consumer goods, luxury items, food, and so forth. George (2001: 48) defined capital as "wealth in the course of exchange" and made the important distinction that nothing can be capital that is not wealth, but not all wealth is capital.

Capital, in a literal sense, is defined by its relationship to labor and can do nothing without the exertion of labor. Capital is put to work by the exercise of human physical or mental exertion. George (1992: 282) said that actual or real wealth is a product of labor. Real wealth consists of things like buildings, livestock, tools, and manufactured goods (George 2001: 41). According to George, wealth can be said to have three basic characteristics. (1) Wealth is made of tangible material things. Anything that is non-material cannot be classed as wealth. (2) Wealth is produced by the exertion of labor—either in its original form, or by changing and adding to it. (3) Wealth is capable of satisfying human desires. In classical economics land is the passive factor and labor is the active factor. It is labor that defines George's (2001: 42) definition of wealth:

> Nothing which nature supplies to man without his labor is wealth, nor yet does the expenditure of labor result in wealth unless there is a tangible product which has and retains the power of ministering to desire.

In the economic sense, it is thus labor conjoining with land that produces material goods, which are not only the fruits of our labors, but the objects that satisfy all humankind's wants and desires.

Adam Smith (1723–1790) identified two types of capital that generate revenue. Fixed capital consists of useful machines, profitable buildings, improvements to land, and acquired and useful human abilities. Circulating capital is more fluid and is "employed in raising, manufacturing, or purchasing of goods and selling them again for a profit" (Smith 1937: 262). Both kinds of capital need human input to spawn interest or profit.

One of the main goals of George was to harmonize the law of production with the law of distribution. In *The Science of Political Economy* he criticized J. S. Mill for the erroneous and vague notion in which "the one set of laws are natural laws and the other human laws" (George 1992: 450–453). Human laws are based on custom and therefore open to change. In opposition to the classical tradition, George maintained that the laws of production and the laws of distribution are both natural laws. The distinction is that, while the laws of production are limited to the physical laws of nature, the natural law of distribution is a moral law and therefore makes reference to ethics:

> And it is this that enables us to see in political economy more clearly than in any other science, that the government of the universe is a moral government, having its foundation in justice. Or, to put this idea into terms that fit it for the simplest comprehension, that the Lord our God is a just God.

The laws of production and distribution unite to form one homogenous path to the comprehension and realization of a just world free of poverty and want. Two things should be noted: first, George (1992: Book I, chapters I–VI) saw labor as being of a spiritual composition; therefore it is always human and personal. Secondly, he severely criticized *Rerum Novarum* and Catholic social teachings for succumbing to the erroneous notion that land is a form of capital.

The First Law of Political Economy

The first law of political economy is that all men seek to satisfy their desires with the least exertion. This axiom is the foundation on which the whole structure of Georgist ethic-economics is based. All human actions aim to satisfy human desires. Desires can be positive or negative, and George said that without them man could not exist. Here "desire" should be seen in its broadest context—material, intellectual, emotional, and spiritual. Some desires are primary, such as the desire for nourishment, maintenance of life, or avoiding injury and pain. The most basic desires he calls "needs": food, clothing, shelter, and so forth. After these basic needs have been met, human desires increase to a higher level, for example, to gain greater love, knowledge, or happiness (George 1992: 81–85).

Desires and their corresponding satisfactions may be divided into subjective and objective. Subjective desires and satisfactions are related to the individual—his or her immaterial thoughts or feelings. Objective desires and satisfactions are always related to the external world. They may be actual material things or objects of thought. George criticized the German philosopher Arthur Schopenhauer (1788–1860) for the view that "wise men should seek the extinction of all desires" (George 1992: 83). In fact, George observed that desires actually increase, at least in quality, "coming higher and broader in their end and aim" (1992: 83). This is the reason why with the advancement in society the capacity for gratification is never static, but dynamic. All human desires and satisfactions evolve, and fall within the scope of political economy.

Work is not an end in itself, but the way in which humans can satisfy their desires. The toil and irksomeness of exertion is the natural condition associated with work or labor. In observing one's own actions or the actions of others, humans seem to take a path of least resistance. This does not mean that that at all times and circumstance we always take the easiest road, but there is a tendency to do so (George 1992: 87):

But whatever be its ultimate cause, the fact is that labor, the attempt of the conscious will to realize its material desire, is always, when continued for a little while, in itself hard and irksome. And whether from this fact alone, or from this fact conjoined with or based upon something intuitive to our perceptions, the further fact, testified to both by observation of our own feelings and actions and by observation of the acts of others, is that men always seek to gratify their desires with the least exertion. This, of course, does not mean that they always succeed in doing so, any more than the physical law that motion tends to persist in a straight line means that moving bodies always take that line. But it does mean the mental analogue of the physical law that motion always seeks the line of least resistance— that in seeking to gratify their desires men will always seek the way which under existing physical, social and personal conditions seems to them to involve the least expenditure of exertion.

There is an important difference between George and other political economists. He particularly criticized Adam Smith for the assumption that humans' primary motive is selfishness or self-interest. He called it a fundamental and great error in the history of political economy. The motivation for physical exertion is not a curse, but an *impulse* that has increased enormously the material wealth of civilized societies.

Work in both its subjective and objective senses is the means by which mankind prospers and societies advance. The ability to find decent employment, receive a fair wage, gain an education, have recreation and leisure time, and be financially able to support self and family is vitally important when discussing the relationship among the nature of human work, economic justice, and social progress. Fittingly, it was not a desire for riches or fame that first sparked George's interest in the laws and principles that govern the production and distribution of wealth. It was the underlying cause of poverty, unemployment, and industrial depressions that first aroused George's fury against the injustice of increasing wealth and want.

The Law of Rent

The Catholic Church may have unfairly criticized George when it interpreted his views as similar to those of Smith and Mill. Liberalism's doctrine of self-interest or selfishness is a way of excusing injustices in society and defends the exploitation of the working class. The Catholic Church, from Leo XIII's *Rerum Novarum* (1891) to the present day, has consistently criticized the excesses of the old capitalist system. George should not be included in this criticism.

Adam Smith rightly suggested that the division of labor allows for great advances in the material wealth of nations. Increased specialization within trades and professions, labor-saving machines and inventions, advances in technology, and efficiencies in methods of production all contributed in the material advancement of our modern age.

Population density and improvements in transportation methods have a general tendency to increase the amounts of goods that labor can buy (George 1992b: 139–147). Manufactured goods and services are generally cheaper in cities than in rural areas. The intensive margin is said to be labor saving. However, it costs more to purchase a parcel of land in a city. Cheaper land is available at the extensive margin, that is, when it is a further distance from a central core, or of a poorer quality. Wages may be higher in the cities, but the cost of living is also relatively higher. In rural areas land is cheaper, but wages tend to be lower. The relationship between the intensive margin, the extensive margin, and the ability to monopolize land and natural resources is one of the reasons industrial progress and economic expansion do not necessarily guarantee a fair distribution of wealth. George did not believe that invention, technological advancement, or improved labor efficiency, in the long-term, increase the general level of wages; he dedicated a good part of his working life writing and speaking on the subject. To some, George's view of technological advancement may seem counter-intuitive. Technology is supposed to help labor, but it is a mixed blessing.

George's argument is basically that, even with all of the different kinds of economic improvements, the result will always be the same: the owners of land (including natural resources) will have a greater share of the wealth than workers and capitalists (George 2001: 252):

> All I wish to make clear is that, without any increase in population, the progress of invention constantly tends to give a larger portion of the produce of labor to the landowners, and a smaller and smaller proportion to labor and capital.

George (2001) adapted David Ricardo's (1772–1823) law of rent to show that wages are affected by the margin of cultivation. Increases in the number and density of a population push up the value of land. Landowners can demand a higher ground rent, affecting the returns to labor and capital. George's (2001: 231) aim was to show that the law of wages (for labor) is a corollary of the law of rent (for land) and harmonizes with the law of interest (for capital):

> Wages depend upon the margin of production, or upon the produce which labor can obtain at the highest point of natural production open to it without the payment of rent.

George observed that Ricardo's law of rent was accepted to be valid by most, if not all, of the economists of his day. He reworked Ricardo's formula to show that as the demand for land increases the ground rent also increases (the reverse is also true). The consequence is that "[w]ages depend on the margin of cultivation, falling as it falls and rising as it rises" (George 2001: 219). Interest reacts in the same way as wages. The first law of political economy is embedded in all three laws (2001: 218):

> The all-compelling law that is as inseparable from the human mind as attraction is inseparable from matter, and without which it would be impossible to previse or calculate upon any human action, the most trivial or the most important. The fundamental law, that men seek to gratify their desires with the least exertion, becomes, when viewed in its relation to one of the factors of production, the law of rent; in relation to another, the law of interest; and in relation to a third, the law of wages.

The first law of political economy is critical to George's program of reforms. As the "golden rule" (of doing unto others as one would have done to oneself) applies to moral law and good actions, so does this axiom apply to the natural laws of economics and just actions. It is the ground on which the laws of production and distribution are based.

The Gift of Nature

If justice and liberty are to be attained it must be through equitable access of labor to the earth's resources, or what George calls the natural opportunities of nature. George emphasized that nature is a gift from the Creator. There is a "natural and inalienable" right of equal access to the natural opportunities that the earth provides (George 2001: 335). The Creator provided in the goodness of nature the means for mankind to live and prosper. Henry George observed that nature does not discriminate among those who wish to use her natural resources (2001: 335):

> She makes no discriminations among men, but is to all absolutely impartial. She knows no distinction between master and slave, king and subject, saint and sinner. All men to her stand upon an equal footing and have equal rights. She recognizes no claim but that of labor and recognizes that without respect to the claimant.

It is through work that we lay claim to the fruits of the earth. Man does not live apart from nature, but in and with nature. It provides the air that he breathes, the ground on which he stands, the food that he eats. It is imperative that everyone has access to nature for his or her survival and well-being. Equal access to nature's bounty is a natural right of existence. George (2001: 338) proclaims it is a universal principle dictated by God:

> If we are all here by the equal permission of the Creator, we are all here with an equal title to the enjoyment of his bounty-with an equal right to the use of all that nature so impartially offers. This is a right which is natural and inalienable; it is a right which vests in every human being as he enters the world, and which during his continuance in the world can be limited only by the equal rights of others.

George's religious convictions are evident in his whole approach to nature, land, and the labor question. Equal title to the goods of the earth has its foundation in the biblical creation story. Since mankind first appeared on this earth all God's "children were to have an equal share" in His creation (George 2001: 420). It is in the creation story, in the opening chapters of the Book of Genesis, that we find the basis for this equality right. Creation was a gift to mankind from God. Man and woman were given dominion over the earth (Genesis 1–3). It was through their labors that man and woman were to furnish their material needs, food, clothing, shelter, and so forth. To do so, man must have access to nature's materials, forces, and opportunities.

Just Reward for Labor: Wages

Remuneration for one's work is usually in the form of wages. George made no distinction between the wages of an employee and those of a self-employed worker: both are compensation paid for one's labor. George (2001: 17) began *Progress and Poverty* with a direct question on the relationship of wages, wealth, and poverty: "Why, in spite of increase in productive power, do wages tend to a minimum which will give but a bare living?" His conclusion was that workers are shut out from the natural opportunities that land provides. No artificial restrictions should inhibit any person from finding work. His attack on the wage fund theory is aimed at reinforcing the principle that all types of exertion, in all their various forms, are but a "return to labor" for the work done.

In the production of wealth, equilibrium should exist between the three factors of production and each should be guaranteed their rightful reward. Restrictive practices, human laws, and customs tend to skew this natural relationship and divert income from one group to another. Wages will never rise to a natural level as long as the owners of land or capital take a greater share of the increase in wealth than is due to them. George (2001: 421) held the provocative view that landowners are not entitled to any share of the economic rent because it is created by the community and not a product of one's labor. This view has been challenged by many Catholic commentators, including Monsignor John A. Ryan (1869–1945) (Ryan 1942; Andelson 2004: 327–329).

Wages, Labor, and Employment

For full employment to occur, George said, labor must have access to the natural opportunities and forces of nature. He said that the real cause of poverty is due to labor being shut out from the natural opportunities land provides. His philosophy is that everyone who wants to work should have work.

For example, forest leases should be structured to allow for a greater share of the timber harvesting to be done by individual operators or small or medium-size companies. Job opportunities would increase with a shift towards labor-intensive tree farming and reforestation. Large capital-intensive multinational forest products companies would not be allowed special privileges by way of long-term leases or taxation policies. In the cities and rural areas, with the introduction of a land-value tax, land prices would stabilize or decline. Lower land prices could help revitalize the idea of the family farm because it would be easier to own, buy, or sell land. One could envision the expansion of small specialized farming operations and market gardens close to urban population centers. Shifting taxes from business and labor and onto land would reduce the costs of hiring employees. It would be more financially and socially advantageous to hire full-time rather than part-time employees.

George believed that giving labor better access to land would increase wages, self-reliance, and an entrepreneurial spirit. There would be greater cooperation between labor, commerce, and industry. But the greatest effects would be the reduction of actual or hidden poverty, the actualization of individual potential, and an end to a misconceived class struggle between different economic classes or groups. George did not see this as a utopian dream, but as the harmonization of natural law with justice and freedom.

George wanted us to make a fundamental shift in our perception of the relationship between the worker and the employer. He asked, should not the one who is providing his labor be seen as providing the more important economic function? It is labor that gives value to commodities and exchange; therefore should not labor be the more valuable, or sought after. He writes (1992b: 131–132), "Why is it that we do not consider the man who does work the obligatory party, rather than the man who, as we say, furnishes work?" An analogy here may help. Any professional sports franchise is made up of owner(s) and players, the players forming a team. Every person on the team is important, but some players have specific skills that are prized more than others. Within the team different players may demand higher wages than others. In the analogy, it is the relationship between owner(s) and players that is central to George's realignment of labor-employer value. Who is more impor-tant—the team or the owner(s)? It is the team because without the team the owner could not put his capital to good use. The owner needs the team to realize the return on capital. George (1992b: 133–134) identifies three things that might limit the earning capacity of labor: the minute division of labor, the concentration of capital, and labor-saving devices. All three tend to restrict workers from directly applying their labor, skills, or initiative in the satisfaction of their desires. Access to land circumvents these problems (George 1992b: 134):

> It being the power of every one able to labor to apply his labor directly to the satisfaction of his needs without asking leave of any one else, that cutthroat competition, in which men who must find employment or starve are forced to bid against each other, could never arise.

True competition between the suppliers and employers of labor permits variations in the supply and type of labor required. The big advantage would be to create a more flexible industrial system, which could adapt quickly to variances in economic output or demand. Labor would be capable of "indefinite expansion," self-directed, and in control of its earning potential. Laborers would be more productive because they would have a greater say in the economic outcome of their own enterprise, or that of their employer. A substantial increase in the number of self-employed trade-persons, business people, and professionals is also likely (George 1992b: 135).

> In such a state of things, instead of thinking that the man who employed another was doing him a favor, we would rather look upon the man who went to work for another as the obliging party.

Capital would be unable to have an "excessive advantage" over labor because of its command of the factors of production. Pius XI (1931) criticizes liberalism capital and the Manchester School for lacking a social conscience in regard to the ownership of productive goods. Rodger Charles (1998: 98–100) summarized the case against radical liberal capitalism:

> Private ownership of productive goods must be the basis of the economy. Liberal capitalism, out of which the modern economy grew, was based on economic freedom and private ownership of productive goods. It warped that institution with its excesses of freedom and lack of respect for the social responsibilities of private ownership, but capitalism itself cannot be dismissed as by nature vicious. Its evil came from the liberal ideology of the time which made it deny workers their dignity and neglect its social responsibilities.

George held a similar view, but blamed monopolistic practices that concentrated capital and power in the hand of a few large landowners and capitalists, which in turn denied workers their natural rights and freedom. George was adamant that under the present system capital has the advantage because it is less susceptible to having to satisfy immediate needs or desires. For example, during a strike or lockout, capital can wait out the conflict, while labor must provide for its basic needs, food, drink, and shelter. As George (1992b: 134) stated, "Capital wastes when not employed; but labor starves." The freedom associated with a free labor market would lead to the possibility of greater employment opportunities. Increased competition for labor would increase the general level of wages. Thus, the CST principle of a family wage could be realized. John Paul II (1981: 46) defines a family wages as the income of one adult that is sufficient to properly maintain a family's present material needs and security for the future.

According to a recent report published by the left-leaning Canadian Centre for Policy Alternatives, the gap between the rich and poor in Canada seems to be widening (Yalnizyan 2007). One explanation is that there is too much low-paid part-time work and not enough full-time work. It is difficult to get an accurate picture of the real rates of unemployment, underemployment, and income levels. Robert Hiscott (2007) criticized how the data were compiled and analyzed, concluding that "[t]here is indeed income inequality and growing polarization over time in Canadian society, but it largely reflects the extreme gains of the top 1 percent of earners rather than income changes for the broader segment of Canadian individuals and families captured in the top income decile." This would indicate that concentration of income at the highest 1 percent is the real problem. This parallels George's observations that over time there is a concentration of land and capital. Under George's economic program, the necessity to have two or three low-paying jobs would be reduced and in a very practical way the plight of the working poor would be addressed.

An increase in the rate of pay for a group of workers or a particular skill may be observed at times when specialists are in demand. For example, leading up to the Y2K scare, employers were offering bonuses to IT specialists and giving recruiting bonuses to their employees. Similarly, in the United States and Canada during World War II, wages in shipyards and airplane and armament factories were higher because of the increased demand for labor due to the war effort. Such would be the general tendency in a free labor economy.

Without oversimplifying the complexities of a nation's economy, the conditions created by freed-up labor would be sustainable and stable and provide the means for full employment. Inequalities in the distribution of wealth are magnified when labor is chasing opportunity. It is when there is fair competition between labor and capital that people will not be subjected to the "wretchedness and despair born of poverty" (Geiger 1933: 3), as explained by George (1992b: 135):

> Where there is always labor seeking employment on any terms; where the masses earn only a bare living, and dismissal from employment means anxiety and privation and even beggary or starvation, these large fortunes have monstrous power. But in a condition of things where there was no unemployed labor, where every one could make a living for himself and family without fear or favor, what could a hundred or five hundred millions avail in the way of enabling its possessor to extort or tyrannize.

The monopolization of land and natural resources leads to unfair competition and the concentration of wealth and power in a few hands. George R. Geiger (1933: 10) in his biography on George wrote:

> That monopoly and "big business," the whole "merger" technique of modern industry is slowly concentrating wealth and power and ever widening the gap between the two extremes in the distribution of the product of economic enterprise.

Mass concentration of capital distorts the real purpose of competition. True competition supports the best use of the land and our natural resources, enhances economic efficiency, encourages self-reliance, and promotes cooperation between individuals and groups—and even between labor and capital.

One of the causes of underemployment or idle labor is when artificial restrictions are placed on workers, whether in the skilled, unskilled, service, business, or professional ranks (George 1992b: 138):

> The supply of labor seems to exceed the demand for labor, springs from difficulties that prevent labor finding employment for itself—from the barriers that fence labor off from land.

There is a natural tendency for the labor market to adapt to changes in the type and amount of workers needed to supply demand. Freeing up labor allows for a quicker response to the needs of industry.

Workers gravitate to areas where employment opportunities are good and wages high. George saw a tendency to equilibrium existing between the demand for and the supply of labor. Having access to the natural opportunities that nature provides allows for a fluid movement of resources and people from one occupation to another more attractive one. For example, Alberta's oil, natural gas, and oil-sands industry is leading to rapid economic growth, that is, the production of wealth is increasing. The demand for all types of workers has increased the general level of wages in the province. Workers are moving to Alberta seeking employment and the high wages that go with it. George believes that the impulse to satisfy one's desires with the least exertion would propel individuals into leaving low-paying jobs or trades and equipping themselves with the necessary skills to be employable in higher-paying jobs. This process happens more quickly when restricted practices are not imposed by custom or law. In short, George wanted the entrepreneurial spirit residing in humans to be set free.

When George (1992b) talked about the necessity of land, he did not mean that everyone ought to become a farmer. Without the material universe, no man or woman could live. We all breathe air, drink water, build shelters, eat food, make or use tools, barter and exchange goods or services. Today, it may be more appropriate to say that everyone is interconnected and dependent on a global economic and social eco-system. However, George's insight remains the same: labor needs equitable and unfettered access to land in its classical economic conception (George 1992b: 136–137):

> Without land no human being can live; without land no human occupation can be carried on. Agriculture is not the only use of land. It is only one of many. And just as the uppermost story of the tallest building rests upon land as truly as the lowest, so is the operative as truly a user of land as the farmer. As all wealth is in the last analysis the resultant of land and labor, so is all production in the last analysis the expenditure of labor upon land.

There is a greater awareness about the economic and environmental footprint humans have left of their world. This may help refocus the arguments for social and economic reform so that the social mortgage or ethical-economical interest we all have in our lands is not overlooked.

Productivity and Technological Change

George was not a Luddite, neither was he dazzled by the promise of technological change. (The Luddites were a gang of craft people who organized riots in several northern England textile towns between 1811 and 1816. They destroyed textile machinery that was displacing their traditional craft skills. Several deaths were reported. In 1813 at trials in York several convicted rioters were hanged and many others faced transportation. By 1816 government repression and a revived economy brought an end to the riots. The relationship between hardship, technological change, tyranny, and prosperity should not be overlooked.) It was George's (2001: 249) opinion that every invention or improvement has a tendency not to increase the general level of wages, but to increase ground rent. He observed two effects of the impact of new technology, systems, or procedures. The "primary effect of labor saving improvements is to increase the power of labor, the secondary effect is to extend cultivation, and where this lowers the margin of cultivation, to increase rent" (George 2001: 245). What this means is that labor-saving machines, improvements in technology, new discoveries, or inventions do initially increase the power of production and the productivity of workers. However, ultimately this drives up the economic rent or the surplus from better-situated land. Any real and lasting benefit to labor or capital is offset by an increase in the ground or economic rent. The monopolization of land allows the landowner to limit supply artificially and demand a higher price for its use.

To make this point, George used the example of the expansion of the railroads. The original advantage was to labor because it opened up markets, but very soon after, with an increase in land prices, it was the landowner who demanded the greatest share of the newly created wealth. This phenomenon may be readily observed in those communities that recently experienced a spectacular increase in land values due to the "high-tech" bonanza. One of the best examples in North America is the Silicon Valley technological "land" rush. Remember that land, in the economic sense, includes all the visible and invisible spatial-temporal resources, forces, and natural opportunities of nature, such as land, water, forests, minerals, electro-magnetic forces, and the broadband spectrum. This latest land rush was not for agricultural or railroad land. High-tech speculation caused a dramatic and speculative increase in the price of stocks and land-site values. The bursting of the "high-tech bubble" resulted in the downturn in the stock and land markets. The after-effects of land speculation had a devastating consequence on the incomes of those working in industry and many working people lost their investments or pensions. Some Silicon Valley employees could not afford the cost of accommodation and did not want to stay in homeless shelters. The solution borders on the surreal. (Read an account of this phenomenon by Fred Harrison 2005: 38 and an eyewitness account of people forced, by necessity, to sleep and ride the 26-mile route of the bus #22, dubbed Motel 22, at http://alienflea.tblo.com/archive/2006/09).

Technology is a mixed blessing under current conditions. More than a century ago, George identified a series of effects on society and individuals. The concentration of capital leads to monopolies and oppression. Workers become more dependent on their employers. Opportunities for training and the freedom to acquire profitable skills are restricted. In turn, this reduces the independent nature of workers, their outlook on life narrows, and they become more sullen and less engaged and vigorous. New techniques and greater efficiencies in production are not in themselves good or bad, but intelligence is needed to limit bad effects and promote good ones. This is a political and an ethical issue. However, because of economic repercussions societies, in general, are reluctant to limit the productivity advantage of technological change. It is usually only after a near catastrophe, such as occurred at the Three Mile Island nuclear facility, that restrictions are placed on new processes, inventions, or discoveries. Debates on the ethical and political consequences of technological change often are limited by the desires for economic growth and development. Seldom is the debate on technological change about how it affects land values, economic rent, and taxation policy. In Canada and the United States rents have increased, but productivity gains have raised wages if deadweight tax burdens are factored out. Two-income families, increased voluntary unpaid work hours, and government social subsidies often obscure the view that the major winners in technological advancement are not wage earners, but the owners of land and natural resources.

George foresaw the Industrial Revolution as being only the first stage of economic and social advancement. The experience of later decades during a Technological Age and leading into an Information Age may lead us to draw similar conclusions concerning the beneficial or detrimental effects of new technologies on the lives of working people. In the emerging economies of Eastern Europe, China, and India the same effects of technological and industrial expansion are placing great pressure on traditional values and social institutions. Technological change and increased productivity have the effect of extending the margins and raising rent not only locally and regionally, but globally. Greater employment opportunities are accompanied by greater risks. George warned of the inevitable outcome if landowners have an unfair advantage. In the long-run, discord between landowners on one side and labor and capital on the other is detrimental to the aims of society in general, and particularly those of working people.

In *Progress and Poverty* (2001: 244–254) and *Social Problems* (1992b: 139–147) George first looked at the effect of labor-saving machinery and then identified why workers are deprived of the reward of their labor. He started with a simple economy and said that in a primitive state each family provides for its individual needs. The introduction of labor-saving machinery opens up two possibilities: producing the same quantity with less labor or producing more with the same labor. The general tendency will be to diffuse the benefits of efficiency throughout the economy. George used the example of improvements in tanning hides or mining ore. The same holds true for improvements in automobile assembly and the impact of computer technology. Over time more can be produced with less energy. (Recall the goal is to produce wealth for the satisfaction of human desires with the least exertion.) The initial effect is always to give labor an advantage over capital because that labor is the active factor of production. Capital aids labor and "is merely its tool and instrument." In philosophical terms the efficient cause is always labor.

Capital's due portion of wealth is received as interest. George (1992b: 142) admitted that risk or good management may have a part to play in the "utilization of improvements." However, he held that the rewards that ought to go to labor, in the form of wages, are often diverted due to monopoly or the concentration of capital. He used the example of the railroad, showing that improvements in transportation first properly benefitted labor, but in the end what really increased were not wages, but land values:

> While labor-saving improvements increase the power of labor, no improvement or invention can release labor from its dependence on land. Labor-saving improvements only increase the power of producing wealth from land. And land being monopolized as the private property of certain persons, who can thus prevent others from using it, all these gains, which accrue primarily to labor, can be demanded from labor by the owners of land, in high rents and higher prices. (George 1992b: 142)

Is it fair to say that wages have not increased in the industrial world? Living standards have improved. There has been an increase in the wealth of nations. Homeowners, business people, developers, and multi-national corporations all have a vested interest in the present system supporting the individual right to the economic rent. The rewards of labor and capital—that is, wages and interest—are being substituted by the ability to take the economic rent. For example, in Canada a homeowner who sells her primary residence pays no capital gains on the increased value of the property. In effect, the economic rent is a tax-free income. But the social organism that creates wealth seems to be in a precarious state. Those at the lower end of the income scale, the working poor, continue to be dependent not on their own skills and resources but on government subsidies. George did not disagree that individual wages do rise or adjust to the supply and demand of the market. He concluded that the general level of wages would be driven down as long as there is unfair competition in accessing land and natural opportunities.

Competition and Cooperation

The torch George carried was for the right of all working men and women, whatever their race, country, or culture, to provide not only for their basic needs but also for the higher qualities associated with a civilization. George's doctrine of "true competition" is antagonistic towards socialism, which wants to limit the return to capital, and "malformed laissez-faire" capitalism, which wants to limit the reward of labor. Legitimate competition has rarely, if ever, existed (Geiger 1933: 273–281). As long as renewable and un-renewable resources and the natural opportunities that land provides are controlled by the few and not the many true competition does not exist. Monopolies support spurious competition whether the enterprise is controlled by individuals, corporations, unions, or governments, as expressed by Geiger (1933: 273–274):

> It must be made clear that George's approach to competition was in no way sympathetic with that specious, fictitious competition that has made the very word almost a travesty. George agreed with the socialist that the "present competitive system" must tend to degradation, insecurity and disaster; but it was a pathological system. That is, Sidney Webb's statement that "an almost complete industrial individualism" had been tried and found wanting could not have been accepted by George. Instead, the fact was that real competition had never existed, legitimate laissez-faire had never been given a trial. The sham "hands-off," devil-take-the hindmost policy was as counterfeit as any of the distorted approaches to economics which ignored the fact that the earth was in control of a privileged few. There could be no free competition with the sources of the production of wealth monopolized and the channels of the distribution of wealth blocked or diverted. A diseased condition of competition had been taken as the norm.

Free and fair competition opens up new possibilities for the advancement of exchange and trade, which ought to benefit the whole of society (George 1992: 403):

> The competition of men with their fellows in the production of wealth has its origin in the impulse to satisfy desires with the least expenditure of exertion.
> Competition is indeed the life of trade, in a deeper sense than that it is a mere facilitator of trade. It is the life of trade in the sense that its spirit or impulse is the spirit or impulse of trade and exchange.

In the closing pages of *Progress and Poverty,* George (2001) linked the laws of production and distribution with the law of human progress. He believed in the power of the mind to advance society. Not an individualist in the strictest sense of the word, he also stressed the interdependency between the individual and society and proposed the law of society to be "each for all, as well as all for each" (George

2001: 435, 475–552). He believed God had given each person the abilities to seek security and freedom, as Hannah Arendt (1958: 80–81) put it, through "the labor of their bodies and the work of their hands." Society has an organic nature and needs to be nourished by the actualization of justice, not for the few, but the many (George 2001: 279):

> Mental powers, the motor of social progress, is set free by association—or perhaps "integration" may be a more accurate term. In this process, society becomes more complex. Individuals become more dependent upon each other. Occupations and functions are specialized.

Basic needs must be met before one's mind can be put to higher uses associated with citizenship and the more elevated goals of an advancing civilization. It is in a higher or mental form of cooperation and association of equals that civilization rises. He proclaims, "association in equality is the law of human progress."

It is the monopolization of land that hastens the fall of civilizations. Justice becomes blurred when human laws and social institutions override the natural laws that govern the universe (George 2001: 517–518).

> The idea of property arises naturally regarding things of human production. This idea is easily transferred to land. When population is sparse, ownership of land merely ensures that the due reward of labor goes to the one who uses and improves it. As population becomes dense, rent appears. This institution ultimately operates to strip the producers of wages.

The principle underpinning George's solution to the labor question has its ground in natural law and is composed of two parts: the confiscation of economic rent through taxation and the reduction of all other taxes except those levied on land values. No other reforms, proposals, or policies could alleviate the underlying problem of industrial progress and economic injustice. A "society grounded upon a basic institution of monopoly" is an unjust society (Geiger 1933: 274). George knew it would be difficult to have his remedy implemented, but he had followers in the Catholic community in Ireland, Great Britain, and the United States and he hoped the Catholic Church would see the justice of his reforms.

Catholic Social Teaching

The first problem that arises when discussing CST and the reforms that George proposed is that the Catholic Church does not offer any technical solutions to the question of land ownership and taxation. No economic or political system is particularly promoted, although liberalism, rigid capitalism, and Marxism are specifically singled out for their errors. The Church sees its role as not to "analyze scientifically" but to call attention to the dignity of the human person and the rights of workers. It condemns situations in which human dignity and workers' rights are violated. The aim is to guide authentic progress (John Paul II 1981: 7). Social encyclicals put forth general principles "which defend the human dignity of the worker in the process of change" (Charles 1998: 291).

In George's open letter to Leo XIII on *Rerum Novarum* he seemed intuitively to understand that the encyclical was a veiled criticism of his philosophy and what came to be known as the "Single Tax." When discussing the nature of work both the economic and ethical side must be considered in relation to economic justice and social progress. George (1891: 22) indicated to the pontiff that he regarded the ethical side of the land question as more important than the economic one. On the 90th anniversary of the social encyclical *Rerum Novarum*, John Paul II wrote his first strictly social encyclical *On Human Work: Laborem Exercens* (1981). Certain sections of *On Human Work* relate directly to our discussion of Henry George and the nature of work. The text is broken into five main sections: (1) *Introduction*, (II) *Work and Man*, (III) *Conflict Between Capital and Labor in the Present Phrase of History*, (IV) *Rights of Workers*, and (V) *The Spiritual Significance of Work*.

The first section of *On Human Work* reviews the history of the workers question since the proclamation of *Rerum Novarum*. Work is defined as an activity of man. Work is a "perennial and fundamental" issue to which we must keep returning (John Paul II 1981: 6). "Work is at the very center of the social question" (John Paul II 1981: 7). In section II on *Work and Man* one sees a number of potential areas for dialogue between Georgists and Catholics. For instance, the Book of Genesis states that work is a fundamental dimension of human existence on earth. Work is the proper subject of man and it is directed towards satisfying needs, wants, and desires through external things. The original ordering of the earth is universally applied to each and every generation. Workers should not be treated as commodities.

One statement that does need clarification is the Church's ethical meaning of work and its relationship to economic justice. The encyclical states (John Paul II 1981: 23):

> If one wishes to define more clearly the ethical meaning of work, it is this truth that one must particularly keep in mind. Work is a good thing for man—a good thing for his humanity—because through work man *not only transforms nature*, adapting it to his own needs, but he also *achieves fulfillment* as a human being and indeed, in a sense, becomes "more a human being."

The expression "more a human being" needs clarification. George's view that work is not an end in itself, but only a means to an end, is built on a foundation of natural law. George wanted the meaning of terms used in political economy to be clear and precise. The Church seems to be saying that all forms of work are beneficial. George would see the attributes of an advanced society, for example, education and the arts, as being posterior to humans first satisfying more basic needs and wants. George saw labor as the economic and ethical means by which individuals satisfy their desires and society progresses. He did not glorify the worker, treat labor as a commodity, or believe that labor should be subjected to spurious competition. He trumpeted cooperation rather than class struggle. For George, it is not work *per se* that transforms and improves society, but human will and actions.

Section III of *On Human Work* addresses the conflict between capital and labor. John Paul II asserts that during the Industrial Revolution small groups of entrepreneurs, by controlling the means of production, exploited the workers by maximizing profits while paying the lowest possible wage. The real problems associated with industrialization were mistakenly characterized as a "systematic class struggle" by Marx. This sets up an ideological battle between Marxism and capitalism. George's analysis demonstrates that there is not a natural conflict between labor and capital. Nor is there a fear of capital. Conflicts arise between landowners, workers, and the suppliers of capital when the harmonious laws of production and distribution become distorted, thus interfering with the equilibrium and the functional distribution of land, labor, and capital. George's doctrine of "true competition" promotes a free labor-business market by encouraging fair exchange, free trade, and distributed justice and stands in close parallel with John Paul II's (1991: 62) comments on "capitalism" and "free economy." Therefore, in George's explanation of tri-factor economics there is no conflict between labor and capital. Labor is the active or human factor in the production of wealth. Capital aids labor in the production of wealth. The first law of political economy is upheld when labor is able to access the earth's natural opportunities and when the laws of production and distribution are not distorted by institutional monopoly in land.

Different economic systems have been promoted to explain the workings of society, its political structure, economic laws, and social ordering. Historically, these debates have had a profound impact on how we view our world and how best we can govern ourselves for the intellectual, physical, moral, and spiritual good of the individual and community. John Paul II's encyclical *On Human Work* (1981: 37) states that the "principle of the priority of labor over capital is a postulate of the order of morality":

> In view of this situation we must first recall the principle that has always been taught by the Church: *the principle of the priority of labor over capital.* This principle directly concerns the process of production: in this process labor is always the primary *efficient cause*, while capital, the whole collection of means of production, remains a mere *instrument* or instrumental cause. This principle is an evident truth that emerges from the whole of man's historical experience. (John Paul II 1981: 28)

George's political economy comports with John Paul II's guidelines. Both George and the Catholic Church agree that social problems result from an injustice in the distribution of wealth. Since the time of the Industrial Revolution, the relationship between landowners, workers, and capitalists has radically propelled the debate about economic, ethics, and social justice.

The Enigma of Progress and Poverty

The image of the mansion on the hill and the shantytown below is a vivid illustration of the chasm that exists between unbridled affluence and destitution. In North America's wealthiest cities, panhandlers ply their trade on the same streets where international property developers, day-traders, and merchant bankers make their millions. The causes of homelessness, welfare dependency, and unemployment cannot properly be explained by depravity, alcoholism, or mental illness; these are proximal causes at best. George saw them as the symptoms of maladjustments in society and not the cause.

In the problem of poverty we find further agreement between Henry George and CST. This includes the declaration that involuntary poverty is an evil. Poverty and the needs of the less fortunate in society ought to be relieved by economic progress, but history shows that they have not been. Workers should not be exploited or seen solely in economic terms. Private property rights should be respected, common property rights should also be upheld. And the universal destination of goods must be guided by what is just and right not only for the individual, but also for the community. On these and other understandings a common ground can be sought.

Cooperation in this field is both urgent and necessary. Where many in the Catholic social-justice movement may see the solution in the redistribution of wealth, Georgists recommend that the cause, effect, and remedy to the enigma of wealth and want lies in a just and lasting distribution of wealth. The social and economic reforms suggested by Henry George and his followers are more critical in light of our growing awareness of the limited nature of land. The human price paid for the unjust distribution of our nation's wealth has been well documented: anxiety, distrust, crime, vice, despair, unemployment, exploitation, insecurity, and fear. Today the plight of the working poor is grave. Business and personal bankruptcy rates are on the rise. There has been a vast increase in the amount of personal debt fueled by cheap money and unsustainable dreams. In the last 50 years, with the growth of government-sponsored welfare programs some of the visible symptoms of the wretchedness of poverty have become hidden, but the causes have not been conquered.

This is one of the reasons why research into the nature of work is of critical import. Society as a whole grows and prospers through human endeavor. Further research is needed into a philosophy and a theology of labor and work. George's writings contain many elements that could be developed more fully in a modern context. He is prophetic in his judgments on how advances in civilization are not guaranteed. Human progress must be nurtured, understood, and defended. The homogenization of economies and cultures is propelled by humankind's dependency on scientific knowledge and information technology. A better understanding of the economic and ethical nature of work will make the transition from one stage of development to the next less confrontational.

Labor, Wealth, and Justice

To summarize, morally and economically all workers are entitled to the fruits of their labors. The world in which we all live is a gift from the Creator. In tri-factor economics, land (defined by George as all the natural resources and forces and opportunities of nature), labor, and capital are the general factors of production. Land and labor are the primary factors of production. Labor is the creator of all wealth and the means by which we secure our livelihood. Remuneration for labor is usually in the form of wages. The right to be awarded a fair wage is fundamental to natural and economic justice. At a very basic level, it is through human exertion that one acquires ownership or private property rights to external goods. Work in all its various forms has an ethical and economic component. An institutionalized land monopoly has distorted the natural laws of production and distribution. Under present conditions true competition does not exist. The taxation of economic rent is often overlooked when discussing workers' rights, wages, self-reliance, and social development.

The Catholic Church, especially since Vatican II, has produced many documents that develop and adapt CST to better reflect the changing interaction between human beings and the world in which they live (Vatican Council II 1996: 162–282; John Paul II 1981, 1987, 1991). In the encyclical *On Human Work*, John Paul II (1981: 10) stated that "human work is a *key*, probably the essential key, to the whole social question, if we try to see that question really from the point of view of man's good." Greater awareness of the negative impact that humans are having on the earth's environment demands creative answers to old problems. John Paul II (1981: 6) wrote that there is a "growing realization that the heritage of nature is limited" and that new question and problems must be addressed. Henry George (2001: 299–330) would wholeheartedly agree. And that real change can only occur when a remedy is administered to cure the cause of the ailment and not just its effects.

George Geiger (1933: 5) observed the following in his biography of Henry George:

> George assumed that there was no distinct dualism between the realms of morals and of economics, that there was no insulation which prevented the one from becoming in contact with the other . . . George's demand for economic and social reform was a demand for a new approach to the foundations of ethical concepts, and it was his moral purpose that gave life and richness to the fiscal details of his economics.

The philosopher and educator John Dewey (quoted in Geiger 1933: 4) thought George to be one of the greatest thinkers that the United States had ever produced and compared his practical wisdom to that of Plato:

> It would require less than the fingers on two hands to enumerate those who from Plato down rank with him. Were he a native of some European country, it is safe to assert that he would long ago have taken the place upon the roll of the world's thinkers which belongs to him, irrespective, moreover, of adherence to his practical plan.

Geiger believes it is some external factor, rather than George's theories, that has limited his exposure and influence on modern social thinking. Slowly, activists of a new generation are again looking to George for guidance in facing new challenges and problems related to economic and social justice because of the explicit link between economics, social and ethical responsibility. Again people are considering how taxation policies may be used positively to direct good actions. The phrase "tax the bad, not the good" illustrates why everyone should be concerned how humans use, or abuse our natural heritage. Socially progressive groups in Canada, such as the Green Party of Ontario, the Canadian Research Committee on Taxation, and the Henry George Foundation of Canada, are campaigning for a greater acceptance of Georgist principles.

If work is the "key" to solving our social problems then it may also unlock the door for the acceptance of Georgist principles into mainstream Catholic economic thought. Georgists and Catholics should embrace a cooperative approach and work towards a new understanding on the nature of work and the distribution of wealth.

References

Andelson, R. V. (2004). "Ryan and His Domestication of Natural Law." *American Journal of Economics and Sociology* 63(2): 319–335.

Arendt, H. (1958). *The Human Condition*. Chicago/London: University of Chicago Press.

Charles, R. (1998). *Christian Social Witness and Teaching: The Catholic Tradition from Genesis to Centesimus Annus, Volume II The Modern Social Teaching Contexts: Summaries: Analysis*. Leominster, Herefordshire: Gracewing.

Chenu, M. D (1963). *The Theology of Work: An Exploration*. Trans. L. Soiron. Chicago: Henry Regnery Co.

Geiger, G. R. (1933). *The Philosophy of Henry George*. New York: MacMillan Company, 1933.

George, H. (1891). *The Condition of Labor: An Open Letter to Pope Leo XIII*. New York: United States Book Company.

———. (1992). *The Science of Political Economy*. New York: Robert Schalkenbach Foundation.

———. (1992b). *Social Problems*. New York: Robert Schalkenbach Foundation.

———. (2001). *Progress and Poverty*. New York: Robert Schalkenbach Foundation.

———. (2003). "The Great Battle of Labor." In *Henry George: Collected Journalistic Writings, Volume III, The Later Years 1890–1897*. Ed. K. C. Wenzer. Armonk, NY: M.E. Sharpe.

Harrison, F. (2005). *Boom Bust: House Prices, Banking and the Depression of 2010*. London: Shepheard-Walwyn.

Hiscott, R. (2007). "The Rich and the Rest of Us: The Changing Face of Canada's Growing Gap." *Canadian Journal of Sociology Online* (March–April). http://cjsonline.ca/reviews/rich.html.

John Paul II (1981). *Laborem Exercens: On Human Work*. Boston: Pauline Books and Media.

———. (1987). *On Social Concern: Sollicitudo Rei Socialis*. Boston: Pauline Books and Media.

———. (1991). *Centesimus Annus: On the Hundredth Anniversary of Rerum Novarum*. Boston, MA: Pauline Books and Media.

Kwant, R. C. (1960). *Philosophy of Labor*. Pittsburgh: Duquesne University.

Leo III (1891). *Rerum Novarum: On the Conditions of the Working Classes*. Boston, MA: Daughters of St Paul.

Philosophy and Spiritual Perspectives on Decent Work (2004). Ed. D. Peccoud. Geneva: International Labor Organization.

Pius XI (1931). *Quadragesimo Anno: Encyclical of Pope Pius XI on Reconstruction of the Social Order.* http://www.vatican.va/holy_father/pius_xi/encyclicals/documents/hf_p-xi_enc_19310515_quadragesimo-anno_en.html.

Ryan, J. A. (1942). *Distributive Justice,* 3rd Edition. New York: Macmillan Company.

Schumacher, E. F. (1979). *Good Work.* New York: Harper & Row Publishers.

Smith, A. (1937). *The Wealth of Nations.* New York: Modern Library.

Vatican Council II (1996). *Pastoral Constitution of the Church in the Modern World: Gaudium et Spes.* Ed. A. Flannery. Northport, New York: Costello Publishing Company, 1996.

Yalnizyan, Armine (2007). *The Rich and the Rest of Us.* Toronto: Canadian Centre for Policy Alternatives.

Human Work in Catholic Social Thought

By Daniel Finn*

ABSTRACT. In Catholic Social Thought, work is at the center of issues related to morality and economic life. It is simultaneously objective and subjective. Workers are the real agents of production, and therefore labor should have priority over capital. The able-bodied have a moral obligation to *work* to obtain the things they need, but everyone has a claim on the basic necessities of life. Hence the property claims of the well-to-do are not to exclude the poor from what they need. The property-right claim of stockholders depends on the firm serving work and the interests of workers. In unions, workers' natural right to form associations aligns with the right to participate in decisions affecting their lives. Numerous groups and organizations have some degree of complicity in workplace injustice and some degree of responsibility to address it.

Introduction

The best place to start in considering the view of work in Catholic Social Thought (CST) is an encyclical written by Pope John Paul II in 1981, *Laborem Exercens*. Encyclicals are called "letters," but practically they are monographs written by a pope on a particular theme. The first famous "social" encyclical of the modern period was written by Pope Leo XIII in 1891, and later popes have regularly written on related themes on the occasion of an anniversary of that document.

John Paul, who himself had been a laborer in Poland before becoming a priest, argued in *Laborem Exercens* that work is "at the center" of the "social question," that wide ranging set of issues related to morality and economic life (John Paul II 1981: 2). For him, work is the door into all these problems for CST. (There is no doubt that much "work" occurs outside the market, unpaid and generally underappreciated. This includes most definitely the work of caregivers, typically

*Daniel Finn is Professor of Theology and Economics at St. Johns University in Collegeville, Minnesota.

American Journal of Economics and Sociology, Vol. 71, No. 4 (October, 2012).

women, in looking after both children and the elderly. There are references in church documents to work in the home, but I will not address unpaid work in this paper as that would raise a number of issues that may lie beyond the scope of this volume.)

In order to address work, John Paul turns to the first of the two creation stories found in the book of Genesis (Genesis 1: 26–31). There he argues that "the church is convinced that work is a fundamental dimension of man's existence on earth" (John Paul II 1981: 4). He interprets God's command to Adam and Eve—to have dominance over the rest of creation—as an invitation, a call to humans to enter into God's creative action through work. Thus work has a dignity arising from its existence even in the Garden of Eden. When, as the story has it, the fall occurs—with humans rebelling against God— work begins to involve toil; work now occurs "with the sweat of one's brow" (Genesis 3: 19). But the basic, noble character of work remains, even in the midst of human sinfulness.

An important part of John Paul's analysis of work is the distinction between its objective and subjective dimensions. Work is "objective" in that it is particular, focused on a particular task at a particular time. Objectively, different workers produce different things, and this is the main source of difference in status and wages in the market. In this vein, the development of technology is the result of human work. John Paul thus shares with partisans on the political left the conviction that both the machines and know-how of modern technology are the products of work, though he persistently rejects both class analysis and any sense that strife is an essential part of relations between workers and the owners of technology. He encourages a struggle for social justice but this is *"for* the common good rather than *against* others" (Hornsby-Smith 2006: 196). As he puts it, "technology is undoubtedly man's ally" (John Paul II 1981: 5).

But work is simultaneously "subjective," in that the worker is the acting subject, the one who exerts a subjectivity. This occurs regardless of the particular time and place where work occurs, and irrespective of what is being produced or the size of the wage. Subjectively considered, all work is dignified and all work contributes to the worker's self formation as an active, deciding person. As John Paul describes the worker, "these actions must all serve to realize his humanity, to fulfill the calling to be a person that is his by reason of his very humanity" (John Paul II 1981: 6). As Michael Naughton (1992: 72) has put it, "as people perform certain acts they fulfill themselves in what they perform." Thus, both the source of the dignity of work and the basis for determining the value of work are "not primarily the kind of work being done but the fact that one who is doing it is a person" (John Paul II 1981: 6). As Thomas Massero (2000: 141) has said: "This is why workers must not be treated as just another cog in the huge machine of production, an attitude that offends the dignity of all." The key here is that the worker as a person is the ultimate purpose of work and should never be subordinated to the objective output of the work done. In fact, John Paul referred to this reversal as the "error of economism," when labor is valued only according to its economic product (John Paul II 1981: 13). The fact that work is the labor of an acting subject makes work the key to the whole social question, and a significant part of that key is understanding the relation of labor to its partner in modern production, capital.

John Paul boldly asserts the principle of "priority of labor over capital," though this principle has been interpreted quite differently on the left and the right. (For more thorough discussion of the interplay between capitalism and socialism in Christian ethics, see Werpehowski 1994: 516–520). For example, Gregory Baum (1982: 80–81) explains that "the economic system proposed by *Laborem Exercens* is a form of socialism." Baum even includes a chapter entitled "John Paul II's Socialism." This Baum (1982: 30) founds on his interpretation of the priority of capital over labor: "Justice means that capital is made to serve labor." It includes "the right of the people who do the work to participate in decisions regarding production, distribution and the use of capital."

Others farther to the right, however, interpret the priority quite differently. As Robert A. Destro (1993: 172–173) sees it, employees' stock ownership and pension funds already represent the way in which capital serves labor in the United States. In addition, he argues that in case of small business, "the physical, emotion, and professional proximity of the 'capitalist' to the persons who are 'the workforce' virtually obliterate the distinction between them." Far from Baum's conception of worker participation in management, Destro interprets

John Paul to be endorsing "a vision of the common good of the enterprise, as defined by the management or ownership and agreed to by those who participate in it."

The source of these different interpretations is John Paul's own double definition of "capital" in *Laborem Exercens*. At times capital means machines and tools of production and at other times it refers to the persons who own them. His commitment here is to the central importance of the person who labors, whether a blue-collar worker or a manager, in comparison to the myriad of inanimate things—from brooms to machine tools to computers—that make humans more productive. At no point, the Pope says, should we allow the people in this process to be treated as mere things. Workers are the real agents of production, even the most humble of them.

Work, of course, is how the vast majority of us who are not "independently wealthy" put food on the table. It is the way we get the things we need. And in the Catholic tradition, we should not talk about this process without stepping back to examine the tradition's view of property, since part of the importance of work is rooted in the guarantee of access to what we need, which itself is based on the understanding of the rights and responsibilities of owners of property.

Work and Creation

Christians hold that the world has been created by God, which of course is what makes it "creation." This conviction about creation by God should not be confused with "creationism," the belief of many fundamentalist Christians today that God's creative acts took place about 6,000 years ago, based on a literal interpretation of the Bible. Catholics and mainline Protestants rejected this belief long ago and today understand God's creation as *embodied in* the physical evolution of the cosmos over the past 14 billion years and in the biological evolution of living species on earth over the past 4 billion or so. As Galileo's friend, Cardinal Cesare Baronio phrased it, "the scriptures tell us how to go to heaven not how the heavens go."

The science has improved since the days when the creation story was first put in writing by Israelite scribes, but Christians today still hold to the religious basics of the story—that God created the earth with a purpose, and meeting the needs of all was part of that divine intention. Of course, the able-bodied have a moral obligation to *work* to obtain the things they need, but everyone has a claim on the basic necessities of life, based in God's intention in creation.

There are two key characteristics of creation particularly relevant to the Catholic view of human work. The created world is good and it is a gift.

The first creation story in Genesis famously describes God's judgment at the end of each of the "days" of creation. God looked at what he had made and "saw that it was good" (Genesis 1: 1–31). In Christianity, the material world is known as good. Unlike some world religions that stress the religious importance of separating oneself from the material world and moving to a more purely spiritual path for life, Christians and especially Catholics have stressed that the material side of our life is just as authentically religious—and important to God—as the spiritual.

Jesus and many others in this tradition warned against putting our confidence in material wealth and taught that the wealthy always risk a "hardness of heart" in their tendency to think themselves self-sufficient and in no need of God or others. But this does not contradict the fundamental conviction about the goodness of the material world. Jesus sometimes fasted but he also ate well on occasion. He changed water into wine according to the story of the wedding feast at Cana—not something a teetotaler would do.

Theologically, Catholics hold a "sacramental" view of the material world—convinced that material things can be "translucent to the divine light"—a conviction that forms the basis not only for the seven sacraments but also for religious art and beautiful churches. For economic life, the meaning of the goodness of creation is that our work—whether growing wheat, doing laundry, or managing a business—has religious significance. It is religiously important, another reason for our reminding ourselves of the dignity of work, even menial work.

The second characteristic of creation—that it is a gift from God—also has critical relevance for work. For Christians, humans have not stumbled upon the planet in a sort of cosmic lottery. The world we have, we have as a gift from God's loving care. And the fact that the goods we work to obtain are also gifts from God has always entailed obligations.

In the Hebrew Scriptures (the Old Testament), the law required that farmers not harvest the corners of their fields. The grain there was to be left standing to be harvested by the poor of the day: the widow, the orphan, and the resident alien. And when an Israelite owner of a vineyard picked grapes, he was not to go back later to pick the ones that ripened late. These too were to be left for the poor (Deuteronomy 24: 19–21; Leviticus 19: 9–10). All the able-bodied were obliged to work, but the point of such laws was that the property claims of the well-to-do were not to exclude the poor from what they need.

Work and Property Ownership

Jesus' teaching of love of neighbor is well known. Less well known is the view in the early church—taught by all the church "fathers"—that Christians must not adopt the predominant Roman view of property ownership. Clement of Alexandria, Ambrose, Augustine, and all the other fathers of the church, East and West, taught that the well-to-do were obliged to assist for the needy from their surplus. The rule was that if I have more than I need and you have less than you need, I am obliged to share my surplus with you—because everything anyone owns is a gift from God. In fact, Saint Augustine (quoted in Avila 1983: 116) spoke in much more striking language: "Those who offer something to the poor should not think that they are doing so from what is their own." It belongs to the poor.

The transition from the traditional economy of the Middle Ages to the industrial economy of the modern world occurred rapidly in historical terms. The Industrial Revolution brought about immense dislocation for ordinary workers beginning in England. Products such as textiles that had been produced for centuries in people's homes in rural areas began to be produced in urban factories once the power of the steam engine and the ingenuity of the Industrial Revolution took hold. As these new products were produced more cheaply, jobs dried up all across rural areas. Large numbers of workers left their traditional homes, moving away from family and community and into the large industrial cities. Once there, workers often lived in economic squalor and, with the bonds of family and tradition broken, often lost their religious faith and the moral compass that went with it. Large numbers of industrial workers no longer went to church the way their ancestors had. And the organizations in the forefront of efforts to challenge this brutal capitalist system were labor unions, which tended to be strongly anti-religious.

It was in this atmosphere of social upheaval and out of intellectual ferment among well-educated Germans and French Catholics that Pope Leo XIII wrote his famous encyclical, *Rerum Novarum*, in 1891. His statement was simultaneously a response to a threat to the Church and a prophetic protest against the unjust treatment of workers throughout the industrializing world.

Leo XIII was keenly aware of the imbalance of power between workers and factory owners in the nineteenth century (Leo XIII 1891: 6). For this reason he gave strong support to "workmen's associations," as a counter-balance to the owner's power. He recognized that an individual worker cannot long withhold his labor—either in search of a different job or in negotiation with his current employer. This has led to consistent, even growing, endorsement of labor unions by popes since Leo's day. As Patricia Lamoureux (2004: 402) has put it, Pope John Paul II in *Laborem Exercens* "provides the strongest affirmation of labor unions to be found in Catholic social teaching with the claim that unions are not just legitimate or important, but are 'an indepensible element of social life.' "

In unions, workers' natural right to form associations aligns with the right to participate in decisions affecting their lives. Solidarity, which is to characterize all Christian life, becomes embodied in a particular way in labor unions themselves. John Paul writes that labor unions ought not become political parties and should not be fixated only on their own interests, but he expresses such caveats in the midst of broad endorsement of unions as the ordinary way for workers to offset the power that modern corporations hold.

Going beyond the question of unions, Leo XIII puts the medieval notion of a "just wage" into modern context. He argues that a just wage should provide the worker and his family with "reasonable and frugal comfort" (Leo XIII 1981: 63) and any wage that falls short of this is an injustice even if the worker gives consent. Here, of course, Leo recognizes what libertarians and many other defenders of the markets have not—that the combination of mutual consent in an economic transaction and the attendant assurance that both parties will improve their lot do not by themselves assure justice. Some exchanges are made out of desperation—for fear of a worse outcome—and thus the standards of justice from a Catholic perspective require more than consent. They require a just wage.

Popes since Leo XIII have consistently upheld Leo's concern for the ordinary worker faced with the pressures of industrial life, at first with traditional remedies. Forty years after *Rerum Novarum*, Pope Pius XI, in *Quadregesimo Anno*, argued for the importance of workers' associations and like Leo held out the hope for a return to a guild-like organization in each industry that would encompass workers, managers, and owners. This position, known as "corporatism," held that industrial strife could be prevented if these kinds of cooperative organizations could be created and cultivated. However, history moved in another direction and later papal thought on the question of the rights of workers stressed instead the role of government in establishing just rules of interaction between unions and firms. (For an account of this transition in the first half of the twentieth century, see Mueller 1984). As Thomas Massero (2000: 138) has put it, "government has become the instrument that now enforces prevailing labor protections."

By the time that Pope John Paul II is articulating his own contribution to this growing tradition in CST, there is great unrest in Eastern Europe, led by the trade-union movement in John Paul's native Poland. Although it is clear John Paul intends his encyclical writings to apply to the universal church, he is thinking actively about the situation in his home country and in other nations of Eastern Europe as he writes. And once the fall of the Soviet Union occurs, he is intimately aware that the nations of Eastern Europe are trying to decide what sort of an economic system they ought to adopt. Thus in his 1991 encyclical, *Centesimus Annus*, John Paul provides the clearest analysis of markets and morality that has yet to appear in papal teaching. And in this document he makes clear his own resolution of meaning of the priority of labor over capital.

John Paul explicitly makes the connection between his two meanings for capital—as inanimate things and as the people who own them—by means of the obligations of owners of capital. Because today a job is the normal way for ordinary people to have the access intended by God to the goods of the earth, having employment is understood as a basic economic right.

But beyond this, relying on the doctrine of property articulated above, John Paul argues that property ownership "should serve labor and thus . . . should make possible the achievement of the first principle of this order, meaning the universal destination of goods and the right to common use of them" (John Paul II 1981: 14). According to John Paul, "ownership of the means of production . . . is just and legitimate if it serves useful work. It becomes illegitimate, however, when it is not utilized or when it serves to impede the work of others, in an effort to gain a profit which is not the result of the overall expansion of work and wealth of society, but rather is the result of curbing them or illicit exploitation, speculation or the breaking of solidarity among working people. Ownership of this kind has no justification and represents an abuse in the sight of God and man" (John Paul II 1991: 43). This is a part of John Paul's position that neo-conservative Catholics—quick to quote him when he praises markets—often pass over in silence. Gregory Baum (1994: 542), on the contrary, reminds all that "title to the ownership of the means of production is legitimate only on the condition that they serve labor."

John Paul recognizes that no government could create all the needed jobs without lapsing into an overly centralized control of the economy such as that criticized in his homeland, Poland (John Paul II 1991: 48). The solution, as we have just seen, is his emphasis on the obligation of the owners of capital to ensure that their capital serves work.

John Paul's view here speaks to the very Catholic insistence that there are many communal responsibilities, only some of which are to be fulfilled through government actions. Some are to be taken up by persons individually, and many others require non-governmental organizations.

In this case, the Pope is clearly identifying a key obligation of corporations. As we have seen, he declares that the property-right claim of stockholders depends on the firm serving work and the interests of workers. This stands as a stark challenge to U.S. corporate law, where boards of directors are legally restricted to serve only the interests of stockholders. John Paul doe not mention the co-determination laws of many European nations—where workers of large firms get to elect up to half the board of directors—but some such institutionalization of this obligation would seem to be implied. Gregory Baum (1982: 42) goes so far as to say that "Pope John Paul II affirms the principle of co-determination in a categorical fashion." He adds that "it is only through such a democratization of the workplace that the priority of labor over capital can be protected."

Looking at this situation more broadly, John Paul conceives of a variety of justice obligations that are to be fulfilled at the level of the individual firm. As always, he encourages moral managers to recognize these obligations and act accordingly in good will. But the Catholic tradition has always understood the positive role of government in sharing institutional structures. John Paul employs two concepts to specify the place of government in relation to work.

First, in he identifies a locus of responsibility in employment relations that he calls "the indirect employer" (John Paul II 1981: 17). The direct employer is the firm that pays the wage. The indirect employer designates a network of relations and forces that condition the interaction of workers and firms. Social custom in any particular nation is a part of this, as is the state, in its responsibility to specify in law the rights and responsibilities of labor and management. As Donald Dorr (1992: 308–311) has argued, the notion of indirect employer means that employment injustice in our world cannot be side stepped. Numerous groups and organizations have some degree of complicity in workplace injustice and some degree of responsibility to address it. Even the conservative commentator Robert Destro (1991: 156) has argued that "if one enjoys the fruits of others' labor, some degree of moral responsibility for their welfare attaches."

The second concept arises in *Centesimus Annus* in a discussion of markets. Here John Paul speaks of the essential role of "the juridical framework" for the market—the laws that define the rights and responsibilities of all market participants, both individuals and organizations (John Paul II 1991: 15). Although the pope defends an arena of freedom in markets, he opposes any completely "free" market by insisting that the market system must be organized to serve the common good.

Under both of these concepts—government as indirect employer and government as provider of the juridical framework for markets—there is ample room for institutionalizing the obligation of owners of capital so that the capital they own serves work as its primary purpose.

CST, particularly at the level of papal statements, has dealt with issues of employment and labor in largely general terms without much specific analysis of more concrete patterns of development. Among the areas needing further attention are issues such as the changing nature of work even in industrialized societies, where fewer and fewer people have lifetime careers. As Michael Hornsby-Smith (2006: 179) has put it, "there has been a commodification of labour and relentless speeding-up of the labour process which have led to a decline in the levels of confidence and trust relations between employers and employees." And J. Milburn Thompson (2003: 43) has argued that "exploitation of the worker has been a social justice issue since the beginning of the Industrial Revolution, and it continues to be a major concern as multi-national corporations comb the earth in search of cheaper labor and higher profits."

Conclusion

The challenges facing workers are more serious than ever and CST, developing as it has over the past two millennia, strives to confront new problems with a corpus of commitments and teaching that has shown itself capable of developing in the midst of new situations. It can only be enriched by dialogue with other perspectives.

References

Avila, C. (1983). *Ownership: Early Christian Teachings*. Maryknoll, NY: Orbis.
Baum, G. (1982). *The Priority of Labor: A Commentary on Laborem Exercens, Encyclical Letter of Pope John Paul II*. New York: Paulist Press.
——. (1994). "Laborem Exercens." In *The New Dictionary of Catholic Social Thought*. Ed. J. A. Dwyer. Collegeville, MN: Liturgical Press.

Destro, R. A. (1991). "Laborem Exercens." In *A Century of Catholic Social Thought: Essays on Rerum Novarum and Nine other Key Documents*. Eds. G. Weigel and R. Royal. Washington, DC: Ethics and Public Policy Center.

——. (1993). "Work: The Human Environment." In *Building The Free Society: Democracy, Capitalism, and Catholic Social Teaching*. Eds. G. Weigel and R. Royal. Grand Rapids, MI: William B. Erdmans.

Dorr, D. (1992). *Option for the Poor: A Hundred Years of Catholic Social Teaching*. Maryknoll, New York: Orbis Press.

Hornsby-Smith, M. (2006). *An Introduction to Catholic Social Thought*. Cambridge: Cambridge University Press.

John Paul II (1981). *Laborem Exercens*. http://www.vatican.va/holy_father/john_paul_ii/encyclicals/documents/hf_jp-ii_enc_14091981_laborem-exercens_en.html.

——. (1991). *Centesimus Annus*. http://www.vatican.va/holy_father/john_paul_ii/encyclicals/documents/hf_jp-ii_enc_01051991_centesimus-annus_en.html.

Lamoureux, P. (2004). "Commentary on *Laborem Exercens*." In *Modern Catholic Social Teaching: Commentaries and Interpretations*. Eds. K. R. Himes, OFM, et al. Washington, DC: Georgetown University Press.

Leo XIII (1891). *Rerum Novarum: Encyclical of Leo XIII on Capital and Labor*. http://www.vatican.va/holy_father/leo_xiii/encyclicals/documents/hf_l-xiii_enc_15051891_rerum-novarum_en.html.

Massero, T. (2000). *Living Justice, Catholic Social Teaching in Action*. Chicago: Sheed & Ward.

Mueller, F. H. (1984). *The Church and the Social Question*. Washington: American Enterprise Institute.

Naughton, M. (1992). *The Good Steward: Practical Applications of Papal Social Vision of Work*. Lanham, NY: University Press of America.

Pius XI (1931). *Quadragesimo Anno: Encyclical of Pope Pius XI on Reconstruction of the Social Order*. http://www.vatican.va/holy_father/pius_xi/encyclicals/documents/hf_p-xi_enc_19310515_quadragesimo-anno_en.html.

Thompson, J. M. (2003). *Justice and Peace: A Christian Primer*, Second Edition. Maryknoll, NY: Orbis Books.

Werpehowski, W. (1994). "Labor and Capital in Catholic Social Thought." In *The New Dictionary of Catholic Social Thought*. Ed. J. A. Dwyer. Collegeville, MN: Liturgical Press.

Going My Way? Wending a Way Through the Stumbling Blocks Between Georgism and Catholicism

By Mason Gaffney[*]

Abstract. This essay surveys the issues between Georgists and Roman Catholics in three classes: issues that are not peculiarly Roman Catholic (RC) but play out across faiths and denominations, issues that are peculiarly RC, and points of similarity and agreement. Addressed in this fashion are the tensions that arise between the social gospel and individual salvation, between specifics and glittering generalities, between _noblesse oblige_ and governmental reform, between the doctrine of original sin and _tabula rasa_, between the rich and the poor, between the dignity of labor and the honor of predation, between democracy and authority, between the regulatory emphasis rooted in the philosophy of Aquinas and free markets, and between plain talk and gobbledegook.

Introduction

There have been and are many Georgist Catholics and Catholic Georgists. The divisions inside each group are perhaps as deep as the divisions between them. This bodes well for future cooperation between at least some Georgists and some Catholics.

Some outstanding Catholic Georgists or fellow-travelers in politics have been Fr. Edward McGlynn (see Gaffney 2000), Governor Al Smith, Mayor and Governor Edward Dunne, Mayor Daniel Hoan, union leader Margaret Haley, presidential advisor Joseph Tumulty, Mrs. Henry George, Governor John Peter Altgeld, and Mayor Mark Fagan. Some current Georgist/Catholics are John Kelly of Peoria, Terry Dwyer of Canberra, Bryan Kavanagh of Melbourne, and David Kromkowski of

*Mason Gaffney is Professor of Economics at University of California, Riverside.

American Journal of Economics and Sociology, Vol. 71, No. 4 (October, 2012).

Maryland. Some of them, like McGlynn and Smith, met stiff resistance from upper echelons of the Roman Catholic Church (RCC) hierarchy, but that is one of the internal divisions we will explore. Some, like Patrick Ford and Terence Powderly, succumbed to the pressure.

The hierarchy has also repressed Catholic land reformers of other stripes: the worker priests of France and the liberation theologists of Brazil, for example. The knee-jerk reaction has been to cry "Marxism" and clamp down. In turn, some Catholic land reformers in power have suppressed the RCC and confiscated its lands, as in Mexico. Catholic King Louis XV of France expelled the Jesuits, who did not return until 1814, under aegis of the Holy Alliance. Either way there has been considerable hostility. The hierarchy has generally allied with big landowners, while many priests, like France's Abbé Pierre, have identified with the landless.

This essay surveys the issues between Georgists and Roman Catholics in three classes: issues that are not peculiarly Roman Catholic (RC), issues that are peculiarly RC, and points of similarity and agreement. I have not come to reopen the Thirty Years' War. My hope and intent is to help the points of agreement override the differences.

Generic Issues Between Georgists and Clerics, and Among Clerics of All Faiths and Denominations

The Social Gospel vs. Individual Salvation

With the ascendancy of altar-calling evangelist Billy Graham, Protestant Christianity leaped far away from the social gospel of, say, Walter Rauschenbusch and Washington Gladden of the Progressive Era and the mild liberalism of *The Christian Century*. The Elmer Gantry phenomenon was of course well known before that, as was the "Monkey Trial" subculture of Dayton, Tennessee, but they were on the downswing. In the Cold War era, however, Protestant Americans suddenly responded en masse and without much discretion, flocking to caricatures of Graham, and televangelists like Bebe Patten, Jim and Tammy Bakker, Paul Crouch, Jimmy Swaggart, Pat Robertson, Gene Scott, Jerry Falwell, and many others of like bent. They attacked the social gospel with as much vigor as they preached individual salvation.

Recently, in heavily churched Protestant Alabama, Professor Susan Pace Hamill, a committed southern Methodist allied with a Baptist school, sought to mobilize the churches to raise the puny property taxes levied on giant holders of timberlands, while raising the personal exemptions for the poor. She allied with popular Governor Bob Riley. They enlisted a substantial minority of the churches, but a majority, with most of the money, turned against them. The richer church leaders argued that a progressive tax system would undercut their role as charity-givers.

Nothing in Georgism makes one oppose individual salvation or embrace sin. George himself was floridly religious, and many clergy of all faiths took his part, while many anti-Georgist academicians sneered at his religious "emotionalism," as they called it. Marxists, too, and those who followed their fashions, belittled George's overt expressions of religious faith and feelings. Most Georgists, however, give priority to some kind of social gospel over individual salvation, which they see as rather narcissistic.

Some leading anti-Georgists, too, were leaders of the social-gospel movement. Protestant Professors John B. Clark and Richard T. Ely were highly visible, but their social gospel stayed well inside the comfort zone of *rentier* mainstays of the collection plate. They preached for privatizing all lands and protecting them from property taxation, while they traduced Henry George and his ideas and allies.

One RCC position on this, expressed by Brian Benestad (2012), is that overcoming evil deserves priority over improving human institutions. It is more than just "priority," but virtual exclusion of any social gospel. Benestad holds that worldly reforms may do more harm than good by misleading people into thinking the world may be saved without overcoming personal sin.

There may be an element of truth in that. Some Georgists grow flippant about their personal behavior, using their underlying Georgism as an excuse. Some speculate in land, saying that institutional wrongs are not cured by individual rights. The problem is that they forget that "where your treasure is, there will your heart be also" (Matthew 6:21). The older they get the tighter they cling to that treasure. If they do not, their wives and children will. I could name names, but so could you. The point here, however, is that this issue is not peculiarly RC.

Some Catholics may believe that it is—that the RCC has the only pathway to salvation. Cardinal Josef Ratzinger said as much in 2000 and later, as Pope Benedict XVI, repeated it in July 2007 (Winfield 2007). Here we meet the problem of evil within the RCC itself. Even if one believes that the sacraments are divine, and that experiencing them will purify one from evil, the moral authority of the RCC and its officers has dropped in the last few years, following a long series of sex scandals, cover-ups, and hardball litigation against complaining victims. The Diocese of San Diego pleaded bankruptcy in 2007, and apparently lied to cover up the true value of its assets, according to Federal Bankuptcy Judge Louise De Carl Adler (Dolbee and Sauer 2007). In one ploy, they listed their landholdings at assessed values, far below market values. The Diocese of Los Angeles in July 2007 agreed to pay out $600,000,000 to victims of abuse (Mozingo and Spano 2007). Protecting the institution and its hierarchs has taken priority over serving the flock and healing the victims—a case of "goal displacement" parallel to what we see in secular institutions.

This is not the time or place to rub salt in these wounds. We seek reconciliation, and appreciate the many good works of the RCC and its communicants. Neither, however, is it the time for RCC spokesmen to preach "holier than thou." Denial and cover-up have been tried and failed; it is time for disclosure and reform—a modern "counterreformation," if you will. We know the RCC can do it, for they did it before, led by the Jesuit Order itself.

Specifics vs. Glittering Generalities

Georgists are specific—some think TOO specific—about reform. Many of the religious, at the other extreme, expound glittering generalities but resist getting down to brass tacks. These religious are of all faiths. It is important to see the stars above, but also to keep our feet on the ground, muddy though it may be.

Rerum Novarum (Leo XIII 1891) (*RN*) and "The Son of RERUM," *Quadragesimo Anno* (Pius XI 1931) (*QA*), were more specific than most religions are at most times. *QA* especially came at a critical time when nations everywhere sought radical reforms, and it pointed a way. The problem was that many of these specifics turned out poorly, and some disastrously.

In the U.S.A., Fr. Charles Coughlin, pioneer radio priest, popularized both the Encyclicals as never before. Irish Catholic laymen like Raymond Moley, James Farley, Joseph Kennedy, and James Byrnes gained great power in the early New Deal, as did also Msgr. John A. Ryan of the National Catholic Welfare Conference (NCWC). Their best-known product was the National Recovery Act (NRA), known by its logo, the Blue Eagle. NRA was a cartelization of American industry supposedly modeled on Aquinas' ideas of guilds, elaborated in *QA*. The Agricultural Adjustment Act (AAA) was the farm counterpart. NRA died, but AAA survives under other names.

Social insurance also fitted with *QA,* although Dr. Francis Townsend, of no distinctive church affiliation, led the movement for old-age pensions. He was considered "screwball" and radical when he began, but Townsend quickly amassed millions of signatures and forced President Franklin Delano Roosevelt (FDR) to coopt his movement with the present Social Security program. In 1936 Townsend allied with Fr. Charles Coughlin, the radio priest who had popularized *RN* and *QA*, to push FDR further. Their politics failed, but their alliance indicates the compatibility of *QA* with Social Security.

Joe Kennedy, father of later President John F. Kennedy, led the new Securities and Exchange Commission (SEC). Generally, FDR depended on votes from big-city machines, many of them run by Irish Catholics, and wove their views into his policies. After Louis Howe died in 1936, Ed Flynn of the Bronx became FDR's chief strategist, urging FDR to the left, but still following signals from *QA*. Raymond Moley, the right-wing Irish Catholic, had pushed business cartels, modeled on Aquinas' merchant guilds (but also drawing on earlier work by Charles Van Hise and Herbert Hoover). After Moley fell, Flynn, the left-wing Irish Catholic, pushed the Wagner Act, empowering labor unions, modeled roughly on Aquinas' craft guilds. Senator Robert F. Wagner of New York was a Catholic, too (of German extraction).

In the postwar period some of the New Deal social safeguards were dismantled, with at least the tacit approval of the postwar "American Pope," Francis Cardinal Spellman of New York. Spellman's gospel was anti-Marxism and raising money; his greatest financial angels were Mr. and Mrs. Nicholas Brady.

At the same time, union organizer Cesar Chavez was inspired by *RN* under tutor Fr. Donald McDonnell, a worker priest, and later enjoyed support from many Catholic bishops. Chavez needed RCC endorsement to fend off the inevitable McCarthyite attacks, backed by Spellman Catholics. Ironically, Fr. McDonnell's friendly persuasion was more weakening in the long run, as the guidance of *RN* focused Chavez on union organizing instead of tax reform, with its grander and more immanent effects.

In Europe, the history of *QA* was unfortunately bound up with the growth of Fascism (Rothbard 2004). Mussolini's "corporate state" supported and was supported by *QA*. Worse, most of the fascist dictators of Europe were cradle Catholics, and weaned on RERUM and later, on its sequel, *QA* (Meyers 2009): Antonio Salazar in Portugal, Francisco Franco in Spain, Adolf Hitler in Germany, Benito Mussolini in Italy, Arthur Seyss-Inquart in Austria, Msgr. Jozef Tiso in Slovakia, Ante Pavelic in Croatia, Admiral Miklos Horthy in Hungary, Marshal Philippe Petain in France . . . it is a long list, unrelieved by many exceptions.

Noblesse Oblige vs. Governmental Reform

We saw above how the Alabama Protestant churches put down Bob Riley and Susan Pace Hamill by arguing that an egalitarian tax system would weaken their character as voluntary donors to the poor. They also worried that the poor would regard welfare as an entitlement, instead of charity, and not be properly grateful.

In Europe, of course, the Catholic Church had been the welfare system of the middle ages, handling charity, medicine, and education. These were to be financed by voluntary contributions, and/or from the rents of church lands, which were extensive and, since the church never sold, growing indefinitely. Private landowners have ever preferred voluntary donations to mandatory, since they may stop voluntary ones at will.

The Catholic welfare system was perhaps workable when there was just one church. Everyone belonged, everyone feared damnation, everyone kicked in. Today, however, Catholics are a minority of the population, with personal wealth and income below the average and falling, as Catholic Latinos enter at the bottom of the ladder. Besides Protestants and Jews there are now members of multiple Asian faiths with higher incomes and better prospects than the Latinos (Singh 2011). Asian-American incomes average higher than European-Americans in California (California Pan-Ethnic Health Network 2012). Conditions are not right to replicate the medieval system of Europe.

RN speaks of worker associations to provide welfare for other workers, with no reference to property owners. Our Social Security system works on that basis, too, which is why it is so egregiously regressive. How about land owners? Should they not contribute to worker pensions? The original tithe that the Old Testament or Torah prescribes is on the produce *of the land*, not on wages and salaries or interest income (Meir 2007). Since *RN*, and perhaps earlier, the church's tithes have been on cash incomes, defined more or less the way the Internal Revenue Service (IRS) defines income in cash, omitting invisible incomes of the rich like unrealized capital gains, and imputed incomes of owner-occupied homes plus vast landed estates held for pleasure. Thus the churches lend their moral authority to the idea of defining tithe-able income the same way the IRS, subject to all manner of unholy lobbying pressures, defines taxable income. The net outcome is to tithe low- and middle-income churchgoers to relieve landowners of their traditional tax and social obligations.

Genetics vs. Unjust Policies as Cause of Inequality and Poverty

Leo XIII (1891) writes in *RN* that differences in wealth arise from differences in "ability," meaning ability to serve mankind by producing more goods and services than others. Given that *RN* is considered a milestone of liberalism in the RCC, one can imagine what attitudes prevailed earlier.

Protestants held similar ideas. James Madison (1787: #10), a Calvinist, wrote as follows:

> The diversity in the faculties of men from which the rights of property originate, is not less an obstacle to a uniformity of interests. The protection of these faculties is the first object of Government. . . .
>
> The latent causes of faction are thus sown in the nature of man; . . . the most common and durable source of factions, has been the various and

unequal distribution of property. Those who hold, and those who are without property have ever formed distinct interests in society. . . .

To secure the public good, and private rights, against the danger of such a faction, and at the same time to preserve the spirit and the form of popular government, is then the great object to which our enquiries are directed.

Such attitudes, coupled with racism, still prevail in the kinds of Protestant Alabama churches that rejected the theology and turned back the egalitarian tax reforms advanced by Professor Susan Pace Hamill and Governor Bob Riley. The (mostly) Protestant champions of eugenics believed the same, although Hitler, the greatest ethnic cleanser of modern times, was a cradle Catholic.

In the French Revolution, the anti-clerical leaders of the 3rd Estate proclaimed the "Theory of previous accumulation," meaning we all started free and equal, and then some saved more, accounting for their wealth—for the 3rd Estate represented successful merchants, not proletarians. This idea harks back at least to the Stoics and Epicureans, who saw it as an ahistorical assumption. It evolved later into a self-evident axiom, requiring no proof. "Rationalism (as of the Stoics) is essentially unhistoric, even anti-historic," said sociologist Franz Oppenheimer (1928).

Since then social scientists have found that differences in wealth are much too great to be explained that way. Marginal differences in height, strength, speed, or intelligence cannot begin to explain quantum differences in wealth, which spring from an acquisitive attitude, not a gene. Economic writer Amartya Sen (1981) has found that death by famine occurs almost solely in nations without democratic governments.

Many modern talk-show pundits preach that academics are "liberals" and "eggheads," meaning at once elitist and egalitarian. Overlooking the oxymoron, the fact is that the Department of History at Columbia University was for years the center of intellectual racism in America, under Professors William Archibald Dunning, John W. Burgess, and Claude Bowers, who dominated the history of Reconstruction until recent times. For an idea of their views, see the 1915 film *The Birth of a Nation* or dip into Bowers' (1929) racist diatribe, *The Tragic Era*. Henry Steele Commager, Amherst historian, was considered a liberal stalwart, but when writing with Allan Nevins of Columbia, in their standard *A Pocket History of the United States* (Nevins, Commager, and Morris 1992), he signed on to the following sentiments, presented as objective history, assigned to millions of students:

> Slavery "was designed to regulate the relationships of black and white rather than of master and slave" and the backwardness of the South was caused by "the presence of cheap and ignorant black labor—a situation that persisted long after emancipation" (p. 196). In 1850, Webster's support of the fugitive slave provisions of the compromise was "statesmanlike," a "great service to the nation," and "required high courage" (p. 201). In 1861, a southern advantage in the civil war was the "efficiency and organization of its agriculture" (pp. 217–281). In 1868, the impeachment of Andrew Johnson was "a disgraceful attack upon the constitutional integrity of the president" (p. 231). Emancipation should have been gradual, and "with due compensation to the slaveholders" (p. 234). Carpetbag regimes were extravagant, thieving and insouciant. Under sharecropping, "Farmers furnished their tenants with . . . land . . . The system seemed to work well and was so convenient" (p. 244). The landlord got 2/3 of the crop.

This is not just pre-civil rights literature. Nevins and Commager's *Pocket History* was reissued in 1996 by the Trustees of Columbia University themselves, acting for the deceased Nevins. Even more recently, academic eugenics is rising again, in works like Herrnstein and Murray's (1994) *The Bell Curve* and Gregory Clark's (2007) *A Farewell to Alms.*

The point here is that genetic determinism is not peculiarly RCC. It may not be RCC at all, any more, for it is not clear that Leo's rationale for inequality represents either a majority or an "official" RCC view today. Georgist Robert Andelson, a professor of philosophy and an ordained Protestant minister, also preached eugenics, but on the whole his views are rare among Georgists. Most of them believe that nurture generally overrides nature in determining the fate of mankind.

Sanctifying Land Tenures Derived from Invasion and Conquest

Europeans of all faiths used religion, among other things, to rationalize their invasion and seizure of heathen and "empty" lands around the globe. Their Bible taught them that God Himself mandated the

Israelites' invasion and seizure of the Holy Land, and vindicated it by promising it to them. Other peoples' gods may have promised it to them, too, but these were lesser gods. Modern Zionists, of course, are replicating this ancient movement, leading to strife without visible end or resolution.

In 1095 Pope Urban II called for the Crusades (Readings in European History I 1904: 312–316): "Wrest the land from the wicked race" quoth he, "and subject it to yourselves." We are paying the price today. In 1208 Pope Innocent III blessed Simon de Montfort's genocidal internal crusade against the cultured but heretical Albigensians and Waldensians of Toulouse and Languedoc. This paved the way for Louis IX to annex southern France and be sainted. Pope Gregory IX then assigned to Dominicans the long task of mopping up remaining heretics, beginning with the Papal Inquisition. It took a century or more. In 1486 Pope Innocent VIII confirmed Tomas Torquemada as Grand Inquisitor of several kingdoms of Spain, which quickly absorbed the entire nation, rooting out Moors, Jews, and various egalitarian heretics, and of course seizing their lands, an important collateral benefit.

In 1494 Pope Alexander VI (Roderigo Borgia) rather immodestly cut the western hemisphere in two, between his native Spain and Portugal, pole to pole. The indigenes were not consulted—heathens were a nullity, and their lands regarded as no-one's. This presumption, however, was not peculiarly RCC. Soon Dutch, French, and English empire-builders (and a few Danish, Norwegian, Swedish, Belgian, and Russian rivals) sent their missionaries to convert the heathen they had "discovered."

Imperialist religion was ecumenical. Protestant England built the widest empire of all, "bearing the white man's burden" of civilizing savages and spreading English versions of the Bible. Among other conquered victims were the Catholics of Ireland, whose lands were divided among the provocatively named "Protestant Ascendancy." Not until the Catholic Emancipation Act of 1829 could Catholics even serve in Parliament; and not for a century after that, if ever, did land reform rid Ireland of the Protestant Ascendancy.

Robert J. Miller's (2006) *Native America, Discovered and Conquered* gives a detailed account of how the doctrine of discovery worked its way into American law.

Original Sin vs. Tabula Rasa

Original sin is not a peculiarly RCC doctrine. It is prominently associated with John Calvin of the Reformation. New England Puritans followed it. James Madison of Virginia was a Calvinist: he believed in original sin, and set up checks and balances to hold it and the popular will in check. The "sin" he most guarded against was the sin of dividing landholdings among all the people. He also tried to guard against an imperial presidency, an issue that hangs in the balance today in spite of all his efforts.

John Locke (1841), whom most Georgists revere, did not believe in original sin. In his classic *An Essay Concerning Human Understanding* he pictured the newborn's mind as a blank slate, or *tabula rasa*, to be filled up with experience and reflection, unbiased by either inborn sin or virtue. Locke also disputed the divine right of kings, who at that time in England were the RCC Stuarts, but there had been and would be Protestant monarchs as well.

It is from this presumption of a free, self-authored mind that Locke's doctrine of "natural" rights derives, and Locke's idea of property. The idea is that we own ourselves, and therefore own what we produce with our own labor.

The *tabula rasa* idea does seem to rule out original sin, but here we must reckon with St. Thomas Aquinas, whose ideas Leo XIII elevated as official RCC doctrine. Aquinas expounded *tabula rasa* long before Locke revived it. Aristotle (disputing Plato) published it even longer ago, and of course Aristotle influenced most of the early churchmen or "scholastics."

George had a more optimistic view of human nature; hence his faith in democracy, as direct as possible. This, however, is not a peculiarly RCC issue, since Calvin and others shared the RCC belief in original sin, and the RCC seer Aquinas expounded *tabula rasa*.

Rousseau believed we are born good; Rome banned his works. Machiavelli apparently believed people are born bad, and Rome also banned his works. Perhaps there is some kind of common principle behind that, but without more evidence it is not clear what it might be.

The Rich vs. the Poor

Cardinal Josef Ratzinger was sent to Latin America to put down liberation theology by tarring it as Marxist and therefore atheist and therefore sinful. He succeeded well, and returned to be chosen as Pope Benedict XVI. Returning to Latin America in 2007, Pope Benedict disappointed hopeful landless Latins by focusing his criticism on political leaders who purport, at least, to represent the landless. He was silent on the slaughter of 200,000 Guatemalans by landlord death squads following the CIA coup overthrowing President Jacobo Arbenz-Guzman, the *Contra* war against the Sandinistas of Nicaragua, the assassination of Archbishop Romero and various nuns and priests, the Colombian war against the peasantry, the violent seizure of lands from Brazilian indigenes to free absentee owners to rape the Amazon, the crimes of Augusto Pinochet advised by faculty at the Catholic University in Santiago allied with Chicago economists, the "disappearances" in Argentina, and similar outrages. Peccadillos of the poor are magnified into menaces to civilization; mortal sins of the rich are overlooked.

One could probably match those Papal faults case by case by looking back in history at England's rape of Catholic Ireland, Russia's rape of Catholic Poland, the Southern Protestant Church's support of slavery, Jackson's expulsion of the Cherokees, and so on. One could cite Jewish evictions of Palestinians.

In recent times the Protestant tyrannies have perhaps become more subtle, more indirect, and worked through remote control, but none the less real. The smuggest, most reactionary sermon I ever heard was in the high-society New York Presbyterian on 5th Avenue near 55th Street. "Storefront" churches for the poor have been diverted from social issues into escapist mythology and, in some cases, orgies of mass hypnosis, while the richer fundamentalists, like those cited earlier, have merged their ideas of personal salvation with a new kind of social gospel that entails taxing the poor to help the rich.

Dignity of Labor vs. the Honor of Predation

Catholics see dignity in work. So do many Protestants: "Work is Worship" is an old Puritan theme, part of the so-called Protestant Ethic.

Georgists certainly preach the dignity of labor; that is why they want to untax it, and why, like John Locke, they want to trace property rights back to labor. Now, academic economists have quietly subverted the working assumption first of George and later of Keynes that "full employment" is a worthy and primary goal of public policy. They slyly rationalize unemployment by calling it "leisure," which they treat as a product in itself—yes, some even want to include it in the measured Gross National Product! Work is a tradeoff with leisure, so the person at work is not much better off than if queuing at the soup kitchen. Sometimes common sense serves us better than clumsy efforts to be philosophical and universal.

Meantime, "work is worship" has also been twisted so as to rationalize exploitation of labor. Joe Hill the union man sang sarcastically in his 1911 song, "Work and pray, live on hay, there'll be pie in the sky in the sweet bye and bye when you die." Even worse was the Nazi's greeting at Auschwitz, "*Arbeit macht frei.*"

Veblen (2006) in *The Instinct of Workmanship* writes that work and the sense of achievement can be gratifying *per se*. As Adele Wick says, a human is more than someone who seeks to satisfy desires with minimal effort, and the social and moral value of those desires should be examined. Veblen went on that wages are not paid so much to overcome the irksomeness of labor as the indignity of it, given the atavistic values of our *rentier*-led society, which labor itself has internalized. These values have us admiring predators and despising producers. George, of course, would turn that around; so would those religious who teach that work is worship. A reasonable combination of religious and economic truths would have it that a society is rich when products are cheap and labor is dear, as Tawney (1961) said, and when jobs are plentiful for those who want them.

Tax-Exemption for Churches and Their Lands

Georgists do not necessarily oppose exempting churches from taxation or publicly supporting church schools. Separation of church and state is not a peculiarly Georgist issue. There is a strong case for exempting churches, since they welcome all comers, contributions are voluntary, they inspire their people to behave better, and they patronize charity and education.

Georgists do opine, however, on *how* best to exempt churches, if that is to be done. What Georgists, along with most economists, object to is exempting institutions from property taxes while continuing to tax them on hiring and paying personnel. Other economists call this the "bricks and mortar" bias, but that name in turn reveals the bias other economists harbor against distinguishing land from buildings. Georgists favor exempting the bricks and mortar, the better to tax the land. What Georgists object to is the parking-lot and prime-location bias. Many a church whose attendance has dwindled occupies prime central land far costlier than its present congregation would pay for against other bidders.

One of the strongest arguments against taxing church buildings is that it is not possible to assess the market value of most of them, anyway. There is little market in used churches, especially those tailored for particular denominations. However, there is always a market for the land under churches.

It may have been this realization that explains the high heat of New York Archbishop Michael Corrigan's persecution of Fr. Edward McGlynn during and after 1886. Fr. McGlynn mobilized a huge following behind Henry George's program of exempting buildings and raising the tax rate on land values. This would have nullified one of Abp. Corrigan's grounds for exempting his (and other) churches from the property tax.

There is also a bias for long-term land speculation. Land appreciates over time and Georgists recognize the wisdom of taking these unearned increments in taxation. A century is but a moment in the life of the Catholic Church, which sees itself as eternal and takes a very long view. The Sisters of the Divine Word, a Catholic order, has owned a vast tract of land west of Winnetka, IL, between Northbrook and Glenview, since 1895, when it was just farmland, and rather swampy too. Now it is one of the most valuable locations in greater Chicago with its own post office, Techny. They lease parcels to major industries and merchants. The Cardinal of Chicago is often seen visiting. They have never had to sell, but if they did they would be exempt, like other eleemosynaries, from any capital-gains tax, as of today. If

Georgists had their say, they would have been taxed not just upon sale, but upon rising market values year after year, for the last 113 years.

This issue is not, to repeat, peculiar to RCC lands. Everything said about Techny can be said in spades about Stanford University, a secular eleemosynary, and in a smaller way about the Loma Linda and California Baptist sectarian campuses in Riverside, California. It is, however, a source of uneasiness in the eleemosynary world, secular and sectarian, which helps explain their coolness to Georgist ideas.

Issues That Are Peculiarly RCC

Democracy vs. Authority

The word "authority" resounds through much RCC teaching, usually with a good ring. To many democrats and libertarians and creative thinkers and scientists the ring is bad. It evokes repression and tyranny and corruption of power and backwardness. It evokes Crusades, persecutions, inquisitions, Falangists, suppression of science, male chauvinism, tortures, burnings, stonings, massacres of Anabaptists and Cathars and Albigensians and witches, superstition, worship of relics and graven images . . . a panoply of evils sponsored by "authority." It sounds un-American and, well, authoritarian.

That is to overstate the case, however. The views of many Catholics are more nuanced than the above suggests. Professor Charles Clark (2001) and others champion the "Principle of Subsidiarity": authority should reside in the smallest units that can handle the functions that require authority. Applied to governments, this principle suggests weakening national governments in favor of local governments.

I wonder, though, if Professor Clark would also apply the principle to church organization? Here, it would seem to suggest less "ultramontanism" and more independence of American Catholics from Rome, as Fr. Edward McGlynn believed. Carried further, it would lead to Congregationalism, obviating the Vatican itself.

Applied to multinational corporations it would suggest breaking them up, as the Progressive administrations once broke up Standard Oil, in the golden age of anti-trust policy. Otherwise, if we weaken national governments by applying Clark's Principle of Subsidiarity, while abiding or fostering corporate giantism, we are left with unbridled corporate rule, which we seem to be approaching at high speed anyway.

As to authority vs. democracy, the choice is not as simple or clear as some of our popular democratic slogans would have it. Democracy can degenerate into plutocracy, as we observe today. Many primitive and half-literate citizens are easily misled into voting against their own interests. The Age of Enlightenment, supposedly democratic, actually fruited in the Age of Benevolent Despotism. A French Catholic monarchical agent like A. J. R. Turgot could see and speak the truth more plainly and directly than "democratic" writers like John Locke and Adam Smith, for in England one needed a rich patron whose personal interests were adverse to most other citizens.

Smith's patron, the Duke of Buccleuch, was England's biggest landowner. Smith had to tiptoe around His Grace to lay it between the lines. He also had to reckon with his friend Charles Townshend, author of the Townshend Acts, excise taxes that helped trigger the American Revolution. Today, extension of our "democracy" into unwilling foreign nations is widely regarded as a sham, a cover for plutocratic imperialism, petrolocracy, and kleptocracy.

Modern public schools, originally so promising, come increasingly under the sway of small-minded petty bourgeoisie who suppress any teaching about economic justice such as the Catholic monarchist Turgot (1913) urged, and instead are reviving the anti-scientific spirit of Dayton, Tennessee and the Scopes Trial.

Turgot and the Physiocrats, some of the clearest economic thinkers of all time, were part of the French monarchy. Turgot championed, among other things, a school system where sound economic studies (like his) would be required of all students. Napoleon, the autocrat, probably did more to spread ideas of economic justice around Europe than any democrat. More recently, some of the best examples of applied Georgism, as in Hong Kong, Kiaochow, Taiwan, and Singapore, were imposed by foreign powers.

The ancient Jews set up a separate class of Levites who owned little land, and whose job was to teach the Covenant to others who did. Thus it is conceivable that the Catholic school system might become a vehicle for conveying Levitical ideas of justice to a new generation of students. If so, however, if would call for a different set of directives from the new Pope Benedict XVI than he has ever uttered. It would call for a new College of Cardinals and probably an entirely new way of screening papal candidates.

Aquinas vs. Free Markets

Aquinas, endorsed by Leo XIII and all of his successors, believed in substantial regulation of free markets, without much or any confiscation or taxation of land rents. This belief was applied with religious zeal in the 1930s in FDR's New Deal, and, with a fascist twist, in Mediterranean and Central European nations. Following the Great War it was reapplied by post-fascists in the social democracies, where leaders like Schumann, De Gasperi, Adenauer, and others had learned their Encyclicals early on. (English and Scandinavian socialism had other roots.)

Ludwig Erhard, father of Germany's free market *Wirtschaftswunder*, was a Protestant. He was an academic product and disciple of Franz Oppenheimer (1928), a scholar whose works criticizing the right of conquest, large landholdings, and the exploitive state contain many Georgist themes. Erhard was often at odds with Adenauer, who aimed to unify the Catholic nations of Europe.

Modern Georgists lean more towards *laissez-faire*, free markets, and the price system. They count on taxing land values to achieve social justice and economic security, reasonably free of regulations and price controls. Let us not overstate this difference, however. Henry George himself remained a labor-union member to the end. He favored public regulation or outright ownership of rails and public utilities—burning issues in his day. So did most politically active Georgists throughout the Progressive Era.

George, married to a Catholic, allied with socialists in the election of 1886. Following that, the extremists on both sides set to feuding until their alliance exploded in faction. (One suspects the work of *agents provocateurs* on both sides.) It is not that modern Thomists would accept the "socialist" label, which to them carries baggage they reject. However, with a little semantic sophistication on both sides, a little distinguishing of the essential from the incidental, and careful avoidance of *agents provocateurs*, it should be possible to unite on a common core of beliefs.

It is worth remembering that the mayors of Milwaukee from 1910–1912, and again 1916–1950, were nominal "socialists" who implemented a good deal of Henry George's program. Morris Hillquit of New York, a doctrinaire socialist, dismissed them and Mayor Dan Hoan with a sneer as mere "sewer socialists." Socialist Mayor Daniel Hoan (originally Hogan) (1916–1940) was also a Catholic. Milwaukee was and is heavily RCC (German, Polish, Italian, and Irish). These good Catholics were not scared by the fright-word "Socialist!" Socialist Norman Thomas always included a Georgist plank in his platform. Upton Sinclair fused Georgism with quasi-socialist programs.

Aquinas believed in "just price" enforced by controls if need be. Georgists who believe in the price system preach against such controls. My advice is, leave that to ordinary neo-classical economists; it is their main stock in trade. Georgist time is too precious and our task is harder. Remember, also, the violent reaction against Turgot when he suddenly decontrolled the price of grain, 1774–1776. Sometimes a good idea must be eased in and explained at length. There are always ignorant and excitable spirits out there, studiously stirred by calculating ones, to make trouble for good leaders.

Aquinas would also cap interest rates, and *RN* and *QA* echo that. This is a tougher nut to crack. My first hope is that most Catholics have moved on from this position. My greater hope is that more people will realize that land speculators, above all men, love low interest rates, because they push up land prices. This is a point on which ordinary neo-classical economists are remarkably obtuse. It wants constant reaffirmation: land rents vary *inversely* with interest rates. In addition, price/rent ratios vary inversely with interest rates, redoubling the effect.

Who Owns Us: Ourselves, God, or the State?

Georgists follow John Locke, who posited that we own ourselves and therefore the things we make. That is the basis of property rights, said Locke.

Brian Benestad (2012) writes that Catholics do not believe we own ourselves. That is why suicide is a sin. However, suicide is so rare that that is hardly the main point. What it does is help rationalize forms of taxation that take from labor. It might help rationalize military drafts.

More recently, the idea we do not own ourselves helped rationalize the payroll tax introduced in the peak of RCC influence on the New Deal. (Francis Townsend, who instigated the system, had wanted a sales tax, which is bad enough, but at least would have raised money from rentiers as well as workers.) Then it rationalized withholding of taxes from payrolls (Beardsley Ruml, a Czech-American Catholic and Rockefeller man, and Milton Friedman, of Jewish extraction but unknown religious views, teamed to introduce withholding). Note that Friedman and Ruml subjected only wage income to withholding. Property income soon evolved into the major tax shelter.

Catholic Georgist economist Terence Dwyer (1980) of Australian National University points out that it is God, not the state, who owns our bodies. He sees the RCC doctrine as a safeguard against state slavery, not an adjunct to it. Surely there are cases in point, from Thomas More to Martin Luther King, Jr. The first *levée en masse* was introduced by anti-clericals in the French Revolution. There are also opposite cases, as when we are urged to pay taxes and support tyrants and murder strangers "for God and Country." One might conclude that neither organized religion nor patriotism can substitute for individual wisdom and judgment and responsibility. This brings us back, however, to the point that we own ourselves, even to the point of choosing when to serve God or the state.

Now, however, rentiers who craft and dominate our public philosophies have reframed them so that property in land is sacred, while labor's civic duty is to pay taxes, including huge debts incurred to enhance land values and spare property from taxes. Thus the state owns a major equity in labor, including unborn laborers, but may not tax property at rates above very low caps. The Catholic Church seems to have gone along with this, at least in part. In 1992 the Catholic catechism was changed to make tax evasion a sin. Perhaps this was aimed at rich evaders, but an article in the *New York Times* by David Cay Johnston (2007) couples this with implied Catholic support for jailing tax-protesting pacifists.

Gender Issues

Clerical celibacy is under increasing attack. It is hardly found in other religious institutions, not even in the Greek Orthodox communion, which considers itself to be the true and original Catholic Church. Critics are linking the pedophilia problem to celibacy (Sommer 2011), although many earnest defenders deny that (Crisis E-Letter 2002). Opposition is nothing new: Fr. Edward McGlynn, the Georgist Catholic, spoke out against it as long ago as the 1880s, and it has withstood other attacks. In our times the growing shortage of priests and nuns may yet force changes. Meantime, clerical celibacy in the RCC remains a "peculiar institution" in modern society. While it sets Catholics apart, it does not by itself block understanding and cooperation between Georgists and Catholics. However, to the extent it is part of a Gestalt denying women's rights, there is an issue.

George and his followers led prominently in movements for women's rights. Carrie Chapman Catt led the successful struggle for the 19th Amendment (votes for women) and went on to found the League of Women Voters. It is less well known that Newton Baker tried in 1920 to enlist her to run with Brand Whitlock or William Gorgas on the Single Tax ticket for vice-president of the U.S.

However, Georgist causes have gone downhill ever since women got the vote, and there may be some causal connection. Many older widows, in particular, are small rentiers since men have the better jobs, and die younger. Women actually own (slightly) more property than men. As women become more independent, and win equal pay for equal work, these attitudes may slowly change, but meantime Georgists face a major problem.

The movement against exploitation of child labor had brought feminist and Georgist leaders together. Jane Addams, Julia Lathrop, Louis F. Post, and Scott Nearing worked together for this cause. *RN*, on the other hand, pulled back from demanding a "family wage" for adult male workers, thus leaving open the interpretation that women and children should join the hired labor force, as children did then, and women do now. Employers were simply not to assign them tasks beyond their capacity, presumed to be inferior. "Rosie the Riveter" did not come along until World War II.

The RC priesthood is closed to women. So then, of course, are all the leadership positions in the hierarchy. It is an exclusive men's club; women may not even exert indirect influence as priests' wives. Female religious are mostly restricted to serving as nuns. To the outsider this seems like an anachronism. Some Georgists would not make an issue of it, so long as the RCC women accept it voluntarily, but others are feminists who see such male bastions as unworthy of tax exemption or subsidies.

One could argue, with RC writer E. Michael Jones (1993), that employer interests fostered feminism in order to lure women into the work force, lowering wages and weakening labor unions. Jones weaves a fascinating thesis combining St. Augustine, Freud, advertising guru Eddie Bernays (Freud's nephew), Freudian A. A. Brill, the Rockefellers, behaviorist John Watson, G. W. Hill of American Tobacco, Protestant and liberal-dominated Madison Avenue, Robert Yerkes, Joseph Goebbels, British agent William Stephenson, Beardsley Ruml, Vance Packard, and Alfred E. Kinsey. On the other hand, Jones does not take into account *RN*'s unwillingness to advocate a "family wage." It would take a career to unravel Jones's interwoven plots, but they contain enough truth to be evocative and challenging. Watson, for example, was the Dr. Spock of the 1920s, yet has now, but for Jones, been thrust down the memory tubes of history. I pass no judgment on Jones' claims, other than that they are novel and challenging. It is true, however, that the combined competition from female, immigrant, and foreign labor, encouraged by employing interests, has lowered normal male wage rates in the last century.

The parochial school system has depended heavily on the work of celibate nuns receiving minimal compensation. The women's liberation movement of the 1960s found a ready audience among many such nuns who began to see themselves as exploited. Some left their orders; recruitment fell off, and schools had to replace them with lay teachers at competitive salaries. Tuition then rose, attendance fell, and the system has shrunk, in spite of the modern political movement for replacing public schools with private and religious ones. The RCC response is to agitate for a voucher system that does not bar the use of vouchers in religious schools. Individual Georgists may support or oppose that for their own reasons, but Georgism *per se* would ask only that the vouchers be financed from taxes on land value.

It is past time the Vatican redirected its energies from damning gay marriage to damning pedophilia and alcoholism among its own shepherds. A few years ago Catholic World News (2002) reported that the rate of AIDS among priests was four times the national average. Catholic novelist Graham Greene has made the "whisky priest" a literary type.

As to abortion, there is no clear "Georgist" position on that tortured question, nor have I authority to declare one. As for my own opinion, it is mixed. I would resist having a child of mine aborted in the womb, but then, I've never had a womb or a pregnancy, which narrows my perspectives. My feelings should carry less weight than the females', for they are more directly involved. I am impressed by some modern feminist writers who document the history of forced maternity in the slave-breeding states, 1808–1863, and who liken modern enforced maternity to the older slave-breeding industry. Like all analogies, however, this one is imperfect, and I will leave it unresolved here.

It would be good if we could somehow make women alone eligible to vote on abortion laws, but that is probably impractical. Meantime, it seems somehow wrong to give much weight to the RCC position so long as it is determined by men alone, and celibate men at that, as now.

Whether Georgists and Catholics can breach these barriers depends on motivation, and the quality of leadership on both sides. The challenges are daunting, but not irresolvable, for there are no irresolvable problems.

Points of Similarity and Agreement

Natural Law, Rights, and Justice

Both Catholics and Georgists give great weight to natural law and rights. These ideas have been rejected by professional philosophers, and much of the intellectual world, leaving Catholics and Georgists as natural allies to defend them.

We are not alone, however. There are millions more Catholics than professional philosophers, and millions more Protestants and Muslims and others who believe in natural rights. These "have legs," going back at least to Lao-tze in 500 B.C., and are firmly embedded in our culture: in Jewish and Christian doctrine, the English Bill of Rights (1689), the American Declaration of Independence (1776), the Massachusetts Declaration of Rights (1780), the French Declaration of the Rights of Man (1789), the 9th and 10th Amendments to the U.S. Constitution (1789), the Gettysburg Address (1863), the United Nations Declaration of Human Rights (1946), and more orations and sermons than you could count. The Declaration of Independence never made it into the U.S. Constitution, but it is found in many state constitutions, including California's. As unlikely a source as Rush Limbaugh opines occasionally that there are natural rights, God-given and unalienable.

Ironically, the Enlightenment philosophers, who are thought to have undermined Catholicism with their Deism, also generally believed in Natural Law and Rights. Turgot the land-tax champion declares it specifically. Some champions of the legal Public Trust Doctrine even claim that it somehow precedes and trumps all man-made laws.

Plain Talk vs. Gobbledegook

Both Georgists and Catholics view much modern economic literature as pretentious trash. Alas, the disdain is mutual, for most professional economists today see us as "outside the mainstream"—mainstream meaning themselves. Their hostility long preceded the rise of tech-nobabble, however, and has other causes like the spontaneous comity of property (Gaffney and Harrison 1994). Our reasons for disdain are nothing new, and were expressed long ago by Erasmus (1876), by Baruch Spinoza (1883), by Jonathan Swift (1892), and by the very John Locke we have been discussing. Here is Locke (1841: The Epistle to the Reader):

> It is ambition enough to be employed as an under-labourer in . . . removing some of the rubbish that lies in the way to knowledge, which certainly had been much more advanced in the world if the endeavors of ingenious and industrious men had not been much cumbered with the learned but

frivolous use of uncouth, affected, or unintelligible terms. . . . Vague and insignificant forms of speech, and abuse of language, have so long passed for mysteries of science . . . that it will not be easy to persuade either those who speak or those who hear them that they are but the covers of ignorance, and hindrance of true knowledge.

Open almost any modern economics journal and you will see how little the world has advanced since 1690, in spite of Locke's efforts. If the intellectuals ever heeded him, they have regressed. It's a massive herd behavior, hard to stem.

The Catholic *Review of Social Economics* is one of the few journals that maintains some readability, and Notre Dame has long been a haven for "heterodox" economists who strayed from the flock. Alas, its administration finally caved under the pressure of methodological correctness and reined in its heterodox department—much as the University of California Riverside Administration did 15 years ago.

The Georgist-inspired *American Journal of Economics and Sociology* is another haven for independent individualistic writers. Perhaps the editors of these two journals should get together and explore their common interests.

Anti-Malthusianism

Georgists and Catholics both deny that population control is the panacea for apparent resource scarcity. The Georgist position goes back to George's long campaign to get good lands used better, with the corollary of constraining settlement sprawl: not just urban, but also rural, sylvan, extractive, hydraulic, and what have you. It needs tweaking today to incorporate the role of taxes based on extraction and pollution. I will let others articulate the RCC position. To an outsider it looks like a tradition too single-mindedly based on the sanctity of the individual human life, without much thought for the aggregate and long-term effects on human or non-human life.

Conclusion

I was pleasantly surprised, as I worked along, how few of the stumbling blocks I had listed are peculiar to Roman Catholicism;

and how many are passable without stumbling. The ones listed in as "Peculiarly RCC" may remain, but I am optimistic that with good will on both sides we may find pathways through, over, around, or under them, to work together towards our common goals. I have not minced words to avoid tough problems, but tried to define issues clearly as a prelude to resolving them. Catholics of good will will not take offense, but detect the search for reconciliation beneath my frank words. I look to Catholic Georgists like John Kelly, Bryan Kavanagh, David Kromkowski, and Terry Dwyer to carry this resolution further.

References

Benestad, B. (2012). "A Catholic Response to Henry George's Critique of Pope Leo XIII's Rerum Novarum." *American Journal of Economics and Sociology* (this issue).

Bowers, C. G. (1929). *The Tragic Era: The Revolution After Lincoln.* New York: Literary Guild of America.

California Pan-Ethnic Health Network (2012). "Median Household Income, (California, 2006)." http://www.cpehn.org/demochartdetail.php?btn_viewchart=1&view_137.x=47&view_137.y=14.

Catholic World News (2002). "The Gay Priest Problem" (June 3). http://www.catholicculture.org/news/features/index.cfm?recnum=20565.

Clark, C. (2001). "Catholic Social Thought and Economic Transition." *Review of Business* (Fall).

Clark, G. (2007). *A Farewell to Alms: A Brief Economic History of the World.* Princeton, NJ: Princeton University Press.

Crisis E-Letter (2002). "10 Myths About Priestly Pedophilia." http://www.catholiceducation.org/articles/facts/fm0011.html.

Dolbee, S., and M. Sauer. (2007). "Judges Tears, Rebuke Close Case." *Union-Tribune* (November 2). http://www.bishop-accountability.org/news2007/11_12/2007_11_02_Dolbee_JudgesTears.htm.

Dwyer, T. M. (1980). "A History of the Theory of Land Value Taxation," Ph.D. dissertation. Cambridge, MA: Harvard University.

Gaffney, M. (2000). *Henry George, Fr. Edward McGlynn, and Pope Leo XIII.* New York: Robert Schalkenbach Foundation.

Gaffney, M., and F. Harrison. (1994). *The Corruption of Economics.* London: Shepheard-Walwyn.

Johnston, D. C. (2007). "Professor Cites Bible in Faulting Tax Policies." *New York Times* (December 25). http://www.nytimes.com/2007/12/25/business/25tax.html.

Leo XIII (1891). "Rerum Novarum." In George, H., 1941, *The Land Question Etc.*, New York: Robert Schalkenbach Foundation: 109–151. Also in Molony, J., 1991. *The Worker Question. A New Historical Perspective on Rerum Novarum.* North Blackburn, Victoria, Australia: Collins Dove.

Jones, E. M. (1993). *Degenerate Moderns: Modernity as Rationalized Sexual Misbehavior.* Fort Collins, CO: Ignatius Press.

Locke, J. (1841). *An Essay Concerning Human Understanding*, 29th edition. London: Thomas Tegg.

Madison, J. (1787). "The Federalist No. 10: The Utility of the Union as a Safeguard Against Domestic Faction and Insurrection." *Daily Advertiser* (November 22). http://www.constitution.org/fed/federa10.htm.

Meir, A. (2007). "Anti-Aristocracy." *Jewish World Review* (August 6). http://www.jewishworldreview.com/jewish/ethicist_tithing.php3.

Meyers, W. P. (2009). "Pius XI and Fascism in Austria." Point Arena, CA: III Publishing. http://www.iiipublishing.com/religion/catholic/popes/pius_xi_austria.html.

Miller, R. J. (2006). *Native America, Discovered and Conquered: Thomas Jefferson, Lewis & Clark, and Manifest Destiny.* Westport, CT: Praeger.

Mozingo, J., and J. Spano. (2007). "$660-Million Settlement in Priest Abuses." *Los Angeles Times* (July 15). http://articles.latimes.com/2007/jul/15/local/me-priests15.

Nevins, A., H. S. Commager, and J. Morris. (1992). *A Pocket History of the United States*, 9th revised edition. New York: Pocket Books.

Oppenheimer, F. (1928). *The State: Its History and Development Viewed Sociologically.* Trans. J. Gitterman. New York: Vanguard Press.

Pius XI (1931). *Quadragesimo Anno: Encyclical of Pope Pius XI on Reconstruction of the Social Order.* http://www.vatican.va/holy_father/pius_xi/encyclicals/documents/hf_p-xi_enc_19310515_quadragesimo-anno_en.html.

Rothbard, M. N. (2004). *Catholicism and Capitalism.* Auburn, AL: Ludwig von Mises Institute. http://www.lewrockwell.com/rothbard/rothbard59.html.

Singh, R. M. (2011). "American Religious Affiliation Versus Household Wealth." http://americanturban.com/2011/05/12/american-religious-affiliation-vs-household-wealth/.

Sommer, J. C. (2011). "Clerical Celibacy and Pedophilic Priests." http://www.humanismbyjoe.com/clerical_celibacy_and_pedophilic.htm.

Spinoza, B. (1883). *Ethics.* Trans. R. H. M. Elwes. Murfreesboro, TN: Middle Tennessee State University Philosophy WebWorks. http://frank.mtsu.edu/~rbombard/RB/Spinoza/ethica-front.html.

Swift, J. (1892). *Gulliver's Travels.* London: George Bell and Sons.

Tawney, R. H. (1961). *Religion and the Rise of Capitalism.* New York: Penguin Books.

Turgot, A. R. J. (1913). "Memorandum on Local Government." In *Oeuvres de Turgot*. Ed. G Schelle. Paris: Alcan. http://chnm.gmu.edu/revolution/d/255/.

Veblen, T. (2006). *The Instinct of Workmanship and the State of the Industrial Arts*. New York: Cosimo, Inc.

Winfield, N. (2007). "Protestant Leaders Upset by Benedict's Vatican II Correction." *Union Tribune* (July 11). http://www.signonsandiego.com/uniontrib/20070711/news_1n11church.html.

A Catholic Response to Henry George's Critique of Pope Leo XIII's *Rerum Novarum*

By J. Brian Benestad*

ABSTRACT. In *Rerum Novarum*, the first of the modern social encyclicals, Pope Leo XIII argued that there is a right to the possession of property, but there are limits on the use of wealth. Christians have an obligation to use their property and talents for the good of others. Private ownership must serve not only the interests of the individual but also the public welfare. The disadvantages of private ownership are not to be corrected by socialism, communism, or the free market, but by the teaching of the Church on faith and morals, the laws of the State, and the action of private associations. Efforts to solve the problems of poverty and unjust working conditions will be in vain unless principles of Christian living drawn from the Gospel are taught to people in all ranks of society.

George's Philosophical Differences with Leo XIII

In the spring of 1891, Pope Leo XIII issued the first of the modern social encyclicals, *Rerum Novarum*. (Leo XIII'S encyclical was made public on May 15, 1891. All references will be to the numbers in this translation, which has been authorized by the Holy See. The text used by Henry George was an unauthorized translation and contains different paragraph numbers.)

Toward the end of the summer (carrying the date of September 11, 1891), Henry George (1953: 1–105) wrote a long critique of that encyclical in the form of an open letter to the pope. George takes Leo XIII to task for defending a limited right to own land, and for limiting the right of private ownership of things produced by labor. While recognizing the right of all to possess (and use) land, George holds that there is no right to own land. He also argues that there is an unlimited right to ownership of things produced by labor. The basis of

*J. Brian Benestad is Professor of Theology at the University of Scranton.

American Journal of Economics and Sociology, Vol. 71, No. 4 (October, 2012).

this unlimited right lies in "the right of the individual to himself" (George 1953: 5). George echoes the teaching of John Locke (1764: 27) that man has a property in his person and, therefore, has a right to the fruits of his personal labor. George (1953: 6) defends the exclusive possession of land only in order to secure "the exclusive ownership of the products of labor."

George's (1953: 8) distinction between possession and ownership of land is meant to serve the common good: "To combine the advantages of private possession with the justice of common ownership it is only necessary therefore to take for common uses what value attaches to land irrespective of any labor on it." George (1953: 12) proposes that government levy a tax on all land equal to its worth, annualized, "irrespective of the use made of it or the improvements on it." As this tax would provide sufficient revenue for the operation of government, George recommends the repeal of all taxes levied on the products and processes of industry. Taxes on the fruits of labor, according to George, violate the moral law, including the right to property.

George's defense of a Single Tax on land is meant to secure equal opportunity to all. Equality of mutual opportunity is the most important of all natural rights (George 1953: 17). George goes so far as to say that his proposals are in conformity with the will of God. More precisely, God intended public revenues to be raised solely by taxing land (George 1953: 15): "That God has intended the State to obtain the revenues it needs by the taxation of land values is shown by the same order and degree of evidence that shows that God has intended the milk of the mothers for the nourishment of the babe." George further believes that his views on economics correspond to Christ's teaching in the Sermon on the Mount:

> We see that Christ was not a mere dreamer when he told men that if the world would seek the kingdom of God and its right-doing they might no more worry about material things than do the lilies of the field about their raiment; but that he was only declaring what political economy in the light of modern discovery shows to be a sober truth. (George 1953: 21)

That "sober truth" is, of course, to abolish all taxes on the fruits of labor and tax land values irrespective of improvement. These two steps are decisive in the quest for justice. George thus puts forth his two-pronged proposal not only as a sound economic policy but as good ethics as well.

George contends that Leo XIII really did not understand the nature of private property. The pontiff supposedly confused property in things produced by labor with property in land created by God. His argument against Leo's defense of property in land can be briefly summarized. Purchase can only give a right to own things that would become rightful property. To justify private property in land is no different from justifying private property in slaves, or the seizure of a spring in the desert to which one would allow access only upon payment. To justify ownership of the earth is to debar some from satisfying their daily needs. George (1953: 34) characterizes as naive Leo's statement that "the earth though divided among private owners ceases not thereby to minister to the needs of all." Why? Some people hoard up land and cause scarcity and thus poverty and destitution. A study of history reveals that land ownership led to lawsuits, maldistribution of goods, slavery, and war. For example, "to the parceling out of land in great tracts is due the backwardness and turbulence of Spanish Americans; that to the large plantations of the Southern States of the Union was due the persistence of slavery there" (George 1953: 42). Furthermore, a study of Scripture, contrary to Leo's assertion, shows that there is not the slightest justification "for the attaching to land of the same right of property that justly attaches to the things produced by labor" (George 1953: 44).

Abolishing taxes on the processes and products of labor in favor of taxes on land values would promote equality of opportunity, thrift, industry, commerce, and "the largest production and the fairest distribution of wealth" by managing individual freedom; it would also reduce the size of government, dispense with oaths, and do away with temptation to bribery, tax evasion, and corruption (George 1953: 48). George further believes that universal affluence would be possible if his ideas were accepted. "But in the state of society we strive for where the monopoly and waste of God's bounty would be done away with and the fruits of labor would go to the laborer, it would be within the ability of all to make more than a comfortable living with reasonable labor." Those unable to work because of disability would receive from the wealth of the state, which would always be sufficient for every need provided the land was taxed.

In brief, George believes that adoption of his land policy would eliminate scarcity, which is the real cause of greed. Land reform, leading to prosperity, would produce moral reform. The following passages from George's major work, *Progress and Poverty*, confirm without a doubt the author's hopes and expectations (George 1942: 373, 382, 387):

> It seems to me that in a condition of society in which no one need fear poverty, no one would desire great wealth at least no one would take the trouble to strive and to strain for it as men do now. . . .
>
> The rise of wages, the opening of opportunities for all to make an easy and comfortable living would at once lessen and would soon eliminate from society the thieves, swindlers and other classes of criminals who spring from the unequal distribution of wealth. . . .
>
> With this abolition of want and the fear of want, the admiration of riches would decay, and men would seek the respect and approbation of their fellows in other modes than by acquisition and display of wealth.

That greed would disappear if scarcity were overcome is a most optimistic view of human nature, not shared by either the classical or Christian tradition and not supported by the results of contemporary social-science research.

George's Critique of Leo XIII's Practical Proposals

George (1953: 70) summarizes Leo's proposals for improving the condition of labor under three headings.

1. That the State should step in to prevent overwork, to restrict the employment of women and children, to secure in workshops conditions not unfavorable to health and morals, and, at least where there is danger of insufficient wages provoking strikes, to regulate wages.
2. That it should encourage the acquisition of property (in land) by workingmen.
3. That workingmen's associations should be formed.

George broadly characterizes all of Leo's proposals as socialistic, though an extremely moderate form of socialism. George does not believe any of Leo's suggestions can be effective. Limiting the hours of labor and the employment of women and children is futile as long as people are living in a penurious condition. Nor can the State cure poverty by regulating wages. According to George (1953: 73), the level of wages depends on the "ease or difficulty with which labor can obtain access to land." The only way the State could override the effect of market tendencies on wages is to provide employment to all who wish it, or to sanction strikes and to support them with government funds.

Furthermore, all efforts by the State to promote ownership of land by working people will prove futile. With the advent of material progress, "land becomes more valuable" and, when this increasing value is left to private owners, "land must pass from the ownership of the poor into the ownership of the rich" (George 1953: 76). The only way to prevent this from occurring is to allow possession but not ownership of land—that is to say, to take the profits of land ownership for the community.

Thirdly, George (1953: 78) takes issue with Leo's endorsement of labor unions. George believes that unions are necessarily selfish; they must attempt to hurt nonunion workers by limiting or even obliterating their natural right to work:

> By the law of their being they must fight for their own hand, regardless of who is hurt, they ignore and must ignore the teaching of Christ that we should do to others as we would have them to do to us, which a true political economy shows is the only way to the full emancipation of the masses.

George (1953: 80) admits that unions may improve the lot of some workers by the use of force or the threat of force. They are in his mind a palliative, not a remedy for poverty amidst plenty. Surely, he says to Leo, true unionism does not have "that moral character which could alone justify one in the position of your Holiness in urging it as good in itself." George believes that Leo had no other alternatives because he insists on justifying property in land.

Another mistake Pope Leo is seen as making is to assume that the labor question concerns the relation between wage workers and their employers. As a matter of fact, says George, most people work for themselves and not for an employer. George contends that the remedies proposed by Leo do not take the self-employed into consideration. Furthermore, Leo assumes that all employers are rich. In fact, says George, many are struggling against their competitors to stay in business.

George also questions Leo's assumption that humanity will always be divided into two classes, the rich and the poor. In George's mind the division of classes into rich and poor stems from a violation of the natural law, from force and fraud perpetrated by some on others. If everyone had access to land, there would no longer be any poverty.

George also chides Leo XIII for seeming to direct his sympathy exclusively toward the poor. George (1953: 85) asks: "Are not the rich, the idlers to be pitied also? By the word of the gospel it is the rich rather than the poor who call for pity, for the presumption is that they will share the fate of Dives." George then proceeds to describe the vices from which the rich often suffer on this earth, implying that they need more spiritual help than the poor. George (1953: 86) refers to the story of the rich young man in the gospel in order to show that Jesus showed concern for the rich: "When Christ told the rich young man who sought him to sell all he had and to give it to the poor, he was not thinking of the poor, but of the young man."

George (1953: 87) further argues that it is "a violation of Christian charity to speak of the rich as though they individually were responsible for the sufferings of the poor." The cause of "monstrous wealth" and "degrading poverty," says George, stems primarily from the existence of private property in land. The answer to the social questions, then, lies not in taxing the rich, no matter how rich they might be. George, like John Locke, even argues that the honest acquisition of wealth necessarily adds to the wealth of the world and thus contributes to the well-being of all.

George (1953: 90) also criticizes Leo for asserting the right of workers to employment and the right to receive from employers "a certain indefinite wage": "No such rights exist." Leo invents these two false rights, according to George, because he defends private property in land, thereby severely threatening the well-being of many people. "The natural right which each man has is not that of demanding employment or wages from another but that of employing himself—

that of applying by his own labor to the inexhaustible storehouse which the Creator has in the land provided for all men." The only way to open up the land to all is by restricting the right of land ownership to the community by means of the "single tax."

As for requiring employers to pay a certain wage to workers, George objects on two grounds: employers should not be obliged to pay any more than the market requires, and workers should never be satisfied with any rate of wage since it is human nature to desire more and more of the comforts of life. George couples a faith in the free market with a skepticism that man's desires for more things can ever be moderated. In another context, George does argue that the abolition of insecurity would moderate people's pursuit of wealth.

George also chides Pope Leo for stressing the role of charity in improving conditions of labor. The stress must be on justice, says George. He further implies that Leo XIII is really commending charity as a substitute for justice with the following results. First, while charity may mitigate somewhat the effects of injustice, it can never get to the root cause. Charity, which does not build on justice, leaves intact an unjust status quo. Secondly, charity "demoralizes its recipients," turning them into beggars and paupers. Thirdly, charity soothes the consciences of those who profit from unjust political and social conditions.

Worst of all, writes George (1953: 93), substituting charity for justice is an occasion for teachers of the Christian religion to "placate mammon" while "persuading themselves that they are serving God." For example, George implies that if American Christians had con-demned slavery as unjust instead of preaching kindness to slave owners, there would not have been a civil war. In short, George believes that "stressing the clear-cut demands of justice" rather than "the vague injunctions of charity" will improve the condition of labor and help preserve the integrity of Christian faith and morals. George does not believe that charity requires Christians to address seriously the social and philosophical problems of the day.

George (1953: 96) further argues that the rich can do little or nothing to improve the conditions of labor by acts of largesse. George specifically rules out the utility of: giving money to the poor; building churches, schools, colleges, hospitals, tenements, workshops for scientific experiments; refusing rent for land or lowering rentals; or beautifying cities. The rich man "can do nothing at all except to use his strength for the abolition of the great primary wrong that robs men of their birthright." That wrong, of course, is the State-sanctioned private ownership of land.

George (1953: 96–97) argues that in applying moral teaching to society "the question, What is wise? may always safely be subordinated to the question, What is right?" George means that people should not rest content with stating wise principles, but advocate measures that will indeed be effective in eradicating unjust situations. For example, George admits that Leo wisely says that "God owes to man an inexhaustible storehouse which he finds only in the land." The pope, however, George believes, does not draw the right conclusion from that principle, *viz.*, that the Catholic Church should no longer defend the right to private property in land. George (1953: 98) applauds Leo's statement that all men are children of God, have the same last end, and are redeemed by Jesus Christ, but criticizes him for justifying the possession of private property in land by a few: "you give us equal rights in heaven but deny us equal rights on earth? It is thus that your encyclical gives the gospel to laborers and the earth to the landlords."

George suggests to Leo XIII that people are turning away from organized religion because it doesn't offer solutions to the problems the world is facing. In particular, organized religion has failed to say clearly what is wrong with the conditions of labor and, of course, has failed to provide satisfactory answers.

George (1953: 100) concedes that Leo XIII has correctly discerned the problem labor is facing: "Reduced to its lowest expression it is the poverty of men willing to work." Workers lack bread. George then argues that Leo XIII has not explained why people lack bread. It is not God's fault, says George. He has provided all the bread people need for life. Some people have thwarted the Creator's benevolent intentions by legalizing private property in land. The solution to the problem of labor is very simple; disallow private ownership of land (George 1953:101): "Any other answer than that, no matter how it may be shrouded in the mere form of religion, is practically an atheistical answer."

George is arguing that one structural change will be sufficient to bring about a just society. He implies that the sins of men, whatever their nature or gravity, cannot pose a new obstacle to the realization of that goal.

A Summary of Leo XIII's *Rerum Novarum*

Leo XIII's position on the ownership of property has more nuances than George's letter reveals. The pope does indeed argue that nature gives a *right* to the ownership of land and the fruits of one's labor. In arguing that people have a right (*ius*) to property, the pope departs from the thought of Thomas Aquinas (1946: II, II, Q. 66, Art. 2), who simply said that it is necessary to possess property. Leo's stress on the natural right to property sounds more like Locke than Aquinas. By asserting that the right to property must be regarded as sacred, Leo XIII invests the ownership of property with more importance and dignity than it had in the mind of Aquinas, who nevertheless contended that ownership serves three important purposes in society: it promotes industry, order, and peace. Aquinas (1946: II, II, Q. 66, Art. 2, Reply Obj. 1) did argue, however, that "the division of possessions is not according to natural right, but rather arose from human agreement . . . Hence the ownership of possessions is not contrary to natural right, but an addition thereto devised by human reason."

Leo's stress on the sacredness of property is balanced by comments on the use of wealth, inspired by the Bible and Thomas Aquinas. Unlike Locke, Leo (1891: #36) holds that there are limits on the use of wealth. Citing Thomas Aquinas, the pontiff writes, ". . . man ought not regard external goods as his own, but as common so that, in fact, a person should readily share them when he sees others in need. Wherefore the Apostle says: 'Charge the rich of this world . . . to give readily, to share with others.' " According to Leo, then, there is no absolute right to the ownership of land or the fruits of one's labor. Christians have an obligation to use their property and talents for the good of others:

> [W]hoever has received from the bounty of God a greater share of goods, whether corporeal and external, or of the soul, has received them for this purpose, namely, that he employ them for his own perfection and, likewise, as a servant of Divine Providence, for the benefit of others.

Leo is not arguing that law should enforce the generous use of property and talent, except in cases of extreme need. These are duties of charity to which all Christians are bound in order to be faithful to God's will. Given these duties of charity, education to virtue or character formation takes on great importance. Without the proper formation, people will not be inclined to share their property or use their intellectual and spiritual talents for the benefit of others.

George does not advert to the limits Leo places on the use of property. This omission is partially understandable because George is intent on maintaining the inviolability of the fruits of one's labor. Since George places limits on the ownership of land, it is surprising that he doesn't point out the similarity between his position and Leo's. George desires to facilitate the access to the possession of land by all through a tax on land; Leo desires to assure access to all goods of the earth by teaching that charity requires Christians to share their wealth and talent. But this is far from all that he teaches on the possession and use of property.

Leo's teaching on the role of the State, as we will presently see, indicates that property in land is not an absolute right of the individual. The pope clearly implies that the State may lay down laws regulating the use and possession of property for the sake of the common good. Pius XI (1957) in *Quadragesimo Anno* (originally published in 1931) is more explicit in asserting the authority of the State over property. He lays down as a principle that property has both an individual and a social character. Private ownership must serve not only the interests of the individual but also the public welfare (Leo XIII 1891: 49): "Therefore, public authority always under the guiding light of the natural and divine law can determine more accurately upon considerations of the true requirements of the common good what is permitted and what is not permitted to owners in the use of their property." By moderating the possession and use of private property for the sake of the common good, the State does no injury to private owners. On the contrary, the State's action is really a friendly service since it "effectively prevents the private possession of goods . . . from causing intolerable evils and thus rushing to its own destruction." By taking property, the State will, ironically, preserve property rights. Without State intervention,

Pius XI implies, the needs of many people would not be met, thereby threatening the stability of the political and social order.

The private ownership of land and other property is admittedly an imperfect social arrangement. The disadvantages of private ownership, in Leo's mind, are not to be corrected by socialism, communism, or the free market, but by the teaching of the Church on faith and morals, the laws of the State and the action of private associations. This teaching is not peculiar to Catholicism but has striking similarities with classical political philosophy. For example, Aristotle (1984: 1263a) clearly prefers private property to a system of community of property, but only in conjunction with the right kind of laws and the proper character formation: "and it will be through virtue 'that the things of friends are common,' as the proverb has it, with a view to use." The education to moral virtue will produce apposite customs in the citizens that together with legislation will serve to obviate the disadvantages of private property.

From this brief summary of Leo XIII'S teaching on property, it should be evident that the pope puts the social problem of the poverty and unjust working conditions of laborers in a much broader context than Henry George. This section of my essay will explain Leo's view that resolution of the social problem hinges on the contribution of religion and the church, the government, and individuals, together with voluntary associations.

Leo (1891: #82) believes that all efforts to solve the problems of poverty and unjust working conditions will be in vain unless principles of Christian living drawn from the Gospel are taught to people in all ranks of society:

> And since religion alone as we said in the beginning can remove the evil, root and branch let all reflect upon this: First and foremost Christian morals must be reestablished, without which even the weapons of prudence, which are considered especially effective, will be of no avail to secure well being.

To be reestablished, Christian morals must be presented clearly and energetically by the ministers of the Gospel.

The Church improves the social order not only by regulating the life and morals of individuals but by instructing the mind (Leo XIII 1891: #40): "she strives to enter into men's minds and to bend their wills so that they may suffer themselves to be ruled and governed by the discipline of the divine precepts." Leo's examples of that instruction, while by no means intended to be complete, are sufficient to be indicative. He first mentions the ineluctability of inequality and the inevitability of evil. Leo teaches that inequality will always be a characteristic of civil society because there are great and many natural differences among men. Inequality is beneficial to society, Leo continues, because of the varied aptitudes that living in community requires. Because of sin there will always be injustice in society. No action by the Church, the government, or voluntary association will be able to remove all tribulations from human life. While moral progress is possible, it is not inevitable. Leo further holds that the belief in the eradicability of evil and the social consequences of sin will eventually lead to greater evils.

The Church also teaches, says Leo, that one class of society is not by nature hostile to another. Through its teaching, the Church always attempts to moderate conflict between any antagonists, especially the rich and the poor. "But for putting an end to conflict and for cutting away its very roots, there is wondrous and multiple power in Christian institutions" (Leo XIII 1891: #28). Leo then goes on to list the duties of the poor and workers, as well as those of rich men and employers. For example, workers are enjoined to perform their work thoroughly and conscientiously. Employers are told that one of their important duties is to pay a just wage. If workers and employers performed their duties, the bitterness and curse of conflict between them would cease.

Leo (1891: #33) then introduces the Church's teaching on eternal life: "We cannot understand and evaluate mortal things rightly unless the mind reflects upon the other life, the life which is immortal." Leo clearly implies that workers and employers will not understand their respective duties unless they see this life as a preparation for eternal life. Only then will both classes have the proper perspectives on riches, deprivation, and earthly sorrows.

Leo (1891: #36) next reminds the rich of the words of Jesus about the obstacles posed by wealth for the attainment of eternal happiness. The pope explains the Catholic position on the use of material goods and the goods of the soul. After satisfying the demands of necessity and propriety, "it is a duty to give to the poor out of that which remains." This duty rests on belief in the social nature of man. Because man is a political or social animal, he has duties toward his neighbors. If he were by nature a radical individual with no natural ties to the community, then it would be reasonable to speak simply of the rights of man, of rights to property. According to Leo XIII, the duty to use property and talents well takes precedence over rights. Any right to property or anything else is derivative from duties.

Catholic teaching not only requires generosity from those who have, but also calls for friendship and brotherly love between the rich and the poor. If the economy of duties and rights according to Christian teaching were widely accepted, then it seems, says Leo, that all conflict would cease.

The purpose of the State is to cause both private and public well-being through its institutions and laws. States achieve well-being through the following (Leo XIII 1891: #48): "wholesome morality, properly ordered family life, protection of religion and justice, moderate imposition and equitable distribution of public burdens, progressive development of industry and trade, thriving agriculture, and by all other things of this nature." Still other factors contributing to the private and public welfare are, of course, peace and good order, punishment for crime, strong citizens capable of supporting and protecting the State, competent, sustained work for the dignity of all people, and a moral and healthy atmosphere in one's place of work. In any case, where these elements of a flourishing State are threatened, "the power and authority of the law, but of course within certain limits, manifestly ought to be employed." The law ought not to attempt more than the remedy of the evil requires. Since the use of material goods is an element of a well constituted State and necessary for virtue, the State must make sure that there is an adequate supply and a just distribution. It is the State's responsibility to protect all citizens "maintaining inviolate that justice especially which is called distributive" (Leo XIII 1891: #49). For example, the State must see to it that workers have adequate housing, clothing, and security, and the State must give special consideration to the poor and the weak.

Other duties of the State are as follows: restrain those who stir up disorder and incite workers to violence; anticipate and prevent the evil of strikes by removing early the causes of discontent; protect the goods of the soul; limit the hours of work so that people will not be crushed in spirit or body; shield women and especially children from physical labor beyond their capacity; intervene, if necessary, to make sure that wages are sufficient to support a thrifty worker and his family, and safeguard the sacred right to private property.

From the protection of the right to property by the State will flow the following benefits: a more equitable distribution of goods, a greater abundance of national wealth, and, as a consequence, a strong incentive to remain in the country of one's birth. Leo explains that the opportunity to possess private property will stir the workers to be more productive, thus making a significant contribution to national wealth. The pope also suggests that the eagerness to acquire property will at length remove the difference between extreme wealth and extreme poverty (Leo XIII 1891: #66, 67).

Not only the Church and government can make a significant contribution to the resolution of the social question but also the employers and workers themselves. In other words individuals can form various kinds of associations in order to promote the well-being of various groups, especially those who cannot help themselves. The pope first praises associations for giving mutual aid, that is those caring for children, adolescents, and the aged and those providing for the families of workers who die prematurely or become incapacitated through sickness or accidents.

Leo ascribes the most importance to associations of workers, either alone or of workers with employers. The purpose of these workers' associations should be to procure for individual members "an increase in the goods of body, of soul, and of prosperity" (Leo 1891: #76). Their principal goal, says Leo XIII, should, be moral and religious perfection. To accomplish this goal, Leo suggests that associations provide opportunity for religious instruction so that workers may understand clearly their duties to God, neighbor, and self. For example, workers must be taught that the sacraments "are the divine means for purifying the soul from the stains of sin and for attaining sanctity" (#47).

Among the most important services to be provided by workers' associations are the following (Leo XIII 1891 #79):

> that the workers at no time be without sufficient work, and that the monies paid into the treasury of the association furnish the means of assisting

individual members in need, not only during sudden and unforeseen changes in industry, but also wherever anyone is stricken by sicknesses, old age, or by misfortune.

So, even though Leo stresses the spiritual role of workers' associations, he expects them to deliver adequate financial help to needy members.

Leo thinks that the existence of associations is very important for the well-being of society. In fact as "man is permitted by his right of nature to form associations, the State does not have the authority to forbid them" (Leo XIII 1891 #72). The State may, of course, regulate or even oppose associations if their objectives are clearly at variance "with good morals, with justice or with the welfare of the State." The pope's position on associations follows from the well-established principle that man is a social animal (Leo XIII 1891 #70): "Just as man is drawn by this natural propensity into civil union and association, so also he seeks with his fellow citizens to form other societies, admittedly small and not perfect, but societies none the less. Without associations, including the commonwealth, people could neither provide for their physical needs nor develop their intellectual and spiritual lives."

Thus we see that there are two bases to Catholic social thought. One, established by theological reflection and philosophical inquiry, is the truth that each individual human person is of unique worth in the economy of all Creation. But every person has an obligation of stewardship *vis à vis* every aspect of Creation. The biblical writer described our relationship to things in the term "stewardship." We have a duty to use our material resources and our talents for the benefit of others.

A Response to George Based on Catholic Political Principles

In the first of the modern social encyclicals expressing the mind of the church on societal problems and in the letter of reply to the pontiff by the American social philosopher, Pope Leo XIII and Henry George really do not communicate with one another. Leo XIII's approach to political reform draws heavily on classical and medieval political philosophy. Henry George, on the contrary, belongs to the tradition of modern political philosophy, with close ties to the thought of John Locke. Following Locke, George argues that one has a property in his or her person and, therefore, is entitled to all the fruits of one's labor. Both Locke and George further contend that there is an unlimited right to wealth one produces or acquires by exchange, and defend unlimited acquisition by one's labor as socially beneficial. George differs from Locke in denying the right to own land. George's denial of the right to own land stems from the instincts of a generous heart, even from a strong moral fervor. If land rent were to accrue to the State by means of the Single Tax, he believed, there would never again be poverty amidst progress. Not only scarcity would be overcome, but also unjust behavior. Wilson Carey McWilliams (1973: 387) explains, "George believed that an abundant love for his fellows would emerge in man were economic scarcity once banished from the earth."

From Pope Leo XIII's perspective on people and society, George's expectations from restrictions on land ownership, coupled with the unlimited right to accumulate all other kinds of wealth, are utopian to say the least. George believes that these two reforms would abolish scarcity and thus injustice and render unnecessary Leo's stress on the role of religion, voluntary associations, and the State in solving social problems. In Leo's mind the problem of social reform is much more complex and intractable than George ever suspected. It requires conversion to virtue, many kinds of public and private initiatives, and the continuous exercise of prudence by leaders in the various sectors of society.

George's defense of the unlimited right to acquire wealth by one's labor rests on a principle that the Catholic Church could never accept. This is the Lockean view that one has a property in one's person. According to Catholic teaching the human being is created in God's image, redeemed by Jesus Christ, and is a temple of the Holy Spirit. No one owns one's person or body but rather receives them as a gift from God. People do not have a right to dispose of themselves as they see fit. Rather they have a duty to have reverence for their person and body, to live their lives in accordance with God's will. No one is allowed to commit suicide, or mutilate oneself, which actions would be permitted if one enjoyed a property in one's person.

George's defense of unlimited acquisition through one's labor or in exchange for one's product further flies in the face of the biblical and Catholic teaching on the proper attitude toward money. Avarice has always been condemned in the Catholic tradition. Jesus said you can not serve God and mammon; Paul argued that love of money is the root of all evil (I Timothy 6: 10). As a result of these teachings and others, the Catholic Church has always stressed the duty to limit one's desires for material goods as well as the duty to share with others.

Furthermore, George's defense of unlimited accumulation of property other than land would, according to Catholic Social Thought (CST), increase the amount of injustice in society. Classical and medieval political philosophies would argue in a similar vein. The only possible justification for George's defense of unlimited accumulation is found in the philosophy of John Locke and Adam Smith. They hold that private vice by an invisible hand produces the public good. If this principle were true, then George could not be criticized for failing to elaborate ethical and political principles that would limit the acquisition of wealth.

There is no real contradiction between Pope Leo's political principles and George's recommendation for land policy. A Single Tax on land, while not required by CST, is surely compatible with it. Whether George's land policy should be adopted by a State is a judgment of political prudence that could vary according to time and circumstances.

In the late 19th century, a priest of the New York Archdiocese, Dr. Edward McGlynn, ran afoul of his religious superiors for advocating George's ideas on land reform and for refusing to submit to discipline. In fact he was excommunicated for a period of six years. On December 23, 1892, Msgr. Francisco Satolli, Pope Leo XIII's ablegate, reinstated Father McGlynn after he and a commission of theologians and canon lawyers examined a doctrinal statement prepared by the priest. About that statement they said, "there was nothing in the land philosophy preached by Father McGlynn that was contrary to Christian faith or to Catholic doctrine" (Bell 1937: 232).

I would accept the judgment of Msgr. Satolli and the commission in this regard. Neither Christian faith nor Catholic doctrine prohibits a Catholic from accepting George's approach to land policy. A Catholic is free to argue that the State should allow possession of land but restrict ownership. Father McGlynn, however, is surely mistaken in arguing that there must only be one right way of raising revenue for the State, a Single Tax on land values. Reasonable Catholics can surely legitimately argue that there are other equally good or better ways of raising revenue. Will not the best method of taxation vary from age to age and from country to country?

On the other hand, George's contention that a Single Tax on land is really the only moral way of raising revenue for the State would be rejected by Catholic political thought as an improper mixing of religion and politics. George's position reminds me of the contemporary tendency of Catholics, both on the left and the right of the political spectrum, to equate their political opinions with Gospel truth. Catholic political principles may suggest in many cases a certain kind of policy, but in others any number of policy options could be chosen. In Pope John Paul II's (1980: 255) words: "In her social doctrine the Church does not propose a concrete political or economic model, but indicates the way, presents principles." Furthermore, George's claim that a Single Tax on land would do away with scarcity and thus injustice in society and produce love in the heart of man could never be reconciled with Catholic doctrine. According to that doctrine, human beings cannot overcome selfishness and learn to love one another without divine grace. Society can never overcome injustice until, at the very least, individuals undergo a conversion. The traditional Catholic view is succinctly and even humorously stated by Thomas More (1955: 34–35) in his Utopia: "But you should try and strive obliquely to settle everything as best you may, and what you cannot turn to good, you should make as little evil as possible. For it is not possible for everything to be good unless all men are good, and I do not expect that will come about for many years."

George does have a point, even on Catholic grounds, in objecting to Pope Leo XIII's strong defense of the right to property; the Pope characterizes that right as sacred. While George does accept the sacred right to the fruits of one's labor, he strongly objects to making sacred the right to own land. Leo's defense of all ownership is somewhat exaggerated in comparison with the treatment of Thomas Aquinas. As mentioned, unlike Thomas, Pope Leo XIII argues that nature has conferred on human beings a right to property. Furthermore, Leo (1891: #14) seems to expect great benefits from private ownership:

"however the earth may be apportioned among private owners, it does not cease to serve the common interest of all." Surely, this far-reaching claim is not true. Some property arrangements will not be conducive to the common good.

Msgr. John A. Ryan attempts to state the longstanding Catholic position on the ownership of property in these terms. He argues that the Christian tradition does not uphold an absolute right to land (Ryan 1916: 23): "Ownership, understood as the right to do what one pleases with one's possessions is due . . . chiefly to modern theories of individualism." The natural right to land is not an end in itself (1916: 35–37): "It has validity only insofar as it promotes individual and social welfare. . . . To interpret man's natural right to land by any other standard than human welfare, is to make of it a fetish, not a thing of reason." Ryan candidly admits that the private ownership of land does not secure perfect justice because it is an imperfect social arrangement. Despite his intemperate praise of private property, Leo also recognizes the limits of this institution. Otherwise, he would not have devoted so much of *Rerum Novarum* to explaining how religion and the Church, the State, and voluntary associations contribute to the resolution of the social problem. Nevertheless, George is correct in noting the extraordinary praise Leo bestows on private ownership of land.

What George and Leo XIII Had in Common

Because of Henry George's respect for virtue, patriotism, and love of God, it is ironic that he and Pope Leo XIII had such different approaches to political and social reform. There is no doubt that George wrote his works in order to promote respect for everything decent and sublime. The words honor, duty, sympathy, virtue, justice, love of God, public spirit and respect for law meant much to George. It pained him to see vice and injustice in the United States. He wrote with great passion and eloquence in order to combat these evils. In their respect for the Christian faith, love of virtue, and hatred of vice, Henry George and Pope Leo XIII had much in common; both men also rejected the materialism and individualism of John Locke.

The reason for the great differences between George and papal social teaching was the former's belief that virtue is not possible until scarcity is overcome. George believed that against temptations to greed, power, and prestige, which appealed to the strongest impulses of our nature, "the sanctions of law and the precepts of religion can effect but little." (Subsequent papal encyclicals came to analyze political and socioeconomic issues from an international perspective.) The only solution for George was to effect reforms in society that would make possible doing away with scarcity by one's labor. Once fear of want was overcome by adoption of his land policy, George believed that virtue and love of God would once again be possible. People would not be vicious, George thought, if they did not fear deprivation. In the Single Tax on land, George felt he had found the solution to society's ills. Convinced that his land policy would lead to prosperity and virtue, George wrote with a passionate moral fervor.

In opting for a certain land policy as a cure-all and in justifying the unlimited acquisition of wealth George revealed himself to be an unwitting disciple of modern political philosophy. I say unwitting because George did not share the low view of human life held by Machiavelli, Hobbes, or Locke. These philosophers did not believe that virtue and love of God perfect the human soul, as George did. Nevertheless, in my judgment, George compromised his Christian beliefs by espousing a political philosophy that promised a solution to political and social problems without prior conversion to virtue. George differs from Hobbes and Locke in arguing that genuine moral conversion and belief in God would flourish if scarcity were overcome.

Where does all this leave George's ideas on land reform? I think the greatest service one could render to the memory of George and his genuine effort to show compassion for the poor would be to separate his ideas on land reform from their philosophical and theological underpinnings. Even if George's land policy would not overcome scarcity, and eliminate vice and produce love of God, it might indeed contribute to bringing about a more just society. George's idea of creating access to the land for all and of promoting the fruitful use of land are surely admirable goals. It is up to economists, political philosophers, and other citizens to decide whether the Single Tax on land values or some variation thereof will indeed contribute to a more just distribution of material goods.

Natural Rights and the Common Good in Catholic Social Thought

Leo XIII's *Rerum Novarum* (1891) proved to be a decisive catalyst for Catholic social thought and action. Subsequent papal encyclicals on political and socioeconomic issues constantly refer to *Rerum Novarum*, mention its great impact, and substantially follow its general outlines (John Paul II 1981: #14). For example, Pope John Paul II (1981: #14) in *Laborem Exercens* explains the Catholic teaching on the possession and use of property in the same framework and in almost the same words as Leo XIII:

> The Church's teaching . . . diverges radically from the program of collec-
> tivism as proclaimed by Marxism and put into practice in various countries
> in the decades following the time of Leo XIII's encyclical [that is, *Rerum
> Novarum*]. At the same time it differs from the program of capitalism
> practiced by liberalism and by the political systems inspired by it. In the
> latter case, the difference consists in the way the right to ownership or
> property is understood. Christian tradition has never upheld this right as
> absolute and untouchable. On the contrary, it has always understood this
> right within the broader context of the right common to all to use the
> goods of the whole of creation; *the right to private property is subordinated
> to the right to common use.*

John Paul II perhaps makes it more clear than Leo XIII that all goods of the earth have a universal destination. Everyone is entitled "to use the goods of the whole creation." At the same time he upholds the right to private property. He is really saying that society should find a way to ensure universal access to material goods, including land, without abolishing private ownership. The popes since Leo XIII have agreed in principle with George's dictum that "we must make land common property." They differ from George in arguing that all external goods should in a sense be common and unlike George they do not endorse one specific mode of making land common.

Henry George and the modern popes have shared a passion for bringing about a more equitable distribution of property. Reading

Henry George and the papal social encyclicals together serves to remind us how important some notion of the common good is for society. In a time when contemporary moral theory is built upon individualistic premises, whether in the form of utilitarianism or deontological liberalism, there is a great need to resurrect thinkers with thoughts out of season.

George rightly sensed that Leo XIII's *Rerum Novarum* was an important document, worthy of commentary. I suspect that few others, if any, realized how important it would be for the development of modern CST in the 20th and 21st centuries. The strengths and weaknesses of that thought depend to a large extent on *Rerum Novarum*. Hence, a reading of that encyclical and the authors who shaped Leo XIII's thought may provide an important key to improving CST. Now that the Vatican archives of Leo XIII's papacy are available for public inspection, the task of unearthing and assessing the origins of Leo XIII's thought will be much easier.

Even without the archives it is possible to shed some more light on CST by extrapolating some of George's criticisms of Leo XIII. While George did not thoroughly examine *Rerum Novarum*, he did make a few remarks that point in the direction of a fruitful analysis. George accuses Leo of inventing both the right to employment and the right to "a certain indefinite wage." George also vehemently objects to Leo XIII's strong defense of the right to property in land. I believe, as already mentioned, that Leo XIII expects too much from the results of private ownership.

Leo XIII's emphasis on the right to property as well as other rights has been reinforced by later popes, especially Pope John XXIII and Pope John Paul II. As there is no doctrine of rights in the thought of Aquinas and Augustine or the Bible, what then is the origin of the Catholic teaching on rights? The question is whether Catholic rights teaching evolved from Catholic thinkers, or from the natural-rights teaching of Hobbes and Locke, or from the philosophy of Kant or from some other source.

This question is very important because CST has focused on rights either to the detriment, or even neglect of duties and the common good. This is understandable because of the stress on rights in philosophical circles and in political discourse and activity.

In its best form, Catholic teaching on rights, while preserving a traditional understanding of duties and the common good, as in the papal social encyclicals, is not widely known nor adequately presented to Catholics, not to mention non-Catholics. Nearly everyone today is educated to think about society and the State in Lockean, Kantian, or egalitarian terms. In its inferior forms, Catholic teaching on rights loses a balanced perspective and adopts one or the other aforementioned philosophical views.

Both Leo XIII and John Paul II properly subordinate rights to duties. In other words, persons are entitled to rights because they have God-given duties to fulfill. Both Leo XIII and John Paul II accept the primacy of the common good over rights. Still, both popes lay more stress on rights than on the common good.

Pope John XXIII's (1963) *Pacem in Terris* has become the classic statement of Catholic teaching on natural rights. While John XXIII also accepts the primacy of the common good and duties over rights, it should be noted that the subordination of rights to duties is not very clearly stated in *Pacem in Terris*. Pope John lays such stress on the rights of man that his comments on duties are hardly noticed. Paragraphs 11 to 27 indicate man's rights. Paragraph 28 says that man has as many duties as rights, and paragraph 29 gives three examples of duties—to preserve life, to live becomingly, and to seek the truth. Paragraphs 30 to 38 mention in general terms the duty to work for the rights of others. This one-sided emphasis on rights could very easily lead people to believe that Pope John's teaching on rights is not essentially different from the United Nations Declaration of Human Rights, the Declaration of Independence, or the French Declaration on the Rights of Man. *Pacem in Terris* makes the Church sound like a proponent of a teaching on rights that is divorced from a teaching on duties.

The advantage of a stress on rights is that most people tend to think about justice and the public interest in terms of rights—political and/or socioeconomic. Respect for rights, enforced by national laws and international covenants, is one of the few barriers against various kinds of injustice. Talking the language of rights provides the Catholic Church with an entry into public discourse and into scholarly debate, and enables the church to promote justice in the world.

While the advantages of rights teachings should not be underestimated, their disadvantages should not be overlooked. There is a profound disagreement about the foundation of rights. Some scholars think there are no solid philosophical grounds for respecting rights. Alasdair MacIntyre (1981), in his widely read book, *After Virtue*, makes that argument with considerable persuasiveness:

> The best reason for asserting so bluntly that there are no such rights is indeed of precisely the same type as the best reason which we possess for asserting that there are no witches and the best reason which we possess for asserting that there are no unicorns, every attempt to give good reasons for believing that there *are* such rights has failed.

Given the pervasive relativism and even nihilism of the present age, widespread societal doubt of the existence of rights could cause considerable disruption. The bonds of society are fragile enough without losing respect for rights. A teaching without foundation, however, will not last indefinitely. Nietzsche's comment about Christian morality is pertinent. He argued that if God is dead in the hearts of people Christian morality is without foundation and would eventually be abandoned. Respect for human rights is subject to the same fate.

References

Aquinas, T. (1946). *Summa Theologica*, tr. Fathers of the English Dominican Province. New York: Benziger Brothers.

Aristotle (1984). *The Politics*, tr. Carnes Lord. Chicago and London: University of Chicago Press.

Bell, S. (1937). *Rebel, Priest and Prophet: A Biography of Dr. Edward McGlynn*. New York: Devin Adair Company.

George, H. (1942). *Progress and Poverty*. New York: Walter J. Black.

——. (1953). *The Land Question*. New York: Robert Schalkenbach Foundation.

John XXIII (1963), *Pacem in Terris*. Boston: Daughters of St. Paul.

John Paul II (1980). *Brazil. Journey in the Light of the Eucharist*. Boston: Daughters of St. Paul.

——. (1981). *Laborem Exercens*. Boston: Daughters of St. Paul.

Leo XIII (1891). *Rerum Novarum*. Boston: Daughters of St. Paul.

Locke, J. (1764). *The Two Treatises of Civil Government*, ed. T. Hollis. London: A. Millar et al.

MacIntyre, A. (1981). *After Virtue.* Notre Dame, IN: Univ. of Notre Dame Press.

McWilliams, W. C. (1973). *The Idea of Fraternity in America.* Berkeley, CA: Univ. of California Press.

More, T. (1955). *Utopia.* New York: Washington Square Press.

Pius XI (1957). "*Quadragesimo Anno.* On Reconstructing the Social Order." In *The Church and the Reconstruction of the Modern World,* ed. T. McGlaughlin. Garden City, NY: Doubleday.

Ryan, J. A. (1916). *Distributive Justice.* New York: Macmillan Company.

Henry George's Perspective on War and Peace

By ALANNA HARTZOK*

ABSTRACT. This essay examines Henry George's perspective on war and peace. With justice added to the foundation in the way that Henry George proposes, the conditions of inequality and conflict that lead to war will no longer prevail. George saw that trade prohibitions furthered elite rule, militarization, and a worldview of "them" versus "us." George's great contribution was to see how these big issues of War and Peace bore directly upon the constellation of rules governing the relationship of people to planet, humans to humus, earthlings to earth. Social arrangements not based on the fundamental and equal human right to the earth lead inevitably to a gross imbalance of political power and thus to government corruption, odious public debt, war, and preparations for further war. Although he warned us of what might befall the United States if it took the imperialist path, George seemed hopeful that the highest and best moral purpose of our nation would prevail. The paper concludes with an assessment of contemporary devices that protect the interests of the few over the many—subsidies, the ballooning national debt, the ever-widening wealth gap, megacities, and the full-spectrum-dominance objective of U.S. imperialism.

Introduction

"We propose to readjust the very foundation of society." Thus stated Henry George (2006: 254) in *Progress and Poverty*. With justice added to the foundation in the way that George proposes, the conditions of inequality and conflict that lead to war will no longer prevail. Humans will relate to one another in just, generous, and cooperative ways. War would be an unthinkable relic of a distant dark past.

*Alanna Hartzok is Co-Director, Earth Rights Institute, Scotland, PA.

American Journal of Economics and Sociology, Vol. 71, No. 4 (October, 2012).

George (2006: 276) did not see war and preparations for war as separate from conditions of economic injustice. Rather he saw these perversions of morality and truth on a continuum, much like an initial mild bellyache turns into agonizing paroxysms leading to death by food poisoning: "Conflict includes not only war or preparation for war; it encompasses all mental power expended seeking gratification at the expense of others, and resisting such aggression."

To George seeking gratification at the expense of others meant the private appropriation of land rent, the monopolization of industry, the subjugation of workers, odious public debt, the domination of women by men, and tariffs and other policies that limited the freedom to trade. The ensuing concentration of wealth and power led to ever greater degrees of organization of lethal force (George 2006: 281):

> This unequal distribution of wealth and power, which grows as society advances, tends to produce greater inequality. Then the idea of justice is blurred by habitual toleration of injustice. . . . As collective power grows, the ruler's power to reward or punish increases. From the necessities of war on a large scale, absolute power arises. The masses are then mere slaves of the king's caprice. . . . When society has grown to a certain point, a regular military force can be specialized.

He traced the origination of early human tribal conflicts to the diverse natural conditions from which came differences in "language, custom, tradition, religion" from which "prejudice and animosity arise" (George 2006: 278). Warfare than becomes "a chronic and seemingly natural relation of society to each other. Power is depleted in attack or defense, in mutual slaughter and destruction of wealth or in warlike preparations." In the same paragraph he states that "[p]rotective tariffs and standing armies among the civilized world today bear witness to how long these hostilities persist."

Trade

The greatest part of George's writings on war and international conflict are to be found in his book *Protection and Free Trade* (George 1992). Of course George (2009) was well aware of the problem of land grabbing as detailed in *Our Land and Land Policy* with its focus on the Mexican land grants and the railroad land grants. But issues of tariff and trade policies were more alive in the public mind during George's time than was concern for U.S. foreign policy regarding land and natural resources. George was only seven years old during the land conflict of the Mexican-American War and he died the year before the Spanish-American War. Had he been alive in 1898 no doubt he would have had something to say about the U.S. victory over the Spanish Empire that allowed the victorious power to purchase the Philippine Islands from Spain for $20 million.

George (2006: 278–279) viewed trade as a great civilizing force: "It is in itself a form of association or cooperation. It not only operates directly—it also builds up interests opposed to war. It dispels ignorance which is the fertile mother of prejudice and hate." The freedom to exchange goods anywhere and anytime was in George's (1992: 46) views a sort of inoculation against war. "Trade is not invasion," he said. "It does not involve aggression on one side and resistance on the other, but mutual consent and gratification."

Protection was simply un-American and wreaked of Old World aristocratic arrangements of power and control. Protection was the antithesis of George's vision of a world of fraternal cooperation beyond the artificialities of nation-state borders and boundaries. One of George's (1992: 47) most famous statements is: "What protection teaches us, is to do to ourselves in time of peace what enemies seek to do to us in time of war."

George (1992: 328) saw that trade prohibitions furthered elite rule, militarization, and a worldview of "them" versus "us":

> Fortifications and navies and standing armies not merely suit the protectionist purposes in requiring a constant expenditure, and developing a class who look on warlike expenditures as conducive to their own profit and importance, but they are of a piece with a theory that teaches us that our interests are antagonistic to those of other nations.

He imagined that many good things would happen if there were free trade between Britain and the United States (1992: 330–331):

> . . . we should become one people, and would inevitably so conform currency and postal system and general laws that Englishman and American would feel themselves as much citizens of a common country as do New Yorker and Californian. . . . And with relations so close, ties of blood and language would assert their power, and mutual interest, general

convenience and fraternal feeling might soon lead to a pact, which, in the words of our own, would unite all the English-speaking peoples in a league "to establish justice, insure domestic tranquility, provide for the common defense, promote the general welfare, and secure the blessings of liberty. . . . Thus would free trade unite what a century ago protectionism severed, and in a federation of the nations of English speech—the world-tongue of the future—take the first step to a federation of mankind.

George was clearly a precursor voice to the movements for world federalism spawned since his time.

George (1992: 329) credits the absence of internal trade barriers as key to the rapid emergence of the United States as a world power. "The true benefits of our Union, the true basis of the interstate peace it secures, is that it has prevented the establishment of State tariffs and given us free trade over the better part of a continent."

Debt

George held deep distrust of the motives of warmongers. He saw that preparations for war and the stirring up of patriot fervor leading to war served elite interests. He wrote at considerable length about the dangers of public debt, warning the middle class people of the United States that this would be a mechanism for their exploitation just as surely as had happened to the British commoners in previous centuries. After a profound exposition of how English public debt corrupted legislatures, supported oligarchies, and crushed civil liberties he tells us how the relationship of war and debt has been a primary instrument of human exploitation and degradation (George 1883: 166):

> . . . the device of public debts enables tyrants to entrench themselves, and adventurers who seize upon government to defy the people. It permits the making of great and wasteful expenditures, by silencing, and even converting into support, the opposition of those who would otherwise resist these expenditures with most energy and force. But for the ability of rulers to contract public debts, nine-tenths of the wars of Christendom for the past two centuries could never have been waged. The destruction of wealth and the shedding of blood the agony of wives and mothers and children thus caused, cannot be computed, but to these items must be added the waste and loss and demoralization caused by constant preparation for war.

George was keenly aware of the opportunities taken by elites to incur national debt during the Civil War. The wealthiest grabbed and gobbled up the government-issued war bonds, which they knew would be paid back to them with substantial interest from the working backs of the common people. In *Social Problems* he makes a scathing attack on William H. Vanderbilt, who he said "expresses the universal feeling of his kind" when he "with his forty millions of registered bonds, declares that the national debt ought not to be paid off; that, on the contrary, it ought to be increased, because it gives stability to the government" (George 1883: 167). "We could have carried on the war without the issue of a single bond, if, when we did not shrink from taking from wife and children their only bread-winner, we had not shrunk from taking the wealth of the rich," said George (1883: 76).

Here is how he put it all together (George 1883: 164–165):

> . . . if, when we called on men to die for their country, we had not shrunk from taking, if necessary, nine hundred and ninety-nine thousand dollars from every millionaire, we need not have created any debt. But instead of that, what taxation we did impose was so levied as to fall on the poor more heavily than on the rich, and incidentally to establish monopolies by which the rich could profit at the expense of the poor. And then, when more wealth still was needed, instead of taking it from those who had it, we told the rich that if they would voluntarily let the nation use some of their wealth we would make it profitable to them by guaranteeing the use of the taxing power to pay them back principal and interest. And we did make it profitable with a vengeance. Not only did we, by the institution of the national banking system, give them back nine-tenths of much of the money thus borrowed while continuing to pay interest on the whole amount, but even where it was required neither by the letter of the bond nor the equity of the circumstances we made debt incurred in depreciated greenbacks payable on its face in gold. The consequence of this method of carrying on the war was to make the rich richer instead of poorer. The era of monstrous fortunes in the United States dates from the war.

George was, as the British would say, "spot on" with his analysis of the Civil War and issues of tariffs and public war debt.

Recent historical research demolishes the view that Lincoln opposed the secession of the South because he wanted to abolish slavery. In his summary of Thomas J. DiLorenzo's (2006) book, *Lincoln Unmasked*, David Gordon (2007) wrote:

> Following his mentor Henry Clay, Lincoln favored a nationalist economic program of which high tariffs, a national bank, and governmentally financed "internal improvements" were key elements. This program, he

thought, would promote not only the interests of the wealthy industrial and financial powers he always faithfully served but would benefit white labor as well.

DiLorenzo (2006: 57–59) found support for his views from a leading abolitionist and libertarian theorist, Lysander Spooner, who saw that the primary motive of Lincoln and the war party was to preserve and consolidate Northern control of the Southern economy. Spooner wrote that the war "erupted for a purely pecuniary consideration," and not for any moral reason. He labeled the economic lifeblood of the Republican Party, Northern bankers, manufacturers, and railroad cor-porations, "lenders of blood money'." To Spooner the Northern fin-anciers of the war who had lent money to the Lincoln government did so not for "any love of liberty or justice," but for the control of Southern markets through "tariff extortion."

DiLorenzo (2006: 126) quoted Lincoln himself to support his views, pointing to his first inaugural address:

> Lincoln shockingly threw down the gauntlet over the tariff issue, literally threatening the invasion of any state that failed to collect the newly doubled tariff . . . "[T]here needs to be no bloodshed or violence, and there shall be none unless it is forced upon the national authority." What was he [Lincoln] talking about? What might ignite bloodshed and violence? Failure to collect the tariff, that's what. He further stated that it was his duty "to collect the duties and imposts; but beyond what may be necessary for these objects, there will be no invasion." In other words, Pay Up or Die.

Spooner said, and DiLorenzo (2006: 59) agreed, that "[t]he Republicans did not end slavery as an act of justice to the black man himself, but only as a 'war measure,' which were the exact words that Lincoln himself used in *The Emancipation Proclamation*" ("as a fit and nec-essary war measure for suppressing said rebellion"—Lincoln 1863). The result of Lincoln's aggressive prosecution of the war was "the killing of one out of four males of military age while maiming for life more than double that number" (DiLorenzo 2006: 28).

George was against borrowing money to wage war, any war, anywhere. This stance naturally follows from the entire sequence of his political-economic analysis. He clearly saw how the land problem related to trade issues, the ever growing divide between the rich and the rest, myriad symptoms of social and economic injustice, government debt, outbreaks of internal conflicts, and war between nations. George's great contribution was to see how these big issues of War and Peace bore directly upon the constellation of rules governing the relationship of people to planet, humans to humus, earthlings to earth. No wonder Leo Tolstoy loved him.

Dwight D. Eisenhower had just begun to glimpse our state of affairs when at the end of his presidency he warned us of the military-industrial complex. Seventy years previously George had loudly and clearly forewarned us of the military-industrial-prison-financial-mortgage-land-and-natural-resource control complex. That's a mouthful so let's just say "neocon"—the "new controllers"—different bunch, same brand.

"The same disease which rotted the old civilization is exhibiting its symptoms in the new," said the seer (George 1992: 165).

War

It had become crystal clear to George that social arrangements not based on the fundamental and equal human right to the earth would inevitably lead to a gross imbalance of political power and thus to government corruption, odious public debt, war, and preparations for further war. With his profound knowledge of the injustice that leads to war, George would have had little use for concepts and considerations concerning "just wars." He would assuredly take offense to the very idea of a "just war" and view anyone putting forth such reasoning as a propagandist for the elite-ruled status quo:

> The passions aroused by war, the national hatreds, the worship of military glory, the thirst for victory or revenge, dull public conscience; pervert the best social instincts into that low, unreasoning extension of selfishness miscalled patriotism; deaden the love of liberty; lead men to submit to tyranny and usurpation from the savage thirst for cutting the throats of other people, or the fear of having their own throats cut. They so pervert religious perceptions that professed followers of Christ bless in his name the standards of murder and rapine, and thanks are given to the Prince of Peace for victories that pile the earth with mangled corpses and make hearthstones desolate! (George 1883: 166–167).

During Viet Nam War days members of my generation who opposed the war were appalled by warmongering Christians. We had a phrase that mocked them—"kill a Commie for Christ." Henry George understood the distortions of Christianity in its mainstream institutionalized form. In *The Science of Political Economy*, George (1962: 174) first describes the several perversions of the field of political economy as developed in Adam Smith's *The Wealth of Nations* that "did away effectually with any fear that the study of natural laws of the production and distribution of wealth might be dangerous to the great House of Have."

Christianity and Empire

In the next paragraph George (1962: 174) stated:

> So far from showing any menace to the great special interests, a political economy, so perverted, soon took its place with a similarly perverted Christianity to soothe the conscience of the rich and to frown down discontent on the part of the poor.

George at all times took the moral high ground. He believed in the "unity of the Creative Mind" (1992: 31) and in natural law spawned from "the All-originating, All-maintaining Spirit" (1962: 174). He greatly treasured not only the teachings of Jesus but nuggets of wisdom that he found in ancient texts of both Eastern and Western philosophy. He was a man who felt and experienced a deep guiding force of meaning, mission, and purpose. But he could not comfortably fit in with the dogmas and doctrines of either the Catholic or the Protestant traditions. Some of us view him as most closely aligned with the teachings of the early patristic period prior to the First Council of Nicaea and the codifications of the Nicene Creed.

The First *Council of Nicaea* was the first of the seven so-called ecumenical councils—bureaucratic exercises of bishops held to codify and regiment the teachings of Christianity, the last one being held in year 787. Note that the word "ecumenical" is from a Greek word that literally means "inhabited" and was originally a figure of speech referring to the territory of the Roman Empire since the earliest councils were all convoked by Roman Emperors (http://en.wikipedia.org/wiki/Ecumenical_council).

The purpose of the First Council of Nicaea, convoked by the Roman Emperor Constantine in year 325, was to resolve disagreements in the

Church of Alexandria over the nature of Jesus in relationship to the Father; in particular, whether Jesus was of the same substance as God the Father or merely of similar substance. Three hundred and eighteen Christian bishops out of 1,800 in the Roman Empire attended the council. In other words, 17 percent of Christian Bishops in the Roman Empire in 325 AD adopted Roman Christianity's official position on the nature of Jesus, the Holy Ghost, and God as the Holy Trinity (Antoine 2002). It was called the Nicene Creed.

The research of theologian Michael Rivage-Seul (2007), put forth in a paper presented at the May 2007 International Philosophers for Peace Conference, shows the Nicene Creed to be a repackaging of the myths of the supreme Roman God Jupiter who, along with the goddesses Juno and Minerva, formed the Holy Triad. The temple of Jupiter on the Capitoline Hill was dedicated in 509 BC to this trinity. As such the Nicene Creed can be viewed as a cooptation of the Jesus movement by the Roman state and a carefully scripted evasion of Jesus' main teaching to love one another in the here and now (Rivage-Seul 2007: 6):

> The Creed jumps from the conception and birth of Jesus to his death and resurrection. It leaves out entirely any reference to what Jesus said and did. For all practical purposes it ignores the historical Jesus and pays attention only to a God who comes down from heaven, dies, rises, ascends back to heaven and offers eternal life to those who believe. It's a nearly perfect reflection of "mystery cult" belief. The revolutionary potential of Jesus' words and actions relative to justice, wealth, poverty and revolution are lost. Not only that, but subsequent to Nicaea, anyone connecting Jesus to a struggle for justice, sharing and communal life is rendered suspect and is very often classified as heretical. That is, mystery cult becomes "orthodoxy." The example and teaching of Jesus (and of the early church) becomes heresy.

Anyone attempting to fully live and embody this teaching became a threat to the elite rule status quo. This Council, convened by a Roman Emperor, was an attempt to tame the wildfire of Christianity and gut its core teachings. The Nicene Creed took the heart, soul, and embodied spirit out of the Jesus movement, eliminating the voice and wisdom of women in the process, as only men participated in these codification Councils.

The Nicene Creed made Jesus a God instead of a highly evolved being guided by a profound moral mission on planet Earth. Jesus came down from heaven, was born by a virgin, killed, buried, and then went back to heaven, end of story. He did this "for us men for our salvation" (Nicene Creed). The Nicene Creed, the core document of faith of organized, institutionalized Catholic and Protestant Christianity, repeated countless millions of times in churches and catechisms since the year 325, gave us bookends only. It tells us nothing of what Jesus actually did and taught during his time on earth. This must have been precisely the point of the exercise. Henry George (2006: Chapter 38) well knew that the forces that "perverted Christianity" were the same ones he was up against in his mission to "readjust the very foundation of society."

The lowest common denominator of love is justice, treating each with fairness during our brief sojourn on earth. This truly Christian ethic bears directly on the human relationship to the basis of physical life itself—the earth. The early Christian land ethic was that of "koinonia." The Creation was for all to share for the "autarkeia"—self-sufficiency—in securing physical needs of each and everyone. The true Christian teachings of love and justice in the here and now were squarely at odds with the Roman land laws of "dominium," which legalized lands gained by conquest and plunder.

When Christianity became the state religion of the Roman Empire, the early Christian teachings on land were overtaken by the Roman land laws. A corrupted Christianity, uprooted from its early teachings on land ownership, too often went hand in hand with the exploitation and degradation of centuries of colonial conquests (Hartzok 2004).

Augustine, writing after the First Council of Nicaea, was in alignment with the early Christian land ethic. According to Charles Avila (1983), Augustine saw that the poor are poor because they have been deprived by the propertied few of the wealth that should belong to all. He laid the blame for this unjust situation squarely on the doorstep of an absolutist and exclusivist legal right of private ownership. He reminded his audience that they were all "made from one mud" and sustained "on one earth" under the same natural conditions, having the same essence, and called to the same destiny. He rejected the legalized status quo as inappropriate for human living. Holding that legal arrangements of property rights were of human origin, he asserted that they should be changed, in theory and in practice, in function of a faith-informed ethic based on the true meaning of ownership.

Unfortunately, Augustine, who also helped bring us the doctrine of original sin, is much better known for his "just war" theory than his land-rights stance. One can surmise that then as now the class with the greatest capacity to promulgate their own interests came to shape and spin the words and thought of Christian theologians in such a way as to not "be dangerous to the great House of Have."

As the Roman emperors were trying to tame, control, and contain Christianity, so perhaps Augustine, with his "just war" theory, was trying to tame the Roman empire. But Augustine thereby compromised and corrupted the pacifist teachings of Jesus who, though he did create a bit of havoc that day in the temple when he overturned the money-changers tables, never threw a stone at anyone let alone amassed an armed force.

The Augustinian corruption of Jesus' teachings via "just war" theory sounds forth to this day from the lips of radical fundamentalist warmongering Christians who thus play nicely into the hands of those holding grossly excessive wealth and obscene powers to manipulate, control, and exploit other human beings. "God is pro-war," said Jerry Falwell (2004), titling an article about Iraq for a fundamentalist web site. Some of the ayatollahs probably preach the same thing to suicide bombers. Former President Jimmy Carter (2005), writing in his book *Our Endangered Values: America's Moral Crisis,* characterized radical Christian fundamentalism as a core threat to America.

Henry George walked with Jesus, not with Augustine. Avila (1983), doing his research into early Christian teachings on land ownership after discovering the plight of landless peasants in the Philippines, considered George to be in the lineage of the patristic pre-Nicene Creed period. Avila searched through the Latin and Greek writings of the early Christians and discovered that imperialist Roman law had indeed corrupted the teachings of Jesus—a tendency shared by modern social thinkers (Avila 1983: 8–9):

> The concentration of property in private hands began very early in Rome and was indeed based on the foundational and legitimizing idea of absolute and exclusive individual ownership in land. This was the same

idea which would come to form the basis of the slave-owning, the feudal, and the capitalist (including the pseudo-socialist, or state-capitalist) economic systems successively. Modern civilization has not yet discarded this antiquated ownership concept, which was originally derived from ancient Rome. In fact, it seems to us, this is one of the main roots of the present global crisis, in which the rich become richer because the poor become poorer. . . . [Modern social thinkers] advocate the promotion of social justice without stopping to think that individual ownership of nature's bounty might be socially unjust in itself. And yet patristic thought insisted long ago that there can be no real justice, or abolition of poverty, if the *koina*, the common natural elements of production, are appropriated in ownership by individuals.

High Hopes for the American Republic

George profoundly grasped the sequence leading from the land problem to unwarranted wealth to unlimited power. Although he warned us of what might befall the United States if it took the imperialist path, he seemed hopeful that the highest and best moral purpose of our nation would prevail, as evinced by the following (George 1992: 329):

> Already in her sixty millions of people, the most powerful nation on earth, and rapidly rising to a position that will dwarf the greatest empires, the American Republic can afford to laugh to scorn any suggestion that she should ape the armaments of Old-World monarchies. . . . The giant of the nations does not depend for her safety upon steel-clad fortresses and armor-plated ships which the march of invention must within a few years make, even in war-time mere useless rubbish; but in her population, in her wealth, in the intelligence and inventiveness and spirit of her people, she has all that would be really useful in time of need. No nation on earth would venture wantonly to attack her, and none could do so with impunity. If we ever again have a foreign war it will be of our own making. And too strong to fear aggression, we ought to be too just to commit it (p. 329). . . . A nobler career is open to the American Republic than the servile imitation of European follies and vices. Instead of following in what is mean and low, she may lead toward what is grand and high. This league of sovereign States, settling their differences by a common tribunal and opposing no impediments to trade and travel, has in it possibilities of giving to the world a more than Roman peace.

If Henry George were alive today, he would note that the tariffs morphed into subsidies, the national debt ballooned to monstrous proportions, and the enormous wealth chasm between the super-rich and the rest is nearly beyond comprehension.

Subsidies

In George's time the federal government gave excessive amounts of public land to railroads and other private corporations. Today we let big landowners and businesses gorge at the public trough. Subsidies are today what the tariff was in George's time. Both protect the interests of the few over the many.

Between 1995 and 2010 the federal government gave out $261.9 billion in subsidies (Environmental Working Group 2011). The top 10 percent of big business farms received 74 percent of all subsidies while more than half (62 percent according to USDA) of all farmers and ranchers receive no subsidies. As a result, small farmers here and millions around the world aren't able to compete. The federal government has paid at least $1.3 billion in subsidies for rice and other crops since 2000 to individuals who do no farming at all (Morgan, Gaul, and Cohen 2006).

National Debt

What would George say of our current state of affairs regarding the national debt? According to the U.S. National Debt Clock (Hall 2012), as of February 14, 2012 the U.S. National Debt was $15,367,058,901,083.27. The estimated population of the United States is 312,220,819. Each citizen's share of this debt is $49,218.53. The national debt has continued to increase an average of $3.98 billion per day since September 28, 2007.

The accumulation of ever larger current-account deficits over the past quarter-century has played an indispensable role in transforming the United States from the world's largest creditor nation into the planet's biggest debtor nation (Cuadra 2011).

Wealth Gap

Although the focal point of George's great work was the wealth gap, he would probably be stunned by the magnitude of the numbers. A

Congressional Budget Office (2011: ix) analysis of income-distribution trends between 1979 and 1997 revealed the following:

- For the 1 percent of the population with the highest income, average real after-tax household income grew by 275 percent between 1979 and 2007.
- For others in the 20 percent of the population with the highest income (those in the 81st through 99th percentiles), average real after-tax household income grew by 65 percent over that period, much faster than it did for the remaining 80 percent of the population, but not nearly as fast as for the top 1 percent.
- For the 60 percent of the population in the middle of the income scale (the 21st through 80th percentiles), the growth in average real after-tax household income was just under 40 percent.
- For the 20 percent of the population with the lowest income, average real after-tax household income was about 18 percent higher in 2007 than it had been in 1979.

All of the Forbes 400 are now billionaires (http://www.forbes.com/forbes-400/). The United States has 412 billionaires while 15.1 percent of the nation's population lived in poverty in 2010 ($17,552 or less for a family of three)—the highest proportion since 1993 (U.S. Bureau of the Census 2010: 61).

Megacities

In its State of World Population report, the United Nations Population Fund (2011: 77) said that "the global rural-urban balance of populations has tipped irreversibly in favour of cities" and "[m]etropolitan areas spreading over large territory are absorbing or overtaking compact cities, sometimes merging with other metros along heavily populated corridors." The report warned that "[w]ithout planning, cities can grow absent-mindedly, spread over every available empty space and overrun the ability of public services, where they exist, to meet demands or cope with the growth of slums."

George would be concerned about the explosive growth of megacities. He viewed this concentration of population with alarm from his own early vantage point of the late 1800s (George 1992: 165):

Population and wealth are concentrating in huge towns and an exhausting commerce flows from country to city. But this ominous tendency is not natural, and does not arise from too much freedom; it is unnatural and arises from restrictions. It may be clearly traced to monopolies, of which the monopoly of material opportunities is the first and most important. In a word the Roman system of landownership, which in our modern civilization has displaced that of our Celtic and Teutonic ancestors, is producing the same effect that it did in the Roman world—the engorgement of the centers and the impoverishment of the extremities.

U.S. Imperialism

If in 1883 George was concerned about the damage that "destructive agents" such as nitro-glycerin could do to destroy the city of London (1883: 5), he would shake in his shoes to learn of the thousands of nuclear weapons poised for immediate launch in this now highly interconnected world. If alive today George would know that we did not solve the land problem and that we did tread the path of imperialism. He would learn that "full spectrum dominance" of the globe on land, sea, air, and outer space is now official U.S. foreign policy. He would be able to peruse maps on the internet showing the 700 to 800 military bases that the U.S. operates and/or controls worldwide with an underlying land surface of 5,443,054 acres making the Pentagon one of the largest landowners on the globe (Dufour 2007). He would learn that the United States has structured the earth as a battlefield divided into five spatial units and four unified Combatant Commands each under the command of a General. Total active-duty military personnel is of the order of 1.4 million (Global Firepower 2012). U.S. defense spending (excluding the costs of the Iraq war) have increased from 404 billion in 2001 to 685 billion dollars in 2011 (United States Department of Defense 2012: 1-1).

But military auditors admit that they cannot account for 25 percent of what the Pentagon spends. And in 2002 then Secretary of Defense Donald Rumsfeld made the astonishing admission that "according to some estimates we cannot track $2.3 trillion in transactions" (Sirgany 2009). This works out to $8,000 for every woman, man and child in America.

This writer believes that if Henry George were alive today he would take a deep look at the evidence surrounding the events of 9/11 and conclude that they did indeed make it happen, the "new Pearl Harbor" (Griffin 2004) event to stir up war fever, thus manipulating the masses into a war on Iraq for the purpose of geopolitical control of Eurasia as a key to the neocon elite power drive for full-spectrum dominance.

Thus Spake Henry George

If George were alive today, after surveying our current dangerous and insane situation and recovering from the shock of what he discovered, he would likely join with movements to abolish war and dismantle the military-industrial-financial complex.

George would rage and rail like the prophet that he was.

He would focus progressive movements on the land problem, knowing as he did that "[p]ublic debts and standing armies historically were products of the change from feudal to allodial (i.e., private) land tenures" (George 2006: 255). He thus might rekindle the hope that "[a]s intelligence and independence grow among the masses, standing armies would soon disappear."

Given what we are faced with at this moment in time, George's words seem overly optimistic. But dark despair and paralyzing pessimism did not rule the spirit of this man who said "[r]eligion and experience alike teach us that the highest good of each is to be sought in the good of others; that the true interests of men are harmonious, not antagonistic, that prosperity is the daughter of good will and peace" and then asked "[c]an we imagine the nations beating their swords into plowshares and their spears into pruning hooks . . . ?" (George 1992: 31).

Yes, Henry, we must imagine the possibility of peace on earth, or else we are doomed.

References

Antoine, K. (2002). "An Essay on the Origin of the Holy Trinity." http://www.kevinantoine.com/holytrinity.htm.

Avila, C. (1983). *Ownership: Early Christian Teaching*. Maryknoll, NY: Orbis Books.

Carter, J. (2005). *Our Endangered Values: America's Moral Crisis*. New York: Simon & Schuster.

Congressional Budget Office (2011). *Trends in the Distribution of Household Income Between 1979 and 2007.* Washington, DC: Congress of the United States. http://cbo.gov/ftpdocs/124xx/doc12485/10-25-HouseholdIncome.pdf.

Cuadra, L. (2011). "List of World's Largest Creditor and Debtor Nations." *Financial Sense* August 31. http://www.financialsense.com/contributors/leslie-cuadra/2011/08/31/list-of-worlds-largest-creditor-and-debtor-nations.

DiLorenzo, T. J. (2006). *Lincoln Unmasked: What You're Not Supposed to Know About Dishonest Abe.* New York: Crown Forum.

Dufour, J. (2007). "The Worldwide Network of U.S. Military Bases." *Global Research* July 2. http://www.globalresearch.ca/index.php?context=va&aid=5564.

Environmental Working Group (2011). "2011 Farm Subsidy Database." http://farm.ewg.org/region.php?fips=00000&progcode=total&yr=2005.

Falwell, J. (2004). "God Is Pro-War." *WND Commentary* January 31. http://www.wnd.com/2004/01/23022/.

George, H. (1883). *Social Problems.* New York: Robert Schalkenbach Foundation. http://schalkenbach.org/library/henry-george/social-problems/spcont.html.

——. (1962). *The Science of Political Economy.* New York: Robert Schalkenbach Foundation.

——. (1992). *Protection or Free Trade: An Examination of the Tariff Question, with Especial Regard to the Interests of Labor.* New York: Robert Schalkenbach Foundation.

——. (2006). *Progress and Poverty.* New York: Robert Schalkenbach Foundation.

——. (2009). *Our Land and Land Policy,* digitized Per Moller Andersen. New York: Robert Schalkenbach Foundation. http://schalkenbach.org/library/henry-george/grundskyld/pdf/George/pe-Our-Land-and-Land-Policy.pdf.

Global Firepower (2012). "United States of America Military Strength." http://www.globalfirepower.com/country-military-strength-detail.asp?country_id=United-States-of-America.

Gordon, D. (2007). "Who Was This 'Great Liberator'?" *Mises Daily* July 12. http://mises.org/daily/2621.

Griffin, D. R. (2004). *The New Pearl Harbor: Disturbing Questions About the Bush Administration and 9/11.* Northampton, MA: Olive Branch Press.

Hall, E. (2012). "U.S. National Debt Clock." http://www.brillig.com/debt_clock/.

Hartzok, A. (2004). "Earth Rights Democracy: Public Finance Based on Early Christian Teachings," presented at Christianity and Human Rights Conference. Birmingham, AL: Samford University. http://www.earthrights.net/docs/samford.html.

Lincoln, A. (1863). "The Emancipation Proclamation." Washington, DC: National Archives and Records Administration. http://www.archives.gov/exhibits/featured_documents/emancipation_proclamation/.

Morgan, D., G. M. Gaul, and S. Cohen. (2006). "Farm Program Pays $1.3 Billion to People Who Don't Farm." *Washington Post* July 2. http://large.stanford.edu/publications/coal/references/morgan/.

Rivage-Seul, M. D. (2007). "The Emperor's God—Recovering the Lost Message of Jesus," presented at International Philosophers for Peace Conference. Radford, VA: Radford University.

Sirgany, A. (2009). "The War on Waste." *CBS Evening News* February 11. http://www.cbsnews.com/stories/2002/01/29/eveningnews/main325985.shtml.

United Nations Population Fund (2011). *State of World Population 2011: People and Possibilities in a World of 7 Billion.* New York: United Nations. http://www.unfpa.org/swp/.

U.S. Bureau of the Census (2010). "Income, Poverty, and Health Insurance Coverage in the United States: 2010," Report P60, n. 238. Washington, DC.

United States Department of Defense (2012). *Fiscal Year 2012 Budget Request.* Washington, DC. http://comptroller.defense.gov/defbudget/fy2012/FY2012_Budget_Request_Overview_Book.pdf.

Just War: A Catholic Perspective

Cui Non Videtur Causa Justa?

By MARGARET MONAHAN HOGAN*

ABSTRACT. Just peace is the desired condition and there exists a presumption against war. That presumption may be overridden by injustice that disrupts the just peace. Once the peace is broken, war is permissible under the following conditions: the war must be declared by the legitimate authority; there must be a just cause (defense against aggression, punishment against guilt, violation of rights, defending the innocent, or protecting those values required for decent human existence); the right intention (pursuit of stated cause, pursuit of lasting peace, and right attitude) must guide the move to war; the response of war must be proportional (producing more good than evil, appropriate to remedy the extent of injustice); success in waging war is probable; conformity to international law; all other attempts to remedy the injustice perpetrated or imminently threatened must have been attempted and exhausted.

Introduction

This essay is about war—and its causes—as understood from a Catholic perspective. It represents the thinking of a woman who is by profession a philosopher and who is, by religious affiliation and deep commitment, a Catholic. It represents my thoughts as I ponder what ought a Catholic mother and professor tell her sons and her daughters as well as her students. While this essay represents my understanding of the Catholic position on war, it makes no claim to speak for the Catholic Church.

As the subtitle "Cui Non Videtur Causa Justa?" suggests, the notion of just war is problematic. The notion of waging war—of any kind of

*Margaret Monahan Hogan is McNerney-Hanson Professor Emeritus of Ethics, Professor Emeritus of Philosophy, and Founding Executive Director, Garaventa Center for Catholic Intellectual Life and American Culture at the University of Portland. She is a Fellow of the Notre Dame Center for Ethics and Culture.

American Journal of Economics and Sociology, Vol. 71, No. 4 (October, 2012).

war—is troubling. It was for Christians from the founding of Christianity whose Lord called the community of believers to peace; it was for Christians in the time of the Empire; it was so for the great humanists of the Renaissance whose great hopes for peace, heralded they thought by the ascendancy of Henry VIII to the throne, were dashed by war; and it is even more so for Christians today as they ponder once again the possibility of nuclear war on a global scale. Two questions persist: (1) Why then war? and (2) Why then a defense of just war?

The attempt to address these issues will proceed by making a few observations about war and its effects and causes, by sketching the development of just war theory from its inception to the present, and then by making a few recommendations—what ought one as a Catholic, a philosopher, a teacher, and a mother do.

Why Then War?

War is terrible . . . Robert E. Lee is recorded as cautioning General Longstreet from the battlefield at Fredericksburg to remember that war is such a terrible thing. War takes the lives of so many of the young—the most precious capital of any nation. War scars and maims in mind and body those who we send to war in our name and for our values. War takes the lives of fathers and mothers and children and in this taking leaves families in sorrowful disarray. War devours the material and economic resources of any nation that prepares for war. Billions of dollars that might have been directed to education, to housing, to feeding, to medical care, to the advancement of science are now spent for the instruments of war.

War is indeed an ugly thing.

But war is not the ugliest of things. John Stuart Mill wrote at the time of the American Civil War: "The decayed and degraded state of moral character and patriotic feelings which thinks that nothing is worth war is much worse . . . a man who has nothing for which he is willing to fight, nothing which is more important than his own personal safety, is a miserable creature and has no chance of being free unless made and kept so by the exertions of better men than himself" (*Dissertations and Discussions* (1868), Vol. 1, p. 26). Peace at any price is a terrible thing.

If war is so ugly and peace the desired condition of rational beings, why then are there wars? The direct cause of war is sin. Sin is to be understood here not as part of a divine-command theory of morality; that is not the Catholic tradition, although all Catholics would acknowledge that to disobey a divine command is surely a sin. The Catholic tradition holds that sin is missing the mark—the failure to accomplish the good of human flourishing. And the name of the sin that is the cause of war is injustice. The injustice is enacted in a variety of ways. The injustice might be nationalism; it might be religious—a crusade; it might be economic gain; it might be territorial expansion; it might be the harvesting of resources; and it might be national or individual glory. But whatever its name, it is the sin of injustice.

What causes such sin—the injustice that leads to war? The major causes of sin are two: lack of knowledge and lack of rectitude. The latter, lack of rectitude, is the disordering of the passions, which is manifest as the inordinate desire for some apparent or real good or as defect in the ability to order the passions toward the good as end. The former, lack of knowledge, is caused by ignorance—either vincible (which can be overcome if open to correct insights) or invincible (impossible to be overcome in the historical or individual circumstances) or by bias—the bias of the big idea, the general bias of common sense, or the bias of culture.

Why Then a Defense of Just War?

In the presence of unjust war—war caused by the sin of injustice—it is sometimes necessary, as the only option—the last resort—to wage war. And war as the remedy for injustice is a good. The denotation of war as good falls strange upon first hearing. But if there is such a thing as just war—war understood as rectification of injustice perpetrated— then surely it must be designated as good. Those who carry out just war must be considered noble and the victory in just war an occasion of celebration.

It is within the context of this understanding that the Catholic tradition has developed the just war theory that directs how we are to tread, when we must, toward the necessity of war because there is injustice such that there cannot be peace. How do we carry out necessary war in such a way that peace be possible? Clearly, just war theory stakes out a position between the claim of *Realpolitik* and the claim of pacifism. The former finds war an acceptable and legitimate means of pursuing national interests. The latter, pacifism, which marked early Christianity and continues as well in this day in the traditional contemporary peace churches, rules out the very possibility of war. Just as clearly as just war theory marks out a difficult path between "realistic" political theory and pacifism, just war theory, as theory, has been developed over time and remains open to development. And just war theory requires careful adherence to all its conditions.

You may recall from your study of history that the early Christians embraced pacifism as part of their belief that the second coming of Jesus was imminent. As their belief in the immediate return of Jesus waned, they became active and full participants in the Roman Empire. And they were left, as we are left, to figure out what it means to "[r]ender to Caesar the things that are Caesar's and to God the things that are God's" (Mark 12: 17). Biblical scholars caution that prooftexting the Scriptures in search of guidance will not work. Focusing on the Old Testament, the Pacifist will say, quoting from Isaiah 2:4 or perhaps Micah 4:3, "God will settle disputes among Nations. They will hammer their swords into plows and their spears into pruning knives. Nations will never again go to war, never again prepare for battle again." The other side will quote Joel 3: 10: "Make this announcement among the nations: Prepare for war; call your warriors, gather all your soldiers and march. Hammer the points of your plows into swords and your pruning knives into spears." Switching to the New Testament gains no advantage. The Pacifist will quote Matthew 5: 39–45: "But I say to you resist not evil, but whosoever shall smite you on the right cheek, turn to him the other also . . . Love your enemies, bless them that curse you, do good to them that hate you . . . that you may be the children of your father. . . . who makes the sun to rise on the evil and on the good . . . and sends his rain on the just and the unjust." The other side will also quote Matthew . . . but at 10: 34–35: "Think not that I come to send peace on earth. I came not to send peace but a sword. For I have come to set man against his father and daughter against her mother."

But the early Christians were not left alone and we are not left alone. Jesus sent the Spirit to be with us until His return and the Spirit operates through wise men and women who arise to lead—both in the Church and in the civil community. Christians of the Roman Empire embraced their situation as citizens of God's kingdom and as citizens in the earthly kingdom and they struggled with their obligations in each city. Along with citizenship came the obligation of military service. With the obligation of military service came the question of appropriate penitential inquiry and appropriate penance for those who as Christian citizens engaged in war. Out of this necessity just war theory was born.

Saint Augustine (354–430) is cited as the Christian originator of just war theory. The theory as it comes from Augustine has its source in the obligation of the ruler to maintain peace. Because the ruler is obliged to maintain peace, war may be required to defend the peace of the nation against serious injury—against injustice. Augustine says: "The natural order conducive to peace among mortals demands that the power to declare and counsel war should be in the hands of those who hold supreme authority . . . a just war is wont to be described as one that avenges wrongs, when a nation or state has to be punished for refusing to make amends inflicted by its subjects, or to restore what it has unjustly seized" (quoted in Aquinas 1946: *Questions. In Hept. Qu. x, super Jos.*). Augustine continues: "The passion for inflicting harm, the cruel thirst for vengeance, an unpacific and relentless spirit, the fervor of revolt, the lust of power, and such things, all these are rightly condemned in war" (Aquinas 1946: *Contra Faust. xxii, 74*). He says further: "We do not seek peace in order to be at war, but we go to war that we may have peace. Be peaceful therefore in warring, so that you may vanquish those whom you war against and bring them to the prosperity of peace" (Aquinas 1946: *Ep. ad Bonf. clcxxxix*).

What points is Augustine making here? He is making at least the following five: (1) in a sinful and broken world war is sometimes necessary; (2) only the legitimate authority may wage war; (3) the reason for war is injustice—a harm has been done and rectification is required; (4) the goal of war is peace; peace is the normal condition; and (5) the conduct of war must be conducive to peace—you have obligations to your enemies.

In the 13th century, Thomas Aquinas (1225–1274) developed his position rooted in Augustine, and grounded in the notion of the common good and in the natural law tradition. As did Augustine, Thomas emphasized legitimate authority, just cause, and rightful intention as the necessary conditions for a just war. For Thomas, the intention of waging war is limited to two possibilities, namely the "furthering of some good or the avoidance of some evil." Thus as befitting the common good tradition, Thomas says, "[j]ust as it is lawful for them [the legitimate authority] to have recourse to the sword in defending that common weal against internal disturbances . . . so too it is their business to have recourse to the sword of war in defending the common weal against external enemies" (Aquinas 1946: II-II, Q. 40).

In the 16th and 17th centuries the just war theory continued to develop. The canonists of this era, including Francis Vitoria (1492–1546) and Francis Suarez (1548–1617), in their development of the theory of law of nations (*jus gentium*) expanded the possible cause of war from one to two possibilities . . . an armed attack against a peaceful society and injurious actions taken against a peaceful society. The first, the response to an armed attack, the classical self-defense position seemed to them to require no justification, but the response to injurious actions seemed to them to require further justification. And they continued to look to just war theory as the test of the moral acceptability of war. Suarez defined the injurious act as "an injury, to the honor of a nation to the natural right of a nation . . . to the rights of a nation under positive law . . . so grave that it outweighs the risks and losses of war" (Suarez 1944, 13,4,1). And he added two more conditions: that the war be fought as a last resort and that the war be fought in a proper manner—the *jus in bello* (Suarez 13,7, 3–15).

As the just war theory continues to evolve, we continue to pray and to call for peace. But this cry for peace remains *Vox clamantis in deserato*. The Popes, the bishops, and the people call for peace and yet all acknowledge the necessity of war. The just war theory, as a theory, is an attempt to use wisdom and to exercise care in a sinful and broken world. It recognizes that all war is terrible, representative finally of human failure. It recognizes that the primary justification for war is to protect the innocent from harm. It rules out wars of aggression and wars of self-aggrandizement. In the contemporary period the Popes and the Bishops have spoken of and hope for peace and have acknowledged the necessity of war. Pope Pius XII wrote in a message in 1948 . . . in the wake of World War II . . . the following: "A people threatened with an unjust aggression, or already its victim, may not remain passively indifferent, if it would think and act as befits Christians" (Pius XII, Christmas Message, 1948, in *The Challenge of Peace, §76*).

The second half of the 20th century finds similar mournful affirmation of just war theory. Despite the optimism of the Second Vatican Council the possibility of war remains a constant threat. In the documents of the Second Vatican Council (1965), *Gaudium et Spes,* (whose title is translated as a set of words—Joy and Hope—which is immediately followed by an opposite set of words—Grief and Anguish) we find these words: "As long as the danger of war persists . . . governments cannot be denied the right of lawful self-defense . . . State leaders have the duty to defend the interests of people and to conduct such grave matters with a deep sense of responsibility . . . Soldiers should look upon themselves as custodians of the security and freedom of their fellow country men; and when they carry out their duty properly, they are contributing to the maintenance of peace" (*Gaudium et Spes, §79)*.

In *Evangelium vitae,* the Great Gospel of Life, Pope John Paul II (1995) wrote: "Legitimate defense can be not only a right but a grave duty for someone responsible for another's life, the common good of the family, or of the state. Unfortunately, it happens that the need to render the aggressor incapable of causing harm sometimes involves the taking of his life. In this case the fatal outcome is attributable to the aggressor whose actions brought it about, even though he may not be morally responsible because of the lack of the use of reason" (*Evangelium vitae §55*).

The Catechism of the Catholic Church (1994) avers the following: "The evaluation of those conditions for moral legitimacy (of just war) belongs to the prudential judgment of those who have the responsibility for the common good" (2309) and "Public authorities . . . have a right and duty to impose on citizens the obligations necessary for national defense" (2310). "Legitimate defense can be not only a right but a grave duty for one who is responsible for the lives of others. The defense of the common good requires that an unjust aggressor be rendered unable to cause harm. For this reason, those who legitimately hold authority also have the right to use arms to repel aggressors against the civil community entrusted to their responsibility" (2265).

This same position was reiterated by the United States Conference of Catholic Bishops in 1993 in *The Harvest of Justice is Sown in Peace* 10 years after the pastoral on peace—The Challenge of Peace.

The history of the theory of just war continues, as does the history of war ever more violent, ever more destructive, ever more sophisticated in technology. In our time the theory that is to serve as a moral guide to permissible war and to the engaging in war is rendered this way. Just peace is the desired condition and there exists a presumption against war. The presumption against war may be overridden by injustice that disrupts the just peace. Once the peace is broken, war is permissible—*jus ad bellum* – under the conditions of *jus in bello*. The requirements for the permissibility of war—*jus ad bellum*—are the following. The war must be declared by the legitimate authority; there may be no wars declared by private citizens. There must be a just cause and among the just causes are the following: (a) defense against aggression, (b) punishment against guilt, (c) violation of rights, (d) defending the innocent, and (e) protecting those values required for decent human existence. The right intention must guide the move to war; right intention requires pursuit of stated cause, pursuit of lasting peace, and right attitude. The response of war must be proportional. Proportionality requires that war should produce more good than evil and should abate more evil, and that the waging of war be appropriate to remedy the extent of injustice. Further, war should not be an appropriate response without the prudential judgment that success in its waging is probable. Furthermore, war should be carried out in due form, which includes conformity to international law and conformity to *jus in bello*. Finally, war must be seen as a last resort; all other attempts to remedy the injustice perpetrated or imminently threatened must be attempted and exhausted.

The requirements of *jus in bello* are three. They are proportionality, discrimination, that is, direct intentional attacks on non-combatants are forbidden, and desire for peace.

To the requirement of *jus ad bellum* and *jus in bello*, a third condition has been added in the contemporary time. That condition is called *jus post bello* and it requires that once the war is brought to conclusion, the victorious party make peace possible by restoring for the defeated party the conditions that allow for the possibility for peace.

Just war theory is prefaced by the *prima facie* obligation to pursue peace . . . to continue the peace, to sustain peace, but if the peace is broken by injustice to wage war until the objective is accomplished and the possibility of peace can be restored. If we have compelling evidence that innocent people who are in no position to protect themselves will be grievously harmed unless coercive force is used to stop an aggressor, then the moral principle of love of neighbor calls us to the use of force.

What Ought We to Be Doing?

Let me return to the question I raised in the beginning: What ought we to be doing in this time between times as we wait for the end time? And let me make some recommendations.

(1) We have an obligation to teach our young people their tradition, including the just war tradition.

(2) We ought to be praying for peace—are we doing that?

(3) We ought to be praying for our president, he is the legitimate authority—can we do that?

(4) We ought to strive to be people of peace: if we cannot be at peace with each other in our institutions, if we cannot be at peace in our families, how can we expect there to be peace in the world?

(5) We ought to work for justice in order that peace prevail, justice, not materialism, justice in the sense of right order; and

(6) Finally, if mournfully, war is undertaken, we ought, at the conclusion of the war, seek justice as aggressively as we engaged in war—justice as distributive justice—for those who have endured the war.

References

Aquinas, T. (1946). *Summa Theologica.* Trans. Fathers of the English Dominican Province. New York: Benziger Brothers.

Catechism of the Catholic Church (CCC) (1994). English translation. United States Catholic Conference, Inc.—Libreria Editrice Vaticana.

John Paul II (1995). *Evangelium Vitae.* http://www.vatican.va/holy_father/john_paul_ii/encyclicals/documents/hf_jp-ii_enc_25031995_evangelium-vitae_en.html.

Mill, J. S. (1862). "The Contest in America." *Fraser's Magazine,* later published in *Dissertations and Discussions* (1868), Vol. 1, p. 26.

Pius XII (1948). *Christmas Message of Pope Pius XII: Radio Message to the World* Given December 23, 1948. Washington, DC: National Catholic Welfare Conference.

Second Vatican Council (1965). *Pastoral Constitution of the Church in the Modern World: Gaudium et Spes.* http://www.vatican.va/archive/hist_councils/ii_vatican_council/documents/vat-ii_cons_19651207_gaudium-et-spes_en.html.

Suarez, F. (1944). *De triplici virtute theoligica; de caritate,* in *Selections from Three Works of Francisco Suarez, S.J.* Oxford: Classics of International Law.

United States Conference of Catholic Bishops (1993). *The Harvest of Justice Is Sown in Peace.* Washington, DC: USCCB Publishing.

Henry George and Immigration

By JOHN H. BECK*

ABSTRACT. Henry George's opposition to free immigration may be surprising in light of his positions on other aspects of economic theory and policy. This essay reviews George's statements on immigration policy, discusses inconsistencies of these statements with his positions on free trade and Malthusian population theory, compares George's views with the neoclassical economic perspective on immigration, and suggests that implementation of George's policy of taxing land values would share the gains from immigration in a manner that might reduce opposition to open borders.

George's Views on Immigration

Henry George's views on immigration policy have received limited attention. Hansen (1969: 65) noted that George's "anti-Asian immigration policy was an exception" to his philosophy favoring freedom of opportunity, opposing monopoly, and supporting free trade. However, George's opposition to immigration was aimed specifically at immigration from Asia. Wenzer (2003, 2: xxii) notes that George's attitude toward immigrants from southern and eastern Europe did not exhibit "the virulent prejudice he turned on the Chinese."

Problems associated with Chinese immigration were an early stimulus to George's study of economics. In *The Science of Political Economy*, George (1992: 200) gave a brief account of how he was led to write *Progress and Poverty* and described his earliest writing on the topic of immigration:

> In 1869 I went East on newspaper business, returning to California in the early summer of 1870. John Russell Young was at that time managing editor of the New York Tribune, and I wrote for him an article on "The Chinese

*John H. Beck is Professor of Economics, Gonzaga University.

American Journal of Economics and Sociology, Vol. 71, No. 4 (October, 2012).

on the Pacific Coast," a question that had begun to arouse attention there, taking the side popular among the working-classes of the Coast, in opposition to the unrestricted immigration of that people.

The *New York Tribune* article voiced concerns about cultural differences similar to arguments of conservative opponents of immigration today, describing the Chinese immigrants as having low moral standards and questioning whether they could be assimilated into American culture. From an economic perspective, George's concern was that Chinese immigration would reduce wage rates. In George's analysis this effect was not simply due to downward pressure on wages from the increased supply of labor associated with any immigration; the reduction in wage rates was uniquely associated with Chinese immigration because the Chinese immigrants would accept a lower standard of living (Wenzer 2003: Vol. 1, 161).

> [T]heir standard of comfort is very much lower than that of our own people – very much lower than that of any European immigrants who come among us. This fact enables them to underbid all competitors in the labor market. . . . [T]hus in every case in which Chinese comes into fair competition with white labor, the whites must either retire from the field or come down to the Chinese standard of living.

George wrote 39 more articles on Chinese immigration published in California newspapers in 1869 and 1870 including one article in the *Oakland Daily Transcript* of November 20, 1869, in which he quoted a letter from John Stuart Mill agreeing with George's conclusion that a large Chinese immigration would reduce wages. However, Mill was more optimistic than George about the long-run potential for education to raise the Chinese to the level of Americans (Wenzer 2003: Vol. 1, 173–177).

George's continued opposition to Chinese immigration is also found in a lecture on "The Study of Political Economy" delivered to students at the University of California in 1877 and published in *The Popular Science Monthly* in 1880:

> In connection with the discussion of Chinese immigration, you have, doubtless, over and over again heard it contended that cheap labor, which would reduce the cost of production, is precisely equivalent to labor-saving machinery, and, as machinery operates to increase wealth, so would cheap labor. This conclusion is jumped at from the fact that cheap labor and

labor-saving machinery similarly reduce the cost of production to the manufacturer. But, if, instead of jumping at this conclusion, we analyze the manner in which the reduction of cost is produced in each case, we shall see the fallacy. Labor-saving machinery reduces cost by increasing the productive power of labor; a reduction of wages reduces cost by reducing the share of the product which falls to the laborer. To the employer the effect may be the same; but, to the community, which includes both employers and employed, the effect is very different. In the one case there is increase in the general wealth; in the other there is merely a change in distribution – whatever one class gains another class necessarily losing. Hence the effect of cheap labor is necessarily very different from that of improved machinery.

This distinction between the effects of labor-saving machinery and the effects of low-wage immigrant labor is also found in George's 1869 article in the *New York Tribune* (Wenzer 2003: Vol. 1, 166).

In his later writings and speeches, George took a much more favorable view of European immigration than he had of immigration from Asia. In response to an anti-immigration article by Terence Powderly, a leader of the Knights of Labor and sometime ally of George, George argued that Americans should welcome immigrants from southern and central Europe (Powderly 1888; Barker 1991: 515; Wenzer 1997: 218–219). In a series of articles on "Labor in Pennsylvania" in *The North American Review*, George argued that Hungarian immigrants, who had been feared as having a depressing effect on wages similar to the Chinese, in fact had shown themselves to be militant labor activists in the successful Connesville coal strike in 1886 (Wenzer 2003: Vol. 2, 129–133).

In "The Democratic Principle: Address of Henry George Before the Crescent Club Democratic Society of Baltimore" (*The Standard*, Sept. 14, 1889), George spoke with regret at the hostile reception accorded European immigrants at the time (Wenzer 1997: 117):

> The gulf stream of European immigration still flows on, for social discontent is rife in Europe, and the conditions that are increasing social pressure here are being felt all over the civilized world. But what is most significant is the change in feeling toward this immigration. . . . [T]he European immigrant is met when he lands by officials, who, if he brings nothing but the power for labor, send him back again. Chronic paupers, criminals, the weak in mind and body are not desirable elements, but [there was a time] when we boasted that this was the country of countries for any one willing to work, and when we welcomed the man who brought nothing but a pair of willing hands as

an addition to national strength, a new recruit for the great army that was to overrun the continent and make the wilderness bloom. But now if the immigrant shows, or, rather if it can be shown, that he has made arrangements to go to work, and has secured employment before coming here, then is he not merely sent back, but the American who made the bargain with him is liable to fine or imprisonment. The trustees of a New York church are even now under sentence of the law for having imported a contract laborer in the shape of an Episcopal minister. It is only one step further to prohibit all immigration of men likely to work for their living. And this is the logical outcome of the system we have adopted. By elaborate laws we strive to keep goods out of the country in order, we have been told, to give Americans more work to do. It is but logical, then, to keep out workmen in order that there shall be fewer to do it.

George attributed the negative effects of immigration to the monopoly power of privately owned land and argued that if his reforms of free trade and land value taxation were implemented the negative effects of immigration would be eliminated. Even with regard to immigration from Asia, George suggested that his reforms would eliminate the negative effects. At a meeting of the Anti-Poverty Society in 1887, in response to a question about Chinese immigration, George answered (Wenzer 2003: Vol. 2, 211–212):

> [U]nder the present condition of things, where competition of men deprived of all opportunity to earn a living for themselves fixes the rate of wages, in my opinion we cannot be too careful to keep out any large immigration from China. But if we were to base our social conditions upon principles of justice, securing to all men their natural rights, then I believe that we would have no need for any restrictions.

Many followers of Henry George have expressed more favorable views of immigration. Albert Jay Nock (1939: 91–92) contrasted George's negative picture of the moral character of Chinese immigrants with the more favorable description in Mark Twain's *Roughing It* and concluded that Twain's view was "the more nearly accurate." Jack Schwartzman (1998) compared the view of George to that of Emma Lazarus, a proponent of free immigration who was herself favorably impressed by *Progress and Poverty*. Schwartzman noted George's opposition to Chinese immigration despite his rejection of Malthusian population theory, which is often used to justify anti-immigration policies.

George's Critique of Malthus's Theory of Population

George's opposition to Chinese immigration was not based on a belief that population growth in general led to reduced *per capita* income. Indeed, he devoted all of Book II of *Progress and Poverty* (George 1942: 75–125) to a critique of the Malthusian theory.

> [E]ven if the increase of population does reduce the power of the natural factor of wealth, by compelling a resort to poorer soils, etc., it yet so vastly increases the power of the human factor as more than to compensate. Twenty men working together will, where nature is niggardly, produce more than twenty times the wealth that one man can produce where nature is most bountiful. The denser the population the more minute becomes the subdivision of labor, the greater the economies of production and distribution, and, hence, the very reverse of the Malthusian doctrine is true; and, within the limits in which we have reason to suppose increase would still go on, in any given state of civilization a greater number of people can produce a larger proportionate amount of wealth, and more fully supply their wants, than can a smaller number.

Whitaker (1997, 2001) expresses George's theory in the terminology of modern economics as diminishing returns offset by scale economies of increased specialization of labor and agglomeration economies. According to Whitaker's (1997: 1899) description of George's view:

> Population growth has three distinct effects. (i) It increases the demand for land, requiring its more extensive and intensive utilization, thus running into diminishing returns. (ii) It increases the efficiency of labor by permitting more specialization and a more complex division of labor, thus increasing the output of any worker on each piece of land. (iii) It leads to increased agglomeration of population and industry, greatly raising the productive advantage of the selected pieces of land which are the sites of such agglomeration by bringing out in land special capabilities otherwise latent, and by attaching special capabilities to particular lands. Pecuniary benefit accrues to the owners of such land and not to the workers employed on it. The last two effects are social or externality effects not observed in the private decisions of individual economic actors. The competitive wage for labor is simply the extra product coming from the first effect—the average product of labor at the no-rent margin—the addition of any one worker exerting only a negligible and uncompensated influence through the last two effects. The addition of these makes it at least possible for output per head to rise while population grows and the real wage rate falls.

George's Contrasting Views on Free Trade and Immigration

Libertarian writers have often linked support for free immigration with arguments for free trade. For example, David Friedman (1996: 207–208) argues as follows:

> One way of looking at immigration restrictions is as barriers to trade; they prevent an American consumer from buying the labor of a Mexican worker by preventing the worker from coming to where the labor is wanted. The comparative advantage arguments . . . apply here as well. The abolition of immigration restrictions would produce a net benefit for present Americans, although some would be worse off—just as the abolition of tariffs would produce a net benefit for Americans, although American autoworkers (and GM stockholders) might be injured.

Based on the above reasoning, one might expect that an advocate of free trade such as Henry George would also oppose restrictions on immigration. However, George's opposition to Chinese immigration was based, at least in part, on the belief that immigration would reduce domestic wages but that the importation of goods would not. He alluded to the different effects of imports and immigration in his 1877 lecture on "The Study of Political Economy" (George 1999: 103–104), and elaborated on this point in *Protection or Free Trade* (George 1980: 201–202):

> The incoming of the products of cheap labor is a very different thing from the incoming of cheap labor. The effect of the one is upon the production of wealth, increasing the aggregate amount to be distributed; the effect of the other is upon the distribution of wealth, decreasing the proportion which goes to the working-classes. We might permit the free importation of Chinese commodities without in the slightest degree affecting wages; but, under our present conditions, the free immigration of Chinese laborers would lessen wages.

Despite George's claim in the above passage that trade has no effect on wages, elsewhere in *Protection or Free Trade* he recognizes that trade policy may increase the wages of some workers relative to the wages of others (George 1980: 209):

> When a duty, by increasing the demand for a certain domestic production, suddenly increases the demand for a certain kind of skilled labor, the wages of such labor may be temporarily increased, to an extent and for a time determined by the difficulties of obtaining skilled laborers from other

countries or of the acquirement by new laborers of the needed skill. But in any industry it is only the few workmen of peculiar skill who can thus be affected, and even when by these few such an advantage is gained, it can be maintained only by trades-unions that limit entrance to the craft.

Thomas Martin (1989: 498) has argued that "Henry George anticipated key elements of the modern theory concerning the impact of trade on relative factor prices." According to Martin (1989: 494):

[T]he Stolper-Samuelson theory predicts that in each country free trade will increase the prices of the abundant factors of production relative to the prices of the scarce factors. Protect some industries against import competition through tariffs or quotas, and a nation's relatively scarce, relatively expensive factors of production will benefit. In addition to consumers, those who pay the costs of "protection" are owners and providers of the relatively abundant, relatively inexpensive factors of production. . . . Henry George's model assumed that the United States had a relatively scarce endowment of capital in the 1880s and 1890s relative to England, and was relatively abundantly endowed with land vis-a-vis labor when compared to the smaller, crowded England. Furthermore, the protected industries in the United States were capital intensive, not labor intensive. Labor was not gaining by protection.

Contrary to George's distinction between the effects of international trade and immigration, neoclassical economic theory concludes that both trade and immigration may affect wages. In particular, neoclassical economists have attributed part of the decline in real wages of unskilled labor in the United States during the 1980s to imports and immigration. Imports competed with domestic goods produced by unskilled workers, reducing the demand for unskilled labor. At the same time immigration that included a disproportionate share of unskilled workers increased the supply of unskilled labor. Borjas (1994: 1699, 1995a: 5–7) cites estimates that immigration explains about one-third of the decline in the relative wage of high school dropouts between 1980 and 1988, and that increased foreign trade between 1976 and 1990 accounted for about one-fourth of the increase in wage inequality during that period. Although Borjas, Freeman and Katz (1996: 250) conclude that immigration was the dominant cause of the decline in wages of high school dropouts, they found that imports and immigration had effects of similar size on the relative wages of high school compared to college equivalents. On the other hand, based on time-series analysis Card (2005: F321) finds that "the wages of native dropouts . . . relative to native high school graduates have remained nearly constant since 1980, despite pressures from immigrant inflows that have increased the relative supply of dropout labour."

Land Value Taxation and Immigration

How would the implementation of Henry George's proposal for taxing land value affect the distribution of the costs and benefits of immigration?

In Book IX of *Progress and Poverty* George noted many beneficial effects of implementing a single tax on land values to replace other taxes that fall directly and indirectly on the productive activities of labor and capital. George (1942: 369) anticipated that these tax revenues "being applied to public purposes, would be equally distributed in public benefits." The potential scope of these public expenditures would expand because George (1942: 363) thought that "the increasing complexity of life makes it desirable" for society to assume more functions. Government might use these revenues to provide schools and universities, telegraph, railroad, and other utilities (George 1942: 382–383).

George (1942: 191) understood that increased population—from immigration or other sources—increases land rents. The implication for immigration policy is that, if the single tax on land values were implemented and these revenues used in a manner to benefit all of society, the native-born workers would share in the economic gains from immigration even if the growth of the labor force by immigration put downward pressure on wages.

However, according to George the tax on land values would alleviate the downward pressure on wages. For George the greatest benefit of taxing land rents was not the redistribution of those rents by using those rents to finance increased government spending or reductions in the burden of other taxes. The greatest benefit of taxing land rents would be the increased demand for labor. In a dialogue with David Dudley Field published in the *North American Review* in 1885, George (1999: 165) said: "The great benefit would not be in the appropriation to public use of the unearned revenues now going to individuals, but in the opening of opportunities to labour, and the stimulus that would be given to improvement and production by the throwing open of unused land and the removal of taxation that now weighs down productive powers." In *Progress and Poverty* George (1942: 370) wrote:

> To take rent in taxation for public purposes, which virtually abolishes private ownership in land, would be to destroy the tendency to an absolute decrease in wages and interest, by destroying the speculative monopolization of land and the speculative increase in rent. It would be very largely to increase wages and interest, by throwing open natural opportunities now monopolized and reducing the price of land.

In George's view, it is the speculative withholding of land from productive use and workers' lack of access to this land that is the source of the downward pressure on wages. In Book III of *Progress and Poverty* George (1942: 178) wrote: "Where natural opportunities are all monopolized, wages may be forced by the competition among laborers to the minimum at which laborers will consent to reproduce."

Similarly, in *Social Problems* George (1930: 208) argued that under a system of land-value taxation taking nearly all of the land rent, "no one could afford to hold land he was not using, and land not in use would be thrown open to those who wished to use it, at once relieving the labor market and giving an enormous stimulus to production and improvement, while land in use would be paid for according to its value, irrespective of the improvements the user might make." George (1930: 210) concluded:

> With the natural opportunities of employment thrown open to all, the spectacle of willing men seeking vainly for employment could not be witnessed; there could be no surplus of unemployed labor to beget that cutthroat competition of laborers for employment which crowds wages down to the cost of merely living. Instead of the one-sided competition of workmen to find employment, employers would compete with each other to obtain workmen.

The implication for immigration policy is that, with the implementation of the tax on land values, native-born workers would have nothing to fear from immigration putting downward pressure on wages. Thus in "The Condition of Labor: An Open Letter to Pope Leo

XIII" George (1982: 35) attributed anti-immigrant feelings to "the artificial scarcity that results from private property in land":

> If you will come to the United States, you will find in a land wide enough and rich enough to support in comfort the whole population of Europe, the growth of a sentiment that looks with evil eye on immigration, because the artificial scarcity that results from private property in land makes it seem as if there is not room enough and work enough for those already here.

Henry George did not just advocate land-value taxation in the United States; he sought to spread this policy throughout the world. What would be the effects on international immigration of the adoption of land-value taxation in countries throughout the world?

Steiner (1992: 89–90) considers the implications of a global tax appropriating all of the rent derived from natural resources and redistributing this revenue in equal amounts to all persons in the world and concludes:

> Perhaps its most obvious probable impact would be to decrease the demand for entry into wealthier societies. Since average per capita land values in such societies are more likely to be higher than in poorer societies, the global application of the single tax should result in an on-balance redistribution of wealth from the former to the latter. And presumably this would greatly tend to reduce a principal motivation for that aforesaid demand.

Actually, Steiner's conclusion that this policy would reduce international migration is not so obvious. The equal redistribution of global land tax revenues would reduce *income* differences across countries, not *wage* differences. The distribution financed by the tax on land values would be independent of where a person lived, whereas wage rates would still depend on location. Therefore, under this policy people would still have an incentive to migrate from low-wage countries in order to increase their earnings from labor. However, if retaining ties to a person's culture and extended family are normal goods, the increase in income from this policy might reduce international migration despite wage differences. However, as Bhagwati (1991: 349) notes, with imperfect capital markets, people with low incomes may not be able to afford the costs of migration. In such cases, an increase in their incomes might cause more of them to migrate.

Although he sought to spread land-value taxation throughout the world, George (1999: 199) spoke of the effect of this policy that "everyone would be equally interested in the land of his *native* country" (emphasis added). This seemed to be an inconsistency in the eyes of George's biographer Charles Albro Barker (1991: 302) who wrote:

> George failed to notice the awkwardness of saying that the land belongs to all the Creator's children, without also recognizing that this argues for the *internationalization* rather than the *nationalization* of land . . . the author who explored so many lines of ethical logic ought to have noticed that only a world organization with power to tax, or at least to distribute the proceeds of land-value taxation, would fit well his ideal scheme.

Global land-value taxation with the revenues shared equally by all persons in the world is such a remote possibility that it will not be discussed further here. Therefore, let us turn our attention to the implications of the adoption of land-value taxation by local or national governments throughout the world, with the revenues disbursed within each nation. From George's perspective, the most important effect on international migration would be that, by alleviating the downward pressure on wages, land-value taxation would reduce the incentive to emigrate from one's home country to find better economic opportunities elsewhere. Thus, in "A Response to 'Mr. Powderly on Immigration,' " George envisioned the effect of land-value taxation replacing tariffs and taxes on production in reducing Americans' hostility to immigrants but also resulting in less motivation for immigrants to leave their home countries when these nations followed the American example (Wenzer 1997: 218–219):

> [I]nstead of looking with jealous, hateful eyes at our kindred from beyond the sea who seek our shores, the cry would go up, "Come over and help us! . . ." All Europe would come? What if they did? We would have room for them, and work for them, and plenty for them. But nothing of the kind would happen. The spectacle of such a republic across the western sea . . . would arouse such a moral force that thrones would totter and fall, and standing armies would disappear, and a United States of Europe, before a generation had passed away, would clasp hands with a United States of America.

The Neoclassical Perspective on Immigration Policy

Modern neoclassical economic theory (Sykes 1995: 165–166) considers the distributional and efficiency effects of international migration for a variety of cases. For example, consider a simple "Heckscher-Ohlin" model with two goods, two factors of production (labor and "capital"), differing factor endowments across countries, and constant-returns-to-scale production functions. Under these assumptions, trade between countries would cause the real wage to rise in the labor-abundant country and the price of the scarce factor in each country to fall according to the Stolper-Samuelson theorem. If there were no international trade but international migration were possible, immigration into the country where labor was relatively scarce would have an effect similar to the opening of international trade. The real wage would fall in the country where labor was scarce and would rise in the labor-abundant country; the price of the other factor of production would change in the opposite direction in each country. In the country from which labor emigrated, the total income to the owners of the other factor falls by more than the increase in earnings of the workers remaining there. In the country to which labor immigrates, the total income to the other factor increases by more than the fall in earnings. Of course, the immigrants gain, and global efficiency is enhanced due to the immigrants locating where the gains from trade are greatest. If international trade occurs along with migration, the analysis is more complex and the distributional effects of migration will be different due to changes in the terms of trade (Sykes 1995: 167).

The complication that is most relevant to the concerns of this essay is the analysis for the case with more than two factors of production. For example, suppose there are four factors of production—unskilled labor, skilled labor, capital, and land—with immigrants being perfect substitutes for native unskilled labor. Then in a closed economy immigration will lower the wage of native unskilled labor, raise the prices of complementary factors of production, and have an ambiguous effect on the prices of factors that are imperfect substitutes (Friedberg and Hunt 1995: 28). Interestingly, Borjas (1995b: 16 n. 12) suggests, "it seems plausible that unskilled workers and some fixed factors of production (such as land) were complements in the U.S. economy at the end of the nineteenth century."

Although Sykes (1995: 159) states that simple models of migration "suggest that migration is a net benefit to the world as a whole and to the country of immigration," he identifies some circumstances in which inefficient migration may occur. One such circumstance is where trade barriers have distorted factor prices in the two countries, and elimination of the trade barriers would be more efficient than the second-best policy of allowing immigration (Sykes 1995: 163). The most likely sources of inefficient migration in Sykes' (1995: 168–175) view are nonpecuniary externalities, including situations in which immigrants impose greater costs on governments in the host country than they contribute in taxes. Yuengert (2003: 37–39) reviews several studies of this topic and concludes that immigrants have a negative fiscal impact on state and local governments in areas with high concentrations of immigrants but have a positive effect on federal government finances.

If international migration is efficient, there is some way to share the gains from migration with those who would be harmed by it such that all are made better off than they would be if immigration were prohibited. Freeman (2006: 165) suggests:

> [B]ecause most of the gains from immigration accrue to the immigrants rather than to the residents of destination countries . . . , there is little incentive for destination countries to ease immigration restrictions. The only way I can think of to increase the receptivity of destination countries to accept more immigrants would be redistribute the benefits of immigration so that a greater share of the benefits flows to natives and a lower share of the benefits to immigrants. The "radical economic" policy here would be to use the price system to equilibrate the market for immigrants rather than to ration entry. An immigrant-receiving country could charge admission fees or auction immigration visas or place special taxes on immigrants, and use those funds to redistribute the gains from immigration to existing citizens.

Although Freeman's proposal appeals to some efficiency-minded economists, Trebilcock (1995: 224) voices concerns that this policy violates norms of distributive justice by limiting opportunities for immigration to those with the ability to pay.

Using revenues from land-value taxation to compensate those harmed by immigration may be more ethically appealing. Neoclassical theory recognizes that immigration benefits the owners of complementary factors of production—including land as well as capital and possibly some types of native labor. The potential for land-value taxation to raise revenues to capture the gains from immigration and compensate the losers depends, first, on the size of these gains and, second, on how much of these gains accrue to landowners.

Hamilton and Whalley (1984) estimated the effects of eliminating immigration restrictions based on the assumption that international migration would then occur until all differences in the marginal product of labor across regions are eliminated. Using 1977 data, they concluded that unrestricted international migration would potentially result in large efficiency gains increasing worldwide output and very substantial reductions in inequality in the worldwide distribution of income. Under some assumptions, they calculate that the efficiency gains could exceed the value of the existing worldwide output, although various adjustments to their calculations result in smaller but still large gains. Moses and Letnes (2004), using 1998 data and a modified version of Hamilton and Whalley's model, found similar results but noted that increased global inequality in 1998 resulted in larger potential gains from labor mobility. Bhagwati (1991: 353–355) and Philip Martin (2004: 445) point out that several of the assumptions in Hamilton and Whalley's calculations—such as no capital mobility and identical elasticities of substitution in production functions among countries—lead to exaggerated estimates of the effects of relaxing immigration restrictions.

In the neoclassical analysis the size of the gain to complementary factors depends on the amount of loss to native-born labor that is a substitute for immigrant labor; if there is no decline in wages of native-born substitutes for immigrants, there is no gain to complementary factors of production. Empirical studies by neoclassical economists have generally not found large reductions in wages of native-born workers as a result of immigration, although there are substantial differences in these estimates. If neoclassical economists have been unable to provide good estimates of the aggregate gains to complementary factors from immigration, they certainly cannot provide much empirical information as to the size of the gain to just one of those complementary factors, land.

From a theoretical perspective, neoclassical economists do offer some insight into how the gains from immigration would be shared by complementary factors of production. In neoclassical theory, *immobile* complementary factors of production gain from immigration. Land is certainly immobile, and people's family and cultural ties limit labor mobility. If capital was perfectly mobile between countries, immigration would be accompanied by capital inflows until the rate of return on capital in the host country was equal to the rate of return on the world market. This theoretical perspective would seem to support the view that a large share of the gains from immigration would go to increased land rents. However, public-choice analyses of immigration policies such as Thum (2004: 426, 440 n. 4) have argued that owners of capital do capture some of the gains from immigration because capital is not perfectly mobile.

Hatton and Williamson's (2005: 101–125) empirical study of the effects of international trade and migration during the late nineteenth century is especially relevant to the Georgist perspective because they attempt to estimate the impact of immigration on land rents. Although there is no rent data for land of comparable quality, they argue that changes in land prices will be similar to changes in land rents. Hatton and Williamson (2005: 118) found:

> . . . from 1870 to 1913. In the New World, the wage-rent ratio plunged. By 1913, the Australian ratio had fallen to one quarter of its 1870 level, and the U.S. ratio had fallen to less than half of its 1870 level. In Europe, the ratio boomed: the British ratio in 1910 had increased by a factor of 2.7 over its 1870 level, while the Irish ratio had increased even more, by a factor of 5.5.

Measuring income inequality by the ratio of the unskilled wage to GDP per worker hour, Hatton and Williamson (2005: 120–121) also found that:

> . . . between 1870 and 1913, inequality rose dramatically in rich, land-abundant, labor-scarce New World countries like Australia and the United States; inequality fell dramatically in poor, land-scarce, labor-abundant, newly industrializing countries like Norway, Sweden, Denmark, and Italy; inequality was more stable in European industrial economies like Belgium, France, Germany, the Netherlands, and the United Kingdom.

Hatton and Williamson (2005: 119) conclude:

> While real wages grew everywhere before 1913, they grew faster in labor-abundant Europe compared with the labor-scarce frontier overseas. Rents surged in the land-abundant New World and plunged in land-scarce, free trading Britain, while remaining relatively stable on the European Continent, which either protected its agriculture or made profound structural changes in farming practice. And the wage-rent ratio increased dramatically in Europe, especially in free-trading countries, while declining equally dramatically in the frontier economies overseas.

Although the changes in factor prices during this period result from the combined effects of international trade and migration, based on a regression estimating the separate effect of trade and migration on income inequality, Hatton and Williamson (2005: 123) conclude:

> Overall, we read this evidence as strong support for the impact of mass migration on distribution trends: the effects were great everywhere in the Atlantic economy where the migrations were large. The evidence offers weak support, however, for the impact of trade on distribution trends, except around the European periphery, where trade lowered inequality.

Although Georgists may be favorably impressed by the stress on the role of land rents in this analysis of the late nineteenth century, Hatton and Williamson (2005: 119), in justifying their approach also qualify its applicability to later periods, arguing that "land and labor were the dominant factors of production a century ago, not skills and capital as is true today." However, in contrast to neoclassical economists' tendency to minimize the role of land rent in the modern economy, Gaffney (2009) argues that there are downward biases in estimates of narrowly defined land rent based on property assessments of land values, IRS measures of rental income, and National Income and Product Accounts measures of rental income. Furthermore, a broader conception of "land" rent would include rents from all uses of natural resources and charges for pollution of the environment. Thus, from a Georgist perspective, "land" rents represent a larger share of national income in a modern economy than suggested by conventional estimates.

The Neoclassical Perspective on Land-Value Taxation

Although neoclassical economists might admit the potential for land-value taxation to raise revenues that could be redistributed to those harmed by immigration, perhaps their biggest disagreement with Georgists would be with the propositions that land speculation withholds land from productive uses and creates downward pressure on wages and that land-value taxation would alleviate this problem. As Hebert (2003: 71–73) has noted, Alfred Marshall agreed that a tax on land values avoided the disincentives to production associated with other taxes and that workers could gain from the redistribution of these tax revenues. But Marshall questioned George's claims that land speculation caused the business cycle and that land-value taxation would provide a great stimulus to production by eliminating this speculation.

Tideman (1999) confirms the neoclassical conclusion that, in a world with perfect markets with land rent appropriately defined, land-value taxation is neutral; taxing land values neither encourages nor discourages earlier development of land. However, in the real world markets are not perfect. In particular, people may have different beliefs about the future and incomplete markets make it impossible to insure against some of the risks associated with the unknown future. Based on a mathematical analysis of this situation, Tideman (1999: 131) concludes:

> In a world with incomplete futures markets for land, the distribution of land among persons with different beliefs about whether it is efficient to develop land now or hold it idle varies with the level of taxes on land. Not taxing land creates a "social winner's curse"—an artificial scarcity of land since land will be worth the most to those who have the most extreme beliefs about future speculative gains from land.

In this situation Henry George was correct; taxing land values will encourage earlier development on land that speculators would have withheld from productive activity.

Tideman's analysis focuses on the microeconomic effects of land-value taxation on speculation and economic development. What about the macroeconomic effects of land-value taxation? Foldvary (1997: 531) has incorporated a Georgist emphasis on the role of land speculation into Austrian business cycle theory: "The geo-economic remedy for the cycle is the public collection of rent (PCR), also known as land-value taxation (LVT). When future rents are collected, the profit is taken away from real-estate speculation."

Foldvary (1997: 525) acknowledges that this theory "focuses only on the approximately 18-year major cycle coinciding with the major depressions. It is not a universal explanation of all cycles." However, modern, mainstream neoclassical economics has not acknowledged even this limited role for land-value taxation in combating the business cycle. From the neoclassical perspective, there would be no reason to expect the taxation of land to alleviate the downward pressure on wages resulting from immigration.

Free Trade and International Migration

As noted above, Sykes (1995: 163) has observed that elimination of trade barriers may be more efficient than allowing immigration. There would be no disagreement between Henry George and most neoclassical economists on the desirability of free-trade policies. The adoption of such policies by the developed countries would reduce the economic disparities between nations that give rise to international migration. In particular, Philip Martin (2004: 449) notes:

> There is a second dimension to increasing economic differences that adds to international migration pressures. . . . Low farm incomes in developing countries encourage rural-urban migration as well as international migration, in part because trade barriers for farm products maintain a demand for migrants in more developed countries while reducing farm prices and farm employment in developing countries.

Although free trade will reduce international migration in the long run, Martin (2004: 464, 469–470) also notes that reduced trade barriers in developing countries may cause a "migration hump," a temporary increase in emigration of displaced workers from industries that were previously protected in these countries.

The Political Economy of Immigration and Land-Value Taxation

As noted above, international migration generally enhances worldwide efficiency by allowing human resources to move to the location where their productivity is greatest. How these economic gains are distributed is critical to winning political support for public policies allowing this movement. Foreman-Peck (1992: 361) describes the circumstances in which this political support will occur:

If all land and capital were distributed equally and the government was elected by universal adult suffrage, then the objective function would depend only upon national factor endowments. A labour-abundant country in these circumstances would place the greatest weight upon wages, whereas electors in a land-abundant country under the same conditions would favour emphasizing rents. The more common historical experience is that the bulk of land and capital is owned by a few. Under a democratic franchise the objective function then only includes wages, regardless of national endowments, because the majority have no income from land or from capital.

Foreman-Peck (1992: 367) contrasts British attitudes toward immigration between 1815 and 1914 with French policy during that period: "the French willingness to absorb migrants may be related to the more equal distribution of land, thanks to the Revolution, and a low natural rate of population increase, further retarded by the impact of the Franco-Prussian War."

This political economy perspective reveals the complementarity between land-value taxation and an open immigration policy. Land-value taxation effectively achieves an "equal distribution of land" by using land rents to finance public goods. In doing so, the economic gains from immigration will be shared by the whole population, broadening political support for an open immigration policy.

Yuengert (2003: 15–16, 2000: 90) has noted some undesirable effects of international migration from the perspective of Catholic social teaching. By weakening ties to family and culture, international migration may cause a decline in morals of young migrants, and emigration is a regrettable loss of a person who might have contributed to the common good in his home country. Therefore, policies that reduce the economic disparities that are an impetus to international migration are desirable.

The policies advocated by Henry George could improve the poor economic conditions in developing countries that compel immigrants to move to the United States and western Europe. The implementation of land-value taxation in developing countries could foster economic growth and reduce inequality of incomes in those countries. Henry George's free-trade policy, if followed by the developed countries, would also reduce the economic disparities between nations that give rise to international migration. However, in cases in which high transportation costs discourage trade, international migration may be the best means of achieving an efficient allocation of resources as well as reducing income disparities among nations. In such cases, Henry George's policy of land-value taxation would allow the gains from migration to be shared by all citizens of the host country.

References

Barker, C. A. (1991). *Henry George*. New York: Robert Schalkenbach Foundation.

Bhagwati, J. (1991). *Political Economy and International Economics*, ed. D.A. Irwin. Cambridge, MA: MIT Press.

Borjas, G. J. (1994). "The Economics of Immigration." *Journal of Economic Literature* 32 (December): 1667–1717.

———. (1995a). "The Internationalization of the U.S. Labor Market and the Wage Structure." *Federal Reserve Bank of New York Economic Policy Review* 1 (January): 3–8.

———. (1995b). "The Economic Benefits from Immigration." *Journal of Economic Perspectives* 9 (Spring): 3–22.

Borjas, G. J., R. B. Freeman, and L. F. Katz. (1996). "Searching for the Effect of Immigration on the Labor Market." *American Economic Review* 86 (May): 246–251.

Card, D. (2005. "Is the New Immigration Really So Bad?" *Economic Journal* 115 (November): F300–F323.

Foldvary, F. E. (1997). "The Business Cycle: A Georgist-Austrian Synthesis." *American Journal of Economics and Sociology* 56 (October): 521–541.

Foreman-Peck, J. (1992). "A Political Economy of International Migration, 1815–1914." *Manchester School of Economic and Social Studies* 60 (December): 359–376.

Freeman, R. B. (2006). "People Flows in Globalization." *Journal of Economic Perspectives* 20 (Spring): 145–170.

Friedberg, R. M., and J. Hunt. (1995). "The Impact of Immigrants on Host Country Wages, Employment and Growth." *Journal of Economic Perspectives* 9 (Spring): 23–44.

Friedman, D. (1996). *Hidden Order*. New York: HarperCollins.

Gaffney, M. (2009). "The Hidden Taxable Capacity of Land: Enough and to Spare." *International Journal of Social Economics* 36: 328–411.

George, H. (1930). *Social Problems*. Garden City, NY: Doubleday, Doran & Company.

———. (1942). *Progress and Poverty: An Inquiry into the Cause of Industrial Depressions and of Increase of Want with Increase of Wealth*. 4th ed. New York: Walter J. Black.

——. (1980). *Protection or Free Trade: An Examination of the Tariff Question, with Special Regard to the Interests of Labor.* New York: Robert Schalkenbach Foundation.

——. (1982). "The Condition of Labor: An Open Letter to Pope Leo XIII." In *The Land Question and Related Writings.* New York: Robert Schalkenbach Foundation.

——. (1992). *The Science of Political Economy.* New York: Robert Schalkenbach Foundation.

——. (1999). *Our Land and Land Policy: Speeches, Lectures and Miscellaneous Writings.* Ed. K. C. Wenzer. East Lansing: Michigan State University Press.

Hamilton, B., and J. Whalley. (1984). "Efficiency and Distributional Implications of Global Restrictions on Labour Mobility." *Journal of Development Economics* 14 (January/February): 61–75.

Hansen, R. R. (1969). "Henry George: Economics or Theology?" In *Property Taxation USA.* Ed. R. W. Lindholm, pp. 65–76. Madison: University of Wisconsin Press.

Hatton, T. J., and J. G. Williamson. (2005). *Global Migration and the World Economy: Two Centuries of Policy and Performance.* Cambridge, MA: MIT Press.

Hebert, R. F. (2003). "Marshall: A Professional Economist Guards the Purity of His Discipline." In *Critics of Henry George.* Ed. R. V. Andelson, vol. 1, pp. 61–82. Malden, MA: Blackwell Publishing.

Martin, P. (2004). "Migration." In *Global Crises, Global Solutions.* Ed. B. Lomborg, pp. 443–477. Cambridge, UK: Cambridge University Press.

Martin, T. L. (1989). "Protection or Free Trade: An Analysis of the Ideas of Henry George on International Commerce and Wages." *American Journal of Economics and Sociology* 48 (October): 489–501.

Moses, J. W., and B. Letnes. (2004). "The Economic Costs to International Labor Restrictions: Revisiting the Empirical Discussion." *World Development* 32: 1609–1626.

Nock, A. J. (1939). *Henry George.* New York: William Morrow & Company.

Powderly, T. V. (1888). "General Master Workman Powderly on Immigration." *Standard* August 18.

Schwartzman, J. (1998). *Henry George and Emma Lazarus: Comparative Views.* New York: Robert Schalkenbach Foundation.

Steiner, H. (1992). "Libertarianism and the Transnational Migration of People." In *Free Movement.* Eds. B. Barry and R. E. Goodin, pp. 87–94. University Park, PA: Pennsylvania State University Press.

Sykes, A. O. (1995). "The Welfare Economics of Immigration Law: A Theoretical Survey with an Analysis of U.S. Policy." In *Justice in Immigration.* Ed. W. F. Schwartz, pp. 158–200. Cambridge, UK: Cambridge University Press.

Thum, M. (2004). "Controlling Migration in an Open Labor Market." *Public Choice* 119 (June): 425–443.

Tideman, T. N. (1999). "Taxing Land is Better than Neutral: Land Taxes, Land Speculation, and the Timing of Development." In *Land-Value Taxation*. Ed. K. C. Wenzer, pp. 109–133. Armonk, NY: M. E. Sharpe.

Trebilcock, M. J. (1995). "The Case for a Liberal Immigration Policy." In *Justice in Immigration*. Ed. W. F. Schwartz, pp. 219–246. Cambridge, UK: Cambridge University Press.

Wenzer, K. C., ed. (1997). *An Anthology of Henry George's Thought*, Vol. 1 *The Henry George Centennial Trilogy*. Rochester, NY: University of Rochester Press.

——. (2003). *Henry George: Collected Journalistic Writings*, 4 vols. Armonk, NY: M.E. Sharpe.

Whitaker, J. K. (1997). "Enemies or Allies? Henry George and Francis Amasa Walker One Century Later." *Journal of Economic Literature* 35 (December): 1891–1915.

——. (2001). "Henry George and Classical Growth Theory: A Significant Contribution to Modeling Scale Economies." *American Journal of Economics and Sociology* 60 (January): 11–24.

Yuengert, A. M. (2000). "Catholic Social Teaching on the Economics of Immigration." *Journal of Markets & Morality* 3 (Spring): 88–99.

——. (2003). *Inhabiting the Land: The Case for the Right to Migrate*. Grand Rapids, MI: Acton Institute.

A Little Common Sense: The Ethics of Immigration in Catholic Social Teaching

By William R. O'Neill, S.J.*

ABSTRACT. Modern Catholic social teaching recurs to the idiom of human dignity and human rights. Our moral entitlement to *equal* respect or consideration, in concert with the ethical ideal of the common good, moreover, justifies *preferential* treatment for those whose basic rights are most imperiled. Thus states are morally bound to respect and promote the basic human rights of both citizen and resident alien, especially the most vulnerable—and of these, in particular, women and children. Indeed, the duty to protect grounds the subsidiary duty to rescue, for example, through diplomatic initiatives, sanctions, and *in extremis*, humanitarian intervention in the case of genocide or mass atrocity. Disciples thus see and have compassion, even as compassion becomes a way of seeing. Compassion, then, not only guides them in the fitting application of universal, essential norms, for example, the rights of migrants, but gives rise to existential (personal and ecclesial) imperatives as they come to the aid of wounded humanity.

Introduction

In Robert Bolt's (1990: 19) play, *A Man for All Seasons*, the aging Cardinal Wolsey admonishes Sir Thomas More: "You're a constant regret to me, Thomas. If you could just see the facts flat on, without that horrible moral squint; with just a little common sense, you could have been a statesman." Wolsey's heirs are quick to upbraid our latter-day Mores for their sentimental "moral squint" at public policy. Yet even statesmen of Wolsey's stripe seldom see the "facts" of migration "flat on." Invariably, our perceptions betray our moral

*William R. O'Neill, S.J. is Associate Professor of Social Ethics at the Jesuit School of Theology in Berkeley, Santa Clara University.

American Journal of Economics and Sociology, Vol. 71, No. 4 (October, 2012).

squints, our tacit prejudices (pre-judgments). (For a non-pejorative interpretation of prejudice (*praejudicium*), see Gadamer 1991: 265–307.)

Beginning with Leo XIII's magisterial teaching on the rights of workers to a living wage, modern Roman Catholic social teaching, we may say, is the moral squint the Church brings to public policy. In its social teaching on dignity and human rights, the Church follows its Lord in proclaiming the "Good News" to the poor (Luke 4: 18). The Synod of Bishops (1971: 289), in a memorable declaration, thus affirmed that "action on behalf of justice and participation in the transformation of the world fully appear to us as a *constitutive* dimension of the preaching of the Gospel, or, in other words, of the church's mission for the redemption of the human race and its liberation from every oppressive situation."

In these pages, I will first consider the principal themes of modern Catholic Social Teaching (CST) and then turn to their implications for immigration policy in a religiously pluralist polity like our own. I will conclude with an assessment of the distinctively Christian obligations borne by citizens of faith in such a polity.

Good News to the Poor

Inspired by the great biblical injunctions of justice or righteousness (*sedaqah*) and right judgment (*misphat*) marking the reign of God, modern CST recurs to the distinctively modern idiom of human dignity and human rights. (For an interpretation of biblical conceptions of justice, see Donahue 1977, 2004.) Since the first modern social encyclical, Leo XIII's *Rerum novarum* (1891), the Church's magisterial teaching has upheld the fundamental, intrinsic worth of persons as created in the "image of God" (*imago dei*). Earlier perfectionist interpretations of human finality, consistent with an organically conceived social hierarchy, have, in recent teaching, ceded to a more deontological appeal to moral persons' equal dignity and rights. John XXIII (1963: 9) thus affirms in his encyclical *Pacem in Terris:*

> Any human society, if it is to be well-ordered and productive, must lay down as a foundation this principle, namely, that every human being is a person; that is, his nature is endowed with intelligence and free will.

> Indeed, precisely because he is a person he has rights and obligations
> flowing directly and simultaneously from his very nature. And as these
> rights and obligations are universal and inviolable, so they cannot in any
> way be surrendered.

Pope John (1963: 10) invokes both norms of reason and of revelation:

> If we look upon the dignity of the human person in the light of divinely
> revealed truth, we cannot help but esteem it far more highly; for men are
> redeemed by the blood of Jesus Christ, they are by grace the children and
> friends of God and heirs of eternal glory.

The recognition and institutional protection of persons' dignity as
fulfilling the divine command of neighbor-love (Luke: 10:27; cf. Leviticus: 19:18, 33; Deuteronomy: 6:4ff.; Mark. 12:30f.; Mt. 22:37f.) sets
the framework of social policy. The equal recognition and respect due
moral persons in virtue of their dignity is, in turn, parsed in terms of
agents' basic human rights. So it is the discourse of human rights and
of correlative duties that serves as a lingua franca in mediating the
Church's theological beliefs regarding covenantal fidelity (*sedaqah*) in
a religiously pluralist context. In the words of the United States
Catholic Bishops (1986: 79) in their Pastoral Letter:

> Catholic social teaching spells out the basic demands of justice . . . in the
> human rights of every person. These fundamental rights are prerequisites
> for a dignified life in community. The Bible vigorously affirms the sacred-
> ness of every person as a creature formed in the image and likeness of
> God. The biblical emphasis on covenant and community also shows that
> human dignity can only be realized and protected in solidarity with others.

The appeal to human dignity "in solidarity with others," that is, near
and distant neighbors, thus serves as a proximate foundation of
human rights, permitting citizens of faith to speak prophetically to the
world. In specifying the "minimum conditions" for the realization of
such dignity, the bishops seek to extend the notion of human rights.
For in CST, basic human rights encompass not merely the "negative"
civil-political rights enshrined in our American tradition, for example,
the freedoms *from* interference or coercion expressed in our rights to
freedom of worship, assembly, and speech, but the "positive" socioeconomic rights of subsistence, employment, minimal health care,
education—rights necessary *for* "a dignified life in community"
(United States Catholic Bishops 1986: 80). The bishops thus conclude

in their 10th Anniversary statement of *Economic Justice for All*, "A Catholic Framework for Economic Life" (United States Catholic Bishops 1996: 370–371):

> All people have a right to life and to secure the basic necessities of life (for example, food, clothing, shelter, education, health care, safe environment, economic security). . . . Society has a moral obligation, including governmental action where necessary, to assure opportunity, meet basic human needs and pursue justice in economic life.

Invoking dignity and human rights, both negative and positive, as a basic moral minimum reveals that in adopting the modern language of human rights the Church charts a *via media* between liberal-philosophical emphasis upon individual "negative" claim-rights of civil liberty and communitarian appeals to the "common good" of particular narrative traditions. In the Roman Catholic tradition, the common good entails neither the collectivist subordination of the individual to a suprapersonal entity such as the State or ethnic group, nor the reductive individualism of modern liberalism. For the common good is conceived distributively, not *en masse*, as "the sum total of those conditions of social living" that protect and promote the dignity and rights of every person (John XXIII 1961: 65; see also John XXIII 1963: 55–61; Second Vatican Council 1965: *Gaudium et Spes*, par. 26). In a similar vein, the principle of subsidiarity provides for the distinctive role of the mediating institutions of civil-society (for example, the churches, unions, and other voluntary associations) so that the structural prerequisites of the common good are both equitably and efficiently satisfied (Pius XI 1929: 79–80; see also John XXIII 1961: 51–58; United States Catholic Bishops 1986: 96–101).

As the foregoing remarks reveal, CST, despite its irenic tenor, offers a richer understanding of the moral aims of social policy than envisioned in much contemporary democratic deliberation. The structural ideal of the common good, mediated by the principle of subsidiarity, gives rise to a substantive conception of justice, whereby it is not so much fair procedures that determine just outcomes, as an antecedent set of material outcomes (that is, the institutional fulfillment of persons' basic human rights) that render procedures just or fair. From the earliest of the social encyclicals, a fair remuneration depended not only upon the contractual agreements of commutative justice, but upon the strictures of distributive and social justice that would ensure a "living wage." (For an analysis of the threefold understanding of justice in modern CST, see Hollenbach 1988: 16–33). The dignity of labor and the rights of workers thus enjoyed pride of place in the encyclical tradition. For work is conceived less in privitive terms than as the characteristic mode of expressing persons' dignity and fulfilling their contribution to the commonweal (John Paul II 1981).

Our moral entitlement to *equal* respect or consideration, in concert with the ethical ideal of the common good, moreover, justifies *preferential* treatment for those whose basic rights are most imperiled—in Camus's (1960: 230) phrase, our taking "the victim's side." (In the present context, the term "victim" is an evaluative moral description referring to those suffering deprivation of their basic rights; as such, it is reducible neither to class membership nor to a particular psychological state. I have developed this analysis in O'Neill (1994).) For if equal consideration does not imply identical treatment, so one may distinguish legitimately between indiscriminate regard for moral persons and discriminate response to their differing situations (Outka 1972: 20; Dworkin 1978: 227). Aquinas's (1946: II-II, Q 31, art. 2) observation that a servant who is ill merits greater attention than a son who is not pertains, *a fortiori*, to equals: the fulfillment of equal basic rights, in materially dissimilar conditions, justifies a discriminate response. In social ethics generally, such a discriminate response is expressed in the graduated moral urgency of differing human rights (that is, the lexical priority of agents' basic rights over other, less exigent claims such as property rights) and in the differing material conditions presumed for realizing the same human rights. A regime of rights may thus embody a legislative or juridical preference for the least favored in society and differential material entitlements corresponding to the differing intrapersonal and interpersonal prerequisites of agency, for example. the greater nutritional needs of pregnant women (Drèze and Sen 1989: 37–42).

These brief remarks permit us, I believe, to "translate" the fundamental motifs of CST into a persuasive, modern idiom, without thereby assuming the burden of keeping "our metaphysics warm" (Eliot 1962: 33). The biblical ideals of covenant fidelity and *agape* (neighbor-love) underwrite our modern teaching on dignity, solidarity, human rights, and the option for the poor as an answer to the lawyer's question, in Jesus' parable of the Good Samaritan, "what must I do to live?"

Immigration Policy

Church teaching, to be sure, is far from a panacea. The broad leitmotifs sketched thus far frame, but do not dictate, policy on such vexed social issues as immigration. And yet, as we shall see, the Church's teaching on migrants' rights is not nugatory.

With respect to the *nature and object* of rights, subjective rights (Shue 1980: 13ff; Gewirth 1978: 65, 1983: 2–3, 1998: 31–70) are warranted claims to social goods (for example, liberties, security, subsistence) that we may legitimately enjoy, assert, or enforce against other social actors (persons, institutions).

The graduated urgency of basic, mutually implicative human rights claims establishes the relative (lexical) priority of migrants' claims. As in modern CST, the legitimate sovereignty of states in regulating immigration subserves the global common good, so that states are morally bound to respect and promote the basic human rights of both citizen and resident alien, especially the most vulnerable—and of these, in particular, women and children. (For magisterial teaching on the moral status of migrants and refugees, see: Leo XIII 1891: 32, 35; Pius XII 1952; John XXIII 1961: 45, 1963: 11, 25, 94–108; Second Vatican Council 1965: *Gaudium et Spes*, pars. 27, 66; Paul VI 1967: 66–69; Sacred Congregation of Bishops 1969; Paul VI 1971: 17; World Synod of Catholic Bishops 1971: 20–24; John Paul II 1981: 23; John Paul II 1987: 24, 38; John Paul II 1990: 37, 82, 1991: 18, 57–58; Pontifical Council for Pastoral Care of Migrants and Itinerant People 2004. For an analysis of the implications of CST in the American context, see: Tomasi et al. 1989; Office of Pastoral Care of Migrants and Refugees 1996; United States Conference of Catholic Bishops 1996; "Love One Another as I love You" (1996); National Conference of Catholic Bishops 2000; United States Conference of Catholic Bishops 2001, 2003; Pontifical Council for the Pastoral Care of Migrants and Itinerant People 2004.) The Catholic Church thus recognizes persons' right to change nationality for social and economic as

well as political reasons, for in view of the "common purpose of created things" (and the mutually implicative character of basic rights), "where a state which suffers from poverty combined with great population cannot supply such use of goods to its inhabitants-
. . . people possess a right to emigrate, to select a new home in foreign lands and to seek conditions of life worthy" of their common humanity (Sacred Congregation of Bishops 1969: 14). Just so, the "new home," even where temporary, must provide for the equitable provision and protection of such basic human rights.

The rhetoric of basic human rights leaves many questions unresolved. Yet recognizing the graduated urgency of human rights and correlative duties does serve to indicate the lineaments of an equitable immigration policy—that is, one that takes due cognizance of the moral priority of relative need (gravity and imminence of harm), particular vulnerabilities (for example, of women and children), familial relationship, complicity of the host country in generating migratory flows (Walzer 1981: 20), historical or cultural affiliations (for example, historic patterns of migration), and a fair distribution of burdens (which countries should offer asylum). The latter consideration applies domestically as well, for the burdens of local integration or resettlement should not fall disproportionately upon the most vulnerable citizens.

With respect to the *subject* of rights, Hannah Arendt (1966: 300) once remarked that "the abstract nakedness of being nothing but human" divests the forcibly displaced migrant of "the very qualities which make it possible for other people to treat him as a fellow-man." Indeed, the right of migrants to have rights (that is, recognizing correlative "positive" duties to fulfill rights) typically remains dependent upon membership (citizenship) in a particular polity. "Positive" obligations extend primarily to fellow citizens privy to the social contract underlying the moral legitimacy of the state.

In such closed social systems, non-citizens are owed the duty of forbearance, but as "aliens" they lack legal title to the primary good of citizenship and its attendant claim-rights (Rawls 1996: 41; Carens 1987, 1998, 1995; Ackerman 1980; Beitz 1983, 1999). Even then with the emergence of a global rights regime, the liberal "*jus cosmopoliticum*" remains highly restricted (Benhabib 2004; Kant 1923). Liberal respect for the "generalized other" fails, in large part, to generate positive (imperfect) moral obligations of *provision*, for example, of welfare rights. Neither is a positive obligation to *protect* potential victims against systemic deprivation generally recognized. Strategic considerations of national self-interest again prevail, so that the "alien" becomes not the exemplar of humanity in general (the generalized other) but "a frightening symbol of difference as such" (Arendt 1966: 297, 301).

Now modern CST bequeaths us a different "moral squint." As we saw earlier, generalized respect for the concrete other lets us chart a critical *via media* between liberalism and communitarianism, adumbrating a different root metaphor: neither "members or strangers" (set by the limits of *philia*), nor "abstract citizens" (generated by the "bracketing" of *philia*), but near and distant *neighbors*. In the words of *Gaudium et spes*, we must "make ourselves the neighbor to absolutely every other person" (Second Vatican Council 1965: *Gaudium et Spes*, par. 27; see also *Catechism of the Catholic Church* 1994: 1825, 2196, 2443–2449). The narrative embodiment or schematization of basic rights and duties, that is, inscribes respect and recognition of the "concrete *other*" within the "latent wisdom" of citizens—a rhetorical *locus communis* restoring migrants' "place in the world."

Recognition of the "stranger" or "alien" *as* neighbor, and thus as a juridical person or claimant, attests to our common "faith in fundamental human rights, in the dignity and worth of the human person" (United Nations 2012)—a faith underwritten by, even as it is expressed within, our differing comprehensive religious traditions. In Frank Michelman's (1996: 203) words, "the notion of a right to have rights arises out of the modern-statist conditions and is equivalent to the moral claim of a refugee or other stateless person to citizenship, or at least juridical personhood, within the social confines of some law-dispensing state." Passing to "the victim's side," as did the Samaritan in Luke's parable (Luke 10: 29ff.), appears, then, as the touchstone of the legitimacy prevailing institutional arrangements, local, national, and global. Indeed, a "well-formed" narrative tradition, far from being merely "local or ethnocentric," will recognize the fitting modes of expressing the *universal* demand for respect. Consonant with an analogical interpretation of the common good, the loss of citizenship, affirms Pope John XXIII (1963: 25), "does not detract in any way from [one's] membership in the human family as a whole, nor from [one's] citizenship in the world community."

Finally, the *duties* correlative to recognizing migrants' rights impose "positive" obligations upon persons, states, and other trans-national actors. Typically, such positive duties of provision, protection, and redress are mediated institutionally; indeed, for CST, their concrete recognition underwrites the legitimacy of state sovereignty. David Hollenbach (2004) proposes an imaginative application of the "Kew Gardens principle," assigning responsibility in terms of the displaced person's relative need, the respondent's proximity to the need, her relative capability to respond, and the determination of last, reasonable resort (see also Loescher 1993: chapters 7, 8; Helton 2002).

As we argued above, it is not, pace Hobbes, finally sovereignty that defines legitimacy, but rather the converse. As David Hollenbach (2002: 65–86, 212–244) has argued, our particular institutional arrangements, including citizenship in a particular polity, are legitimate only if they subserve the global common good, that is, our "moral citizenship" in a world community. Yet it is just this "cosmopolitan" citizenship that is mediated in and across our concrete, particular polities, so that victims of forced migration, even if "undocumented," are never rhetorically effaced, never "rightless."

John XXIII (1963) thus properly affirms not only the commonly recognized right to emigrate, but the right to immigrate as well, for "when there are just reasons for it," every human being has "the right to emigrate to other countries and to take up residence there." In a similar vein, Paul VI (1971: 17) urges acceptance of "a charter which will assure [persons'] right to emigrate, favor their integration, facilitate their professional advancement and give them access to decent housing where, if such is the case, their families can join them." In a world ever more interdependent, citizens must seek a "continual revision of programmes, systems and regimes" so as to guarantee the full and effective implementation of the basic human rights of the most vulnerable, for example, those condemned to stateless existence in camps of first asylum (John Paul II 1980: 17).

Finally, virtue of solidarity with both near and distant neighbors in CST seeks not only to protect and extend the legal rights of migrants, but to redress the "oppression, intimidation, violence and terrorism" (John Paul II 1979: 17) that all too often impel them to migrate against their will (see also Christiansen 1996). The duties falling upon states and NGOs to aid and protect migrants presume the antecedent duty of preserving an international social order (the global common good) in which the basic rights of the most vulnerable are recognized (Paul VI 1971: 17). Indeed, the duty to protect grounds the subsidiary duty to rescue, for example, through diplomatic initiatives, sanctions, and *in extremis*, humanitarian intervention in the case of genocide or mass atrocity (Himes 1994, 2004; International Commission on Intervention and State Sovereignty 2001; Moore 1998).

The Surplus of Christian Meaning

The rhetoric of human rights permits us to "translate" the biblical motifs of justice, solidarity, and hospitality in the public reasoning of complex, religious pluralist polities like our own. And yet, there remains a surplus of religious meaning. *Agape* is never less than just. Yet if the Christian "justices" (Hopkins 1970: 90) in her moral deliberations, so justice bears the mark of "loving tenderly, compassionately" (Luke 10:37). To the lawyer's question in the parable, "who is my neighbor?"—seeking a precise delimitation of rights and duties— Jesus replies with a question of his own, "Who is it that proved himself neighbor?" (Donahue 1992).

The lawyer's reply, "the Samaritan," is richly ironic, for the Samaritan, a despised schismatic, not only proves himself neighbor, but in exemplifying neighborliness as the fulfillment of the law, is the one whom the lawyer must imitate: "Go and do likewise!" (Luke 10:37). For the question posed in Jesus' reading of the law is not finally "Whom shall I love?" but rather "Who shall I become (prove myself to be) in loving?" In Kierkegaard's (1962: 38) words, "Christ does not speak about recognizing one's neighbor but about being a neighbor oneself, about proving oneself to be a neighbor, something the Samaritan showed by his compassion." And this makes all the difference.

In salvific irony, Jesus thus answers the lawyer's first question, "What must I do to inherit eternal life?" in reversing the second. For the command to "love the Lord, your God, with all your heart, with all your being, with all your strength, and with all your mind, and your neighbor as yourself" (Luke 10:27) is fulfilled not in this or that particular deed of love (Rahner 1966: 453, 1974a, 1974b), but in one's "selving as neighbor" (Hopkins 1970): if the disciple is to live, she must enter the world of the *an_wîm*, of the half-dead stranger. In Christ, such "anamnestic solidarity" (Benjamin 1968: 253ff; see also McCarthy 1991) in remembering the Covenant implies not merely taking the victim's side (the "essential" requirement of ethics), but taking the victim's side *as* our own—in Rahner's (1963) terms, the formal, existential demand of love. Gutiérrez (1984: 125–126) observed that "[c]ommitment to the poor means entering, and in some cases remaining in that universe with a much clearer awareness." Such solidarity, he writes, "can therefore only follow an asymptotic curve. . . . ," that is, an ever richer "seeing and having compassion."

The distinctively Christian virtue of solidarity with the *an_wîm*—with those "broken and oppressed in spirit"—thus defines the disciple's moral squint, for "to be a Christian," says Gustavo Gutiérrez (1984), "is to draw near, to make oneself a neighbor, not the one I encounter in my journey but the one in whose journey I place myself." For an ethics of discipleship, then, "What I must do to *live*" (my *metanoia*) is to "turn" to the world of the poor, of the half-dead stranger—in the martyred Archbishop Romero's (1990: 298) words, "becoming incarnate in their world, . . . proclaiming the good news to them," even to the point of "sharing their fate."

In the words of Simone Weil (1951: 115), the disciple must cultivate a compassionate "way of looking . . . attentive" to the migrant "in all his truth." She must come, that is, to see the migrant "not only as a unit in a collection, or a specimen from the social category labeled "unfortunate," but as a man, exactly like us, who was one day stamped with a special mark by affliction." In "anamestic solidarity" with migrants, disciples thus express a sense of the fitting, so that they "see and have compassion" (*esplanchnisthe* signifies being moved in one's inmost heart), even as compassion becomes a way of seeing. Compassion, then, not only guides them in the fitting application of universal, essential norms, for example, the rights of migrants, but gives rise to existential (personal and ecclesial) imperatives as they walk humbly with Jesus, who, as Augustine wrote, is our Good Samaritan, coming to the aid of wounded humanity.

References

Ackerman, B. (1980). *Social Justice in the Liberal State*. New Haven, CT: Yale University.

Aquinas, T. (1946). *Summa Theologica*. Trans. Fathers of the English Dominican Province. New York: Benziger Brothers.

Arendt, H. (1966). "The Perplexities of the Rights of Man." In *The Origins of Totalitarianism*. New York: Harcourt, Brace, & World.

Beitz, C. R. (1983). "Cosmopolitan Ideals and National Sentiment." *Journal of Philosophy* 80(10): 591–600.

——. (1999). *Political Theory and International Relations*. Princeton, NJ: Princeton University Press.

Benhabib, S. (2004). *The Right of Others: Aliens, Residents and Citizens*. Cambridge, UK: Cambridge University Press.

Benjamin, W. (1968). *Illuminations: Essays and Reflections*. Ed. H. Arendt. New York: Harcourt Brace Jovanovich, Inc.

Bolt, R. (1990). *A Man for All Seasons*. New York: Random House.

Camus, A. (1960). *The Plague*. New York: Alfred A. Knopf.

Carens, J. H. (1987). "Who Belongs? Theoretical and Legal Questions About Birthright Citizenship in the United States." *University of Toronto Law Journal* 37(4): 413–443.

——. (1988). "Immigration and the Welfare State." In *Democracy and the Welfare State*. Ed. A. Gutmann, p. 215. Princeton, NJ: Princeton University.

——. (1995). "Aliens and Citizens: The Case for Open Borders." In *Theorizing Citizenship*. Ed. R. Beiner, pp. 229–255. New York: SUNY Press.

Catechism of the Catholic Church (1994). Liguori, MO: Liguori Publications.

Christiansen, D. (1996). "Movement, Asylum, Borders: Christian Perspectives." *International Migration Review* 30(1): 7–17.

Donahue, J. (1977). "Biblical Perspectives on Justice." In *The Faith That Does Justice*. Ed. J. C. Haughey, pp. 68–12. New York: Paulist Press.

——. (1992). "Who is My Enemy? The Parable of the Good Samaritan and the Love of Enemies." In *The Love of Enemy and Nonretaliation in the New Testament*. Ed. W. M. Swartley, pp. 137–156. Louisville, KY: Westminster/John Knox Press.

——. (2004). "The Bible and Catholic Social Teaching: Will This Engagement Lead to Marriage?" In *Modern Catholic Social Teaching: Commentaries and Interpretations*. Ed. K. R. Himes, pp. 9–40. Washington, DC: Georgetown University Press.

Drèze, J., and A. Sen. (1989). *Hunger and Public Action.* Oxford: Clarendon.

Dworkin, R. (1978). *Taking Rights Seriously.* Cambridge: Harvard University.

Eliot, T. S. (1962). "Whispers of Immortality." In *The Complete Poems and Plays: 1909–1950.* New York: Harcourt, Brace and World.

Gadamer, H. (1991). *Truth and Method,* 2d. ed. Trans. J. Weinsheimer and D. G. Marshall. New York: Crossroad.

Gewirth, Alan. (1978). *Reason and Morality.* Chicago: University of Chicago Press.

———. (1983). *Human Rights: Essays on Justification and Applications.* Chicago: University of Chicago Press.

———. (1998). *The Community of Rights.* Chicago: University of Chicago Press.

Gutiérrez, G. (1984). *We Drink from Our Own Wells: The Spiritual Journey of a People.* Trans. M. J. O'Connell. New York: Orbis.

Helton, A. C. (2002). *The Price of Indifference; Refugees and Humanitarian Action in the New Century.* New York: Oxford University Press.

Himes, K. (1994). "The Morality of Humanitarian Intervention." *Theological Studies* 55: 82–105.

———. (2004). "Intervention, Just War, and the U.S. National Security." *Theological Studies* 65: 141–157.

Hollenbach, D. (1988). *Justice, Peace, and Human Rights: American Catholic Social Ethics in a Pluralistic World.* New York: Crossroad.

———. (2002). *The Common Good & Christian Ethics.* Cambridge, UK: Cambridge University Press.

———. (2004). "Humanitarian Crises, Refugees, and the Transnational Good: Global Challenges and Catholic Social Teaching." Presented at the Katholieke Universiteit Lueven Centre for Catholic Social Thought. Leuven, Belgium.

Hopkins, G. M. (1970). "As Kingfishers Catch Fire." In *The Poems of Gerard Manley Hopkins,* 4th ed. Eds. W. H. Gardner and H. M. MacKenzie, p. 90. New York: Oxford University.

International Commission on Intervention and State Sovereignty (2001). *The Responsibility to Protect.* Ottawa: International Development Research Centre.

John XXIII (1961). *Mater et Magistra.* http://www.vatican.va/holy_father/john_xxiii/encyclicals/documents/hf_j-xxiii_enc_15051961_mater_en.html.

———. (1963). *Pacem in Terris.* http://www.vatican.va/holy_father/john_xxiii/encyclicals/documents/hf_j-xxiii_enc_11041963_pacem_en.html.

John Paul II (1979). *Redemptor Hominis.* http://www.vatican.va/holy_father/john_paul_ii/encyclicals/documents/hf_jp-ii_enc_04031979_redemptor-hominis_en.html.

———. (1980). *Dives in Misericordia.* http://www.vatican.va/holy_father/john_paul_ii/encyclicals/documents/hf_jp-ii_enc_30111980_dives-in-misericordia_en.html.

——. (1981). *Laborem Exercens*. Boston: Daughters of St. Paul.

——. (1987). *Sollicitudo rei Socialis*. http://www.vatican.va/holy_father/
john_paul_ii/encyclicals/documents/hf_jp-ii_enc_30121987_sollicitudo-
rei-socialis_en.html.

——. (1990). *Redemptoris missio*. http://www.vatican.va/holy_father/
john_paul_ii/encyclicals/documents/hf_jp-ii_enc_07121990_redemptoris-
missio_en.html.

——. (1991). *Centesimus Annus*. http://www.vatican.va/holy_father/
john_paul_ii/encyclicals/documents/hf_jp-ii_enc_01051991_centesimus-
annus_en.html.

Kant, E. (1923). "Zum Ewigen Frieden: Ein philosophischer Entwurf." In
Immanuel Kants Werke. Eds. A. Buchenau, E. Cassirer, and B. Keller-
mann. pp. 425–474. Berlin: Verlag Bruno Cassirer.

Kierkegaard, S. (1962). *Works of Love*. Trans. H. and E. Hong. New York:
Harper and Row.

Leo XIII (1891). *Rerum Novarum*. Boston: Daughters of St. Paul.

Loescher, G. (1993). *Beyond Charity: International Cooperation and the
Global Refugee Crisis*. New York: Oxford University Press.

McCarthy, T. (1991). *Ideals and Illusions: On Reconstruction and Deconstruc-
tion in Contemporary Critical Theory*. Cambridge, MA: MIT Press.

Michelman, F. (1996). "Parsing 'A Right to Have Rights'." *Constellations* 3(2):
200–209.

Moore, J. (1998). *Hard Choices: Moral Dilemas in Humanitarian Intervention*.
Lanham, MD: Rowman and Littlefield.

National Conference of Catholic Bishops (2000). *Welcoming the Stranger
Among Us: Unity in Diversity*. Washington, DC: United States Conference
of Catholic Bishops.

Office of Pastoral Care of Migrants and Refugees (1996). *Who Are My Sisters
and Brothers? Reflections on Understanding and Welcoming Immigrants
and Refugees*. Washington, DC: United States Conference of Catholic
Bishops.

O'Neill, W. R. (1994). "No Amnesty for Sorrow: The Privilege of the
Poor in Christian Social Ethics." *Theological Studies* 55(4): 638–656.

Outka, G. (1972). *Agape*. New Haven: Yale University.

Paul VI (1967). *Populorum Progressio*. http://www.vatican.va/holy_father/
paul_vi/encyclicals/documents/hf_p-vi_enc_26031967_populorum_en.
html.

——. (1971). *Octogesima Adveniens*. http://www.vatican.va/holy_father/
paul_vi/apost_letters/documents/hf_p-vi_apl_19710514_octogesima-
adveniens_en.html.

Pius XI (1929). "*Quadragesimo Anno*: On Reconstructing the Social Order."
In *The Church and the Reconstruction of the Modern World*. Ed.
T. McGlaughlin. Garden City, NY: Doubleday.

Pius XII (1952). *Exsul Familia Nazarethana*. http://www.papalencyclicals. net/Pius12/p12exsul.htm.

Pontifical Council for Pastoral Care of Migrants and Itinerant People (2004). *Erga Migrantes Caritas Christi*. http://www.vatican.va/roman_curia/ pontifical_councils/migrants/documents/rc_pc_migrants_doc_20040514_ erga-migrantes-caritas-christi_en.html.

Rahner, K. (1963). "On the Question of a Formal Existential Ethics." In *Theological Investigations* 2. Trans. K. H. Kruger, p. 221. Baltimore: Helicon Press.

Rahner, K. (1966). "The 'Commandment' of Love in Relation to the Other Commandments." In *Theological Investigations* 5. Trans. K. H. Kruger, pp. 439–453. New York: Seabury, 1966.

——. (1974a). "The Theology of Freedom." In *Theological Investigations* 6. Trans. K. and B. Kruger, pp. 178–196. New York: Seabury.

——. (1974b). "Reflections on the Unity of the Love of Neighbour and the Love of God." In *Theological Investigations* 6. Trans. K. and B. Kruger, pp. 231–249. New York: Seabury.

Rawls, J. (1996). *Political Liberalism*. New York: Columbia University.

Romero, O. (1990). "The Political Dimension of the Faith from the Perspective of the Option for the Poor." In *Liberation Theology: A Documentary History*. Ed. Alfred T. Hennelly, pp. 292–303. Maryknoll, NY: Orbis Books.

Sacred Congregation of Bishops (1969). *Instructions on the Pastoral Care of People Who Migrate*. Washington, DC: U.S. Catholic Conference.

Second Vatican Council (1965). *Pastoral Constitution of the Church in the Modern World: Gaudium et Spes*. http://www.vatican.va/archive/hist_ councils/ii_vatican_council/documents/vat-ii_cons_19651207_gaudium- et-spes_en.html.

Shue, H. (1980). *Basic Rights: Subsistence, Affluence, and U.S. Foreign Policy*. Princeton: Princeton University.

Synod of Bishops (1971), "Justice in the World." In *Catholic Social Thought: The Documentary Heritage*. Eds. D. J. O'Brien and T. A. Shannon, pp. 287–300. Maryknoll, NY: Orbis Books.

Tomasi, S. M., D. Chriastensen, D. Liptak, J. P. Fitzpatrick, and L. J. Hoppe. (1989). *Today's Immigrants and Refugees: A Christian Understanding*. Washington, DC: United States Conference of Catholic Bishops.

United Nations (2012). *The Universal Declaration of Human Rights*. http:// www.un.org/en/documents/udhr/.

United States Catholic Bishops (1986). *Economic Justice for All: Pastoral Letter on Catholic Social Teaching and the U.S. Economy*. http://www. usccb.org/upload/economic_justice_for_all.pdf.

United States Catholic Bishops (1996). "A Catholic Framework for Economic Life." *Origins* 26(23): 370–371.

United States Conference of Catholic Bishops (1996). *Love One Another As I Love You.* http://old.usccb.org/mrs/pilla.shtml.

———. (2001). *Asian and Pacific Presence Harmony in Faith.* http://usccb.org/issues-and-action/cultural-diversity/asian-pacific-islander/asian-and-pacific-presence-harmony-in-faith.cfm.

———. (2003). *Strangers No Longer Together on the Journey of Hope.* http://usccb.org/issues-and-action/human-life-and-dignity/immigration/strangers-no-longer-together-on-the-journey-of-hope.cfm.

Walzer, M. (1981). "The Distribution of Membership." In *Boundaries: National Autonomy and Its Limits.* Eds. P. Brown, and H. Shue. Totowa, NJ: Rowman and Littlefield.

Weil, S. (1951). "Reflections on the Right Use of School Studies with a View to the Love of God." In *Waiting for God.* Trans. Emma Craufurd. New York: G. P. Putnam's Sons.

World Synod of Catholic Bishops (1971). *Justitia in Mundo.* http://catholicsocialservices.org.au/Catholic_Social_Teaching/Justitia_in_Mundo.

Development and Wealth: A Georgist Perspective

By H. WILLIAM BATT[*]

ABSTRACT. This essay addresses concerns of economic and wealth distribution, especially as they challenge the developing world. The foundation for any new framework of economic thought must embody a structure that allows for a sustainable future, not only for individuals but also for whole societies and economic units, and the assurance of minimal standards of living for the entire world's people. The Georgist position is that all the natural resources of the earth and sky should require payment back to society for the privilege of their use. Hence the recovery of rent is the proper source of finance for government services, restoring what is otherwise an imbalance between the public and the private realms of society. The Georgist philosophy offers economic justice and clarity of vision, restoration of and protection for the commons, and protection for the environment of the earth in a deft and gentle way that is within the capacity of governments to implement.

Introduction

Just over a century ago American journalist and economist Henry George offered to the world a remedy for economic justice and market efficiency that reached beyond all extant social philosophies even as it built on them. He came to be regarded as a hero to some, a crackpot to others. Yet his grand theory of society has continued ever since to lurk in the wings of public-policy discourse. Claim is made that his ideas, even more than Marxism, were so powerful a threat to vested interests that he had to be discredited by whatever means necessary, and this, arguably, accounts for his near obliteration from historical veneration (Gaffney and Harrison 1994).

*H. William Batt is Executive Director, Central Research Group, Inc., Albany, New York.

American Journal of Economics and Sociology, Vol. 71, No. 4 (October, 2012).

For a time it appeared that his arguments would disappear from serious discourse entirely. But in recent years a convergence of forces has given the Georgist solution new life. The possibility of wholesale collection and aggregation of data, the arrival of computers to provide powerful analysis of that data, and the ability of the internet to spread findings have given a renewed promise to a compelling and visionary idea. It is now possible to provide substantive argument, both technically and politically, to what has for so long been simply a plausible theory.

This essay addresses concerns of economic and wealth distribution, especially as they challenge the developing world. But it inevitably speaks to all political and economic systems because the ideals are indeed universal and have applicability everywhere. The findings and lessons that come from study in the industrial societies of the "North" have no less value for the impoverished world of the "South." What is attractive to populations and their leaders of industrialized economies should be equally attractive to rural agricultural communities of impoverished nations.

The world today faces challenges that Henry George never anticipated: skyrocketing population growth, environmental despoliation, blighted and degraded cities of tens of millions, and huge disparities in national wealth. Students of George argue that he succeeded in harmonizing and reconciling the political and economic tensions between labor and capital, between the private and the public realms, between equity and efficiency, and between the demand for public finances and the resentment of taxes. He effectively made laborers and capitalists partners in harnessing the productivity of natural resources. That notables as diverse as Winston Churchill, Leo Tolstoy, Mark Twain, John Dewey, Sun Yat Sen, and Theodore Roosevelt could all understand and appreciate the import of what was offered in the Georgist promise makes it puzzling why today the agenda is so difficult to sell.

Georgists today, however, are now offered another chance. The world stands ready, for few if any other candidates for so comprehensive a remedy exist. Confidence in the validity of the idea compels Georgist adherents to press on; indeed, studies during the past two decades now provide more validation than existed throughout the 20th century.

Political and Economic Development in Context

The word development has been employed since World War II in successive iterations of discourse to bolster national strategies of economic and political transformation worldwide (Meier 2004). Conversations began with experiences taken from post-war Europe's Marshall Plan, and President Truman thereafter inaugurated a program in 1949 known as "Point Four." They were based largely on the success of America's capital investment in nations devastated by the war and inspired by a new world vision. The lessons learned were intended to achieve the same success in third-world nations as had transformed Europe. The first program began with substantial investment in Israel and the Middle East, but it lost support in the Eisenhower Administration and was formally abolished in May 1953.

One can trace the idea of programmed development earlier still to President Franklin Roosevelt's address to Congress in January 1941, wherein he outlined four basic freedoms to which all peoples of the world should be properly entitled: freedom of speech and expression, freedom of worship, freedom from want, and freedom from fear. These principles have in various guises formed the basis of political and economic development strategies ever since.

The literature on development exploded in the last half of the 20th century, followed by a substantial number of program initiatives. But it is questionable whether the world is better off today than at the time of their inspiration. There is a general consensus that political and economic development designs should go hand-in-hand, but palpable and demonstrable progress in their implementation has for the most part been wanting.

The consequence of the world's inability to face the challenge of the enormity of world poverty and the disparity of wealth among its peoples is that remedies are sporadic and ad hoc in nature. The developed world tires of reading and hearing about the tragedies of poverty and dislocation in what have been called "aid and donor fatigue." The result is that policies at the national and international levels have become exhausted, and the burden is left to various private charities. There is a tradition that maintains that only charity can adequately respond since want and suffering are inevitable.

Religious institutions are frequently identified with this view (Pontifical Council for Justice and Peace 2005; Sider 1984). The Georgist argument is that poverty is a result of injustice and poorly designed institutions. George wrote: "There is in nature no reason for poverty" (1992: Ch 8, 77). The same religious institutions that have long carried on campaigns for charity seem now to be basing their arguments more on justice.

Economic Development

The greatest debates have unfolded in reference to the economic dimensions of development. What lessons are to be had from the multiplicity of experiments over the past half century are not easily generalizable. Much of what transpired in the early post-war years needs to be interpreted against the backdrop of the colonial era and cold-war tensions. In the past 30 years, with the cold war now over and yet ironically without the intellectual or financial resources of the earlier years, nations have adopted a multiplicity of approaches to economic development. Most reflect disillusionment with strong government initiatives, whether because of a newly discovered faith in markets and the private sector or from simple lack of public resources. Significantly, however, there is little consensus about such strategies, and ideologies continue to dominate development studies. What is called for is examination of the problems at the systemic level rather than in terms of development's outward manifestations.

The nations of the developing world, once freed from much of their colonial past, were fortunate at least in some instances to have inherited reasonably competent bureaucracies, and sometimes considerable infrastructures. Former British colonies, especially those in Asia, were positioned to capitalize on a legacy of an educated elite, cosmopolitan exposure, and a cadre of English speakers that proved to be no small advantage over succeeding years. Other post-colonial regimes have been less advantaged, although explanations for evolving patterns vary. In almost all instances, however, the colonial policies were based on an economic philosophy known as mercantilism, wherein manufactured goods were sold to native peoples, who were in turn harnessed in extractive enterprises to provide raw materials to the mother country. Local elites with control over natural resources built insular appurtenances to service their growing western tastes, but that further isolated them from the broad masses in their own nations. These patterns of agricultural and mineral extraction did little to foster market economies on a broad scale, and left most emerging nations with compromised political systems as well.

The imposition of western law upon most of these nations was another profound transformation of their sociopolitical arrangements, often as a counterpart to what market regimes were instituted. One could argue that the legal systems were, and continue to be, some of the most radically disruptive factors in the changes wrought, constituting what Max Weber (1968) called the growing organization, rationalization, and "disenchantment" of their worlds. For whatever reason, however, the focus of development today has been more on the economic than upon the legal dimensions of change.

Equally significant, if not more so, has been the transformation of nature into a commodity (Linklater 2002). Historians have now begun to give this phenomenon the attention that it deserves, even though, in the words of one venerable account, it constitutes the "great transformation" of western society (Polanyi 1957). Not only did land come to be regarded as an economic asset in financial accounts, Americans especially, and then others began to rely on it to generate wealth and for speculative gain. The realization of profit that could be had from land speculation led shortly to the "great land rush" worldwide, which shortly thereafter altered economic theory as well as the manner by which spatial relationships would unfold (Weaver 2003; Freeman 2000; Wright 1992; Aron 1996; Banner 2005; Kluger 2007; Chandler 1945). Mention is made here because of its relevance for later discussion.

It is against this setting, I believe, that the recent ideas of economic development need to be understood. I personally came to the early economic-development field during the heyday of its greatest explication and optimism, coming as it did during my tenure in graduate school and early academic experience. Returning to the United States in early 1965 after spending two years' service as one of the earliest Peace Corps Volunteers, I was showered with generous offers from various schools willing to pay for my graduate study. I had every expectation that I would end up working for the US Agency for International Development or some similar program, and ride the cusp of this unfolding world promise of rising expectations.

As it happened, personal circumstances eventually led me in different directions, and I remained at most at the periphery of the development-administration dialogue for the next several years. I was close enough to both the literature and the people, however, to have witnessed the growing disillusion and decline of excitement surrounding this subject in the 1980s and after. Many of those with whom I shared the early years of optimism and idealism left in disappointment. They left not from the lack of success in those early efforts, but as a result of the turn away from faith in a strong public-sector role in such initiatives toward an unwavering faith in privatization led by Chicago-school economists. Those of us whose interest was public administration and political design were left in a subordinate role in the ensuing discourse, if indeed there was any place at all. It was just as well that I followed new directions.

Defining and Re-Defining Development

For the first several decades of economic and political development discussion, utilitarian measures tended to dominate, and ideas of distributive justice seemed to have languished. John Rawls' (1971, 2001) breakthrough essay "Justice as Fairness" renewed interest in the moral dimension of development policies. It posed the question of what rightfully should be one's lot in political arrangements and market exchanges under a "veil of ignorance." In arguments similar to what in economics is called Pareto optimality, anyone's "original position," it argued, should be like anyone else's. But even if all members of a community are entitled to justice, Rawls' scheme did not incorporate future members, that is, those not yet living and non-human claimants. Furthermore, it was not clear whether the equality Rawls had in mind constituted equality of opportunity or equality of outcome. It was all very static and abstract.

One could surmise that development approaches had ignored distributive justice because of faith in what has come to be known as "trickle down economics." This is the idea that support, essentially through tax design, for wealth-producing investments will redound to the benefit of populations at all levels. Sometimes originally attributed to Andrew Mellon in the 1920s, it is often also expressed in the idea that a "rising tide lifts all boats." John Kenneth Galbraith (1982) relates the rejoinder to trickle down during the Roosevelt administration's New Deal as "the horse-and-sparrow theory: If you feed the horse enough oats, some will pass through to the road for the sparrows." There is little evidence that the trickle-down approach really assures optimal distribution, but it has nevertheless dominated both literature and practices of development administration. It has often been accepted as a matter of course that disparities of wealth and resources settle out in natural and inevitable gradations. Just as often encountered is the argument that increased population will generate economic activity and increased wealth commensurate with, perhaps even greater than, investments made (Simon 1981, 1984). Although this latter view is increasingly regarded as quaint if not dangerous, it is much closer to the view of Henry George as he viewed the open American frontier in the post Civil War era. Arguably, the economic development in the "South" has been most successful when birth rates have been reduced. On the other hand, there is considerable alarm about some European nations' shifting age distribution, and in some cases absolute population decline. It stands to reason, however, that increasing populations are likely to make more difficult maintaining well-being compared to those that have succeeded in stabilizing population growth. (The classic test is being played out in China, which has aggressively limited birthrates, and India, which has made less effort to do so. Note is also taken of some European nations that face steeply declining birth rates, and a census only equilibrated as a result of immigration.)

More recent and exciting than the approach of Rawls is the capability approach developed by economist Amartya Sen (1999), who in 1998 was awarded the Swedish Bank Prize for bringing an "ethical dimension" to a discipline that had largely lost sight of such considerations in its contemporary and dominant "neo-classical" tradition, and philosopher Martha Nussbaum (2000). Here development is understood as the extent of personal freedom available to people, not only in terms of their basic needs but also with respect to their opportunities for self-actualization and communal fulfillment. On these perspectives economically wealthier nations appear to fare less well. Where people are constrained by work demands, health, security, access to the means of growth and enrichment, opportunities for social sharing, and so on, certain dimensions of growth are a liability. They are effectively locked into a social and economic system that demands of them certain behavior patterns. Access to resources is also a central consideration. I recently had occasion to use a metaphor that builds upon an adage often used in development literature (Smiley, Batt, and Cobb 2010: 4). "Give a man a fish, the story goes, and he will eat for a day. Teach a man to fish, and he will eat for life." But that's not true unless the man has access to a fishpond. And in many regions of the world, he does not.

Recovering a Framework of Analysis and Direction

For the moment, however, things seem to be at an impasse. In the half-century since economic theory took on an applied dimension directed especially toward developing regions of the world, three perspectives seem worthy of particular note. The first is recognition that the earth is finite, and that the principle of limits as applied to natural resources has had ever-greater moment as its implications become apparent. The second is that free-market, and especially neoclassical economic, theory does not guarantee greater and more equal distribution of wealth. Contrary to the conventional wisdom of its many apologists, a rising tide definitely does not lift all boats. The third significant realization is that the discipline of economics, as with all the other social sciences, does not rest on the same epistemological premises as the natural sciences. The social sciences, it is important to appreciate, were established at the end of the 19th century by fiat, with the hope and expectation that by emulating the "scientific method" of the physical and biological sciences similar progress in the growth of human knowledge would eventuate. Considerable work has amply demonstrated since that not only was that view of science misunderstood, but that social sciences, if they can succeed at all, must develop their own philosophical grounding. The idea that there are laws of human behavior in the same way that there are laws of physics is highly questionable, and attempts to emulate physical sciences by simply applying formulas to numerical data are very much open to debate. During the post-war period, social science was generally enthralled by the philosophical school of logical positivism, particularly by a group identified as the Vienna Circle. Economics came under its sway more completely than any other of the social science disciplines with the possible exception of psychology. Yet the majority of today's Georgists argue, as did George himself, that economic behavior can be explained using a still earlier framework of natural law. Yet notable exceptions to this view include John Dewey. Indeed, there is a real question whether the Swedish Bank Prize in economics, belatedly added in 1969 to the list of awards given by that august Swedish body, would today be given that same status (Bergmann 1999; Gittens 2005; Hudson 1970). Recent years have seen the economics Nobel move far from its early "scientistic" model and take on instead a far more political and ideological character (for example, the 1998 award to economist Amartya Sen and the 2009 award to political scientist Elinor Ostrom).

The environmental movement took a leap forward with the benchmark study by the Club of Rome's Report on the Predicament of Mankind, *The Limits to Growth* (Meadows 1972). That study, and others that followed, spawned a whole stream of new literature and, arguably, led ultimately to the establishment of a radically different paradigm known as Ecological Economics (Daly and Farley 2003; Common and Stagl 2005) and to devastating attacks upon the current neoclassical school (Georgescu-Roegen 1971; Daly 1991, 1996; Nelson 1991, 2001; Fulbrook 2004). Although much of the methodology and data simulation done in the Club of Rome Report soon proved to be faulty, sufficient concerns were raised that the United-Nations-established World Commission on Environment and Development was formed, and issued a report entitled *Our Common Future* (1987). It defined sustainable development as the ability of societies to "meet the needs of the present without compromising the ability of future generations to meet their own needs." The Club or Rome team wrote a sequel (Meadows, Meadows, and Randers 1992) with new and better data, published as *Beyond the Limits: Confronting Global Collapse, Envisioning a Sustainable Future*. Today, with the stream of books issuing almost weekly, and with the growing expert consensus about global warming (Intergovernmental Panel on Climate Change 2007), it should be obvious that the economic paradigm that has dominated the past century cannot survive, and needs urgent replacement (Stern 2007). (To see the clash of conflicting economic paradigms and the extent to which neoclassical economics is on the defensive, see Leonhardt 2007.)

The second failing of the extant neoclassical school is its inability to solve the persistent continuance of poverty. Studies and books are issued almost daily showing how inequitably the 6.5 billion people on earth today share its fruits. The World Bank (2012) estimated that in 2008 22.4 percent of the world's population was living on less than U.S. $1.25 per day and the World Hunger Education Service (2012) reported that 925 million people were hungry in 2010. Probing analyses have been issued as the gravity and seeming intractability of the problem continues (Collier 2007, 2010; Easterly 2006; Prosterman, Mitchell, and Hanstad 2007). The imbalance exists not only between rich countries and poor countries: even in wealthy nations like the United States, roughly 15 percent of the population lived below the government-designated poverty line in 2010, "the largest number in the 52 years for which poverty estimates have been published" (United States Census Bureau 2011). Life is becoming more precarious rather than more secure for many people. The literate and aware population knows all this, as books and news articles recount it. But, in what Thurman Arnold (1937) famously called the "folklore of capitalism," belief persists that the failure of people to sustain themselves economically is not typically a systemic one but due rather to individual lack of resourcefulness.

The foundation for any new framework of economic thought must embody, at the least, a structure that allows for, and even requires, a sustainable future, not only for individuals but also for whole societies and economic units. It must also offer, and perhaps guarantee, the assurance of minimal standards of living for the entire world's people. And in view of the fact that the earth and its resources are finite, any such design should assure that the impact of human life will promise that future citizens of the world will have undiminished, and even perhaps increased, opportunities for survival. This last has been empirically and also graphically portrayed in an easily comprehensible concept of the "ecological footprint." If indeed people are morally entitled to no greater return for their industry than what their ecological footprint prefigures, some radically altered lifestyle patterns are in store for us. Americans, for instance, are estimated to consume so much of the earth's fruits that some 3.5 "earths" would be required to allow everyone to be similarly entitled (Wackernagel and Rees 1996). This is especially well illustrated with the statistics on oil consumption, where the United States consumes 22.5 percent of the world's petroleum with only 6 percent of the population (Davis, Diegel, and Boundy 2011). The disparities in consumption are reflected also in the impact on the environment, as with fish consumption, the use of certain toxic substances, and in pollution emissions.

How might it be possible to reconfigure the world's political and economic systems in a way that is consistent with not only distributive justice but also sustainable development? This is the charge assumed not just for this venue but also for the world. One view is that individuals, once persuaded, can be depended upon to adopt personal choices and lifestyles that will be consistent with these requirements. Many people who have the choice to do otherwise have accepted this challenge and elected to live in ways that are consistent with the kind of steady-state environment of which Herman Daly (1996, 2007) writes. Leading lives of "voluntary simplicity" (Elgin 1993; Shi 1986) has a virtue of its own, offering at the least a feeling of righteousness and perhaps even moral superiority in a world that seems to have run amok. But it is difficult in environments where social and economic environments require the satisfaction of certain minimal demands to reduce needs to such a level. The infrastructures of our society necessitate certain indulgences and consumption patterns; life outside such systems is, practically speaking, impossible, and can only be achieved, if at all, in different social environments.

Any changes in lifestyle that can make a real difference in achieving a sustainable future need to be accomplished collectively. This means by government policy initiatives. But what government actions are possible, either technically, constitutionally, or politically? Only now is serious exploration beginning about how, in programmatic ways, governments might institute policies that can and will make differences in our behavior, both collectively or individually. Some measures taken by various nations and states are significant and incrementally sound. (Illustrative of some creative thinking in this area are the tax policies instituted by European nations. See particularly the website of Green Budget Germany: www.eco-tax.info.) There is much less thinking at levels that can and should guide policy decisions. Thinking about such measures broadly and conceptually will help facilitate movement toward such goals, especially as past paradigms disintegrate when facing changing and challenging demands.

The Necessity of Government Policy

Constitutionally speaking, governments have only two instruments to effectuate policy, referred to in constitutional law as police powers and tax powers. In reality there is a third constitutional power that has no immediate consequence or relevance to this discussion, and that is the power to make war. Even though governments often subsume certain functions otherwise precluded under the rubric of emergency war powers, only the first two above are germane as broad policy instruments.

Tax powers are typically taken to mean all measures through which governments raise revenue to support the general purposes of government. To be sure, the lines have been blurred in recent years insofar as governments have elected to use this power as means to further other public purposes. But such provisions are largely of recent origin, at least as far as they have been employed consciously and explicitly. The classic understanding of taxation is largely, if not solely, to generate revenue. President Ronald Reagan enunciated this view explicitly in 1981, when he avowed that "the taxing power of the government must be used to provide for legitimate government purposes. It must not be used to regulate the economy or bring about social change" (Baumol and Blinder 1991: 693).

Police powers, in contrast, include all those other measures that governments use to direct, channel, discourage, or prohibit behavior. Governments are hard-put to induce behavior, and there are only limited instances where they attempt to do so. A military draft might be one instance; certain taxes might be another. (One could argue, however, that the inducement then comes in such instances only by the threat of imposing some other measure that constitutes a prohibition. The subject/citizen then is faced with a trade-off choice: to comply or relinquish certain freedoms.) This is an important realization, and is something that policymakers have frequently lost sight of: that is, that police powers are better at stopping than they are at inducing. Given, then, that both tax powers and police powers are limited in their abilities to effectuate change, it becomes particularly important that public policies be designed to make best use of what limited resources are at their command.

All this must be borne in mind when designers of government policy consider the efficacy of government policies, particularly with reference to the scope, domain, and weight of government. Scope involves all those things or interests in which government concerns itself; the domain is the area or number of people over which it has exercise; and the weight, or intensity, is the degree to which a people or an area feels itself imposed upon, heavily or only lightly. If a government in some way over-extends itself, or imposes itself too much upon people, it will prove to be ineffectual, illegitimate, and have a difficult time maintaining itself. It is not difficult to find instances in the United States and elsewhere where that limited police power capacity is squandered, that is, where laws are flouted or circumvented. It is even more the case for taxing powers, where estimates are that as much as half the population believes it is legitimate to cheat if they can do so (Bartlett and Steele 2000: 12). Poor design of government administration has the effect of undermining the legitimacy of public authority and is costly in every sense of the word. Authors David Osborne and Ted Gabler (1993) have such concerns in mind when they exhort policy makers to employ measures that rest lightly on society, that do not require so much "muscle," what they call "Catalytic Government: Steering Rather than Rowing."

When referring to the various powers and instruments of government, it is usually the case to refer to "command and control" approaches and "fiscal" approaches rather than tax powers and police powers. This is because many revenue streams are really authorized by law under the constitutional rubric of police powers. This is so particularly when the intention is less to collect revenue than it is to influence or direct economic behavior in certain ways. Even when revenues explicitly labeled taxes are employed to induce some behavior pattern or other, they do so more often by imposing or alleviating a penalty or burden than they do by any positive inducements. This should be obvious in light of discussion above concerning their limited power to exert positive influence.

It must also be borne in mind that many, indeed most, taxes have consequences that impede economic activity and discourage constructive behavior. Tax theorists have over the years been successful in developing a number of textbook principles that together constitute the basis of sound tax theory. Among them are efficiency, neutrality, equity, administrability, stability, and simplicity. An ideal tax is neutral and efficient with respect to markets and progressive in so far as those who have fewer resources will pay less. A sound tax is also easily administered, simple to understand, stable, and provides a reliable revenue stream. It is certain in the face of any attempts at evasion. Many students hold the view that all taxes have downside attributes so that any revenue system must necessarily make compromises and trade-offs. This claim is very much open to challenge. It is important here only to emphasize that taxes impact behavior in ways that go far beyond their purposes of supporting public services. To this extent, their architecture needs to be carefully designed and understood (Batt 2005, 2010).

Instituting Practices on a Georgist Paradigm

A Georgist approach to politics, administration, economics, and law addresses and tries to solve the challenges and obstacles alluded to in the foregoing discussion. There is a strong tradition among the political-science profession, of which I am a part, which sees its greatest challenge as architectonic design. By this is meant that political configurations and institutional structures need to be designed in ways that larger principles and purposes are well served. The study of politics, then, is not about discovering laws of politics and human nature; it is rather about building a political system that works. It is squarely in the tradition of the American founding fathers, who were called upon to conceive government in ways that would measure up to all the pressures and tests to which we have since seen it put. In the intervening two centuries since its inception, governmental structures have been modified several times. Consideration of changes that might improve upon the constitutional framework is a proper subject of inquiry and debate. The task entails examination of questions ranging from the most theoretical and abstract to the most instrumental and concrete.

Implicit in the Georgist vision, first of all, is the view that humanity owns the world in common and is entrusted with its stewardship. Government responsibility assures that it is used and watched over properly under principles of environmental soundness as well as political and moral justice. Arguably, concern for safeguarding the physical and natural world itself comes even before justice, lest there otherwise be no world assured for future inhabitants. This means that the lands, the air, the water, and all the other elements of nature need to be protected by whatever means governments have at their command. Alluded to earlier are the two principal powers granted by constitutional authority: police powers and tax powers. Governments, as sovereigns, may delegate these responsibilities or not, but they remain essential and primary if our earth is to survive. Sometimes, therefore, flat prohibition of certain behaviors may be called for, as when chlorofluorocarbons that threatened the existence of the ozone layer were banned not too long ago. No one doubted that governments acted properly to institute such actions.

The public has the right to expect that governments will take similar actions with any other threats to the integrity of the earth, and they should do so by employing its police powers as occasions fit. They may do so by outright curtailment or by other suitable measures, such as rationing, regulation, or assignment (Prugh et al. 1995: Ch. 6). Imposing such rules, however, needs to be considered with respect to the scope, weight, and domain of government limits, else they overextend themselves. Flat prohibitions are not necessarily the answer in all circumstances where economic behavior needs attention. Fiscal measures, properly designed, can be a far more refined and a deft tool with which to attend policy. They are adjustable because pricing leaves discretion to users. The variety of such instruments continues to grow: user fees, impact fees, fines, tolls, Pigou charges, licenses, and permits are only the best known. Such charges can generate a substantial amount of revenue by themselves.

In addition, the Georgist position is that all the natural resources of the earth and sky should require payment back to society for the privilege of their use, as this is indeed a privilege and a simple means of understanding the philosophy. If the earth is a common birthright, there is every reason to expect that those who use it most should compensate the rest of us. Following the tradition of classical economics, this payment takes the form of rent. Unlike the conventional use of the word rent in the English language, economic rent, or ground rent, is a term of art. It is typically defined as a payment beyond what is necessary to retain its use. As long as there exist accessible resources beyond what the economy demands, rent for their supply will be nil. But as soon as resources are called into play above the supply margin, rent attaches to those resource units as a matter of course and awaits collection by government. It becomes, in effect, a form of rationing, but relies on pricing rather than command-and-control approaches. Land rent is perhaps more easily understood when it is capitalized into a "lump sum" payment at title transfer, when it becomes the "present value" of all anticipated future payments for use of a natural resource site. ("Present value" is another term of art among economists, defined by one economics dictionary as "the worth of any future stream of returns or costs in terms of their value now"—Pearce 1992.) Since rents are socially rather than individually generated, George argued that they should by right be returned to government. Hence the recovery of rent is the proper source of finance for government services. And because the provision of such services is for the most part spatial and reflects the worth of those provisions, it gives them much of their market value to boot.

The existence of rent is also a function of a community's investment in locations—usually in the form of infrastructure. Locations have rental value not due to anything that a titleholder of a parcel does but rather on account of what activity and investment is made in proximate and neighborhood sites. Rent therefore is a socially created value, and it is this that gives a community the primary claim on its recapture.

The Georgist paradigm maintains that all economies have rent, and that it should properly be recaptured rather than left to appreciate in the market prices of the sites on which it comes to rest. Absent its recapture by government, it has many detrimental effects upon the economy generally as well as constituting an unearned windfall for fortunately situated titleholders. First, the detrimental economic effects of rent accretion need to be understood. There are first the distortionary effects at the margin, among the three factors of production, so that resources are not employed in the most optimal way. There are in addition the debilitating effects of rent accretion so that the economy is hampered in its operation. Lastly, there are environmental impacts upon society beyond economic factors that are difficult to identify and calculate but become apparent with its full understanding.

Unlike labor and capital, the other factors of economic production, natural resources, or "land" in classical economics terminology, normally have a fixed supply, or are "inelastic" in economic parlance. This means that any increase in demand for their use raises their market price disproportionately relative to the other factors. The titleholder to such commodities may, and usually is, the accidental beneficiary of such increases in price. Should that party choose to sell, the return is a windfall gain explained more by the common activity and economic vitality of the neighborhood or region than by anything due to that titleholder. In American urban localities as well as in many other nations of the world, speculation in land, whether in the form of locations, air, water, electromagnetic spectrum use, airport landing and take-off time slots, or even more abstruse forms, has evolved into a high art form, at the same time often causing irreparable harm and cost to proximate interests. Its most palpable harm comes from distortions in land parcel prices and the consequent urban sprawl configurations that would not exist if the public captured the rents. Another illustration arises from the wasteful allocation of valuable airport runway time creating congestion because time-slot rents are not auctioned to those for whom they are most economically valuable. These illustrations reveal inefficiencies in use of time and other resources.

In a sense, it is sometimes helpful to understand ground rent as a "deposit" that either flows or accretes in land sites and that, when not removed, constitutes a profound economic drag on the vitality of a community. This drag could at times be equated with the friction of a mechanical apparatus, and has two names to economists: excess burden and deadweight loss. These distortions lead to less than the "perfect competition" modeled by economists. The uncollected rent surplus accreting to resource sites often induces titleholders to keep it outside the market's reach and out of play; the inefficiency of its being on the sidelines may or may not be apparent. Those parties seeking opportunities to use such sites, however, are forced thereby to choose suboptimal and second-best locations that put the whole community at less advantage. Economic efficiency is thereby reduced so that everyone (except perhaps the titleholder to a land site with passive rent accretion) must work harder as a consequence for the same level of comfort and satisfaction.

The Distributional Impact of a Georgist Regime

The moral dimension of the Georgist paradigm is even more compelling. The first question often raised is why is it right to collect the economic rent in the form of taxes from landsites that people regard as their bought-and-paid-for property. If one could make a compelling case for total ownership then that argument might hold. But one would be hard put to find an instance in which real property ownership constitutes an absolute title in fee simple. The argument more often recalls Pierre Joseph Proudhon's (2008) comment over a century ago that "property is theft!" All titles to real property originate in some manner through force or fraud if traced back, even though current owners typically see their titles as legitimate (Miller 2006; Miller et al. 2010). Therefore, the reality is, as courts have decided, somewhere in the middle: ownership of title is always conditional.

Law books (for example, Friedman, Harris, and Lindeman 2005) refer to real property ownership as a "Bundle of Rights," among them, possession, use, alienation (the power to give away), consumption, modification, destruction, management, exchange, and profit taking. One does not see it given the blindness of neoclassical economics, but it could also include the right to the retention of the economic rent. Were the right to keep rent protected by law, the real property tax as presently constituted would certainly be challenged. Any market value that "land" possesses owes its price to the present value of rent, and were such ownership titles to acquire the nature of absolute freeholds, taxing it would constitute a "taking." Yet one sees nothing of the kind: in fact taxes on land were the first this nation ever experienced, and the collection of land rent has a tradition going back 6,000 years (Webber and Wildavsky 1986). The Georgist view is that since rent is a socially created value it should be the moral right of society to reclaim it as the most suitable source of public revenue. Henry George (1962: 405) wrote:

> I do not propose either to purchase or to confiscate private property in land. The first would be unjust, the second needless. Let the individuals who now hold it still retain, if they want to, possession of what they are pleased to call *their* land. Let them buy and sell, and bequeath and devise it. We may safely leave them the shell, if we take the kernel. It is not necessary to confiscate land; it is only necessary to confiscate rent.

Already alluded to is the fact that the existence of rent is a consequence of a community's efforts and not that of any one titleholder, gainfully employed or not. The stronger moral case rests, therefore, with those that would recover all rent to support services for society. John Stuart Mill (2000: Book 5, chapter 2, section 5) recognized that "landlords grow richer in their sleep without working, risking or economizing. The increase in the value of land, arising as it does from the efforts of an entire community, should belong to the community and not to the individual who might hold title." After reading Mill, Henry George made this the core of his economic philosophy. He argued that taxes on labor and capital were both inefficient and unjust, and that the only proper source of taxation was the surplus rent that otherwise links to land.

Because neoclassical economics conflates land with man-made capital to comprise a two-factor theory, capital appreciation of real property is likely to be more in land than not. This becomes even more apparent when one realizes that buildings typically depreciate from 0.5 percent to 1.5 percent yearly (Davis and Palumbo 2006), and capital equipment—motor vehicles, computers, and factory equipment—can typically be written off entirely in an even shorter time period. Peruvian economist Hernando de Soto (2000) has received a good deal of recent acclaim for arguing that improved titling of real estate in developing nations would substantially improve economic growth. Securing better titles, he argues, would provide banks more adequate collateral for the loans that start-up enterprises need to be successful. The assurances of a capital base in real estate offers to borrowers the leverage they need to obtain the further capital that allows them to grow. To de Soto, therefore, land titling is the critically lacking ingredient holding back the development of third-world nations.

Consider this argument from another perspective, however, one looking beyond the simple investment stratagem on which de Soto would grow the economy, to its impact upon the whole society. More than just enterprise ventures are needed to induce development; what about stable government and bureaucracy, reliable infrastructure, quality education, assured health care, and other elements that make for an economy that grows? If leveraged land becomes the basis for private-sector development, the surplus rent created is paid to financial institutions as interest. Rents could not then be the basis of taxation to support public services, and revenue practices would have to emulate the tax structures of Europe and the U.S., that is, income, sales (or VATs), corporate franchise, or real property taxes. These taxes have downside effects that are far more drastic: the rate of evasion is high, the costs of collection and administration are high, and the deadweight loss is high. One can anticipate de Soto's answer being similar to that typically voiced by mainstream neoclassical students of taxation: that all revenue designs have downside effects and there is no perfect tax. The Georgist position is that a land-value tax, and the collection of rent in all its guises, is really in fact an ideal tax, with few if any downside effects at all (Batt 2005).

One needs to ask how much rent is there in a nation's economy. With all the advantages to be had by removing rent from the markets, just like removing sand from the gears of a machine, what kind of productivity surplus does it constitute? Estimates are difficult because even with the advent of computers and data, the neoclassical economics profession has not pressed governments for the financial data compilation that would allow us to measure it adequately. The U.S. National Income and Product Accounts list a figure of roughly 1 or 2 percent, a figure that we know is ridiculous. Even back-of-the-envelope calculations suggest that it is many times this. Moving beyond contemporary attempts at its calculation, one finds references to rent payments of this amount for many societies and times. Historically, rent payments were usually made in other forms than money. It was often the case that payment was a proportion of a farmer's yield or in a specified number of days of corvée labor. Based on practices of the period, classical economic theory took as a given that rent surplus constituted about a third of a society's economy (Bloch 1970: 72; Bennett 1971: 97–125; Bairoch 1991: 283). An old English nursery rhyme (traceable to France as well, as far back as the 17th century) reflects this common practice when feudal arrangements were at their peak: "Bah, bah black sheep, have you any wool? Yes sir, yes sir, three bags full. One for my master, one for my dame, one for the little boy that lives down the lane."

One quick study (Cord 1985), tabulating just based on the potential of a full land tax, excluding rent from pollution rights, the spectrum, landing slots, corporate charters, internet addresses, and other sources, suggested that it amounts to about 28 percent of GDP. A far more detailed and sophisticated study of land rent in Australia (Dwyer 2003: 40) estimated that total rent is well above 30 percent of GDP, and it concluded that "the 'bottom line' reinforces the overall conclusion . . . that land-based tax revenues are indeed sufficient to allow total abolition of company and personal income tax." An enumeration of sites where additional rent situates would take enormous effort, but Mason Gaffney (2004) has suggested 15 major sources as a start, all of which by their private capture reduce economic productivity. When all is said and done, Gaffney (2009) suggests that "The Hidden Taxable Capacity of Land [is] Enough and to Spare" in supplanting all present taxes. This is a significant finding because we know from various studies how much the deadweight loss from the current taxes is. Harvard economist Martin Feldstein (1999) estimated that the burden from the income tax alone is more than 30 percent, and about 50 percent if social security taxes are added. The sales tax is in all likelihood just as inefficient (Diewert and Lawrence 1997). Looked at another way, substantial proof has now been developed to show, as George (1962: 406) originally argued, that:

In every civilized country, even the newest, the value of the land taken as a whole is sufficient to bear the entire expenses of government. In the better-developed countries it is much more than sufficient. Hence it will not be enough merely to place all taxes upon the value of land. It will be necessary, where rent exceeds the present government revenues, commensurately to increase the amount demanded in taxation, and to continue this increase as society progresses and rent advances.

In the past 30 years, such major economists as Swedish Bank Prize Laureates William Vickrey and Joseph Stiglitz have demonstrated the validity of what has come to be called the Henry George Theorem. Gilbert Tucker (2010), a self-taught student of Henry George, foretold the case decades earlier in a short book titled *The Self-Supporting City*. In it, he boldly argues (Tucker 2010: 1):

Municipal taxation as now levied can and should be a thing of the past: the American city can be a self-supporting corporation, meeting its expenses from its rightful income. Taxation is unnecessary, because the city has, in its physical properties, acquired through the years, by the expenditure of its people's moneys, a huge capital investment from which it collects only a very small part of the return earned.

The question, then, begs: why tax those revenue bases that create significant efficiency loss in an economy when alternatively one could tax something else that not only removes the inefficiency from the market but can actually be collected for public service and be adequate for its total support at no loss to the general economy? From a strictly economic viewpoint, leaving aside for the moment any moral arguments, this makes perfect sense! Even more so than in the economies of the developing world generally, it is the public sector that is most starved. Given the common arguments offered about the importance of infrastructure investment as a vehicle for development "take-off," this is the "natural tax" to facilitate it. (The term "natural tax" was a common substitute for the "single tax" that was espoused by the Georgists a century ago; see Shearman 1897; Fillebrown 1917.) Yet, if de Soto's approach is applied, the economic rent pledged to banks as collateral is just as likely, perhaps more so, to be siphoned off for the benefit of extra-national institutions as used as resource capital within a country for its own public development (George 1988, 2004; Perkins 2004; Hudson 2007).

The moral argument is even more compelling: economic rent is windfall income to the titleholder of the site on which it sits, a surplus that is demonstrably the result of community effort and has nothing to do with the behavior of any owner. Mention was made earlier of John Stuart Mill's observation but one could as well cite the widely read story about "Mr. Dooley" in *Plunkitt of Tammany Hall* (Riordan 1905):

> There's an honest graft, and I'm an example of how it works. I might sum up the whole thing by sayin': "I seen my opportunities and I took 'em." Just let me explain by examples. My party's in power in the city, and it's goin' to undertake a lot of public improvements. Well, I'm tipped off, say, that they're going to lay out a new park at a certain place. I see my opportunity and I take it. I go to that place and I buy up all the land I can in the neighborhood. Then the board of this or that makes its plan public, and there's a rush to get my land, which nobody cared particular for before. Ain't it perfectly honest to charge a good price and make a profit on my investment and foresight? Of course, it is. Well, that's honest graft.

Henry George was quite emphatic about this kind of thinking: to him it was theft! One of his most easily understood and therefore widely reprinted speeches (1887) was titled "Thou Shalt Not Steal." In *Progress and Poverty,* he viewed owning land in freehold as the moral equivalent of owning slaves (George 1962: Ch. 27). Looking once more at the morality of taxation, compare the logic of taxing wage labor, which one earns with one's own hands or mind, or the taxation of capital goods, which are produced by sweat and inspiration, with the recapture of economic rent. In the one case it is wrung out from a person's hard-earned labor under threat of punishment; in the other the taxation is the painless collection of socially created windfalls to sites. King Louis XIV, Jean-Baptiste Colbert, had it right when he said that the art of taxation consists in so plucking the goose as to get the most feathers with the least amount of hissing. But for some reason his maxim is not followed; with proper public understanding of the nature of rent—that it is in no instance an owner's entitlement to begin with—there should be no hissing at all!

There is also the distributional issue in any economy that professes to rest on free markets, of which Henry George was certainly a proponent. In his time much of the wealth captured by the American moguls and tycoons was a consequence of their having cornered a source of rental income from land. A review of the titans of the era shows that the sources of early American fortunes were due to their having done just that. Consider the Fortune 400 of the time: Astor (furs and real estate), Field (land), Sage (lumber), Rockefeller (oil), as well as many others like Gould who through their control of railroads extracted rent, Carnegie, whose coal mines facilitated his steel manufacturing, and Morgan, whose banking empire relied upon passed-through rents for further speculation (Myers 1936). The recapture of rent, he argued, removed the phenomenon of unearned income from land to be used for the support of public services.

Absent the ability of such figures to reap the windfall gain of rents, it would be interesting to know how their fortunes would have compared with others. Can one in any way conclude how much of their income was explained by the sweat of their hands and brow or the returns to what manufactured capital they came to own? One might look at today's counterparts for a partial answer. Many of the "world's top billionaires" are software developers like Bill Gates, Steve Ballmer, and Paul Allen who had the good fortune to capture the rent from computer codes, language that is every bit as "natural" in its own way as the land of classical economics. Warren Buffett has always had the prescience in his Berkshire-Hathaway Corporation to invest in ventures that had strong rent features. Ted Turner owes his wealth to his capture of a satellite orbit, which is largely capitalized rent. Several other family fortunes exist largely, if not exclusively, because of investments in real estate, that is, rent returns.

Concern needs to be expressed as well about the preservation of the commons. In classical and feudal societies, the existence of the commons was a given. Only in modern society is it threatened with demise, largely perhaps due to the misreading of many classical economists, and especially of Adam Smith. The notion that the economy is a self-regulating system overseen by an "invisible hand" of natural equilibration is simply false, and the specter of the commons being over-run by private avarice is a misreading of the classic article by Garrett Hardin (1968). Professor Robert Andelson (1991: 41) in response pointed out that pre-modern societies appreciated the limits to growth, and knew that by collection of economic rent, private impulses overwhelming the commons could be kept in check. He pointed out that "the only way in which the individual may be assured what properly belongs to him is for society to take what properly belongs to it: the Jeffersonian ideal of individualism requires for its realization the socialization of rent." Rent, he argued, is every bit as much a part of the commons as any of its correlatives in land, water, or air.

We are witnessing a rebirth of interest in the protection of the commons, especially in light of the looming disappearance of so many parts of it—such as wildlife and fisheries. A word that had for all practical purposes become archaic has now suddenly been given new life. The burgeoning interest in protection of the commons is reflected not only in the recent literature but also by the award of the Swedish Bank Prize in 2009 to Indiana University Professor of Political Science Elinor Ostrom. She was long thought of as working in the proverbial wilderness with little acclaim or recognition in her chosen field of academe or beyond (Ostrom 1990; Buck and Ostrom 1998; Burger et al. 2001; see also Baden and Noonan 1998). The award came very much as a surprise, especially the economics Nobel, as her work was not thought of particularly even as "economic" in nature! The movement toward privatization of natural resources has at least been served notice now, even as inventory of its rightful dimensions as a commons proceeds. Recognition of the phenomenon of economic rent as an element of the commons opens opportunities for additional ways of thinking about common property, open-access regimes, common-pool resources, privatization designs, and so on. Indeed, institution of a program of rent recapture allows for the possibility of protecting public entitlements and interests where the proverbial "horse" is otherwise already "out of the barn." Where rent is to be regarded as part of the commons its collection restores what is otherwise an imbalance between the public and the private realms of society (Batt 2008).

Spatial Configurations with Rent Recaptured

Even if it is clear that rent is recovered from sites where it locates, it needs to be asked who would pay rent. When David Ricardo (1911) originally worked out the theory of economic rent in 1817, he applied it to the productivity of agricultural land and the growing of corn. Today, land-rent calculation has far greater applicability to urban spatial configurations and the differential site values due to strategic access. Looking solely at real property, it is apparent that the market value of land sites is a function of where people choose to gather, and the most valuable sites, therefore, are in urban centers. Typically, these sites are commercial markets or else close to common arenas where people congregate in any case. The land value gradient falls very quickly as one recedes from core areas until coming ultimately to areas where the site values are unmeasurable if not trivial. Looking at land-use configurations one typically finds residential plots outside the commercial core, and farms or forests at the farther reaches. The land value per acre in a typical city core can be as much as 100 times that in residential areas. Much of the theory worked out for this was done in 1826 by a German geographer, Heinrich von Thünen (1966), whom some have ranked among the great economists of the 19th century. Along with Ricardo, he worked out many formulas calculating economic rent. The differential market value of land is most clearly understood when visualized on land value maps. (For an account of the history of land-value maps, see Batt 2009.) His models are now being applied in various ways today because they have proven to be so apt.

In localities where a tax is imposed on land value alone, rather than upon both buildings and land as the conventional property tax prescribes, it is clear how the payment burden is shared. Following von Thünen's formulas, the overwhelming proportion of land rent is in cities, and one typically finds that about half of this rent is on sites that are commercial in nature, the other half on residential sites. (Farmers' land has so little market value—unless it is located inappropriately in urban areas—that it has trivial market price.) This means that, in the United States, where about 65 percent of all households own their own home, the 35 percent remainder who are tenants pay no tax at all. This is because land, being inelastic, capitalizes rent in its market price and does not pass it through to others. Tenants pay nothing at all under a land-value tax regime. All this makes a land-value tax highly progressive. Indeed, if comparative studies of tax incidence were done, there is a good likelihood that a land-value tax would be most progressive of any.

This leads to the third set of consequences of applying land-value taxation, especially in urban localities where the site rents are highest. It neutralizes and even reverses the centrifugal forces of sprawl development that have plagued many cities in the world, especially where motor-vehicle transportation has become the primary means of mobility. By taxing away the site rent, parcels with the highest market value (or rent flow), are induced to develop first in order to recover their carrying costs. Rather than sit idle and wait for speculative gains, thereby driving prospective developers to peripheral and second-best locations, these parcel owners are moved to invest in them—or else to sell to those who will. If one assumes that the "highest and best use" of parcels obtains through the application of a land-value tax, development would unfold in much more concentrated areas.

Site rent is also often easily understood as capitalized transportation cost, because whatever isn't paid for location is likely to be paid (even if assumed by society rather than individuals) for access and mobility (Batt 2003). This relieves the pressure for development in peripheral localities and thereby lessens the costs in terms of time and resources for transportation. Given that public transit services typically need a certain minimum density to be economically viable—about 10 to 12 households per acre, or the commercial equivalent—it means that motor-vehicle dependency is mitigated, and all the expected consequences for pollution, health and safety risks, social disamenities, and so on, are profoundly reduced.

Looking Beyond Land Rent Broadly Defined

Until now the focus has largely been on land-rent recapture, "land" in its contemporary vernacular meaning rather than the sense in which it was used by the classical economists—that is, any element and dimension of nature that had market value as a resource. The advantages of collecting economic rent from other sources should also be apparent, mainly in the way by which it increases the liquidity of the commodity or resource employed. Two illustrations should illustrate the point. First, the electromagnetic spectrum is now treated as "property" by its titleholders, whether used for electronic media presentation, communication, monitoring of various natural or social phenomena, or whatever. Were it paid for at its full marginal cost of operation rather than kept in abeyance for whatever future purpose titleholders saw fit, its use would be far more efficient and its service would have greater reach. To take a second example, the time slots at airports are, in effect, now "owned" by the airlines for their scheduling of take-offs and landings. Regardless whether they are used, or used efficiently from a flight-management perspective, they constitute a "property asset" to an airline. The London-based Institute for Public Policy Research has proposed that those time slots be opened to periodic auction so that the scheduled flights in and out of U.K. airports would be arranged in such a way as to relieve the congestion (O'Connell 2003). Applying the same principle to relieve congestion in the center of London by the institution of a congestion charge proved to be very effective and has since been expanded twice.

A third, and partial, instance where the application of the value of rent has been recognized is in the institution of "pollution rights" in many of the developed nations of the world. In the United States and in the European Community, the air is appreciated as property for its capacity, within limits, to absorb a certain amount of emissions from power plants. The utility companies, identified by the amount of NOX, SO2, and other pollutants into the air, have been given the rights to do so in statute law. Following this, they have been able to trade these "rights" among themselves in a way that balances the costs of investment in scrubber technology and other emission-control measures with the costs of owning pollution rights. Arguably, the use of pricing as a means of achieving the optimal deployment of resources for pollution abatement is an improvement over the earlier "command-and-control" approaches. But the same result, with a far more principled basis, could have been reached had it been recognized that the public is the rightful "owner" of the atmosphere, and that any payment for its use should redound to the public in the form of rent collection. Relinquishing public ownership of the air to the use of utilities to use as a "dump" for their effluents is not only economically inefficient but morally reprehensible as well. Peter Barnes (2001) has proposed something close to this logic: returning the rental dividend directly to each citizen rather than using it to pay for public services. If the threshold level of emissions were set at a level comparable to currently acceptable limits, each American could receive a yearly dividend check of roughly $1,000. Each recipient would then be better positioned to decide how much of this entitlement to pay to government in taxes. Proponents of a citizens' dividend, sometimes called a "basic income guarantee," argue that placing the collected resource rents equally in the hands of all members of society would ensure that a more balanced set of choices would eventuate between public expenditures and private enjoyments. It would be comparable to the design of the Alaska Permanent Fund that distributes a portion of petroleum royalties to every citizen of the state as a matter of entitlement. This distribution now typically amounts to about $1,000 annually for every resident of the State of Alaska. Several American planners and statesmen, including former Secretary of State George Schultz, proposed a similar plan for Iraq with respect to its oil royalties.

All these examples have applicability worldwide, in developing nations as well as advanced industrial nations. In fact, comparatively speaking, it may be easier to apply them in circumstances where other measures are less possible. In the Soviet Union, just before its collapse, where *perestroika* called for the creation of a revenue structure *de novo*, a tax on natural resources and "land" would have been the simplest of all from a technical and equitable point of view. A group of notable western economists, including several past Nobel Prize winners, wrote a letter to then President Gorbachev, urging him to implement a tax on land values (Tideman et al., 1991). The interest in the approach at the highest levels grew to a point where Georgist advocates made as many as nine visits to Russia to advise leaders on its feasible implementation (Banks 1994). No doubt this was aided by the fact that a century earlier, Count Leo Tolstoy was an ardent follower of Henry George (Redfearn 1992). Despite the fact that titles to land in Russia had been dissolved long ago and there were no vested interests in defense of private property, the advice was not heeded for political reasons. It doesn't detract, however, from the fact that it was technically quite feasible.

Georgism as an Answer for Our Time

Presently it appears that the political discourse of western nations has reached an impasse. Radical free-market capitalism, despite a current resurgence of interest, has demonstrated its limitations, and doctrinaire socialism, whether of the Marxist variety or any other, has been shown to be unworkable. There have been many proposals for a "third way," and numerous proposals have sought to seize that mantle. But despite the many approaches offered, none to date has achieved any strong tractability. In most cases its proponents have sought to sell it rather as a "radical middle," rejecting both top-down redistribution and hands-off laissez faire capitalism. The number of political leaders claiming to be the inheritors or apologists for the third way have been legion—Bill Clinton, Tony Blair, Gerhard Schroeder, and Jean Chrétien. Among the more scholarly advocates have been the U.K.'s Anthony Giddens (a prolific author identified with the British think tank Policy Network) and the U.S. communitarian movement's Amitai Etzioni. (Although decrying the "communitarian" label, those most closely identified with its thinking are Harvard political scientist Michael Sandel, Boston College political sociologist Alan Wolfe, Canadian philosopher Charles Taylor, Harvard Law's Mary Ann Glendon, California sociologist Philip Selznick, Scottish philosopher Alisdair McIntyre, and Princeton's Michael Walzer, with Professor Etzioni seemingly the central figure and driving force.) The communitarian movement, however, seems not able to address the question of what ought to be public and what ought to be private. It entreats people to be more mindful and considerate of others and of the social community, but at least to this reader's thinking to date, it has yet to offer a compelling grounding for such action. It does not, or at least has not been able to, build its political philosophy on interests rather than upon expectations. On the other hand, its concerns are very much on the mark with reference to the vitality of community and the need for its revival.

Closer to the Georgist approach perhaps, indeed somewhat a sister to it, is the public-trust doctrine, most recently amplified and edified by author and activist Peter Barnes (2006). Barnes is alarmed by the imbalance between the public interest and the growing power of corporations, having become disillusioned with the capacity of government to serve as a countervailing force for its protection. In response, he proposes that not-for-profit corporate bodies be established to govern and assert the positions of sectors in need of protection against the aggressive forces of corporate power. These bodies would be governed and maintained by elected boards that serve as the guardians of trust interests according to their charters. Their control over resources would be both "propertized" (his word) and privatized. The problem, however, is that these bodies cannot guarantee that they will serve any interest wider than their own. As happens among established trusts of this order, they have often become enclaves of elite and privileged populations. A Georgist approach, in contrast, collects rent not for any private community but by and for the entire society. (For a review of the Barnes book, see Batt 2007.)

Solving the Political Impasse for Nations in Transition

Instances abound, particularly in developing nations, where common resources have been seized either by authoritarian governments or else by powerful corporate interests, and are then seemingly beyond the reach and responsiveness of the public at large. Two instances recently in the news serve well to illustrate the dilemmas, one involving Cuba, where public ownership of land resources may well be in jeopardy with the death of Fidel Castro, the other in Thailand, where monopoly control of almost the entire telecommunications industry was amassed privately and then sold to a corporate body beyond the nation's borders.

Cuba's economic development has been impressive under the almost half-century of the Castro regime. By many standards it measures favorably even with the most developed of nations. Life expectancy, literacy and education levels, and general quality of life are high. On the dimension of sustainability, Cuba has largely weaned itself from fossil-fuel energy sources, has preserved much of its forestland, and prospered in many other ways. There is no question that the legitimacy of the Castro government is not in any jeopardy from any challenges by the resident population. However, there continues to be a large expatriate community, mostly based in Miami, which is eager for the day when it will be able to return to its ancestral homeland and recover its historical position in the political and social scale. This would be a fanciful dream except for the fact that the United States is perhaps willing to support such change when Fidel Castro is no longer on the scene. The expatriate Cuban community dreams of recapturing titles to property that were either seized or abandoned with the arrival of the Castro government decades ago. With the sanctity with which property is held in the United States and with its willingness perhaps to impose this value on a Cuba restored to status quo ante, this is not an unrealistic expectation.

A Georgist solution offers a possible compromise, one that would restore a greater dimension of free-market rule to the Cuban economy as well as recognize some legitimacy to property titles, if push comes to shove. It is not really titles that the erstwhile landowners and property owners are covetous of; rather it is the rent yield from those properties. If a tax regime were instituted in Cuba whereby the rents were collected from any and all the "propertized" parcels, titles would have meaning only for their use value and not for their rental value. Recognizing use value would grant former titleholders the power to choose the purposes to which such lands might be put, and at the same time relieve the puissance of their demands. At the same time, the inheritors of the Castro legacy would be able to accept the equity of the design in as much as this was their greatest concern in the original seizure. This approach is not beyond possibility; representatives of the American Georgist community have had occasion to visit Cuba and talk with officials at the highest level, and there is at least one expatriate Cuban living in America who is a strong supporter of the Georgist agenda. (Tomas Estrada Palma IV is the great grandson of Cuba's first president, 1902–1906, of the same name. He has a website that not only chronicles much of the Cuban political activity, both in the U.S. and in his home of origin, but strongly supports Georgist measures to remedy the nation's economic challenges; see http://tomasestradapalma4today.blogspot.com/.)

Thailand has, to many observers, been a success story of development for the past 30 years, having attained the status of one of the emerging "little tigers" of Asia. Thai government and business control has always been heavily concentrated, belying the outward appearance of a free-market society. The hierarchical order that nests all its institutions and enterprises has roots in the patrimonial structure that marked the society for centuries and gave it much of its stability. In the modern era, enterprises like radio and TV, electric power, and rail transport were owned either by military branches or by the government directly. Other businesses like cement, beer, oil, and insurance were owned by a small network of families or by the king. But stupendous economic growth in the 1970s and 1980s led to binge spending on entertainment emporiums, hotels, resorts, and other ventures, over-extending much of the nation's credit system and leading to a spectacular financial crash in 1997. This crisis shook the economy to its roots. Pressure in response from the World Bank and the IMF resulted in the wholesale privatization of companies, often at fire-sale prices. Many of Thailand's flagship companies thus ended up in the hands of new owners, some under a considerable degree of foreign control.

A strong national educational system along with a cadre of trained civil servants and a resurgent tourism trade gave the country the strength to recover quickly. The nation was viewed as an emerging democracy when, to the surprise of many, the military stepped in to sack the incumbent and popularly elected Prime Minister Thaksin Shinawatra. Sickened by the realization that this was necessary, the urban middle class reluctantly condoned the action, even greeted the military with gratitude by tossing flowers in the paths of soldiers. It realized that Thaksin had become a demagogue, if not worse. The rural population was the base of Thaksin's support, even to the point where had he stood for re-election once more he would have won. He had risen very quickly to power, only in the year 2001, having fortuitously invested in the mobile-phone industry just at the moment that it was exploding in use. (As an illustration of how strategically placed Thaksin's Shin Corporation was, one needs only to recognize that telephone service through landlines was practically non-existent when suddenly cell phone technology burst forth. This allowed the country to install signal towers across the land and essentially leapfrog over existing technologies at a far lower investment cost. When I was first in Thailand in 1962 in a rural Peace Corps post, the only way I could have asked for help, had I needed it, would have been to rely on the police radio service to contact Bangkok. Today cell phones are as ubiquitous in Thailand as they are in any advanced industrial nation.) In a period of a decade Thaksin came to be worth billions. From there he expanded his empire to include other communications enterprises such as radio, television, satellite, newspapers, and of course real estate, and was able on that basis to essentially buy his way to political power. As in the typical Thai way of doing things, he formed his own political party, had his own newspaper, his own media network, and his own coterie of attendants.

To be sure, Thaksin had instituted many measures for which the public was grateful, the most important being the institution of universal health care. For the price of roughly 75 cents a visit ($US), any citizen in the country could have medical treatment. On the other hand, Thaksin had opened even wider the floodgates of the country for foreign investment, and gave international companies attractive opportunities to snatch up hundreds of businesses at bargain-basement prices. Then, suddenly, still as prime minister, Thaksin sold his own cell-phone business for an estimated 4 billion dollars to Temasek Holdings, an international conglomerate in Singapore partially owned by its government. This not only gave control of one of Thailand's key industries to an organization beyond its own borders, but the sale was done in a way that allowed Thaksin to avoid any tax payments to the Thai government.

The politically aware elements of the Thai population, already uncomfortable with this arriviste's control of so much of the country's essential services and fearful and sickened by much of Thaksin's demagoguery, were outraged by this behavior. It was then that the military stepped in with the tacit blessing of the Thai monarchy to seize governance of the nation while Thaksin was in New York at the opening of the UN Session. After a history of military coups going back to the 1930s, it was a move that Thailand watchers, both within and beyond its borders, thought they had moved beyond and hoped would never happen again. Sadly, it was not the case.

The military cabal held new elections soon, following the drafting of a new constitution, one that hopefully would not allow so much power to be amassed by a prime minister. But the general population was mobilized and polarized for the first time in Thai history: the rural people favoring Thaksin for the health program and low interest loans he initiated, and the middle class cognizant of his more egregious financial corruption. The military leadership that stepped in was initially somewhat ham-handed in its rule, one instance of controversial policy being an attempt to rewrite the rules about how much control international corporations should be allowed to have over Thai businesses. National leaders came to be alarmed about threats to Thai sovereignty by the new forces of globalization. Instead of requiring a certain proportion of corporate directors to be Thai citizens, it chose to stipulate that a majority of capital be owned within the country. The globalizers abroad roundly condemned this proposal, and the rules soon collapsed in the face of pressures by international political and business interests. Meanwhile, the government also sought to recover control of the privatized telecommunication monopoly that had fallen into foreign hands.

As matters now stand, a struggle continues over property titles and governing structures and it is by no means clear which factions will prevail. The world community, claiming to be the forces of enlightenment, is on the side of increased free trade. But one can understand how Thai people, and many of their leaders, are concerned that they are about to lose control of their own country, and in effect become a latter-day colony of international corporate interests. (GRAIN, an international organization, has formed to raise awareness about the extent to which land parcels, both urban and rural, are being purchased by individuals and corporations in outside countries. This practice is nothing less than a latter-day land-grab and is being promoted by the World Bank. Dozens of grass-roots organizations worldwide, including several in Thailand, have joined this coalition and have put forth principles to guide national awareness. The largest of these in Thailand is the Land Reform Network of Thailand.) As noted earlier, Thailand has a strong cadre of government experts in finance and economics, and the banking community is equally well staffed with worldly western educated professionals. But these officials, both in government and outside, are totally immersed in conventional neoclassical economic philosophy. They are as blind to the concept of economic rent as are most economists working for international banks, American government agencies, and others.

But there is a Georgist solution to Thailand's dilemma. Were the nation to collect the economic rent from the internationally owned businesses, there would be less incentive for them to be captured, less leverage over Thai government and economy, less tax revenue needing to be taken from Thai people themselves from other sources, and greater recovery of the "commons" the country is now at the risk of losing. Collection of economic rent is the natural defense against the seizure of resources by international businesses on a worldwide basis, a logical protection against the pressures of globalization, and the best protection against corporate power overwhelming political sovereignty. How to help Thailand appreciate this realization is a challenge for not only the international Georgist community but for those in Thailand that have become fascinated with the Georgist paradigm. The one long-time active Georgist in Thailand is retired Admiral Suthon Hinjiranon, who has translated Henry George into Thai, has written his own book for Thai readers (2002), and who maintains a website (http://utopiathai.webs.com/) to promote the Georgist message. (Admiral Suthon was exposed to the ideas of Henry George decades ago when he was stationed in New York as a naval officer and elected to practice his English at the Henry George School in New York. With the support of the Schalkenbach Foundation, he printed copies of his translation of *Progress and Poverty* in 2003, as well as his own book, *The Unjust Poverty*.)

It is almost beside the point to ask what happens to democracy and distributive justice in circumstances where corporate power becomes the prevailing force in a country's operations. This appears increasingly to be the case in world affairs, as elucidated earlier in this paper. Thomas Friedman, foreign-policy columnist for the *New York Times* and an effective chronicler of globalization trends, is as much a journalistic apologist for globalization as Columbia University economist Jagdish Bhagwati (2005) is among economists. Friedman (2006) argues that in a world that is "flat"—that is, where capital and labor are on a level playing field worldwide and where trade offers the efficiency of the lowest common denominator—no two countries having

McDonalds are likely to go to war against one another. Perhaps so, but this is a world where corporate hierarchies are beginning to dominate over political democracies (if they do not already), where wealth and power threaten to prevail over distributive justice, and where freedom and initiative are in danger of becoming subordinate to the "iron cages" of organization that Max Weber dreaded in a coming rational and bureaucratic age. A century ago, Henry George (1966) defended the open market free-trade policies first advocated by David Ricardo as means by which to enhance competitive advantages and raise the quality of markets to the full extent of their reach. When his book on the subject was written, however, labor and capital were for the most part immobile; there was no way he could have envisioned the prospect of worldwide money transfers by wire in an instant. This practice invites reconsideration of George's defense of open markets, at least until such time, should it ever arrive, that economic rent is first and fully collected from land in all its natural forms (Daly 2002; Braund 2005: Ch. 9).

In the final analysis, the Georgist philosophy and its very practical agenda has both wide applicability and moral force. It offers an answer, perhaps the only answer, to a world increasingly captured by private interests, by corporate power, and by distant elites. It offers economic justice and clarity of vision, restoration of and protection for the commons, all critically necessary dimensions if politics is to prevail over economics. Lastly, it offers protection for the environment of the earth in a deft and gentle way that is within the capacity of governments to implement. If the Georgist vision is to be successful, however, it requires a level of altruistic thinking that represents a challenge to political discourse at a local, a national, and a global level.

References

Andelson, R. (1991). *Commons Without Tragedy: Protecting the Environment from Overpopulation—a New Approach.* London: Shepheard-Walwyn.

Arnold, T. W. (1937). *The Folklore of Capitalism.* New Haven: Yale University Press.

Aron, S. (1996). *How the West Was Lost: The Transformation of Kentucky from Daniel Boone to Henry Clay.* Baltimore: Johns Hopkins University Press.

Baden, J. A., and D. S. Noonan. (1998). *Managing the Commons*, 2nd ed. Bloomington: Indiana University Press.

Bairoch, P. (1991). *Cities and Economic Development: From the Dawn of History to the Present*. Chicago: University of Chicago Press.

Banks, R. (1994). "The Mirage of State Planning." *Land and Liberty* November–December.

Banner, S. (2005). *How the Indians Lost Their Land: Law and Power on the Frontier*. Cambridge: Harvard University Press.

Barnes, P. (2001). *Who Owns the Sky? Our Common Assets and the Future of Capitalism*. Washington, DC: Island Press.

———. (2006). *Capitalism, 3.0: A Guide to Reclaiming the Commons*. San Francisco: Berrett-Koehler.

Bartlett D., and J. Steele. (2000). *The Great American Tax Dodge*. Boston: Little, Brown & Co.

Batt (2003). "Stemming Sprawl: The Fiscal Approach." In *Surveying Sprawl: Culture, Ecology, and Politics*. Ed. M. J. Lindstrom and H. Bartling. New York: Rowman & Littlefield.

———. (2005). "The Fallacy of the 'Three-Legged Stool' Metaphor." *State Tax Notes* 35(6): 377–381. Available at: http://www.wealthandwant.com/docs/Batt_3legged.html.

———. (2007). "Reclaiming the Commons." Available at: http://www.progress.org/2007/barncap.htm.

———. (2008). "Saving the Commons in an Age of Plunder." Presentation to the Albany Torch Club, May 5. Accessible at: http://www.wealthandwant.com/docs/Batt_Saving_the_Commons_Plunder.htm.

———. (2009). "Land Value Maps are Not New, But Their Utility Needs to be Re-Discovered." *International Journal of Transdisciplinary Research* 4(1): 108–158.

Batt, H. W. (2010). "Principles of Sound Tax Theory as Have Evolved Over 200 Years." *Groundswell*. Available at: http://commonground-usa.net/battprincip02.htm.

Baumol, W., and A. Blinder. (1991). *Economics: Principles and Policy*, 5th ed. New York: Harcourt Brace Jovanovich.

Bennett, H. S. (1971). *Life on the English Manor: A Study of Peasant Conditions, 1150–1400*. Cambridge, UK: Cambridge University Press.

Bergmann, B. (1999). "Abolish the Nobel Prize for Economics." *Challenge* 42.

Bhagwati, J. (2005). *In Defense of Globalization*. New York: Oxford University Press.

Bloch, M. (1970). *French Rural History: An Essay on Its Basic Characteristics*. Berkeley: University of California Press.

Braund, M. (2005). *The Possibility of Progress*. London: Shepheard-Walwyn.

Buck, S., and E. Ostrom. (1998). *The Global Commons: An Introduction*. Washington: Island Press.

Burger, J., E. Ostrom, R. B. Norgaard, D. Policansky, and B. D. Goldstein. (2001). *Protecting the Commons: A Framework for Resource Management in the Americas.* Washington, DC: Island Press, 2001.

Chandler, A. N. (1945). *Land Title Origins: A Take of Force and Fraud.* New York: Robert Schalkenbach Foundation.

Collier, P. (2007). *The Bottom Billion: Why the Poorest Countries are Failing and What Can Be Done About It.* Oxford, UK: Oxford University Press.

——. (2010). *The Plundered Planet: Why We Must—And How We Can—Manage Nature for Global Prosperity.* Oxford, UK: Oxford University Press.

Common, M., and S. Stagl. (2005). *Ecological Economics: An Introduction.* New York: Cambridge University Press.

Cord, S. (1985). "How Much Revenue Would a Full Land Value Tax Yield?" *American Journal of Economics and Sociology* 44(3).

Daly, H. E. (1991). *Steady-State Economics.* Washington, DC: Island Press.

——. (1996). *Beyond Growth: The Economics of Sustainable Development.* Boston: Beacon Press.

——. (2002). "Sustainable Development: Definitions, Principles, Policies." Speech to World Bank, April 30. Available at: www.earthrights.net/docs/daly.html.

——. (2007). *Ecological Economics and Sustainable Development: Selected Essays of Herman Daly.* Northampton, MA: Edward Elgar.

Daly, H., and J. Farley. (2003). *Ecological Economics: Principles and Applications.* Washington, DC: Island Press.

Davis, M. A., and M. G. Palumbo. (2006). "The Price of Residential Land in Large U.S. Cities," Finance and Economics Discussion Series, Washington: DC: Federal Reserve Board.

Davis, S. C., S. W. Diegel, and R. G. Boundy. (2011). *Transportation Energy Data Book,* 30th ed. Oakridge, TN: Oakridge National Laboratory.

de Soto, H. (2000). *The Mystery of Capital: Why Capitalism Triumphs in the West and Fails Everywhere Else.* New York: Basic Books.

Diewert, W. E., and D. A. Lawrence. (1997). "The Deadweight Costs of Capital Taxation in Australia." Paper presented to Treasury Seminar Series, Canberra, Australia, December 19.

Dwyer, T. (2003). "The Taxable Capacity of Australian Land and *Resources.*" *Australian Tax Forum* January.

Easterly, W. (2006). *The White Man's Burden: Why the West's Efforts to Aid the Rest Have Done So Much Ill and So Little Good.* New York: Penguin Books.

Elgin, D. (1993). *Voluntary Simplicity: Toward a Way of Life that is Outwardly Simple, Inwardly Rich.* New York: William Morrow Press.

Feldstein, M. (1999). "Tax Avoidance and the Deadweight Loss of Income Taxes." *Review of Economics and Statistics* November.

Fillebrown, C. B. (1917). *Principles of Natural Taxation: Showing the Origin and Progress of Plans for the Payment of All Public Expenses from Economic Rent.* Chicago: A.C. McClurg & Co.

Freeman, V. (2000). *Distant Relations: How My Ancestors Colonialized North America.* Toronto: McClelland and Stewart.

Friedman, J. P., J. C. Harris, and J. B. Lindeman. (2005). *Dictionary of Real Estate Terms.* Hauppauge, NY: Barron's Educational Series.

Friedman, T. (2006). *The World Is Flat.* New York: Farrar, Straus & Giroux.

Gaffney, M. (2004). "Sounding the Revenue Potential of Land: Fifteen Submerged Elements." *Groundswell* September–October. Available at: http://www.progress.org/cg/gaff1004.htm.

———. (2009). "The Hidden Taxable Capacity of Land: Enough and to Spare." *International Journal of Social Economics* 36(4): 328–411.

Gaffney, M., and F. Harrison. (1994). *The Corruption of Economics.* London: Shepheard-Walwyn.

Galbraith, J. K. (1982). "Recession Economics." *New York Review of Books* 29(1).

George, H. (1887). "Thou Shalt Not Steal." Address delivered to the Anti-Poverty Society, New York City, May 8. Available at: http://www.wealthandwant.com/HG/George_TSNS.html.

———. (1962). *Progress and Poverty.* New York: Robert Schalkenbach Foundation.

———. (1966). *Protection or Free Trade: An Examination of the Tariff Question, with Especial Regard for the Interests of Labor.* New York: Robert Schalkenbach Foundation.

———. (1992). *Social Problems.* New York: Robert Schalkenbach Foundation.

George, S. (1988). *A Fate Worse than Debt.* New York: Grove Press.

———. (2004). *Faith and Credit: The World Bank's Secular Empire.* Boulder, CO: Westview Press.

Georgescu-Roegen, N. (1971). *The Entropy Law and the Economic Process.* Cambridge: Harvard University Press.

Gittens, R. (2005). "An Economics Fit for Humans." *Australian Economic Review* 38(2): 121–127.

Hardin, G. (1968). "The Tragedy of the Commons." *Science* 162: 1243–1248.

Hinjiranon, S. (2002). *Unjust Poverty.* New York: Robert Schalkenbach Foundation.

Hudson, M. (1970). "Does Economics Deserve a Nobel Prize?" *Commonweal* 93 (December 18).

———. (2007). "The Baltic Miracle's Neoliberal Road to Serfdom." *Nation* May.

Intergovernmental Panel on Climate Change (2007). *Climate Change 2007: The Physical Science Basis: Summary for Policymakers.* Geneva, Switzerland. Available at: http://www.ipcc.ch/publications_and_data/ar4/syr/en/main.html.

Kluger, R. (2007). *Seizing Destiny: The Relentless Expansion of American Territory.* New York: Random House.

Leonhardt, D. (2007). "Amid Ivy: A Battle About the Climate." *New York Times* February 21: 1.

Linklater, A. (2002). *Measuring America: How an Untamed Wilderness Shaped the United States and Fulfilled the Promise of Democracy.* New York: Walker & Co.

Meadows, D. H. (1972). *The Limits to Growth: A Report for the Club of Rome's Project on the Predicament of Mankind.* Washington, DC: Universe Books printing for Potomac Associates.

Meadows, D., D. Meadows, and J. Randers. (1992). *Beyond the Limits: Confronting Global Collapse, Envisioning a Sustainable Future.* Vermont: Chelsea Green Publishers.

Meier, G. M. (2004). *Biography of a Subject: An Evolution of Development Economics.* New York: Oxford University Press.

Mill, J. S. (2000), *Principles of Political Economy with Some of Their Applications to Social Philosophy.* Indianapolis, IN: Liberty Fund, Inc. Available at: http://www.econlib.org/library/Mill/mlP.html.

Miller, R. J. (2006). *Native America, Discovered and Conquered: Thomas Jefferson, Lewis & Clark, and Manifest Destiny.* Westport, CT: Praeger.

Miller, R. J., J. Ruru. L. Behrendt, and T. Lindberg. (2010). *Discovering Indigenous Lands: The Doctrine of Discovery in the English Colonies.* New York: Oxford University Press.

Myers, G. (1936). *History of the Great American Fortunes.* New York: Random House.

Nelson, R. (1991). *Reaching for Heaven on Earth: The Theological Meaning of Economics.* Lanham, MD: Rowman & Littlefield.

——. (2001). *Economics as Religion: From Samuelson to Chicago and Beyond.* State College, PA: Pennsylvania State University.

Nussbaum, M. (2000). *Women and Human Development: The Capabilities Approach.* Cambridge: Cambridge University Press.

O'Connell, D. (2003). "Report Calls for Auction of UK Airport Slots." *Sunday Times* May 18. Available at: http://www.dotecon.com/publications/Sunday%20Times%20slots%2018-05-03.pdf.

Osborne, D., and T. Gabler. (1993). *Reinventing Government.* New York: Addison Wesley.

Ostrom, E. (1990). *Governing the Commons: The Evolution of Institutions for Collective Action.* Cambridge, UK: Cambridge University Press.

Pearce, D. (1992). *MIT Dictionary of Modern Economics,* 4th ed. Cambridge: MIT Press.

Perkins, J. (2004). *Confessions of an Economic Hitman.* San Francisco: Berrett-Kohler.

Polanyi, K. (1957). *The Great Transformation: The Political and Economic Origins of Our Time.* New York: Beacon Press.

Pontifical Council for Justice and Peace (2005). *Compendium of the Social Doctrine of the Church.* Washington, DC: U.S. Conference of Catholic Bishops.

Prosterman, R. L., R. Mitchell, and T. Hanstad. (2007). *One Billion Rising: Law, Land and the Alleviation of Global Poverty.* Amsterdam: Leiden University Press.

Proudhon, J. P. (2008). *What is Property? An Inquiry into the Principle of Right and of Government.* Charleston, SC: Forgotten Books.

Prugh, T., with R. Costanza, J. H. Cumberland, H. E. Daly, R. Goodland, and R. B. Norgaard. (1995). *Natural Capital and Human Economic Survival.* Solomons, MD: ISEE Press.

Rawls, J. (1971). *A Theory of Justice.* Cambridge: Harvard University Press.

———. (2001). *Justice as Fairness: A Restatement.* Cambridge: Harvard University Press.

Redfearn, D, (1992). *Tolstoy: Principles for a New World Order.* London: Shepheard Walwyn.

Ricardo, D. (1911). *The Principles of Political Economy and Taxation.* London: E.P. Dutton Everyman's Library.

Riordan, W. L. (1905). *Plunkitt of Tammany Hall.* New York: Dutton.

Sen, A. (1999). *Development as Freedom.* New York: Random House.

Shearman, T. G. (1897). *Natural Taxation: An Inquiry into the Practicability, Justice and Effects of a Scientific and Natural Method of Taxation.* New York: G.P. Putnam. Available at: http://archive.org/stream/ naturaltaxationi00shearich#page/n5/mode/2up.

Shi, D. (1986). *In Search of the Simple Life.* Layton, UT: Peregrine Books.

Sider, R. J. (1984). *Rich Christians in an Age of Hunger: A Biblical Study, Revised and Expanded.* Downers Grove, IL: Intervarsity Press.

Simon, J. (1981). *The Ultimate Resource.* Princeton, NJ: Princeton University Press.

———. (1984). *The Resourceful Earth.* New York: Blackwell Publishers.

Smiley, D., with H. W. Batt, and C. Cobb. (2010). *Crumbling Foundations: How Faulty Institutions Create World Poverty.* New York: Robert Schalkenbach Foundation.

Stern, S. (2007). *The Economics of Climate Change: The Stern Review.* Cambridge: Cambridge University Press.

Tideman, N., W. Vickrey, M. Gaffney, L. Harris, J. Thisse, C. Goetz, G. Wunderlich, D. Fusfeld, C. Kaysen, E. Clayton, R. Dorfman, T. Scitovsky, R. Goode, S. Rose-Ackerman, J. Tobin, R. Musgrave, F. Modigliani, W. Samuels, G. Orcutt, E. Smolensky, T. Gwartney, O. Oldman, Z. Griliches, W. Baumol, G. Renis, J. Helliwell, G. Pontecorvo, R. Solow, A. Kahn, and H. Levin. (1991). "Open Letter to Mikhail Gorbachev." In *Now the*

Synthesis: Capitalism, Socialism, & the New Social Contract. Ed. R. Noyes, pp. 225–230. London: Shepheard-Walwyn, Publishers. Available at: http://www.earthsharing.org.au/2006/09/15/letter-to-gorbachev/.

Tucker, G. (2010). *The Self-Supporting City.* New York: Robert Schalkenbach Foundation.

United States Census Bureau (2011). "Income, Poverty and Health Insurance Coverage in the United States: 2010. Washington, DC. Available at: http://www.census.gov/newsroom/releases/archives/income_wealth/cb11-157.html.

Von Thünen, J. H. (1966). *Von Thünen's Isolated State.* Trans. C.M. Wartenberg (1966). Oxford: Pergamon Press.

Weaver, J. C. (2003). *The Great Land Rush and the Making of the Modern World, 1650–1900.* Montreal: McGill-Queen's University Press.

Webber, C., and A. Wildavsky. (1986). *A History of Taxation and Expenditure in the Western World.* New York: Simon & Schuster.

Weber, M. (1968). *Economy and Society: An Outline of Interpretive Sociology.* Eds. G. Roth and C. Wittich. New York: Bedminister Press.

World Bank (2012). "Poverty Picture 1990–2008." Washington, DC. Available at: http://web.worldbank.org/WBSITE/EXTERNAL/TOPICS/EXTPOVERTY/0,,menuPK:336998~pagePK:149018~piPK:149093~theSitePK:336992,00.html.

World Commission on Environment and Development (1987). *Our Common Future.* London: Oxford University Press.

World Hunger Education Service (2012). "2012 World Hunger and Poverty Facts and Statistics." *Hunger Notes.* Available at: http://www.worldhunger.org/articles/Learn/world%20hunger%20facts%202002.htm.

Wright, R. (1992). *Stolen Continents: 500 Years of Conquest and Resistance in the Americas.* New York: Houghton Mifflin Mariner Books.

From *The Wealth of Nations* to *Populorum Progressio* (On the Development of Peoples): Wealth and Development from the Perspective of the Catholic Social Thought Tradition

By CHARLES M. A. CLARK*

ABSTRACT. Catholic social thought (CST) looks at economic development from the broader framework of authentic human development. It is only by viewing both man's dignity and his social nature that we include the full nature of the human being. In CST wealth is understood based on its role in promoting authentic human development. Wealth is a gift from God, with humans participating in its creation, and its creation, distribution, and its use must be carried out in a manner that respects God's law (justice and charity). Furthermore, man should never place wealth above God or above humans. Those who control wealth have special responsibilities with regards to their use of it; thus the right of private property is always restricted by the social responsibility to use it towards the common good. The goal must be the development of the whole person and all people. Wealth is socially created and thus must be distributed, at least partially, among the entire community. Economic development needs to be grounded in social justice and its two co-principles, charity and justice. Grounding economic development in the authentic development of the person means placing the people of the poor countries at the center of their development drama, both as the leading actors and as the directors.

A philosophy begins with Being, with the end and value of a living thing; and it is manifest that materialism that only considers economic ethics, cannot cover the question at all. If the problem of happiness were solved

*Charles M. A. Clark is Senior Fellow, Vincentian Center of Church and Society and Professor of Economics, the Peter J. Tobin College of Business, St. John's University.

American Journal of Economics and Sociology, Vol. 71, No. 4 (October, 2012).

by economic comfort, the classes who are more comfortable would be happy, which is absurd. (G. K. Chesterton)

Introduction: The Challenge of Catholic Social Thought

From the perspective of most economists the problem of economic development is typically seen as a problem of exceedingly low *per capita* income, derived by dividing some measure of total output by some measure of population. Variations among the competing theories generally emphasize either the numerator or the dominator, with the more "comprehensive" explanations taking both into consideration. Framed in this manner, the problem of economic development historically has been presented as a problem of inadequate production (here Adam Smith is the starting point), excessive population (Malthusian theories), or both (the grand synthesis achieved under John Stuart Mill). Economic theories that go beyond the limitations of the grand neoclassical synthesis will often examine the social and historical factors that have played a role in either the inadequate levels of production or the excessive population. A few (Andre Gunnar Frank) will state that the problem is not necessarily inadequate production but how the benefits of world production are distributed. They note that those who control world production use the labor and natural resources of the poor to enrich the already affluent. Yet even in these heterodox theories, for the most part, development is seen as a mostly or exclusively economic story. Here the line dividing conservative neoclassical economics and radical Marxism are rather thin, as both are almost exclusively materialist explanations.

Catholic social thought (CST) offers a different perspective, one that looks at economic development from the broader framework of authentic human development. It is not hostile to economic development, or even the materialistic aspects of economic development, but instead places economic development in its proper perspective. This alternative perspective is based on CST's challenge to neoclassical economics as a means for understanding economic and social issues, including the problem of development. These challenges are: (1.) economic activity is also social, political, cultural, and spiritual activity, and thus one needs to take a broad, rather than the overly narrow "economistic," perspective; (2.) market values do not supersede all other values and the "laws of the market" are not, and do not supplant, the "natural law" or God's divine law; (3.) the inherent dignity of each and every person needs to be the foundational value in understanding and evaluating economic and social actions (Clark 2008). These three statements directly contradict the core of mainstream economic theory. For Christians they are the starting point of any attempt to understand and alleviate economic and social problems. Yet they represent more than just a Christian perspective on economic issues because they also present a more meaningful philosophical foundation upon which to understand economic life, and thus provide a perspective that helps secular investigators better to understand these issues. The fact of the matter is that economic orthodoxy (neoclassical economics): excludes historical and social context from its analysis (Clark 1992); incorrectly represents market values (and its underlying psychology of utilitarianism) as being natural and "positive" (meaning value free), relegating all other perspectives to being based on "normative" analysis (implying less scientific); and reduces the human person to "rational economic man," thus empting the humanity from human nature. These limitations of current economic orthodoxy reduce its ability to understand economic phenomena and thus to offer helpful suggestions on how to improve the performance of the economy and alleviate much human suffering.

The significance of a Christian understanding of economic development comes out in the policy suggestions each approach offers. Christian policies center on the development of the whole person, and each and every person, whereas materialistic theories quite often propose "means" to the "ends" of economic development that do not respect the dignity of the person. Some of these materialistic development strategies concentrate on reducing population (for example, via forced abortions, which are common in China) or forced labor and unsafe working conditions to increase production. It is also common to keep living standards of the poor low to increase the surplus going to investors to increase future investment. A Christian approach to economic development looks at the person as the "ends" and never as "means to an end."

The Scope of the Problem

Few contemporary problems facing humanity are more pressing than the vast multitude that are forced to live in conditions that can only be described as below the requirements of human dignity. The statistics are well known but worth repeating: 1 billion of our fellow humans live on $1 a day; almost 3 billion live on $2 a day. What these statistics represent are hundreds of millions living in hunger, malnutrition, and illiteracy, lacking adequate shelter, medical care, clean water, or security, suffering political and social marginalization, and the list could go on and on. One of the most outstanding characteristics of the stark facts of poverty is that they are both causes and effects, reinforcing and perpetuating the misery of the poor.

There has been progress, especially in the more extreme levels of poverty ($1 per day Purchasing Power Parity); by some calculations "[t]he number of people in the world living in absolute poverty has fallen by more than half since the 1950s" (Shermer 2012). However, success at the higher $2 per day has been less impressive. In fact, a considerable amount of the success at the $1 per day level is due to China—both its economic success and the unreliability of its early 1980s estimates (Chen and Ravallion 2007). Yet the success that has been achieved is very unevenly distributed, being mostly confined to East and South Asia. East Europe, and Central Asia; Latin America and the Caribbean and Sub-Saharan Africa have seen little progress or, worse, increases in poverty levels. If we contrast the plight of the poor with the abundance, and in many cases the decadence, of the inhabitants of the rich countries, the situation looks worse, for the lack of progress in many of the poorest regions coincided with increased wealth in the richest (Clark and Alford 2010).

The affluent countries account for 20 percent of the world's population, yet consume 86 percent of the produced goods and services (United Nations Development Programme 1998). "A mere 12 percent of the world's population uses 85 percent of its water, and these 12 percent do not live in the Third World" (Barlow 2001). Furthermore, the gap between the rich and the poor has increased considerably over the past two centuries (United Nations Development Programme

1999) from rich countries' incomes being three times those of poor countries in 1820 to 72 times in 1992:

- 3 to 1 in 1820
- 11 to 1 in 1913
- 35 to 1 in 1950
- 44 to 1 in 1973
- 72 to 1 in 1992

World economic production continues to grow, but the poorest of the poor are, for the most part, excluded from the benefits of economic growth.

From a purely materialist or economic perspective, the efforts to reduce world poverty have been a mixed bag. In materialistic terms, clearly some areas (notably China, India, and Brazil)) have had great successes, while other areas (Africa, Eastern Europe, and Latin America) have struggled considerably. Yet our purpose here is to not reduce the problem of poverty to purely materialistic terms. Looked at from a personalistic perspective, many of the problems of poverty get ignored when it is reduced to purely materialistic terms. CST helps us go beyond the merely material aspects of poverty. It does not offer a "Catholic" development strategy *per se.* What it does do is present principles that can keep the authentic development of the person and peoples as the primary focus of development policies. It is a necessary reminder that the quest for development is a moral issue and not merely a matter of getting the right economic incentives and institutions. This rethinking of development was one of the primary goals of Paul VI's encyclical *Populorum progressio: On the Development of Peoples* issued in 1967. It called for a new approach to the problem of economic development based on a more complete understanding of the nature of the human person. Basing our understanding of social and economic issues on Christian Anthropology, I will argue, leads to a more realistic understanding of society, a necessary first step if we want useful economic policies. Its underlying proposition is that the problem of development is not merely or solely an economic issue, but at heart a moral issue. To be meaningful and to be successful, development strategies must seek the authentic development of the whole person, not merely improvement in economic statistics such as *per capita* income or gross domestic product.

The purpose of this essay is to suggest some benefits of developing a broader, more human approach to economic development. This approach is contrasted with the narrow, economistic approach that dominates most development discussions. I will do this by first looking at the underlying anthropology of the Catholic approach. Second I will show that this anthropology leads to different conception of what is wealth. Third, I will review Paul VI's call for a new approach to development, looking at its impact on how the problem of development is addressed.

Philosophical Anthropology

Any conceptualization of an economic or social issue starts with a view of the nature of the human person and society. These constitute part of what has been called the "vision" that underlies the social analysis (Veblen 1919; Schumpeter 1954; Stark 1959; Clark 1992)—the often unexamined philosophical preconceptions that provide the foundation upon which social theories are constructed. All social theory is based on a "vision" of a just society and this vision starts with a philosophical anthropology—an understanding of the nature of the human person. Most economic theory is based on the "rational economic man" view of the human person and much of that analysis flows directly from this philosophical anthropology. This view assumes that each individual is an autonomous utility-maximizing individual, whose social interaction is understood exclusively through the mode of market exchange. Every question and answer in neo-classical economic theory starts with this perspective. Furthermore, the only valid way to achieve utility maximization is through market exchange; thus, from the perspective of neoclassical economics the only truly valid human activity is market exchange. Within neoclassical economics, life in the family, political life in the community, and religious life, as well as the economic life of the individual, are all understood through the lens of individuals maximizing their utility through market exchange. This gives an excessively narrow view of all aspects of social life, for it excludes all other human motivations and influences. It also raises market/materialistic values to an exalted position, excluding all non-market values and valuations. This view of the human person produces both bad ethical analysis and bad economic theory (as non-economic factors are always in operation) and naturally leads to an understanding of wealth that is limited to terms of market valuations.

CST is built upon a different "vision" of a just society and economy. Unlike neoclassical economic theory, the CST tradition openly and explicitly states its "vision" and its values. The vision is grounded in the Old Testament and comes to life in the Gospels, and it has been deepened philosophically by 2,000 years of reflection and experience. These principles form the explicit underpinning for the various Encyclicals and other Church documents that make up the modern CST tradition. At the heart of this vision is the following belief, as articulated by Sean Healy and Brigid Reynolds (1983: 5–6):

> God speaks to every reality. Whatever we are looking at whether it is an issue such as world hunger . . . or an economic system such as Capitalism, God does have something to say to that reality. Our world either is or is not in accord with God's ideal for it. Consequently it is important for us to come to know what God is saying to whatever reality we are examining. God speaks to these issues or situations in various ways: through the Bible, through the teachings of His Church, through the signs of the times and through the prophets who interpret those signs.

The CST perspective makes a clear distinction between individual and person. Whereas neoclassical economics takes the individual in isolation from the community as its starting point, CST starts with the idea of the person. As one of the leading 20th-century proponents of personalism, Jacques Maritian (1947) noted:

> [T]he human being is caught between two poles; a material pole, which, in reality, does not concern the true person but rather the shadow of personality or what, in the strict sense, is called individuality, and a spiritual pole, which does concern true personality. . . . As an Individual, each of us is a fragment of a species, a part of the universe, a unique point in the immense web of cosmic, ethnical, historical forces and influences— and bound by their laws. Each of us is subject to the determinism of the physical world. Nonetheless, each of us is also a person and, as such, is not controlled by the stars. Our whole being subsists in which is in us a

principle of creative unity, independence and liberty. . . . [Furthermore the] person requires membership in a society in virtue both of its dignity and its needs.

It is only by viewing man as a person, emphasizing both his dignity and his social nature, that we include the full nature of the human being.

The Catholic understanding of the nature of the human person starts at the beginning, with Genesis 1: 26–28:

Then God said, "Let us make man in our image and likeness to rule the fish in the sea, the birds of heaven, the cattle, all wild animals on earth, and all reptiles that crawl upon the earth." So God created man in his own image; in the image of God he created him; male and female he created them.

The significance of *Imago dei*, of being made by God in God's image and likeness, is paramount for Christian Anthropology, for it is here that we get the chief characteristics of human nature. First, being made by God, and being made in His image and likeness, gives each human his or her inherent dignity. Each person, from conception to natural death, has an innate dignity that both the divine and natural law assert, which must be respected. (This is also why no Christian can accept the morality of abortion or assisted suicide.) The human dignity comes from both our origins and our destination; we come from God and our natural final end is God. Here also we find the Christian basis of all assertions of human rights that supersede civil rights. (It is worth noting that the Christian defense of human rights balances all rights with responsibilities—see John XXIII 1963: #8–32). A person's value does not come from her or his usefulness or function, and it certainly is not based on whether s/he is wanted. The value of each and every person comes from God and cannot be taken away by man.

Secondly, being made in the image and likeness of God gives humans their free will and their ability to reason, especially in terms of moral reasoning (right and wrong)—two characteristics of God that He has implanted in us, admittedly in a very limited sense. This, of course, means that humans are morally responsible for their choices. Furthermore, being made in God's image implies that humans necessarily exist in relationship with others, just as the Father, Son, and Holy Spirit exist in relationship. The economic idea of an autonomous individual is a mental fiction, completely contrary to human reality.

Thus all humans exist in relationship—first with God, second with other human beings, and third with creation. (Humans have a natural longing for God, the source of their creation. This natural longing for the infinite is often perverted in our society into a desire for infinite wealth, yet this desire can never be satiated by material goods, for only the truly infinite can fill this void. This perversion of the innate desire for God into economic greed is the greatest threat to God's creation, the environment.) Humans only fully achieve the authentic development of their humanity in community; that is, humans have an inherently social nature and can only achieve their development and happiness through social interaction.

As John Paul II (1999: #2) has stated:

> The dignity of the human person is a transcendent value, always recognized as such by those who sincerely search for the truth. Indeed, the whole of human history should be interpreted in the light of this certainty. Every person, created in the image and likeness of God (cf. Gn 1: 26–28), is therefore radically oriented towards the Creator, and is constantly in relationship with those possessed of the same dignity. To promote the good of the individual is thus to serve the common good, which is the point where rights and duties converge and reinforce one another.

The Importance of Wealth

Wealth, what it is, how it is distributed, and how it is used, is critically important for the well-being of any community (see Clark 2006 for an extended discussion of this topic). Its importance comes from the control of the productive assets of the community, and thus affects the well-being of all, and not merely the well-being of those who happen to own or control it. Yet wealth is not a natural phenomenon, that is, it is not a natural category, but is instead socially defined. From a capitalist perspective, wealth is understood as assets, most often individually owned, that yield a stream of purchasing power (income) or can be exchanged for purchasing power. This definition comes directly from the "rational economic man" view of the human person mentioned above. The accepted anthropology of neoclassical economic theory leads directly to the scarcity view of wealth.

The Development of the Scarcity View of Wealth

Léon Walras (1954: 65) best summed up the neoclassical view of wealth: "[B]y social wealth I mean all things, material or immaterial (it does not matter which in the context), that are scarce, that is to say, on the one hand, useful to us and, on the other hand, only available to us in limited quantity." This scarcity view of wealth eventually came to dominate economic thinking:

- "Wealth is not such for economic purposes, unless it is scarce and transferable, and so desirable that some one is anxious to give something for it" (Bagehot 1888: 132).
- [Wealth] . . . These sources of human welfare which are material, transferable and limited in quantity" (Clark 1899: 1).
- "Wealth is not wealth because of its substantial qualities. It is wealth because it is scarce" (Robbins 1932: 47).

Unlike the classical economists, who understood wealth in relation to abundance, neoclassical economists have separated it from the production of goods and services; thus increases in wealth are no longer connected with improving the well-being of the whole population, especially the lot of the poor. John Bates Clark (1886: 107) stated this: "That mankind as a whole shall become richer does not, of necessity, involve an increase in human welfare."

In neoclassical economics wealth is defined as any asset that yields an income, or can be exchanged for purchasing power, and the asset's value is based on its yield and its scarcity. Furthermore, the economic value of the yield is tied to scarcity, for it is based not only on the yields of the asset in question, but also the yields of competing assets. Thus wealth can "grow" by increasing its yield, which often means an increase in production, but it can also be increased by limiting output and increasing its scarcity. Furthermore, wealth is only counted as wealth when it is privately owned. Thus you can increase the measured wealth of a community by transferring public assets into private hands, even though you may not increase total well-being by such a transfer. Hence the long-recognized disconnect between wealth and well-being.

The View of Wealth in Catholic Social Thought

Starting from the Christian understanding of the nature of the human person directly influences how we view wealth. This comes out most clearly when we examine the purpose or goal of economic activity. In neoclassical economic theory the final end of economic activity is achieving utility though consumption. This level of utility will be determined by the scarcity of the goods and services. Thus, as we have seen above, the concept of scarcity is central to how most current economists understand wealth. In CST wealth is understood based on its role in promoting authentic human development.

Wealth and the Bible

The Catholic understanding of wealth is based on the treatment of wealth in the Old and New Testaments. In both it is clear: (1) that wealth needs to be understood as a gift from God (with humans participating in its creation); (2) that this creation must be carried out in a manner that respects God's law (justice and common good); (3) that the distribution and use of wealth must also follow God's law— the gift of creation (the ultimate source of wealth) was freely given by God to all humanity; and (4) that man should never place wealth above God.

We see this clearly in the new Jerusalem passages in Isaiah:

- "The riches of the sea shall be lavished upon you and you shall possess the *wealth of nations*" (Isaiah 60: 5).
- "You shall be named priests of the Lord, you shall be named ministers of our God; you shall enjoy the *wealth of the nations* and in their glory you shall glory" (Isaiah 61: 6).
- "Rejoice with Jerusalem, and be glad for her, all you who love her; rejoice with her in joy, all you who mourn over her—that you may nurse and be satisfied from her consoling breast; that you may drink deeply with delight from her glorious bosom. For thus says the Lord: I will extend prosperity to her like a river, and the *wealth of the nations* like an overflowing stream; and you shall nurse and be carried on her arm, and dandled on her knee.

> As a mother comforts her child, so I will comfort you; you shall be comforted in Jerusalem" (Isaiah 66: 11–13).

The phrase wealth of nations, of course, is the title of the most import book in the history of economics (Smith's *An Inquiry into the Nature and Causes of the Wealth of Nations*). Much like Isaiah, Adam Smith's main point in the *Wealth of Nations* is that if countries follow the economic laws depicted in his book they will experience material prosperity.

However, the gift of wealth comes with a warning, which we find clearly stated in Ecclesiastes (5: 10–13):

> Whoever loves money never has money enough; whoever loves wealth is never satisfied with his income. This too is meaningless. As goods increase, so do those who consume them. And what benefit are they to the owner except to feast his eyes on them? The sleep of a laborer is sweet, whether he eats little or much, but the abundance of a rich man permits him no sleep. I have seen a grievous evil under the sun: wealth hoarded to the harm of its owner."

And again in Ezekiel (28: 4–10):

> By your wisdom and understanding you have gained wealth for yourself and amassed gold and silver in your treasuries. By your great skill in trading you have increased your wealth, and because of your wealth your heart has grown proud. Therefore this is what the Sovereign LORD says: "Because you think you are wise, as wise as a god, I am going to bring foreigners against you, the most ruthless of nations; they will draw their swords against your beauty and wisdom and pierce your shining splendor. They will bring you down to the pit, and you will die a violent death in the heart of the seas. Will you then say, 'I am a god,' in the presence of those who kill you? You will be but a man, not a god, in the hands of those who slay you. You will die the death of the uncircumcised at the hands of foreigners. I have spoken, declares the Sovereign LORD.' "

The New Testament carries forward the idea that wealth is a gift from God, but presents a more developed analysis as to how wealth can be a barrier to understanding and following God. In the New Testament the pursuit of wealth is seen as a distraction from the real goal of mankind. Jesus tells us:

- "Do not lay up for yourselves treasures on earth, where moth and rust consume and where thieves break in and steal, but lay up for yourselves treasures in heaven, where neither moth nor rust consumes and where thieves do not break in and steal. For where your treasure is, there will your heart be also" (Matthew 6: 19–21).

- "No one can serve two masters; for either he will hate the one and love the other, or he will be devoted to the one and despise the other. You cannot serve God and mammon (riches)" (Matthew 6: 24).

This view of wealth is reinforced in one of the most vivid statements from Jesus:

- "Truly I say to you, it will be hard for a rich man to enter the kingdom of heaven. Again I tell you, it is easier for a camel to go through the eye of the needle than for someone who is rich to enter the kingdom of God" (Matthew 19: 23–24).

The need to share wealth, especially with the poor, is also frequently mentioned in the New Testament. As St. Paul notes in *2 Corinthians* 8: 13–15, when he tells the new Christians that they should strive for equality: "I do not mean that others should be eased and you burdened, but that as a matter of equality your abundance at the present time should supply their want, so that their abundance may supply your want, that there may be equality."

Creation, Distribution, and the Use of Wealth in the Papal Encyclicals

From its biblical roots the Catholic social tradition carries forward the idea that wealth consists of goods and services to meet human needs, and that these goods and services derive from God's gift of creation to all. This is the promise of abundance. Yet the abundance does not come without effort, for we are called to be "collaborators" in creation through work. As John Paul II (1981: #4–7) has noted, through work we produce the goods and services that form the social wealth of a nation, but more importantly, through work we develop ourselves to our fullest potential. The value of work has more to do with the effect it has on the authentic development of the worker (subjective dimension of work) than on the output produced by the worker (objective dimension of work).

That the subjective dimension of work is more than the objective is seen in John XXIII's (1961: #82–83) earlier encyclical, *Mater et magistra*, when he notes:

> Justice is to be observed not merely in the distribution of wealth, but also in regard to the conditions under which men engaged in productive activity have an opportunity to assume responsibility and to perfect themselves by their efforts. Consequently, if the organization and structure of economic life be such that the dignity of workers is compromised, their sense of responsibility is weakened, or their freedom of action is removed, then we judge such an economic order to be unjust, even though it produces a vast amount of goods whose distribution conforms to the norms of justice and equity.

According to Pius XII, social justice requires us to look at the relationship between wealth and the community as analogous to that of blood to the body: "Wealth is like the blood in the human body; it ought to circulate around all the members of the social body" (Naughton 1992: 21). This is why the right to private property must be subordinated to the created reality of the "universal destination of material goods." It is not enough, as John XXIII (1961: #113) argued, "to assert that man has from nature the right of privately possessing goods as his own, including those of productive character, unless, at the same time, a continuing effort is made to spread the use of this right through all ranks of the citizenry."

The Church also asserts that those who have control of wealth have special responsibilities with regards to their use of it. In *Rerum novarum*, Leo XIII (1891: #18) warns:

> [T]hose whom fortune favors are warned that freedom from sorrow and abundance of earthy riches are no guarantee of that beatitude that shall never end, but rather the contrary; that the rich should tremble at the threatening of Jesus Christ—threatening so strange in the mouth of our Lord; and that a most strict account must be given to the Supreme Judge for all that we possess.

Leo XIII (1891: 19) further states the principle of the "right use of money," a rule that is supported by reason as well as by faith. This principle states that "it is one thing to have a right to the possession of money, and another to have a right to use money as one pleases."

The right of private property is always restricted by the social responsibility to use it towards the common good. Part of the "right use of money" is the duty of charity, to give to those who are less fortunate out of one's surplus. Later social encyclicals have extended this duty of charity to a duty to change unjust social structures that create inequality—which creates the need for charity (Paul VI 1967: #66–75; United States Catholic Bishops 1986: #357–358). We should remember that, as St. Thomas Aquinas notes, charity and justice are virtues that require each other and can never be fully separated. In his most recent encyclical, Benedict XVI states that "charity goes beyond justice" (2009, CV #6), thus the requirements of justice come first. Furthermore, CST asserts that one cannot look at the issues of wealth and poverty as completely separate. As John Paul II (1987: #28) notes in *Sollicitudo Rei Socialis*:

> A disconcerting conclusion about the most recent period should serve to enlighten us: side-by-side with the miseries of underdevelopment, themselves unacceptable, we find ourselves up against a form of superdevelopment, equally inadmissible, because like the former it is contrary to what is good and to true happiness. This superdevelopment, which consists in an excessive availability of every kind of material goods for the benefit of certain social groups, easily makes people slaves of "possession" and of immediate gratification, with no other horizon than the multiplication or continual replacement of the things already owned with others still better. This is the so-called civilization of "consumption" or "consumerism," which involves so much "throwing-away" and "waste." An object already owned but now superseded by something better is discarded, with no thought of its possible lasting value in itself, nor of some other human being who is poorer.

The problems caused by consumerism are threefold. First, the pursuit of more and more goods, especially when all legitimate needs and wants are being met, becomes a false god and distracts us away from the real God. This is a main point of the Old and New Testaments, as we have seen. The second problem stems from metaphysics and not religion. It is the problem of seeking to have instead of seeking to be: "what is wrong is a style of life which is presumed to be better when it is directed toward 'having' rather than 'being' and which wants to have more, not in order to be more, but in order to spend life in enjoyment as an end in itself" (John Paul II 1991: #36). This is, of course, the essence of the neoclassical vision of human nature and utility as the ultimate good. In fact, it is impossible to find happiness in such an existence, for one can never fulfill the unlimited wants neoclassical economics assumes. Humans have a desire for the unlimited; however, nothing limited (such as material goods) can ever satisfy that desire. Much of the success of large corporations can be traced back to their ability to co-opt this craving for the unlimited, which is a craving for God, into a craving for goods. Here consumerism becomes a substitute for God, exactly the distraction the Old and New Testaments warn us about. The third problem caused by consumerism and "superdevelopment" is that the greed of the affluent promotes scarcity for the poor, contributing to the problem of poverty. John Paul II noted that the essential problem with our modern economy is its substitution of "having" for "being," thus exposing what is at heart a metaphysical issue.

One of the most controversial points of CST's views on wealth is that wealth can be created in ways that also create poverty. This is not an insight that is exclusive to CST as it was made by economists John Maynard Keynes and Thorstein Veblen (Clark 2006). As we already stated, when wealth is defined with the concept of scarcity then an obvious way to increase wealth is by increasing its scarcity. Wealth can also be increased by shifting costs on to others and by artificially increasing the demand for things (conspicuous consumption—Clark 2002).

CST has developed a different perspective on economic development because it recognizes that it has to be understood in light of the larger issue of human development and because it recognizes that economic development and wealth creation do not necessarily promote human happiness, and can often retard it.

Catholic Social Thought and Development

CST is concerned with an economy of persons; its goal is not economic growth for economic growth's sake, but instead authentic human development. From a Catholic perspective: "Development cannot be limited to mere economic growth. In order to be authentic, it must be complete: integral, that is, it has to promote the good of every man and of the whole man. As an eminent specialist has very rightly and emphatically declared: "we do not believe in separating the economic from the human, nor development from the civilizations in which it exists. What we hold important is man, each man and each group of men, and we even include the whole of humanity" (Paul VI 1967: 14). This is a very different goal. It calls us to look beyond man as a consumer and recognize that there are many aspects of human development that we need to be promoted. As the primer encyclical on human development, *Populorum Progressio* (On the Development of Peoples) states (Paul VI 1967: #15–19): "In the design of God, every man is called upon to develop and fulfill himself, for every life is a vocation. At birth, everyone is granted, in germ, a set of aptitudes and qualities for him to bring to fruition." Thus human fulfillment is a right and "constitutes, as it were, a summary of our duties." In keeping with the view of society in CST, human fulfillment is not merely for individuals, but for societies as well: "[E]ach man is a member of society. He is part of the whole of mankind. It is not just certain individuals, but all men who are called to this fullness of development" (1967: 17). Paul VI places human development in a historical context, noting the link between the past and present, as well as the responsibilities of development:

> Civilizations are born, develop and die. But humanity is advancing along the path of history like waves of a rising tide encroaching gradually on the shore. We have inherited from past generations, and we have benefited from the work of our contemporaries: for this reason we have obligations toward all, and we cannot refuse to interest ourselves in those who will come after us to enlarge the human family. The reality of human solidarity, which is a benefit for us, also imposes a duty. (1967: 17)

Limiting our understanding of development to a solely economic one becomes a barrier to authentic human development:

> Increased possession is not the ultimate goal of nations nor of individuals. All growth is ambivalent. It is essential if man is to develop as a man, but in a way it imprisons man if he considers it the supreme good, and it restricts his vision. Then we see hearts harden and minds close, and men no longer gather together in friendship but out of self-interest, which soon leads to oppositions and disunity. The exclusive pursuit of possessions thus becomes an obstacle to individual fulfillment and to man's true greatness. Both for nations and for individual men, avarice is the most evident form of moral underdevelopment. (1967: #19)

John Paul II (1987: #28) has often noted the danger of the one-sided or exclusively economic conception of human development:

> At the same time, however, the "economic" concept itself, linked to the word development, has entered into crisis. In fact there is a better under-standing today that the mere accumulation of goods and services, even for the benefit of the majority, is not enough for the realization of human happiness. Nor, in consequence, does the availability of the many real benefits provided in recent times by science and technology, including the computer sciences, bring freedom from every form of slavery. On the contrary, the experience of recent years shows that unless all the consid-erable body of resources and potential at man's disposal is guided by a moral understanding and by an orientation towards the true good of the human race, it easily turns against man to oppress him.

In one of his first encyclicals, *Redemptor Hominis*, John Paul II (1979: #19–20) poses the questions of the purpose of development:

> The development of technology and the development of contemporary civilization, which is marked by the ascendancy of technology, demand a proportional development of morals and ethics. For the present, this last development seems unfortunately to be always left behind. Accordingly, in spite of the marvel of this progress, in which it is difficult not to see also authentic signs of man's greatness, signs that in their creative seeds were revealed to us in the pages of the Book of Genesis, as early as where it describes man's creation (Genesis 1–2), this progress cannot fail to give rise to disquiet on many counts. The first reason for disquiet concerns the essential and fundamental question: does this progress, which has man for its author and promoter, make human life on earth "more human" in every aspect of that life? Does it make it more "worthy of man"? There can be no doubt that in various aspects it does. But the question keeps coming back with regard to what is most essential—whether in the context of this progress man, as man, is becoming truly better, that is to say more mature spiritually, more aware of the dignity of his humanity, more responsible, more open to others, especially the neediest and the weakest, and readier to give and to aid all. Indeed there is already a real perceptible danger that, while man's dominion over the world of things is making enormous advances, he should lose the essential threads of his dominion and in various ways let his humanity be subjected to the world and become himself something subject to manipulation in many ways—even if the manipulation is often not perceptible directly—through the whole of the organization of community life, through the production system and through pressure from the means of social communication. Man cannot relinquish himself or the place in the visible world that belongs to him; he cannot become the slave of things, the

slave of economic systems, the slave of production, the slave of his own products. A civilization purely materialistic in outline condemns man to such slavery, even if at times, no doubt, this occurs contrary to the intentions and the very premises of its pioneers. The present solicitude for man certainly has at its root this problem. It is not a matter here merely of giving an abstract answer to the question: Who is man? It is a matter of the whole of the dynamism of life and civilization. It is a matter of the meaningfulness of the various initiatives of everyday life and also of the premises for many civilization programs, political programs, economic ones, social ones, state ones, and many others.

Thus our goal must be the development of the whole person and all people. This goes beyond the limiting concept of development as economic growth in neoclassical economic theory. It asserts that we cannot propose merely economic goals without asking important moral questions. It also asserts that we cannot separate ends and means, for the goal of increased production can be a valid and worthy one, but the process of production must take into account the development of the whole person.

Universal Destination of Material Goods

Just as CST emphasizes that the dignity of the person must be respected in the creation of wealth, it recognizes that the rights and dignity of all persons must be respected in the distribution of wealth. As John Paul II (1991: #31) stated in *Centesimus Annus*: "The original source of all that is good is the very act of God, who created both the earth and man, and who gave the earth to man so that he might have dominion over it by his work and enjoy its fruits." This is the basis of the principle of the Universal Destination of Material Goods, which is referred to in *Rerum novarum* ("the earth, though divided among private owners, ceases not thereby to minster to the needs of all"—Leo XIII 1891: #7) and is carried forward in *Quadragesimo Anno* (Pius XI 1931: #58):

Each class, then, must receive its due share, and the distribution of created goods must be brought into conformity with the demands of the common good and social justice. For every sincere observer realizes that the vast difference between the few who hold excessive wealth and the many who live in destitution constitute a grave evil in modern society.

Paul VI (1967: #22), supporting this principle, notes: "All other rights whatsoever, including those of property and of free commerce, are to be subordinated to this principle. They should not hinder but on the contrary favor its application. It is a grave and urgent social duty to redirect them to their primary finality."

The principle of the Universal Destination of Material Goods recognizes that wealth is socially created and thus must be distributed, at least partially, among the entire community, meeting the needs of all. This is not a rejection of market forces, but a recognition that a higher morality exists, and that due to numerous market failures, markets will not adequately value all contributions, past and present, to wealth creation. The distribution of wealth and incomes cannot be left entirely to the market. John Maynard Keynes (1936: 372) noted as much when he wrote: "The outstanding faults of the economic society in which we live are its failure to provide for full employment and its arbitrary and inequitable distribution of wealth and incomes." Keynes (1936) notes in *The General Theory of Employment Interest and Money* that inequality in wealth and income was one of the central causes of mass unemployment and thus was harmful to the health of the economy.

Social Justice and Development

[E]very program, made to increase production, has, in the last analysis, no other *raison d'etre* than the service of man. Such programs should reduce inequalities; fight discriminations, free man from various types of servitude, and enable him to be the instrument of his spiritual growth. To speak of development is in effect to show as much concern for social progress as for economic growth. (Paul VI 1967: 34)

After analyzing the challenge of development and the need to ground economic development in the nature of the human person, Paul VI argues that economic development needs to be grounded in social justice, specifically in the two co-principles of social justice—charity and justice. The call for charity notes the responsibility of the rich to help the poor, a responsibility that has been a cornerstone of Christian ethics from the beginning. (Many of St. Paul's missions included raising money for the Christian community in Jerusalem.) Yet the purpose of charity goes further (Paul VI 1967: 47):

The struggle against destitution, though urgent and necessary, is not enough. It is a question, rather, of building a world where every man, no matter what his race, religion, or nationality, can live a fully human life, freed from servitude imposed on him by other men or by natural forces over which he has not sufficient control; a world where freedom is not an empty word and where the poor man Lazarus can sit down at the same table with the rich man.

The underdevelopment status of the world's poor is based partly on historical context, the path of world development in which the West developed using the resources of the third world, and in which the economy of the current era is built upon unequal trading relations. One aspect of this path was the accumulation of debts by the poor countries, which had become (noticeable even then) an obstacle to their future development.

Another aspect of the historical context of world economic development has been the development of unequal terms of trade, which place the poorest countries at an unfair disadvantage in world trade, a disadvantage that increases in the era of globalization. This disadvantage is more than the consequence of unequal development. Certainly being affluent gives the countries of the West an advantage. Higher education levels, greater capital intensity, and more development-friendly social institutions give rich countries a great competitive advantage, not to mention the advantages of more stable and honest governments and greater political and legal security. Adam Smith (1976) noted the great economic benefits provided by law and order. Yet the disadvantages extend to the unfair rules that regulate international trade. One example of this is that the rich countries can protect agriculture from foreign competition, which is where the poor countries have the possibility for expanding their share of trade, yet the poor countries are forced to open their markets to all. The subsidization of agriculture in the West leads to a great over production of some agricultural products, which are then dumped on the world markets, greatly reducing world prices and the incomes of third-world farmers. This unfair competition prevents third-world farmers from benefiting from world economic growth. Justice in trade, long noted by St. Thomas Aquinas, requires equity: both countries need to benefit from trade. Economists cite David Ricardo's "theory of comparative advantage" as support for their argument that free trade benefits both counties, yet Ricardo's theory assumes full employment in both countries (thus allowing for no net employment gains or losses). This assumption rarely holds.

Lastly, grounding economic development in the authentic development of the person means placing the people of the poor countries at the center of their development drama, both as the leading actors and as the directors. Their path of development must be laid out by them before it is walked by them. Development aid that continues and encourages further dependency will not help the authentic development of the poor and will do little to promote their material development.

Sustainability

The principle of the Universal Destination of Goods is not limited to those who are currently living on the planet, but applies equally to the generations who will follow us. They too are God's children, and they too share in our divinely given human dignity. Concern for the environment has become a central issue in CST, just as it has in many other traditions.

The approach to environmental issues in neoclassical economics is to view it as essential a problem of property rights. Resources are not being properly valued because no one has the exclusive rights to them. Thus air pollution is caused by air being a free good; no one can prevent others from polluting the air around them because no one has exclusive right to that air. The private-rights approach to pollution and other environmental problems requires that the assumptions of a perfect market exist. It is only with such assumptions that one can argue that private property rights will lead to an efficient allocation of resources. However, there is a major weakness to this approach, besides the obvious lack of perfect markets, information, and costless transactions—the people most affected by environmental problems are not yet alive and thus cannot have any legal standing. How could future generations trade their property rights with those currently living to get a neoclassical general equilibrium? While the neoclassical analysis of market failures, especially the analysis of externalities, does provide useful tools for explaining and in some cases dealing with environmental problems, their analysis in many ways misses the point. Care for the planet requires a value system that is fundamentally different from that which underlies neoclassical economic theory.

As John Paul II (1990) has noted, the environmental crisis is essentially a moral issue. It is the result of the failure of humanity to adequately fulfill its stewardship of God's creation. Failure to care for a gift shows a lack of respect for the giver, and thus the environmental crisis must be seen as also a sin against the creator as well as a self-destructive path for humanity.

> The most profound and serious indication of the moral implications underlying the ecological problem is the lack of *respect for life* evident in many of the patterns of environmental pollution. Often, the interests of production prevail over concern for the dignity of workers, while economic interests take priority over the good of individuals and even entire peoples. In these cases, pollution or environmental destruction is the result of an unnatural and reductionist vision which at times leads to a genuine contempt for man. . . . *Respect for life, and above all for the dignity of the human person, is the ultimate guiding norm for any sound economic, industrial or scientific progress.* . . . These principles are essential to the building of a peaceful society; *no peaceful society can afford to neglect either respect for life or the fact that there is an integrity to creation.* . . . *Finally, the aesthetic value of creation cannot be overlooked.* . . . I wish to repeat that *the ecological crisis is a moral issue.*

From a CST perspective, the environmental crisis is not a scientific or economic problem, but it is at heart a moral problem. Furthermore, it must be understood and addressed in its historical and social context. At the root of the problem is the application of the instrumental logic of neoclassical economics to every aspect of society. To find the causes of the problem we need only look at the lack of respect for life and the dignity of the human person and God's creation, the placing of narrow self-interest ahead of solidarity, and the striving for individual wealth and consumerism over the interests of the poor. Any workable solution to this problem, that is, any move towards creating a just economy, which is necessarily sustainable, will require a rejection of the logic of neoclassical economics as applied to these moral issues, and the adoption of respect for life, solidarity with others, and especially with the poor and marginalized. In the 1960s an argument was presented that Christianity was the cause of the environmental crisis. On the contrary, the Christian view of the human person is the only starting point for adequately addressing this crisis.

Conclusion

CST is not a set of answers or models for promoting economic development, or for managing an advanced capitalist economy. It is a set of principles and insights into the human condition and social living. Its aim is to focus attention on the true end and purpose of human activity. It teaches us to look at the problem of economic development, and the phenomenon of wealth, from a broad perspective, keeping in mind the importance of historical and social context, and promoting the need to uphold the requirements of justice and equity in all economic and social affairs. History has taught us the folly of ignoring these great insights, to the determent of human happiness in the West, material sufficiency in the third world, and the possibility of environmental ruin for the planet. Now more than ever there is a need to bring ethics into the analysis. This is the gift of the Church to humanity.

References

Bagehot, W. (1888). *Economic Studies.* New York: Longmans, Green, and Co.

Barlow, M. (2001). "Water as Commodity—The Wrong Prescription." *Food First* 7(3). Available at: http://www.foodfirst.org/en/node/57.

Benedict XVI (2009). *Caritas in veritate* (Charity in Truth). Available at: http://www.vatican.va/holy_father/benedict_xvi/encyclicals/index_en.htm.

Chen, S., and M. Ravallion. (2007). "Absolute Poverty Measures for the Developing World: 1981–2004." *Proceedings of the National Academy of Sciences of the United States of America* 104(43): 16757–16762.

Clark, C. M. A. (1992). *Economic Theory and Natural Philosophy.* Aldershot: Edward Elgar.

——. (2002). "Wealth and Poverty: On the Social Creation of Scarcity." *Journal of Economic Issues* 2 (June): 415–421.

——. (2006). "Wealth as Abundance and Scarcity: Perspectives from Catholic Social Thought and Economic Theory." In *Rediscovering Abundance: Interdisciplinary Essays on Wealth, Income and Their Distribution in the*

Catholic Social Tradition. Eds. H. Alford, C. M. A. Clark, S. Cortright, and M. Naughton. South Bend, IN: University of Notre Dame Press.

———. (2008). "What Economists Can learn from Catholic Social Thought." *Storia Del Pensiero Economico, Nuova Series Anno* 1: 25–51.

Clark, C. M. A., and H. Alford, OP (2010). *Rich and Poor.* London: CTS Press.

Clark, J. B. (1886). *The Philosophy of Wealth.* Boston: Ginn and Company.

———. (1899). *The Distribution of Wealth: A Theory of Wages, Interest and Profits.* New York: Macmillan Company.

Healy, S., and B. Reynolds. (1983). *Social Analysis in Light of the Gospels.* Dublin: CORI.

John XXIII (1961). *Mater et magistra.* Available at: http://www.vatican.va/ holy_father/john_xxiii/encyclicals/documents/hf_j-xxiii_enc_15051961_ mater_en.html.

———. (1963). *Pacem in terris.* Available at: http://www.vatican.va/holy_father/ john_xxiii/encyclicals/documents/hf_j-xxiii_enc_11041963_pacem_en. html.

John Paul II (1979). *Redemptor hominis.* Available at http://www.vatican.va/ holy_father/john_paul_ii/encyclicals/documents/hf_jp-ii_enc_04031979_ redemptor-hominis_en.html.

———. (1981). *Laborem exercens.* Available at: http://www.vatican.va/ holy_father/john_paul_ii/encyclicals/documents/hf_jp-ii_enc_14091981_ laborem-exercens_en.html.

———. (1987). *Sollicitudo rei socialis.* Available at: http://www.vatican.va/ holy_father/john_paul_ii/encyclicals/documents/hf_jp-ii_enc_30121987_ sollicitudo-rei-socialis_en.html.

———. (1990). *Message of His Holiness Pope John Paul II for the Celebration of the World Day of Peace.* Available at: http://www.vatican.va/holy_father/ john_pau http://www.vatican.va/holy_father/john_paul_ii/messages/ peace/documents/hf_jp-ii_mes_19891208_xxiii-world-day-for-peace-en. html   l_ii/messages/peace/documents/hf_jp-ii_mes_14121998_xxxii- world-day-for-peace_en.html.

———. (1991). *Centesimus annus.* Available at: http://www.vatican.va/ holy_father/john_paul_ii/encyclicals/documents/hf_jp-ii_enc_30121987_ sollicitudo-rei-socialis_en.html.

———. (1999). *Message of His Holiness Pope John Paul II for the Celebration of the World Day of Peace.* Available at: http://www.vatican.va/holy_father/ john_paul_ii/messages/peace/documents/hf_jp-ii_mes_14121998_xxxii- world-day-for-peace_en.html.

Keynes, J. M. (1936). *The General Theory of Employment Interest and Money.* Cambridge, UK: Cambridge University Press.

Leo XIII (1891). *Rerum novarum.* Available at: http://www.vatican.va/holy_ father/leo_xiii/encyclicals/documents/hf_l-xiii_enc_15051891_rerum- novarum_en.html.

Maritian, J. (1947). *The Person and the Common Good.* Trans. J. J. Fitzgerald. New York: Charles Scribner's Sons. Available at: http://maritain.nd.edu/jmc/etext/cg.htm.

Naughton, M. (1992). *The Good Stewards.* New York: University Press of America.

Paul VI (1967). *Populorum progressio: On the Development of Peoples.* Available at: http://www.vatican.va/holy_father/paul_vi/encyclicals/documents/hf_p-vi_enc_26031967_populorum_en.html.

Robbins, L. (1932). *The Nature and Significance of Economic Science.* London: Macmillan and Co., Ltd.

Schumpeter, J. (1954). *History of Economic Analysis.* Oxford, UK.: Oxford University Press.

Shermer, M. (2012). "Defying the Doomsayers." *Wall Street Journal,* February 22, p. A13.

Smith, A. (1976). *An Inquiry into the Nature and Causes of the Wealth of Nations.* Chicago: University of Chicago Press.

Stark, W. (1959). *The Sociology of Knowledge.* New York: Fordham University Press.

United Nations Development Programme (1998). *Human Development Report 1998.* New York: Oxford University Press.

——. (1999). *Human Development Report 1999.* New York: Oxford University Press.

United States Catholic Bishops (1986). *Economic Justice for All: Pastoral Letter on Catholic Social Teaching and the U.S. Economy.* Washington, DC: United States Conference of Catholic Bishops. Available at: http://www.usccb.org/upload/economic_justice_for_all.pdf.

Veblen, T. (1919). "The Philosophical Preconceptions of Economic Science, I, II and III." In *The Place of Science in Modern Civilization and Other Essays.* Ed. T. Veblen. New York: B.W. Huebsch.

Walras, L. (1954). *Elements of Pure Economics.* Trans. Jaffe. Homewood, IL: Irwin.

Neighborhood Revitalization and New Life: A Land Value Taxation Approach

By JOSHUA VINCENT*

ABSTRACT. When a neighborhood declines, the poor get poorer, crime rises, and those who can leave the area. The tax base shrinks, so the rates paid by those least able to pay increase. The prevailing system of a low tax on land values leads to land speculation and private land banking, assuring that the landowner can hold out for a very high price for a very long time. A higher tax on land values (coupled with reduction in building taxes) creates an incentive to sell that land or do something with it rather than waiting. In cities that use land-value taxes, real-estate markets start to work again and neighborhoods recover. Clairton, Pennsylvania's adoption of a land-value-taxation system demonstrates the neighborhood revitalization to which it leads, as owner-occupied residences and multi-family units saw a relief in their tax burden. In contrast, vacant properties' contribution to the city budget tripled, providing the resources to pay for the education of Clairton's children and liberate working and middle-class families from the bonds of labor and capital taxation.

Introduction

This essay is not a debate or a defense, but rather a statement of practice derived from a theory. What success the neighborhood (that is, locally applied) role of Georgism enjoys is most often in alliance and conjunction with disparate groups and individuals. Cooperation and team building are the bywords of local Georgism.

We work with the local tax system for two reasons—first, the bad. Most cities (with a few exceptions) rely to a great degree on the property tax. As a source of revenue, it is stable, predictable, and easy

*Joshua Vincent is Executive Director, Center for the Study of Economics in Philadelphia, Pennsylvania.

American Journal of Economics and Sociology, Vol. 71, No. 4 (October, 2012).
© 2012 American Journal of Economics and Sociology, Inc.

to administer. Unlike wage, business, or sales taxes, it is hard to avoid. Yet, one part of the property tax has problems equal to other taxes on labor and capital: the property tax on buildings. Countless studies and economists have shown that high tax rates on buildings have a corrosive effect on investment, construction, and rehabilitation of existing structures. Old but classic industrial and commercial properties that might have been warehoused or mothballed while waiting for a new use were knocked down by the dozen, so that the (often absentee) owner could avoid taxes. A prospective homeowner deciding where to live would logically choose a site in the lower-taxed exurbs.

Now for the good. The other part of the property tax is a tax on land values. The effects of a tax on land values are very different. First, a homeowner or a business does not create land values. The community, most often through government investment and services, creates land values. If the community creates those values, the justification for the community recouping those values is clear. Second, the current system of a low tax on land values leads to land speculation and private land banking. The holding cost of land under our current tax system assures that the landowner can hold out for a very high price for a very long time. Third, a higher tax on land values (coupled with reduction in building taxes) creates an incentive to sell that land, or do something with it rather than waiting. In other cities that use land-value taxes, real-estate markets start to work again. Neighborhoods recover.

What is a Neighborhood?

A neighborhood is a gathering of human beings who seek the energy and solidarity that more dispersed arrangements lack. A neighborhood is a willing act of cooperation, or at least mutual toleration of sometimes-dissimilar cultures and subcultures. A neighborhood is a place—in either its origin in history or currently—where people want to be. In the modern, US sense, neighborhoods can also be known as places that are empty, declining, dangerous, or poor.

A neighborhood is also an economic unit. In my experience bringing Henry George's ideas into cities and smaller towns, a neighborhood can be as prosaic as a hill or an alley, but usually it's a self-contained area bounded by several major streets with significant automobile traffic. Those streets have the shops, eateries, places of worship, and civic parcels that help people decide, "This is my place," along with the all-important proviso "This is OUR place." A neighborhood contains enough people to make a viable association that has some clout at City Hall.

The size of a neighborhood once was determined by, say, the parish church and its reach. Even today, the closing of a Catholic parish in an older urban neighborhood is perceived as a sign of a neighborhood's pending demise. The existence of meeting places, churches being a notable example, is to me a crucial indicator of that cohesion that neighborhoods provide. The future might hold fewer churches, but replacement by coffee houses and other gathering spots may provide needed stability and continuity.

The popularity of using census tracts to define places and neighborhoods is coming under scrutiny (Clapp and Wang 2005), something that from the perspective of the Center for the Study of Economics (CSE) is long overdue. Yet, our studies are by necessity based on census-tract measures of median income, so for now we are stuck with that.

In conclusion, I assert that the neighborhood ought to be small enough to create a possible link between the people that live there and those who govern, most often expressed through neighborhood watches, civic associations, or homeowners' groups.

Why Do Neighborhoods Decline?

Theorists have expounded many theories as to why, some linking decline to the starvation of lending capital. Examples include VA/FHA lending for the suburbs (redlining) but not the cities and the notorious neighborhood "life-cycle" theory, which holds that abandonment of neighborhoods is a planned concept to empty out troublesome areas, in order to repopulate and revive areas that are viewed as troublesome by the established order (Metzger 2000).

Blaming racism too often gets its due, as it is simple and satisfying, especially since the turmoil of the 1960s seemed to have a direct cause and effect. A burning Newark equaled flight to Hopatcong and Hackettstown in the neat package of this analysis (Hayden 1967), but in reality the decline of Newark neighborhoods (and other US cities) was already in full swing by 1967.

This pernicious insistence on social rather than economic externalities as the cause of neighborhood decline is deeply rooted. For example, "everyone knows" that neighborhoods in decline (or extant ghettoes) have high numbers of racial minorities. Actually, while the majority of poor people in an urban setting *are* African-American or Hispanic, the majority of them live in non-poor neighborhoods (Jargowsky 1997). So it's instructive to note that many of the neighborhoods in decline the CSE works with and in are often overwhelmingly non-minority. Although Harrisburg has an African-American population of 54.8 percent and a Hispanic share at 11.7 percent and Clairton has 28.3 percent African-Americans in its population, we can also see the struggling cities of Titusville, 97.6 percent, Altoona 96 percent, or Dubois 98.2 percent white.

A bad education system is often blamed for the decline of a neighborhood. This seems to put the cart before the horse. A decline in population and jobs has been the trigger for school closure or failure. Losing the middle class certainly triggers the decline of parent involvement in schools. Lack of parental involvement leads to decisions made by centralized school systems with little knowledge of local conditions. The half-century trend of closing neighborhood schools in the name of efficiency has led not only to very expensive transportation solutions in getting students into school, but has produced the anomie seen in the extreme Columbine-style disappearance of self-identity (Kunstler 1999).

Loss of community meeting places plays an often unquantifiable, but anecdotally powerful reminder of negative change. Before a neighborhood goes into decline, there are lodges, churches, corner stores, safe transit stops, and other places where neighborhood communication and business gets done. The disappearance of these meeting places, often replaced, at best, by Plexiglas-enclosed beer joints and fast-food counters, is an overt indicator of danger, dinginess, and mistrust.

What Happens to Neighborhoods When They Decline?

The benefits and definitions of a neighborhood point us to what happens to a neighborhood when it declines. The area gets poorer. It becomes neglected by the loss of political power that poverty brings. As an area becomes poorer, crime rises. As crime rises, those who can leave do leave. Coupled with globalized competition and the corresponding loss of jobs, neighborhoods can become devastated rapidly. In Philadelphia, for example, the statistics haunt: 500,000 loss in population and 250,000 jobs lost since 1950.

The outflow of humanity has led to vacant lots and abandoned buildings on a monumental—though negative—scale, much like the broken statue in *Ozymandias*. Philadelphia at last estimate has 40,000 vacant parcels of land, reducing citywide property values by 6.5 percent (an average of $8000 per household in the city), costing the city $2 million per year in maintenance and resulting in massive tax delinquencies (Econsult Corporation 2010).

So, with the loss of people and commerce what happens to those left? First, and most directly, the tax base shrinks, so the rates paid by those least able to pay increase. As the advocacy group Philadelphia Forward (2012) notes: "The typical city resident's tax burden is more than 50% higher than the tax burden for a suburban resident at a similar income level." The Philadelphia Tax Reform Commission (2003) goes into greater detail in its final report.

As a matter of social justice, the irony is that the declining city or neighborhood becomes cut off; as those most able to keep it healthy flee, we are left with a city of extremes, not just in rich and poor, but in simple levels of taxation (Galster, Cutsinger, and Booza 2006).

An example, readily apparent to a casual observer, is the tax disconnect between aging cities and sprawling—but "hot"—suburban counties. The Baltimore Metro region is instructive as an example because the major governmental "engines" are the counties. When Baltimore City's property tax rates—both real and personal—are compared to surrounding jurisdictions, the problem is apparent—see charts 1 and 2 (Maryland Department of Assessments and Taxation 2012).

Taxes on capital, savings, and labor force those things to leave, in a matter of rational economic decision-making. Labor and capital markets are, like water, a liquid asset. *Like water, they flow to the level at which they are most comfortable.* So, why do taxes matter in our discussion?

Chart 1

Baltimore Metro Real Property Tax Rates 2007

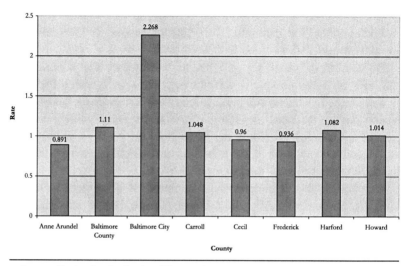

Source: Center for the Study of Economics.

1. Taxation on construction capital penalizes investment, especially of sweat equity, the small-scale rehabber, and homesteader.
2. Taxation on personal property penalizes savings and investment on items particularly mobile.
3. Taxation on reinvestment signals unfriendliness to new pioneers (unless they manage to hustle handsome tax breaks).
4. Taxation forces the poor but hard-working inner city citizens to start to pay for their temerity in trying to help themselves and their families the minute they reach a level of "success" deemed worthy of the taxman's prying hands.
5. Solutions, such as top-down, selective abatements meant to drive renewal—read "gentrification"—can force out original and long-term stakeholders in a neighborhood and city.

From the Henry George perspective, we have the dynamics of what is a neighborhood (in the traditional and citywide sense), and what

Chart 2

Baltimore Metro Personal Property Tax Rates 2007

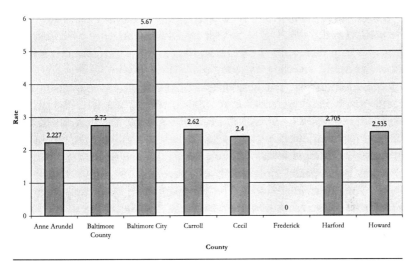

Source: Center for the Study of Economics.

are the problems facing them. The issue IS one of economics and justice, inextricably wed.

Why Does the Georgist Approach Differ from Other Tracks?

When we speak of neighborhood revitalization, it is a *Rashoman* scenario (http://www.cosmoetica.com/B385-DES323.htm) where determining the truth is inevitably impossible when up against human subjectivity. Experiences of recent decades, however, make it possible to identify what makes a neighborhood ripe for revitalization. Proximity to transit modes and public transit—ideally rail-oriented—makes for an attractive feature in an age of choked highways, long commutes, and high gas prices. Historic or architecturally unique features of a neighborhood attract those tired of the classic cookie cutter McMansions of sub- and exurbia. A perceived and actual increase in public safety has made most US cities safer since the breakdown of police effectiveness of the 1970s; empty nesters no longer fear the urban fabric and street traffic equals new commercial opportunities.

Traditional approaches to revitalization are classically piecemeal. In Philadelphia, the effect of a 10-year tax abatement on new construction was to produce, in the years leading up to the recent economic crisis (possibly overheating the market), a boom in construction (Chamberlain 2006). Resentment has followed closely behind in the tradition-rich neighborhoods that tried to stick it out over the years. According to a study led by John Kromer, most of the benefits of the 10-year tax abatement went to the richest developers in the city's strongest housing markets (Couch 2006). I have seen this specific program build social resentment of "yuppies" by impoverished or elderly long-time inhabitants. The forgiveness of taxes for a firm or industry to come into a town has also raised hackles, especially among the established business community still suffering from high vacancy rates.

The Georgist approach is different. We propose that the existing tax structure be used to reward all investment, past, present, and future. We propose that all citizens, rich, middle-class, and poor be treated with (tax) equality under the law. We propose that the one species of taxable asset that is not created by an individual—land—be the source of community resources. In so doing, we liberate not only the employer, but also the employee. We reward not the sharp rent-seeker (for our purposes, rent-seeking is the extraction of personal or corporate gain by manipulation of economics, laws, or governments rather than production), but the plodding but productive shop owner.

How Does the Georgist Approach Work?

Using Pennsylvania cities as a template, this is how Georgism is translated into a specific action: the real property tax is broken apart, and reformed with an emphasis on community-created land values. The Georgist approach can be best understood when we realize most revitalization plans, whether Habitat for Humanity projects (which has built 30,000 homes in the US since 1978—http://www.habitat.org/intl/na/218.aspx), targeted tax breaks for improvements, or blight designations, are meant to help the financing issues of revitalization by easing the tax burden in a narrowcasting manner.

Georgism is less an application than a removal. Georgism removes the penalty of taxation on the properties of those least able to pay taxes. The effects are direct and immediate. The effect is on the whole community. How does this happen?

The traditional property tax garners anywhere from 45 percent to 65 percent of a city's revenue (Monkkonen 1988: 134). Traditionally levied the tax falls equally on land and buildings. Casual observers (and most officials) assume that that means half the revenue comes from land, half from buildings. This is not the case. In fact, as the data for several cities CSE studied in 2006 and 2007 demonstrate, the equal application of rates results in nearly all the property tax coming from buildings (labor and capital) (see Table 1).

The impact is clear in our experience speaking to community groups. When we ask, "when you fix your house or renovate, what happens?" the answer is swift and universal in all situations: "My taxes go up." Similarly, when we ask, "what do you think happens to the tax bill for an absentee-owned rental property that has deteriorated or indeed been razed?" it takes a moment, but most realize "their taxes go down." In a nutshell, that is our tool for revitalization: reward the community for "doing" and penalize those who profit on poverty and blight.

How is the Georgist Program Used?

Nineteen jurisdictions in Pennsylvania use the land-value tax (LVT), as shown below (Table 2).

Some of the towns are more successful than others, particularly Harrisburg, which has stabilized and reversed its decline from the mid-1970s (Vincent 2005). This essay concentrates on one city that uses our program.

Clairton, Pennsylvania, once a prosperous steel town in Southwestern Pennsylvania, is now a struggling city with 2009 statistics (City-Data.com 2012) revealing significantly more poverty (23.0 percent) than the Pennsylvania average (12.5 percent). In 1987, Clairton was reeling. The United States Steel Corporation (USX) mill contracted

Table 1

Tax Rates and Revenues of Various Pennsylvania Cities

City	Land Rate	Building Rate	Land Revenue	Building Revenue	Total Revenue	Percent Revenue From Land	Percent Revenue From Bldgs.
Erie, PA	0.01021	0.01021	6,262,477	20,302,309	26,564,787	23.57%	76.43%
Johnstown, PA	0.03644	0.03644	1,120,233	4,063,377	5,183,610	21.61%	78.39%
Altoona, Pa	0.03844	0.03844	1,044,318	7,091,066	8,135,385	12.80%	87.20%
Sharon, PA	0.04055	0.04055	676,307	3,637,024	4,313,331	15.68%	84.32%

Data Sources: City Assessment Rolls, Analysis by the Center for the Study of Economics.

Table 2

Pennsylvania Municipalities Analysis
Center for the Study of Economics

Land Tax Date	City	Land Tax Rate	Building Tax Rate	Ratio Land: Building Tax	Population
1913	Scranton	9.6701%	2.1030%	4.5982	76,089
1975	Harrisburg	3.0970%	0.5196%	5.9604	49,528
1980	McKeesport	1.6500%	0.4260%	3.8732	19,731
1982	New Castle	2.6556%	0.7508%	3.5370	23,723
1985	Duquesne	1.9000%	1.3470%	1.4105	5,565
1985	Washington	0.1076%	0.0035%	30.7514	13,363
1988	Aliquippa	8.4000%	0.1440%	58.3333	9,438
1989	Clairton	3.3000%	0.2220%	14.8649	6,796
1989	Oil City	9.1500%	2.7100%	3.3764	11,504
1990	Titusville	7.1250%	2.0173%	3.5319	6,146
1991	DuBois	8.8000%	0.2000%	44.0000	8,123
1991	Lock Haven	2.0800%	0.4120%	5.0485	9,149
1993	Aliquippa School District	20.2000%	0.3250%	62.1538	9,438
1997	Allentown	4.1950%	0.8930%	4.6976	118,032
1997	Pittsburgh Improvement	0.3710%	n/app	N/A	n/a
2000	Ebensburg	2.5000%	0.7500%	3.3333	3,351
2002	Altoona	37.3213%	n/app	N/A	46,320
2006	Clairton School District	8.7000%	0.3500%	24.8571	6,796

Source: http://www.newpa.com/get-local-gov-support/municipal-statistics and telephone calls to municipal finance officials, 2009.

with employment at the self-contained "works" declining from 7,500, and the demolition of industrial buildings, coupled with the disappearance of businesses in the Central Business District, forced those left—the retired, unemployed steelworkers and their families—to foot

Chart 3

Clairton, Pennsylvania Pre-LVT

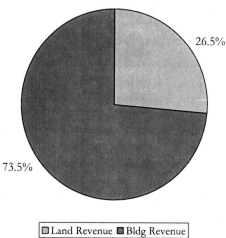

26.5%

73.5%

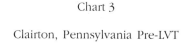

☐ Land Revenue ■ Bldg Revenue

Analysis by Center for the Study of Economics, data from Clairton Assessment Rolls provided by the Clairton School District certified assessment roll of Allegheny County, PA.

the tax bill. From a post-war high of 19,650, the population plummeted to 8,491 in 2000. In the late 1980s, streetlights disconnected for lack of payment, police and fire forces slashed, and crumbling basic infrastructure from lack of maintenance led the litany of despair, entropy, and corrosion.

Like the above cities, property tax revenue from structures was high see Chart 3.

In 1989, the State of Pennsylvania declared Clairton a Distressed Community under Act 47, which forced the city to put several measures in place to put the city back on a sound financial footing (Local Government Commission 2005: 185–188). The Pennsylvania Economy League (http://pelcentral.org/) and the CSE recommended land-value taxation (LVT) as a way to provide "right now" tax relief, as well as to stabilize city revenues. The City of Clairton duly adopted LVT. The tax rate adopted was 2.105 percent for building assessments and land assessments at 10 percent instead of both at 3.7 percent.

LVT provided a tax shift that made city property taxes progressive: newly unemployed homeowners and retired seniors saw healthy tax reductions. The loss was staunched and home construction resumed. Within three years, taxable building permit issuance increased 8.5 percent in Clairton, exceeding the national decline of 5.8 percent (Cord 2003: 3)

However, the LVT program lacked strength in its application: other taxing jurisdictions (the schools and Allegheny County) wielded a combined greater share of tax revenue (see Table 3).

In 2005, land sitting idle was still a bane. The old downtown sat abandoned. Businesses that needed open land (rather than employees and structures) found Clairton still attractive. Think of junkyards and auto wrecking yards. Without school taxes being part of the LVT, the city portion would be able to have only a moderate effect on spurring good economic choices for Clairton, although still providing moderate tax relief for homeowners, and moderate tax increases for vacant or poorly used land. Clairton had the good luck that its school district was qualified to use LVT under Act 16 (1993) allowing school districts, which are coterminous with third-class cities, to levy heavier property taxes on land values than on building values.

The beginning of change occurred when Fran Geletko, former steelworker, finance chief, and public works director for the City of

Table 3

Tax Revenue

Jurisdiction	Property Tax Revenue in 2006	Percent
School	$2,666,549	62.55%
City	$1,028,122	24.12%
County	$568,440	13.33%
	$4,263,111	100.00%

Analysis of percentages derived from Clairton assessment rolls, with tax rate multiplied by total assessments, certified assessment roll of Allegheny County PA.

Clairton, became a member of the Clairton Board of Education. Convinced that LVT in its limited application was a success, he invited the CSE to give a presentation to the district in September 2004. That first meeting was lively; many basic questions about the impact of taxation on a local economy arose. The difference between a tax on movable capital (a building) and an immovable resource (land value) became apparent.

One board member was quite concerned about the impact on United States Steel (USX). The steel firm still had a productive presence in Clairton, as the home of a coke mill that served the whole US steel industry (http://www.uss.com/corp/facilities/clairton-plant.asp). The board member was concerned that Clairton would seem ungrateful to USX for its continued presence. Other board members responded that USX had been appealing it assessments for years (on the buildings), was not paying its fair share of city services, and refused to sell its hundreds of vacant acres to prospective industrial investors.

The first chance to adopt LVT for the school district in 2005 did not happen. Several factors came into play. A squabble erupted between the Allegheny County school districts and the County Executive Dan Onorato over what year's assessments to use for tax purposes. To keep the story short, the Executive wanted to use a "base year" system of assessments (2002) rather than annual updates. In the melee, LVT was lost for a year.

In addition, questions arose as to what kind of economic development would occur. CSE's experience in Pennsylvania, along with independent study by academics and policy groups over the years (Plassman 1997; Oates and Schwab 1997; Hartzok 1997), indicated that residential rehabilitation and new construction would take place only if the jurisdictions involved marketed the idea competently, and the rates were high enough on land and low enough on buildings to effect both "good" and "bad" behavior. (The City of Aliquippa—which has city and school taxes on the LVT program—has done little or nothing to market the advantages of LVT to business, industry, or prospective homeowners. As a result, Aliquippa's tax shift exists in a vacuum, with anemic results and little awareness in government or without.)

In the winter of 2005, CSE returned to present a case for LVT. This time, factors weighed in favor of LVT adoption. Appeals by USX—on structures—over time had drained revenue from school operations and increased taxes on everyone else. More tax-delinquent property popped up, and new not-for-profit housing paid little or nothing in taxes. In May of 2006, the Board of Directors decided to adopt LVT.

The matter moved forward, and William Boucher, the Finance Director for the Clairton School District then had to decide what rates to set. CSE recommended, over the course of several years, that the district take very gradual steps to introduce LVT. The rationale was built on experience: when two Pennsylvania towns, Hazelton and Uniontown, brought in LVT in the early 1990s, they went too fast, introducing high land tax rates and very low building rates.

Although LVT cut taxes for most significantly, it is axiomatic that the squeaky wheel gets the grease, and loud complaints from downtown landowners reversed LVT in both cities after one year. Similarly, in Connellsville, PA the quick shift to high land rates led to enmity from downtown vacant lot owners that never went away, to the point that LVT was finally done away with in 2003 by a neophyte city administration under pressure from a coalition of business leaders even though many saved greatly with LVT.

After a close examination of the impact of the actual tax, Mr. Boucher decided that putting the tax rates in harmony with the city tax was preferable, and would provide dramatic, significant tax reductions for those least able to afford it. There have since been mighty objections from vacant and poor land-use owners, but the district and Mr. Boucher are so far standing firm, essentially chiding and shaming those that have been taking from Clairton for years, and not giving back.

In June 2006, LVT rates were set at 75 mills on land values and 3.1 mills for buildings. In one move, the school district went from 26.5 percent of revenue from land to 89.6 percent. Combined with the city LVT, the rates are 104 mills on land (10.4 percent) and 4.32 mills on buildings (0.432 percent). Even with the obsolete Allegheny County property tax in the mix, the revenue "take" from land is currently

Chart 4

Clairton, Pennsylvania Post-LVT

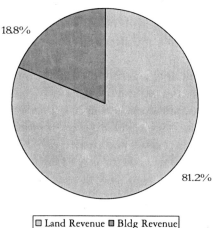

18.8%

81.2%

☐ Land Revenue ■ Bldg Revenue

Analysis by Center for the Study of Economics, data from Clairton Assessment Rolls provided by the Clairton School District certified assessment roll of Allegheny County, PA.

81.2 percent, as can be seen in Chart 4. If there were no LVT, the revenue from land would be 26.5 percent.

Make no mistake: the recent adoption of land-value taxation by the School District of Clairton to complement the city's 1989 adoption has turned the traditional property tax on its head. This action also puts LVT advocates on notice: if LVT in a localized setting is to have an impact, it had better happen here. The ground is fertile. We have a city government and a school board that seems to understand LVT, and wants to use it as an economic development tool and as a way to free the vulnerable from the taxman's hand.

In Allegheny County, indeed in the SW Pennsylvania region, Clairton now has the lowest tax burden on labor and capital, with a large amount of developable open commercial/industrial land, as well as a downtown that is at present woefully underused. The opportunity for Clairton is as great as it has been for decades.

Theory Meets Reality: The Numbers

LVT is supposed to be a fairer tax, meant to reward work and investment and help forgotten neighborhoods. What is the actual outcome? What happens when we look at the city/school tax bill of various properties and classes? To find out, CSE and Clairton studied the assessed values provided by Allegheny County, PA, which create the only legal assessed real estate values for Clairton (http://www.county.allegheny.pa.us/opa/index.aspx). The comparisons in this section are between the traditional property tax rates of 29.5 mills (or 2.95 percent at full market value as determined by Allegheny County, PA) and the rates at the time of writing of 103 mills on land values (10.3 percent) and 4.32 mills on building values (.0432 percent).

Residential

CSE's parcel-by-parcel study of residential property confirmed that homestead (owner-occupied) properties benefited significantly more than absentee-owned (that is rental) properties. There are 3,319 residential parcels in Clairton. Like many older cities in trouble, the number of owner-occupied (OO) homes dropped from the industrial era: 48 percent are now OO, while 52 percent are absentee-owned (ABS), as determined from the "Homestead" key in the assessment roll.

Under LVT, 69.3 percent of OO properties see at least some reduction in tax burden, while only 56.4 percent of ABS sees a reduction (Chart 5). This may confirm the anecdotal assertion that absentee landlords put little investment into the building, while an owner does. The raw dollar shift in tax burden shows greater benefit to OO: the average savings is $283 annually, and the median is $256. With ABS, the average reduction is $271 and the median is $236 (Chart 6). Many of these units—OO and ABS—are actually abandoned shells, so the shift would be greater if more care taken with assessments.

Multi-Family

With 886 properties, multi-family units ranging from two-family to four-family are a significant component of the housing inventory. With

Chart 5

Percent Annual Decrease in Owner-Occ. Tax Liability, Clairton 2006

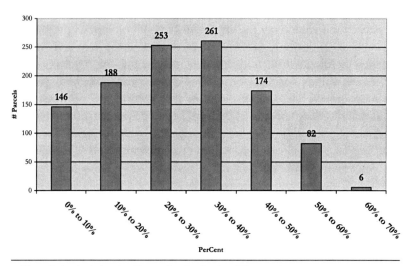

Chart 5, Analysis by the Center for the Study of Economics.

the presumed intensity of lot development, there is no surprise in the 75.6 percent of the parcels that see a tax reduction, with the class seeing a 37 percent average and 40.5 percent median drop in annual tax burden.

Tax progressivity has a home in Clairton. Yet, as the Center always recognizes:: "If all these people save, who pays?" This oft-heard note in defense of the status quo deserves examination, particularly with corporate-owned vacant, industrial, and vacant land sites.

Commercial/Industrial

After the collapse of the industrial era in Clairton, and the resulting decline of the residential sector's presence and buying power, it is not surprising to learn that most of the non-residential sector is now raw land, or abandoned shells on St. Clair Avenue and 3rd Street. This reality agrees with LVT theory in practice: of 455 parcels, 41 percent

Chart 6

Percent Annual Increase in Owner-Occ. Tax Liability, Clairton 2006

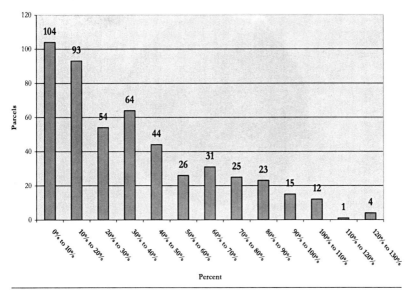

Chart 6, Analysis by the Center for the Study of Economics.

are vacant land, 38.7 percent see increased tax, and only 20.3 percent see a decrease. The biggest savers are big apartment complexes, and some remnant retail.

Vacant Land

The major rationale for elected officials adopting LVT is the increased tax incidence on vacant land. The last thing a town in trouble needs is a tax system that subsidizes private-land hoarding and speculation. Indeed, redevelopment plans often go awry when private-land banking co-opts civic land banks. Of vacant land parcels 100 percent, of course, see an increase. The value of vacant land in Clairton is $3.9 million or 12.2 percent of all taxable land value; yet without LVT it comprised only 4.3 percent of property-tax revenue.

Chart 7

United States Steel: Share of Total Land Value, Clairton, PA

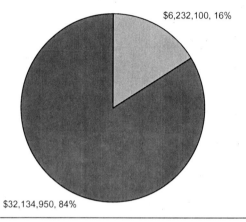

$6,232,100, 16%

$32,134,950, 84%

Chart 7, Analysis by the Center for the Study of Economics.

The current LVT rates increase vacant land tax levies by 249 percent. That results in vacant land now paying 15.15 percent of property tax revenue. With land values generally under-assessed, this revenue share could be much higher. Most of that liability is assumed by Clairton's largest landowner both in size and value, United States Steel (USX). Even though USX lowered its building assessment over the past few years (Vincent 2006), the land value was still significant. USX owns a significant share of total land value that is taxable (see Chart 7).

The 25 vacant parcels will pay for the education of Clairton's children, and liberate working and middle-class families from the bonds of labor and capital taxation.

Conclusion

The efforts to induce LVT are met with many barriers. Political inertia, bad property assessment, and the lack of voice that poorer communities and neighborhoods have all militate against quick or easy adoption of the Georgist approach. Yet, the trend has been inching upwards as far as recognition of what the Georgist approach is, and where it can spread, and how the potential benefits to those communities that need help can be demonstrated by analysis of urban datasets.

References

Chamberlain, L. (2006). "Tax Breaks Drive a Philadelphia Boom." *New York Times* January 8. Available at http://www.nytimes.com/2006/01/08/realestate/08nati.html?_r=1&ex=1184904000&en=8fec50435263bc46&ei=5070.

City-Data.com (2012). "Clairton, Pennsylvania (PA) Poverty Rate Data—Information About Poor and Low-Income Residents." Available at http://www.city-data.com/poverty/poverty-Clairton-Pennsylvania.html.

Clapp, J. M., and Y. Wang (2005). "Defining Neighborhood Boundaries: Are Census Tracts Obsolete?" *Social Science Research Network* August 26. Available at http://papers.ssrn.com/sol3/papers.cfm?abstract_id=478642.

Cord, S. B. (2003). "22." *Incentive Taxation.* Available at http://heartland.org/sites/all/modules/custom/heartland_migration/files/pdfs/12508.pdf.

Couch, A. (2006). "Toward a More Equitable Housing Policy." *Philadelphia Independent Media Center.* Available at http://www.phillyimc.org/en/node/45119.

Econsult Corporation (2010). *Vacant Land Management in Philadelphia: The Costs of the Current System and Benefits of Reform.* Philadelphia: Penn Institute for Urban Research.

Galster, G., J. Cutsinger, and J. C. Booza (2006). "Where Did They Go? The Decline of Neighborhoods in Metropolitan America." Brookings Institution. Available at http://www.brookings.edu/reports/2006/06poverty_booza.aspx.

Hartzok, A. (1997). *Pennsylvania's Success with Local Property Tax Reform: The Split Rate Tax.* Scotland, PA: Earth Rights Institute. Available at http://www.earthrights.net/docs/success.html.

Hayden, T. (1967). *Rebellion in Newark: Official Violence and Ghetto Response.* New York: Vintage Books.

Jargowsky, P. A. (1997). *Poverty and Place: Ghettos, Barrios, and the American City.* New York: Russell Sage Foundation.

Kunstler, J. (1999). "Where Evil Dwells: Reflections on the Columbine School Massacre." Presented at Congress for the New Urbanism, Milwaukee, June 6. Available at http://www.kunstler.com/spch_milw.html.

Local Government Commission (2005). "Municipal Fiscal Distress and Recovery." In *Pennsylvania Legislator's Municipal Deskbook*, 3rd edition. Harris-

burg: Pennsylvania General Assembly. Available at http://www.lgc.state.
pa.us/deskbook06/Issues_Taxation_and_Finance_11_Municipal_Fiscal_
Distress.pdf.

Maryland Department of Assessments and Taxation (2010). *2011–2012
County Tax Rates.* Available at http://www.dat.state.md.us/sdatweb/
taxrate.html.

Metzger, J. T. (2000). "Planned Abandonment: The Neighborhood Life-Cycle
Theory and National Urban Policy." *Housing Policy Debate* 11(1): 7–11.

Monkkonen, E. H. (1988). *America Becomes Urban: The Development of U.S.
Cities and Towns 1780–1980.* Berkeley: University of California Press.

Oates, W. E., and R. M. Schwab (1997). "The Impact of Urban Land Taxation:
The Pittsburgh Experience." *National Tax Journal* 50(1): 1–21. Available
at   http://ntj.tax.org/wwtax/ntjrec.nsf/893168271A5088AD85256863004
A5942/$FILE/v50n1001.pdf.

Philadelphia Forward (2012). "Philadelphia Needs Tax Reform." Available at
http://www.philadelphiaforward.org/node/38.

Philadelphia Tax Reform Commission (2003). *Final Report: November 15,
2003.* Available at http://www.philadelphiataxreform.org/.

Plassman, F. (1997). *The Impact of Two-Rate Taxes on Construction in
Pennsylvania,* Ph.D. dissertation. Blacksburg: Virginia Polytechnic Institute and State University. Available at http://scholar.lib.vt.edu/theses/
available/etd-61097-13834/.

Vincent, J. (2005). "Land Value Property Tax Under Consideration in Seven
States." *Heartlander* June 1. Available at http://news.heartland.org/
newspaper-article/2005/06/01/land-value-property-tax-under-
consideration-seven-states.

——. (2006). "Pennsylvania School District Embraces Land Value Taxation
Reform." *Heartlander* December 1. Available at http://news.
heartland.org/newspaper-article/2006/12/01/pennsylvania-school-
district-embraces-land-value-taxation-reform.

An American Catholic Perspective on Urban Neighborhoods: The Lens of Monsignor Geno C. Baroni and the Legacy of the Neighborhood Movement

By JOHN A. KROMKOWSKI* and JOHN DAVID KROMKOWSKI†

ABSTRACT. This essay reviews insights and actions that were prompted by a contemporary crisis of American development that was not entirely unlike the earlier crisis of growth that inspired Henry George's diagnosis and prescription for relief, reform, and renewal. It traces Catholic underpinnings of social, economic, and political thought and action and their applications to American urban life. It highlights new themes of a developing Catholic tradition that engages new problematic conditions and situations. These new themes and practices became imperatives related to current dynamics of urban and metropolitan growth. Thus this essay addresses the sources of this approach to the crisis of development found in the neighborhood movement and locates the particularly pivotal participation the Monsignor Geno C. Baroni and his vision and action regarding people and places in our time.

Introduction

People don't live in cities; they live in neighborhoods. Neighborhoods. Neighborhoods are the building blocks of cities. If neighborhoods die, cities die. There's never been a Federal policy that respected neighborhoods. We destroyed neighborhoods in order to save them.

I used to think I wanted to save the world. Then I got to Washington, and thought I'd save the city. Now I'd settle for one neighborhood.

—Msgr. Geno Baroni

Today's disparities and inequities occasioned by irrational land uses, inequitable land distribution, and dislocations of communities recalls

*John A. Kromkowski is Associate Professor, Department of Politics, the Catholic University of America.

†John David Kromkowski is an attorney in private practice in Baltimore, MD.

American Journal of Economics and Sociology, Vol. 71, No. 4 (October, 2012).

in some respects the Georgist tradition of critique of domestic policy and the attendant invention of new formulations and designs of justice. However, this account of contemporary social thought and action seeks to widen the horizon of that early critique. It outlines the fluid and broad definition of a neighborhood and the operations of neighborhoods, providing examples of neighborhood-based approaches and action that address the deeper crisis of our time caused by even higher levels of urbanization.

This essay recovers the archeology and anthropology of the Catholic social thought (CST), the origins of neighborhood movement, and the insight of Monsignor Geno C. Baroni. It recounts how they engaged the crisis of our time and articulated a new approach that Georgists may find attractive, complementary, and entirely relevant to the deepening crisis of urbanization and need to move beyond the reform of taxation and its claims and pretense as a sufficient remedy.

To be sure such reform is necessary, but the addition of a fuller vision and deeper therapy found in following accounts of thought and action bodes a renewal of founding impulses of Georgism and the revival of Georgist action for the 21st century. Like Henry George we should make no small-scale plans nor take on small-scale projects, but we should recover the small-scale building blocks of neighborhood and community action as the ground from which the work of justice in urban life can transform the American reality and its landscape into the country that always promised liberty and justice for all. Without this vision and action driven by this expectation our ongoing tasks will wither into routines and acts of the human spirit become even more rare and in the long run, we all know what even the most hopeful economists have foretold.

The Challenge and Opportunity

In the 1960s, the civil rights movement served notice that after almost two centuries an American ideal of equal treatment before the law must become a reality. It also reminded us that America was the special nation that promised hope, dignity, and justice for all. Yet the translation of these profound desires, first embodied by the heroic actions of the civil rights movement, into the civil rights laws, these laws into programs, and these programs into the bureaucratization of the civil rights movement and civic impulses is a sobering tale of the unexpected consequences of focusing on legalistic strategies and state-imposed remedies. Such unanticipated and disallowing outcomes suggest that the promises of the American covenant cannot be achieved merely through the sound of great and prophetic words or through legal authorization by the stroke of a pen. The tasks of justice emerge from the specific injustices encountered.

An additional stunning irony of this era was the expectation that the urban crisis could be resolved by strategies designed to combat racism. Msgr. Geno Baroni, who marched with Rev. Martin Luther King, Jr. in Selma and was the Catholic Coordinator for the march in Washington at which he delivered his "I Have a Dream" speech, was among the first civil rights activists to perceive the bankruptcy of racialism and classism in the politics and policy of the late 1960s. Baroni and his associates at the National Center for Urban Ethnic Affairs (NCUEA) developed an alternative approach to urban economic and cultural contradictions (Kromkowski, Naparstek, and Baroni 1976). This approach implied a critique of the civil rights movement and its advocate governmental agency, the U.S. Commission on Civil Rights. At bottom this difference involved ethnic and racial culturalism as opposed to a white versus black/majority versus minorities vision of America and the relative importance and emphasis on place and community rather than individual rights and the universal claim of social justice. These advocates for urban neighborhoods and cultural pluralism argued for the creation of a National Neighborhood Commission that would promote the renewal of urban life and more adequately address the pluralistic character of American culture.

Baroni and his cohorts were bridge-builders and mediators. Hence, the "neighborhood movement" that they created was not specifically "Catholic." Indeed, it always sought to reach beyond mere Catholic "parish" revitalization, beyond a movement and concrete strategies that were only concerned about predominately Catholic urban neighborhoods. Justice for all obviously meant community and neighborhood revitalization for all. As a part of the Catholic social-justice tradition going back to the lawyer who asked Jesus, "Who is my neighbor," the use of this language and the incorporation of the concept of neighbor has always been affirmed in dogma and theory. While the extension of this concept into a universal that would include the whole of humanity has not been practiced completely nor applied thoroughly throughout the history of the church, the centrality of teaching and prescription of care for the needs of one's neighbor are unquestionable central Catholic social thought.

What we think is notable is that, on one hand, unlike Henry George, the Catholic perspective does not and cannot reduce the issue to economics and tax policy. On the other hand, we can see a striking similarity in stature and mission between Monsignor Geno C. Baroni and Father Ed McGlynn, Henry George's friend, supporter, and organizer (Adreassi 2000).

Moreover, Henry George's motivations to seek the causes for and remedies to poverty and injustice are not entirely different from the motivations of the Catholic social-justice theory and its prescriptions for action. This congruence is especially vivid in the motivations of the neighborhood movement and its principal advocate in Catholic action in America, Monsignor Baroni. George's proposition of a method and public policy that taxes should fall more heavily and perhaps exclusively on land value, rather than on wages or other sources of income and wealth, is not antithetical *per se* to Catholicism, nor the American neighborhood movement. But we think that it lacks the breadth and scope of the neighborhood movement. Moreover, the striking difference in the neighborhood movement is part of a long line of Catholic social justice put into actual action. The successes, though imperfect and unfinished, of the neighborhood movement are tangible, not just theoretical. The general failure of Georgists to get land-value taxation implemented, much less see the fruits, cannot be ignored. The zenith of "Georgism" was when Henry George teamed up with a Catholic advisor who was a man of moral conviction as well as a doer and a man of action. It is worth recalling that Fr. McGlynn did not close down the St. Stephen's Anti-Poverty Society that he founded while waiting for the Single Tax to be enacted.

The Underpinnings of the Neighborhood Movement—
The Catholic Perspective

This section explores several sources and the themes comprise the intertwining of central concepts, texts, and structures that constitute the core features of CST and its unique blending of philosophical anthropology, attention to the sociality of human organization, and the ethical imperatives of Judeo-Christian religious traditions. The following sources are illustrative of core values and explicative of the foundational and universal elements of this approach to social practice, the underpinnings of the social thought and practice of this world-view, as well as the particular application of such perspectives to and within the American context and the particularities of American history and demography: the parish structure of the Catholic Church, the principle of subsidiarity, Baroni's 1969 Statement to the Bishops, Baroni's 1970 "Ethnic" Conference, the American Catholic Bicentennial process (1973–1983), Kaptur's principle's from Humbold Park East work in 1976.

The Parish

The parish is central to Catholic spiritual and temporal life because that is where the sacraments are received. Sources for the governance of parishes are found in Canon Law (Canon Law Society of America 1999). This corpus of regulations, directions, and admonitions is a textual superstructure that expresses optimum behaviors. Moreover the normative and prescriptive, directive tone of the following canons on parishes is particularly attentive to the well-being of persons in particular communities and places. For example:

> Can. 515 §1 A parish is a certain community of Christ's faithful stably established within a particular Church, whose pastoral care, under the authority of the diocesan Bishop, is entrusted to a parish priest as its proper pastor.
>
> Can. 518 As a general rule, a parish is to be territorial, that is, it is to embrace all Christ's faithful of a given territory. Where it is useful however, personal parishes are to be established, determined by reason of the rite, language or nationality of the faithful of a certain territory, or on some other basis.

That a parish is generally synonymous with a certain location or territory, or nationality or language, means that it has always been a focal point for charitable and social organizing activities, including neighborhood revitalization.

That the neighborhood movement of the 1970s grew out of and was greatly influenced by priests and organizers from urban parishes is surprising only because Catholic social organization has been overlooked due to the paucity of attention to social religiosity. The congregational and associational models of memberships and the free-church traditions that are dominant in America and their long-term "quietistic" avoidance of public affairs eclipsed the relevance of this factor in mainstream behavioral research. This era ended with the rise of the "Moral Majority" of the 1980s and its issue focus, which included its inattention to urbanization and its consequences and its espousal of an individualistic piety and critique of modernity and its secular hedonism and depravity, which were masterfully linked to the rise of the administrative state and destructions of rural culture. Fuller attention to this aspect of the topic is beyond the scope of this paper, but attention to other features of CST will illustrate the stark contrast between a fully urban spirituality and institutionalized religious and philosophical anthropology and theory of sociality with origin in the ancient Mediterranean urbanism. The following canons illustrate such features and their full normative thrust (emphasis supplied in *italic* face):

> Can. 528 §1 The parish priest has the obligation of ensuring that the word of God is proclaimed in its entirety to those living in the parish. He is therefore to see to it that the lay members of Christ's faithful are instructed in the truths of faith, especially by means of the homily on Sundays and holydays of obligation and by catechetical formation. *He is to foster works which promote the spirit of the Gospel, including its relevance to social justice.* He is to have a special care for the catholic education of children and young people. With the collaboration of the faithful, he is to make every effort to bring the gospel message to those also who have given up religious practice or who do not profess the true faith.
>
> Can. 529 §1 So that he may fulfil his office of pastor diligently, the parish priest is to strive to know the faithful entrusted to his care. *He is therefore to visit their families, sharing in their cares and anxieties and, in a special way, their sorrows, comforting them in the Lord.* If in certain matters they are found wanting, he is prudently to correct them. He is to help the sick

and especially the dying in great charity, solicitously restoring them with the sacraments and commending their souls to God. *He is to be especially diligent in seeking out the poor, the suffering, the lonely, those who are exiled from their homeland, and those burdened with special difficulties.* He is to strive also to ensure that spouses and parents are sustained in the fulfilment of their proper duties, and to foster the growth of christian life in the family.

§2 The parish priest is to recognize and promote the specific role which the lay members of Christ's faithful have in the mission of the Church, fostering their associations which have religious purposes. He is to cooperate with his proper Bishop and with the presbyterium of the diocese. *Moreover, he is to endeavor to ensure that the faithful are concerned for the community of the parish,* that they feel themselves to be members both of the diocese and of the universal Church, and that they take part in and sustain works which promote this community.

The Principle of Subsidiarity

The influence of the Catholic principle of subsidiarity is another source of guidance to governance that has been deeply etched into the texture of CST. The following texts from teaching documents, not canon law, provide another glimpse into the origins of a world-view steeped in the complexity of large-scale orders and their layers, levels, intersections, convergences, along with the need for guidance in avoiding conflict and resolving contentions regarding the authoritative allocation of resources, values and fair distributions of burdens, and benefits of large-scale social, economic, and cultural orders. While the tradition of this concept is contemporaneous with the time of Henry George, recent expression of the principle of subsidiarity in teaching text follow. These two selections are paradigmatic of both the universal and country-specific articulations of this aspect of social theory and practical guidance.

The "principle of subsidiarity" must be respected: "A community of a higher order should not interfere with the life of a community of a lower order, taking over its functions." In case of need it should, rather, support the smaller community and help to coordinate its activity with activities in the rest of society for the sake of the common good. (John Paul II 1991: 48)

The primary norm for determining the scope and limits of governmental intervention is the "principle of subsidiarity" cited above. This principle states that, in order to protect basic justice, government should undertake only those initiatives which exceed the capacities of individuals or private groups acting independently. Government should not replace or destroy smaller communities and individual initiative. Rather it should help them contribute more effectively to social well-being and supplement their activity when the demands of justice exceed their capacities. This does not mean, however, that the government that governs least, governs best. Rather it defines good government intervention as that which truly "helps" other social groups contribute to the common good by directing, urging, restraining, and regulating economic activity as "the occasion requires and necessity demands." (United States Catholic Bishops 1986: 124)

Baroni's 1969 Statement to the Bishops

Another level of social thought can be found in the expression of consecrated teachers. Such texts are clearly different from those found in canon law and those issued under the auspices of church authority and the collective statements cited above. This level of personal reflection and assessment has interesting weight owing to the impact of this Catholic teaching voice. Monsignor Baroni's biographer, Lawrence M. O'Rourke, chronicled Baroni's assignment to help produce a plan of urban action for the U.S. Catholic Bishops. O'Rourke's (1991: 73) account follows:

> In the late 1960s, the bishops watched with growing concern as the United States drifted into two societies, one rich, one poor: one black, the other white: one with opportunity, the other a boiling cauldron of despair. What Baroni [in his DC parish] and his allies [in urban parishes across the country] experienced underscored the need for national action. The bishops saw the growing division with their own ranks. As they promoted the just cause of blacks, they felt counter-thrust from alienated whites. From Catholic whites across the country, the bishops got a message that, like it or not, they were part of the urban scene too.

As O'Rourke noted, the Kerner Commission's report in March of 1968 spelled out the magnitude of the situation. Baroni was asked to put modern Catholic social-justice theory into proposals for action. In the summer of 1968, he met in Canada with other priest friends who made up the Catholic Committee for the Urban Ministry (CCUM). Returning to Washington, he worked closely with Father Don Clark of Detroit, the president of the Black Catholic Clergy Caucus, Andrew Gallegos, representing the Spanish-speaking community, and Monsignor Aloysius Welsh, staff director of the U.S. Catholic Conference task force. O'Rourke (1991: 74) writes:

> Perhaps liberalism had run its course. At the very least, Baroni observed that the social welfare programs promised by Johnson's War on Poverty had failed. . . . The priest started to rethink his own political philosophy. He had always believed government could do it all, but now he began to wonder about the possibility of a cooperative effort involving government, the private sector and the community.

Clark, Gallegos, and Baroni had become identified as advocates for his particular group so as the deadline for delivering a report to the bishops approached, they decided to draft an overall statement as well as submit individual statements at the November, 1969 meeting of the bishops (O'Rourke 1991: 74):

> [T]he Catholic Church has traditionally been an urban church [they jointly reminded the bishops]. Indeed, it was an inner-city church, with a body of knowledge and techniques useful to achieving the assimilation of poor people into the mainstream. This knowledge is relevant today and adaptable to the new urban poor.

They sought from the bishops a creation of another task force to give direction and support that Baroni felt needed to be as great as the task of going to the moon and that involved each diocese that coordinated church officials, agencies, and parishes. Baroni had the experience to speak about such coordination since he had done it, and more. Baroni's statement set the stage for the Catholic neighborhood movement (O'Rourke 1991: 73–75). As O'Rourke (1991: 75) compellingly argued:

> At 39, Baroni had more practical experience with the problems of contemporary urban America than anyone else in the room that day. In many ways—impact, timing and setting, innovation, Baroni's own career—this was the most important statement that Baroni was to make.

To all who knew him, his 1969 statement to the bishops was classic Baroni. And while he borrowed many ideas from others, he was the first "street priest" of the urban crisis of the 1960s and 1970s to win a national forum and to articulate effectively—and as it turned out, somewhat successfully. This is what he read to the bishops, as excerpted by O'Rourke (1991: 75–82):

Agenda for the '70s

The mission of the Church, a believing institution, in today's world, must be developed in a constantly evolving metropolitan and urban society. Whether a person lives in the center of our cities, or in the suburbs, or in a farm village, his life and the life of his community are significantly shaped by the metropolitan and urban character of our modern world.

What Are the Dynamics of Urban Growth?

Nearly one-half of all people in the United States in the year 2000 will live in dwelling units that have not yet been started and on land that has not yet been broken. . . . Every month in the United States we are adding roughly 300,000 people, a city the size of Toledo. Every year we add a new Philadelphia. . . . Such are the dynamics of our urban growth. It has been said that in the remainder of this century we will build, new, in our cities, the equivalent of all that has been built since Plymouth Rock. What a challenge and opportunity this presents for the Church in an increasingly metropolitan and urban society.

The Urban Crisis—"Inevitable Group Conflict"

"The urban crisis"—at its core, is a human crisis. "The urban crisis" has become our major domestic issue and had focused on those minority groups which have been left at the bottom of the social scale. Now, there is a need to pay new attention to the white urban ethnic groups as well, if we are to move toward the reduction of "inevitable group . . . conflict." Little attention has been given to the anguish of the socially and politically alienated "middle American". . . . As probably the most ethnic and cultural pluralistic nation in the world, the United States has functioned less as a nation of individuals than of groups. This has meant inevitable group competition, friction and conflict. There is a desperate need to reduce and prevent the confrontation—the group conflict—the polarization—between the white urban ethnic groups and the minority poor.

The New Coalition

If we are to develop a new agenda for the 1970s: We must go beyond the civil rights struggle of the '60s. We must stop exploiting the fear of the ethnic, middle Americans. We must bring together a new coalition to press for new goals and new priorities for all the poor and the near poor, including the blacks, the Appalachians, the Indians, the Spanish-speaking, and the white urban ethnic groups. . . . Then we can develop a true cultural pluralism in this country and reduce the "inevitable group conflict."

The Moral Response

At the heart of the urban crisis, a human crisis, is a moral crisis. While we admit that our nation has the material resources, the technology, the economic and industrial know-how and the wealth to provide a more human existence for every man, woman and child, something spiritual is lacking—the heart, the will, the desire on the part of affluent America to develop the goals and commitments necessary to end the hardships of poverty and race in our midst. This is the greatest scandal of our affluent society: that we tolerate millions of poor people living in our midst without hope, some because of poverty, some because of race, and some because of both.

The National Will

This lack of national will, this lack of a national purpose or desire, this lack of a moral response to develop goals and commitments to meet our substantive problems of housing, education, health, unemployment, discrimination and so on, has created a crisis of belief on the part of the poor and youth, including many younger priests and nuns, in our democratic system of government and other institutions of society, including the Church.

We may respond "that much had been done," and much has been done by government, labor, business and the religious community to meet the suffering caused by poverty. But our combined efforts, including the numerous programs sponsored by the Church and its institutions, have not sufficiently affected the causes of our problems. Much more remains to be done.

The most crucial item on the agenda of the 1970s is a moral question: What can we, the nation, or how can we, the Church, develop a spiritual response to meet our urban crisis? How can we help to develop a national will, a desire, that supports the conviction that "we, as a nation, must clearly and positively demonstrate our belief that justice, social progress, and equality of opportunity are rights of every citizen"? Can we lead our people to respond, not out of guilt or fear, but as Christians who believe that "the American people must reorder national priorities~ with a commitment of resources equal to the magnitude we face"? Can we develop the moral commitment necessary to recognize that our human crisis requires a new dimension of effort in both the private and public sectors, working together to provide for the human needs of the poor, for the human needs of a growing urban society? . . .

Urban Mission Policy—The Church and the Evolving Urban Society

The Church in the United States must develop an urban mission policy to meet contemporary human needs . . . We urge the National Council of

Catholic Bishops to establish an annual collection for human development in the United States. A national response by the U.S. Church would be a concrete initiative in leading the nation by way of example to develop new priorities and new efforts in meeting human needs in our society. . . . Such a national campaign might well serve as an educational instrument in developing a domestic social consciousness. . . .

Diocesan Response

Each diocese must provide leadership in developing a moral response to the human needs of the poor by setting up and staffing an urban task force to coordinate church officials, agencies and parishes to develop a new agenda for the 1970s. The development of a local urban mission policy needs concrete data and analysis to be able to set priorities and to have a documented base upon which to determine parish and diocesan positions regarding planning, poverty, human relations, urban renewal, economic development, city services, and other problems in our urban society. . . . Above all, an urban mission statement needs to develop a process whereby the blacks, the middle-American, the Spanish-speaking, the Appalachian, all our people, can participate in developing goals and priorities that go beyond the fears of racism. An urban mission policy needs to develop a spiritual response that is informed, sensitive and well-directed to creating a "national will," that will meet the human needs of the poor and otherwise alienated.

National Task Force

At the level of the National Task Force diocesan and regional goals and plans can be collected and developed into long-range planning and program development. . . . Only by developing a national and local urban mission policy based on concrete data and analysis can the Catholic Church in the United States overcome any temporary lack of direction and give moral and spiritual leadership to demonstrate in a renewed effort, the Church's concern for its mission of service to the poor. . . . The agenda for the 1970s is the same for every follower of Christ: How do we feed the hungry? How do we clothe the naked? How do we house the homeless? How do we multiply the loaves and fishes in a modern and evolving metropolitan society?

The Baroni proposal for an annual human development collection was adopted immediately by the bishops, who voted to create a National Crusade Against Poverty and pledged $50 million. The poor in America need much more than alms, the bishops said. "They need self-respect. They need the door of opportunity to open equally for them. They do not need cast-off housing and inferior education but the quality housing and education that is available for all Americans" (O'Rourke 1991: 73). And while the bishops appointed Bishop Michael R. Dempsey of Chicago to head the Crusade instead of Baroni, the bishops also decided that the issue of urban problems needed further study and Baroni was the one to head up such a task force for studying the issue and making further recommendations. Over the next six months, Baroni traveled to New York, Boston, Detroit, Cleveland, Baltimore, Pittsburgh, Youngstown, Toledo, Providence, and Chicago, and saw firsthand how the Catholic community was handling—or not handling—the urban crisis.

1970 Baroni Conference on "Ethnics" at Catholic University and Mikulski

O'Rourke's (1991: 87) chronicle of Baroni's 1970 Conference at Catholic University sheds light on the passion of the working-class urban ethnics and how Baroni sought to channel and mediate that passion into action consonant with Catholic teaching and the upshot of this effort, the creation of the neighborhood movement:

> Then Baroni's conference came to life. A nervous young social worker from Baltimore named Barbara Mikulski stepped onstage and effectively voiced the anger of white ethnics. . . . "America is not a melting pot," Mikulski said. "It is a sizzling cauldron for the ethnic American who feels that he has been politically courted and legally extorted by both government and private enterprise. The ethnic American is sick of being stereotyped as a racist and dullard by phony white liberals, pseudo black militants and patronizing bureaucrats. He pays the bill for every major government program and gets nothing or little in the way of return. Tricked by the political rhetoric of the illusionary funding for black-oriented social programs, he turns his anger to race—when he himself is the victim of class prejudice. . . . He does not have fancy lawyers or expensive lobbyists getting him tax breaks on his income. Being a home owner, he shoulders the rising property taxes—the major revenue source for the municipalities in which he lives. Yet he enjoys very little from these unfair and burdensome levies. . . . He is tired of being treated like an object of production. The public and private institutions have made him frustrated by their lack of response to his needs. At present he feels powerless in his daily dealings with and efforts to change them. Unfortunately, because of old prejudices and new fears, anger is generated against other minority groups rather than those who have power. What is needed is an alliance of white and black,

white collar, blue collar and no collar based on mutual need, interdependence and respect, an alliance to develop the strategy for new kinds of community organization and political participation.

Baroni was a priest who understood tensions within big cities. As a result Monsignor Higgins at the U.S. Catholic Conference invited him to join in writing a Labor Day statement for the bishops. It rejected "the widespread accusation" that urban ethnics "are the primary exponents of racism in our society, although we do not deny that racism exists in their ranks" (O'Rourke 1991: 88). And it called on government, business, labor, the academic community, citizens' organizations, and churches to look for opportunities for social, cultural, and economic community development that served to unite whites, blacks, and Hispanics in big cities. O'Rourke (1991: 88) continues: "Newsweek magazine in 1970 dubbed Baroni 'chief strategist' for the nascent ethnic movement. Priests and community organizers across the nation invited Baroni to their neighborhoods to help solve their pressing problems before the neighborhoods collapsed."

American Catholic Bicentennial Process (1973–1983)

Another type of teaching that is exemplary of the Catholic tradition can be seen in the American Catholic Bicentennial process. This dialogical process may be modeled by its intentionality, which was to weave a Catholic message and ministry into the texture of temporal and secular affairs. At its optimum, it is rooted in a Catholic principle that affirms a form of holism and integration into the country culture within which the Church is located.

On one level this seems clear, but the process simultaneously affirms the capacity to fashion equivalences in the multitude of cultural contexts without essential contradiction and compromise. This distinction is captured in the difference between homogeneity and catholicity and in the complexes suggested by unity/diversity and one-and-many. This process of enculturation can be modeled to include the following key procedural elements: social listening, observing, judging, deliberating, and deciding on ways of proceeding with collective action. This process in microcosm and for short horizons is illustrative of another dimension of Catholic action and thought. Reviewing aspects of this process in the events leading to the U.S. celebration of the Bicentennial of the American Revolution in 1976 opens another source of Catholic patriotism and how this process accessed the deep texture of the American founding and its capacity to render a usable past and significantly valid teaching moment related to liberty and justice for all.

This process included the beginning of a new legitimated form of urban pluralism in a country bereft of a philosophical anthropology and saddled with broken mechanisms of guidance found in fractionated administrative techniques. In this context and in anticipation of the country's bicentennial celebration and growing on the urban movement set in motion by Baroni and others in 1969, the U.S. Catholic Conference established a Bicentennial Justice Committee to monitor the America Catholic Bicentiennial process. The process was deliberately linked to Pope Paul VI's (1967) encyclical *Populorum Progressio*, his (1971) Apostolic Letter *Octogesima Adveniens*, and the World Synod of Catholic Bishops' (1971) *Justitia in mundo*. Rev. J. Bryan Hehir of the United States Catholic Conference and the Bicentennial Committee noted, in 1974, the dual process of the celebration:

> [Its purpose] is to stimulate a process of reflection, examination, planning and action by the Catholic community in the United States on the topic of freedom and justice in our society [as well as] to allow us to pass from a knowledge of principles to a level of practice. [This] second objective . . . flows from the first. If we carry out the process of moving from principles we carry on a kind of dialogue with the structures, systems of power organization, influence and wealth in our country and in the globe today. (Committee for the Bicentennial 1975: 5)

The process had three stages. Stage one involved a grassroots collection of individual responses, parish and diocesan meetings, regional "justice hearing," and eight writing committees along eight themes: church, ethnicity and race, neighborhood, family, personhood, work, nationkind, and humankind. The second stage consisted of a national Catholic assembly held in Detroit in 1976, the Call to Action Conference, at which time the conference debated and eventually passed a list of 182 recommendation along subthemes that were considered by the National Conference of Bishops between 1977 and 1981. In the third stage, the Bishops responded to the proposals via committees, which assigned a directive to: (1) study; (2) act immediately; (3) support existing activities; or (4) "respond in light of the universal law of the Church."

The proposals regarding the "neighborhood" theme as well as the Bishops' directives are enlightening. Baroni and his allies played a strategic role during the bicentennial process with respect to matters of economic justice, neighborhoods, and ethnicity. But other forces shaped proposals in other areas. Sociologist Joseph Varacalli (1980: 38) in his study of this process comments:

> Such Bicentenial participants as Monsignor Geno Baroni, Michael Novak, Monsignor Silvano Tomasi, Father Andrew Greeley and [others] are representatives of a socio-theological position that is consistent with the position that "we, though many, are one body in Christ and individually members of one another" (Romans 1: 2). While such a moderate group was continually overwhelmed by the forces advocating an almost exclusively socio-political role for the Church, it is precisely such a moderate group— one approaching the role of a "Catholic detached intelligentsia"—that may serve as mediators in an every increasingly complex and pluralistic Church.

Hence, the legacy of the Call to Action Conference is at best mixed. On one hand, to the casual observer it has become associated with the group (CTA) that took the name. While the conference delegates voted that the Catholic Church should reevaluate its positions on issues like celibacy for priests, the male-only clergy, homosexuality, and birth control, those proposals really formed no basis for the Bishops' product that emerged in response (United States National Conference of Catholic Bishops 1978), entitled *To Do the Work of Justice*. Thomas Fox (1978: 746) noted the following just after the Call to Action Conference:

> What began two years ago as an effort to find out what troubles Catholics and what they wanted Church leaders to do in areas of social justice had, by the time the conference ended, snowballed. The conference became a national forum for priests, sisters, and layperson to call for radical change, taking the Bishops call and the Church teachings as the ground for that change.

Nonetheless, the cooption of the name and process by what became CTA and similar groups overshadowed the economic-justice, neighborhood, and ethnicity discussions produced during the process, much of which was through the work of Baroni and his cohorts, especially through a Mini-Conference on Ethnicity, Race and Neighborhoods held in Newark, NJ as part of stage one. If the aftermath of the process highlighted a divide between the so-called liberal and conservative wings of the American Catholic Church, the process also gave evidence to a dichotomy within the so-called liberal Catholic wing.

As Fr. Greeley (1975: 7) would describe, in anticipation of this potential liberal split, a demarcation arose between the "old Catholic social action" and the "new Catholic social action" or the "pre-Berrigan" and "post-Berrigan" approaches to activism: "The old social justice action is in the tradition of labor schools, labor priest, community organizing and Catholic inter-racial councils that mastered the politics of coalition building with the system." Leading figures in that "old" tradition for Greeley were John Ryan, George Higgins, John Egan, and Geno Baroni. On the other hand, the "new" Catholic action came out of the Berrigan experience and the peace movement and was heavily involved in protest. Greeley's observations are instructive:

1. The old Catholic social action was practical and project oriented. It dealt with short-range problems, short-range goals. It was pragmatic partly by choice and partly because the personalities and training of the people involved did not predispose them to any other style. The new social action is systematic, principled and ideological. It has mystique that inclines it to system-wide criticism and system-wide programs for reform.
2. The old Catholic social action was flexible, prone to compromise, ready—perhaps even eager—to tolerate the imperfections of the world. It is fundamentally accepting of the American social and economic system. The new Catholic social action is concerned with moral deals and moral vision. It dreams of a neat and perfect world in which justice reigns supreme. It wants no part of compromise, seriously raises the question as to whether socialism might just be a preferable alternative in American society to capitalism.
3. The old Catholic social actionists by and large respect American society and the American way of doing things. They are not unaware of the imperfections of American society but they look inward for the principles, the traditions, the methods by which American society can be both criticized and transformed. The new Catholic activists are rigidly anti-American. They look outside American theology to Marxism, socialism and third world liberation theology for their principles and methods. They feel ashamed of the American people and seek to "raise their consciousnesses" preparatory to conversion.

4. The old social actionists are largely men of action: doers, not talkers. The new social actionists are intellectuals. They are masters at manipulating words and sometimes ideas. . . . They are fervent crusaders. Winning strikes, forming unions, organizing communities are not their "things", they are much more concerned about creating world economic justice.

5. The old social actionists are listeners, soaking up, absorbing everything they hear. New social actionists tend not to be listeners; they are rather preachers intent on converting you or raising your consciousness. Dialogue with them is extremely difficult, if not impossible.

6. Finally, the old social action was self-consciously Catholic. It drew its principles from the Catholic social encyclicals and from the Catholic social teachings shaped in the early decades of this country in the United States. The new social action is relatively little concerned with Catholic tradition, though it may occasionally quote a papal encyclical. Its positions, its programs, . . . its rhetoric are drawn from the currently fashionable liberal or "radical chic".

The following list identifies the Call to Action proposals regarding neighborhood and provides the directive that Bishops assigned in parentheses at the end of each statement: (1) study, (2) act immediately, (3) support existing activities, and (4) "respond in light of the universal law of the Church" (Committee for the Call to Action Plan 1978):

120. That parish liturgies must be celebrations of community life; that the sacramental life of the neighborhood church should reflect the relationship between Christian commitment and community realities; that the parish personalize its outreach into the neighborhood community; that the parish community educate itself in its role of "neighborhood servant," and that in the selection and tenure of parish personnel great consideration should be given to the needs of the neighborhood. (2)

121. That the neighborhood parish ought to make available to competent neighborhood action groups needed facilities and resources; that a budgetary item of every parish to financially support competent neighborhood action groups be considered a necessary investment; that the Church should initiate and be actively involved in the development of community organizing projects among all peoples; that each diocese shall establish an office for community affairs or shall expand its existing office; that the Church should commit itself to the concept of "open neighborhoods," whereby new residents of any race, ethnic group, cultural background or religious faith would be welcomed as brothers and sisters in Christ; and that the urgent need in the inner-city situations mandates that the Church recognize inner-city neighborhoods as territories demanding priority attention. (2)

122. That each diocese recognize the vital responsibility of ministry to Catholics and other persons who ask for our ministry at colleges and universities and allocate a fixed portion of its personnel and resources to assist those people in effective Christian action in their collegiate neighborhoods. (2)

123. That the Church develop an urban social policy that is based on the concept of equality of persons, races, ethnic and culturally diverse groups, and recognize the commitment in every diocese that community development must flow from the needs of the people as identified by the people. (1, 2)

124. That social justice courses in the area of neighborhood parish community development, community organization and multi-cultural education be mandatory in the training of seminaries and in the continuing education of clergy and religious. (1)

125. That in each diocese the decision whether or not to close parishes and schools should include the involvement of the neighborhood community. (2)

126. That each diocese and state conference should develop a staff position whose major responsibility shall consist of the monitoring and reporting of local, state and federal policy and program initiatives which have impact on the parish/neighborhood community. (2)

127. That the United States Catholic Conference (U.S.C.C.) establish a similar office to coordinate the actions on behalf of social justice and community development of all organizations and institutions of the Church, with special emphasis on housing and employment needs. (3)

128. That there be initiation and continued development of effective advocacy with the poor through the support and expansion of the Campaign for Human Development. (3)

129. That the National Conference of Catholic Bishops (N.C.C.B.) continue its support of the National Rural Life Conference as the American Church's voice for land, town and country related concerns, and that it urge grassroots support adequate for carrying out this role. (3)

130. That there should be an evaluation of Church structures and programs of ministry to the rural community in the light of the present needs for social action, religious education and social services. (1)

131. That the Bishops reevaluate their policies, disbursements of funds and personnel placement in rural communities. (2, 3)

132. That our Bishops be encouraged to address a pastoral letter to the people of their diocese on the dignity of rural life for Christian living. (1)

133. That the Bishops in consultation with the larger Catholic population, develop new structures and ministries appropriate to the needs of rural communities, such as mobile teams of resource persons and new forms of lay leadership and ministry. (1)

134. That national Church organizations consider the needs of more rural dioceses in the location of meetings and allotment of funds. (1)
135. That a special task force be set up through the National Catholic Rural Life Conference to address and develop legislative action relative to the problems of rural poverty, rural health and housing; land use and theology of stewardship; estate, property, and income tax reform; rural financing (redlining); corporate tax deduction (loss) farming; use of food products as a national and international political tool. (2)
136. That the Church support the God-given rights of the poor rural wage earners, immigrants, sharecroppers, and family farmers, and the rights of . . . independent businessmen; and that the Church recognize and encourage their rights to organize. (3)
137. That the N.C.C.B. through the Bicentennial Office establish a representative task force to sustain the Call to Action momentum; to promote the implementation of all the recommendations; and to set in motion another consultation within five years to evaluate the results of this program and to suggest goals for the next period. (1)

1976 East Humboldt Park and Kaptur

A brief look at the 1976 East Humboldt Park proposal of Marcy Kaptur, as recalled by O'Rourke (1991: 119–120) in Baroni's biography, is also instructive of principles guiding Catholic-styled neighborhood revitalization. Of Polish background and technically skilled as a planner, Kaptur was sensitive to urban ethnic values and goals but also had planning skills and expertise in workable approaches. When an opening came in a Chicago project supported by the Center and the Campaign for Human Development, Baroni helped Kaptur get the job in the predominately Polish neighborhood of East Humboldt Park on the northwest side of Chicago, two miles west of Lake Michigan. The neighborhood, which was predominantly Catholic, contained three large Catholic churches. It included a post-War influx of blacks, Mexican Americans, and Puerto Ricans. The city cut a new expressway in the 1950s that forced the eviction of people along eastern border. And many younger people moved to the suburbs in the 1960s. The Catholic parishes called on Cardinal Meyer, archbishop of Chicago, for assistance to stem the outmigration, who gave the assignment to Monsignor John Egan, director of the archdiocesan Office of Urban Affairs. Egan called upon Saul Alinsky, executive director of the Industrial Areas Foundation, to organize the community. It was not long before the Egan/Alinsky team and the area's politicians were in conflict. In response to Mayor Richard J. Daley's Chicago 21 plan, the residents of East Humboldt Park asked what the plan meant for them. So in 1975, residents created a committee to hire a planning consultant to draft a realistic, workable program to improve the area. Baroni's NCUEA was awarded a contract in public bidding and Baroni asked Kaptur to leave the planning board in Toledo and go to East Humboldt Park as his representative. Kaptur's job included guiding the local planning committee and brokering disputes among contending organizations. Working over several months, the committee produced a report, with Kaptur the major author, although in frequent consultation with Baroni and his colleagues back at the Center. As O'Rourke (1991: 121–122) observed, it had these major elements of Baroni's philosophy:

> The basic objective . . . is to insure the residents of the community their right to stay in the neighborhood.
>
> The primary concern is upgrading of the community through repair of older buildings and construction of new homes and apartments on vacant lots without pricing current residents out of the neighborhood. . . .
>
> If there is one underlying theme throughout, it is that the neighborhood unit is recognized as the primary form of human settlement and placed in the special context it deserves. . . . Residential neighborhoods must be protected over time.
>
> The concerns that have surfaced in this community through the planning process revolve mainly around how to keep this a working class area in the face of major rehabilitation and development efforts. This is a particularly important issue here because so many of this community's residents work in the industrial park south of Grand Avenue and are convenient to their place of employment.
>
> In order to keep money that is already here in this area and attract a limited amount of additional wealth, there is a commitment in this plan to provide housing, either new or rehabbed, for the middle income market.

Neighborhood Definition: Beyond Economics

At a conference on the 10th anniversary of Baroni's death sponsored by the Eisenhower Foundation, Representative Kaptur was quick to stress that Baroni insisted that the neighborhood revitalization was more than just "bricks and mortar" redevelopment, it was also about "spirit." Indeed, viewing the neighborhood movement through a Catholic and

Baroni lens requires an understanding that neighborhoods are not merely census tracts or economic units of analysis. As such the neighborhood movement has always drawn on a multitude of approaches and disciplines for defining and looking at neighborhoods.

There is not a single city in the United States without at least some sort of community or neighborhood organization. The daily press overflows with examples of these groups successfully attacking and solving urban problems. They have stopped highways from plowing through their environment. They have closed down or forced changes in companies whose toxic wastes, emissions, and sewage have polluted their neighborhoods. They have used zoning to leverage a stake in how the land in their neighborhood is to be used. Their relationship to each other and to other institutions varies even within apparently similar metropolitan conditions. Various political cultures and emphasis on bureaucracy, conflict, and cooperation influence the consequence of neighborhood leaders and community-based organizations.

The time for systematic policy development and civic/political formation on behalf of neighborhoods as the essential social entities of modern societies has come. The enormity of this task is daunting. For example, despite the validity of developing an ethic of local neighborhoods that seeks to safeguard the entire planetary ecosystem, the experiential reality is echoed in a battle cry that has become increasingly familiar in the last two decades, "Not in my backyard!" While many progressives shake their heads and condescendingly bemoan such small-minded parochialism, the real challenge is to focus communitarian energy in ways that shape and share the burden. To revitalize urban economies and promote peaceful resolution of conflict, one neighborhood at a time, is a radically fresh approach to the relationship between state and civil society, which is constituted by thousands of neighborhoods. How large a task is neighborhood and civic renewal? Discovering what sorts of neighborhood exist in America is among the most important steps toward defining civil society.

In 1979–1980, for the first time, the U.S. Bureau of the Census offered to supply neighborhood statistics to any municipality of 10,000 or more residents that met certain requirements. Information was supplied on 27,000 neighborhoods or 1,252 jurisdictions that requested it. Participation in the Census Bureau's Neighborhood Statistic Program was contingent upon three criteria in addition to the 10,000-plus population size. First, all neighborhoods for which statistics were provided must be official, that is, recognized by the municipality or a central neighborhood council. Secondly, neighborhoods must be distinct: their boundaries could not overlap. Finally, advisory representation was required from each neighborhood. Though the Census data indicate the size and number of neighborhoods as well as social-economic indicators, the issue of neighborhood definition is not entirely resolved. The U.S. Census Neighborhood Statistics Program enabled jurisdictions to design their own approach to neighborhood definition.

Broden et al. (1979) identified six major approaches to defining neighborhoods: (1) homogenous, (2) intimate, (3) political, (4) functional, (5) economic, and (6) citizen perception. Each approach to the neighborhood elucidates dimensions of its essential and local reality.

The homogenous approach generally assumes: a) that cities can be divided into distinct areas using physical boundaries, and b) that there is a tendency for people of similar ethnic and/or demographic characteristics to populate those distinct areas. Cities are viewed as a collection of distinct areas, each with its own homogenous populations, so that each neighborhood tends to act in its own distinct way. A popular variation of this approach is found in Michael Weiss (1989), *The Clustering of America*. Forty types of neighborhoods based on income, home value, and education and other consumer preferences, capacities, and social indicators as well as the prevalence of each of the types were developed by Weiss and his associates at Claritas Corporation.

The intimate definition sees neighborhoods as "urban villages," which are sociological antidotes to the anonymous and impersonal urban industrial life. Primarily sociological, this approach searches for social bonding or networks, which may be based upon familialism, friendship, religion, ethnicity, social interaction, value consensus, and/or the common use of physical facilities. In general, this approach defines a neighborhood as a set of intense and intimate relationships between individuals in a certain locale. The type of communal life or association that creates these bonds or networks influences the degree to which an "intimate" neighborhood is spatial or merely sociological.

The political approach suggests political alliance as the basis for defining neighborhoods, which implies some kind of collective action and commitment. Saul Alinsky argued that cities should respond to community organizations that develop out of specific issues that are not geographic in domain. This approach implicitly and explicitly rejects geographically defined neighborhoods. However, other politically defined notions of neighborhood argue that whenever political power is granted, even through enacted boundaries, real community will arise. A second non-issue political view recognizes geographic boundaries, but generally believes that residents know those boundaries. Democracy breeds community; thus, the political neighborhood results when governance is transferred. A third political approach suggested by governments in nations like China and Cuba is that neighborhoods are urban units of control. These neighborhood-level governmental agencies help decide who goes to college, provide health care, and allocate housing. In addition they promulgate propaganda and act as an intelligence unit to limit dissent.

Another approach believes that neighborhoods are foci of functional common interest. The functional perspective sees neighborhoods as a spatial area whose residents are bound together by common function and institutions: schools, shopping districts, parks, and health care clinics. However, this binding is on a less intense scale than the political or intimate approaches. For example, strong neighborhoods can exist without social intimacy among neighbors when there are strong expectations of property maintenance. The functional approach was very influential in town planning in England, where planners influenced by the Dudley report on town planning (Central Housing Advisory Committee 1944) attempted to create neighborhoods in new towns by such centrally located common services as schools or shopping areas in each area of a city. As a tool for analyzing existing cities, the functional approach locates amenities. User residences then may be mapped to see if geographic clusters emerge.

Broden et al. (1983) identify the economic approach to neighborhood definition and delineation as one that utilizes the perspective of housing markets:

> This approach places heavy emphasis upon the individual consumer who evaluates housing in terms of the physical structure and the environment surrounding it. The "neighborhood" is the locale around a structure which defines the burdens and benefits associated with owning a house in a given location. These burdens and benefits include crime, pollution, schools, parks, zoning provisions, property repair, etc. "Neighborhood viewed in this way is regarded as a distinct housing submarket."

This definition incorporates some of the other perspectives on neighborhood definition because the area that has either very intimate ties or a strong set of functional ties will be identified as a distinct housing submarket. Roos and Swartz (1972) have defined neighborhood as a domain of localized externalities. They suggest that certain activities at the neighborhood level produce costs and benefits for everyone in that area, not just the actor. These positive and negative externalities have spatial domains that define the neighborhood. In addition, housing demands, land use, physical boundaries, and other factors place limits on actual domain.

Finally, a citizen-perception model of neighborhood relies upon boundaries perceived by the citizens. Although this definition may include many of the other perspectives discussed, it is more appropriately a methodology for delineating neighborhoods. While a strict application requires individuals in isolation to draw boundaries from which researchers look for commonalities, a less formal citizen perception approach has been used most notably in Ahlbrandt's and Cunningham's Pittsburgh Neighborhood Atlas. The Atlas was developed through neighborhood group discussions, meetings, and consensus, supplemented by randomly mailed questionnaires, which, in addition to demographic information, asked the respondent for the name of his/her neighborhood. This information was used to map areas by similar responses.

Regardless of the approach used to define neighborhoods, the activities of neighborhood organizations reveal a variety of capacities. The following section identifies generic forms of action that can be regularly found in neighborhoods and indicates the characteristics and limitations of various activities. An inventory of roles and functions provided by neighborhood organizations indicates their potency as a bridge between the governmental and private sectors and their pivotal importance for civil society and its constructive operations. These neighborhood operations are the social products of neighborhood organizations. The importance of this form of social invention cannot be underestimated in any discussion of state and civil society. Understanding this level of social innovation is essential for pathology related to urban life and the realization of multi-ethnic accord in America.

Neighborhood Operations

Safety, Security, and Social Order

This operation consists of activities such as neighborhood crime watch, fostering anti-crime attitudes among residents, cooperating with/monitoring law-enforcement agencies, arson-prevention programs, school-violence prevention activities, and community pressure and sanctions to combat a variety of detrimental social behaviors (dropping out of school, teenage pregnancy, buying stolen property, vandalism, etc.). These activities make the community safe for investments, increase the social and economic participation of residents, and reinforce positive growth-oriented social behavior. The safety, security, and social-order operations help transform the neighborhood by preventing the flight of individuals and families with rising incomes and providing an environment where other operations can be performed effectively.

Neighborhood Improvement/Sanitation

This operation consists of activities such as block clean-up campaigns, community gardens, garbage-collection contracts with local government, and increasing neighborhood amenities such as parks, picnic areas, trees, and shrubs. These activities make the neighborhood look better and residents feel better. The improvement/sanitation operation helps transform the neighborhood by increasing the sense of belonging among residents and increasing their participation in the total revitalization process. Furthermore, visible signs of resident pride and concern in the neighborhood help increase the service response of municipal agencies.

Family Support and Adjustment

This operation consists of activities such as day-care and elder-care programs, youth recreation and development programs, family counseling, drug- and alcohol-abuse assistance, social-service advocacy and guidance. These activities are geared to each subpopulation that requires support to participate in, and contribute to, the economy or needs support to establish or maintain healthy social functioning. This operation helps transform the neighborhood by breaking what many social theorists refer to as "maladaptive, lower-class social pathologies." In addition, family support and adjustment activities form the core of social-service enterprises at the neighborhood level.

Human Capital Development

This operation consists of activities such as employment and training programs, entrepreneurial training, literacy programs, and activities to support public and private elementary and secondary schools that serve neighborhood residents. These activities increase the earning power of local residents. The human-capital-development operation transforms the neighborhood by increasing the immediate marketable skills of residents and enabling neighborhood children eventually to attain higher income levels than their parents. Human-capital development is one prerequisite for increasing community income available for maintaining property, home ownership, and improved cash flows in local enterprises. Distressed communities are characterized by having the local public school as the primary (or sole) vehicle for human-capital development for the overwhelming majority of children and having no major human-capital development efforts for adults.

Income Production

This operation consists of all activities that produce cash income and other financial assets for people residing in the neighborhood. (A neighborhood enterprise that provides income to a nonresident owner/operator and nonresident employees would not be considered an income-production activity in the neighborhood context.) The income-production operation helps transform a distressed neighborhood by maximizing the income of residents by shifting them from a jobless status or welfare dependency to employment and from low-wage to higher-wage jobs. Minimizing participation in antisocial activities such as the sale of illegal drugs also increases income production by reducing the presence in the neighborhood of items or activities that destroy earning and educational capacities and fostering an environment conducive to maintaining middle-income families. Increasing income is a prerequisite for successful human-capital development, property maintenance, and support operation. Government subsidies and private-sector grants for human-capital development, property maintenance, and family services can improve conditions temporarily, but long-term success is dependent on increasing the income residents can devote to these operations.

Property Maintenance

This operation consists of activities such as facade improvements, house-painting programs, landscaping programs, tool-lending libraries, home-improvement and maintenance workshops, low-interest renovation loans, and other activities that preserve, maintain, or improve the value of residential and commercial property in the neighborhood. These activities increase the financial assets of the residents and provide a basis for maintaining an influx of new families with incomes equal to or surpassing the incomes of existing residents. Property is second in improvement only to the residents themselves as a neighborhood asset.

Health

The operation consists of activities such as prenatal-care classes and clinics, health-maintenance organizations, hospital services, and home health care for the elderly. These activities decrease health problems that impede resident participation in the work force, education, or training. Adequate access to good health-care facilities is an important factor influencing the mobility patterns of middle-income families or families rising out of poverty. Furthermore, health-care services are a major source of jobs that can be located in the neighborhood.

Transportation

This operation consists of activities to increase the mobility and economic participation of residents as consumers and wage earners. Activities such as van pools to transport local residents to suburban jobs, transportation services for the elderly, and political activities to influence mass-transit routes and fares are common in revitalizing neighborhoods. (Revitalizing neighborhoods were observed to be characterized by a high percentage of car ownership by families, or numerous mass-transit routes through the neighborhood, or community-owned van-pool or mini-bus services.)

Neighborhood Organizations

Activities and accomplishments by neighborhood organizations in American neighborhoods give a more complete picture of how neighborhood organizations fulfill their purposes. The following are examples of some specific approaches:

The Broadway-Fillmore Neighborhood Coalition in Buffalo, New York, has sponsored various forums and meetings among residents, city officials and private interests to assure that renovation of the local Broadway Market runs smoothly and meets the ongoing needs of residents, including the elderly. This market is more than just a food distribution facility to long-time residents; it is a longstanding neighborhood institution and landmark.

Citizens to Bring Broadway Back in Cleveland's near southeast side has worked on several issues which relate directly to the quality of life of the local elderly. They worked diligently to see that a new fire station was built in the neighborhood, they worked with other local groups and agencies to catalyze the development of a $3 million, 70-unit, elderly highrise in the neighborhood, and they have worked for several years on issues relating to crime prevention, fuel cost containment, and the provision of adequate human services for residents.

Kensington Action Now in Philadelphia has maintained the membership of senior-citizen associations over the years and has worked on specific issues relating to seniors through an ongoing Senior Committee. Activities have included convincing the Philadelphia Corporation to plan a "meals on wheels" program in the neighborhood, work on various crime and arson prevention issues that led to, among other things, increased police patrols, and work to establish a senior-citizen center in the neighborhood.

The Human Action Community Organization (HACO) of Harvey, Illinois, responded to a growing crime rate affecting its elderly by organizing an all-volunteer Victim/Witness Assistance Program which included quarterly meetings with police, prosecutors and judges to assure cooperation, a quarterly accountability meeting with the State's Attorney's Office, the assignment of only one prosecutor to each case in order to ensure continuity in each case, notices to victims/witnesses a week before court dates, an escort service to transport and protect elderly victims and witnesses, a nightly patrol of the homes of victims/witnesses by HACO's crime Stop Patrols, and presentation meetings with the prosecutor's office.

The Washington Heights/Inwood Coalition in Manhattan provides a Community Mediation Service which helps residents, including the elderly, to deal with conflict on an intra-family, inter-family, or intra-neighborhood level.

United Seniors in Action, in both Minneapolis and Indianapolis, carried out city-wide campaigns to win discounts on prescription drugs of 10–25 percent from major regional stores.

Asylum Hill Organization in Hartford, Connecticut, is a coalition of seniors, tenants and issue groups which work on the problems of housing, crime, health care, youth and unemployment. Its member group, Seniors for Action in Asylum Hill, has focused recently on increasing police foot patrols, reducing prostitute activity, developing better elderly transportation services, and keeping open a local medical clinic that serves 3,000 elderly and low-income residents.

The way in which neighborhood organizations assist in the provision of human services to their communities are varied, but the basic approaches and strategies common to all multi-issue, multi-based neighborhood organizations involve empowering neighborhood resources. Whether one targets youth, families, tenants, homeowners, or the elderly for assistance in a neighborhood, neighborhood organizations offer the opportunity for residents to join together on specific, immediate, and realizable issues and projects that, in the end, will benefit everyone.

To simply isolate a certain group, for example, the elderly, as a specific "consumer" of human services is to overlook a number of their most important needs as residents in the community. They need to feel some degree of control over their lives. They also want to feel that they are a part of the mainstream of the community. And they need those natural support systems that come through interaction with other generations and groups in the community. Multi-based neighborhood organizations can fulfill these needs and others simply through basic processes that are common to all organizing efforts (Broden et al. 1983; Cunningham and Kotler 1983; Boyte 1984; Hollman 1984).

Beyond the organizing processes themselves, neighborhood organization successes often include either new, expanded, or improved service for all in the community–from the most vital and active ones to those most dependent on others for basic needs. Not the least important of these needs are economic development and housing fostered by development.

Neighborhood Development Corporations

Neighborhood development corporations are growing in both their numbers and in their capacity as catalysts for development and revitalization in American neighborhoods. As with multi-issue neighborhood-based organizations, these institutions undertake activities that relate to a variety of constituent groups in a community. The ventures they develop generally cut across generational and ethnic lines, often including the entire community, from the earliest planning phases to such end results as an improved flow of goods and services in and out of the community and the revitalization of buildings, residences, and facilities.

Factors that ensure a steady rise in production, distribution, and ownership within a community form a complex equation that depends largely upon localized characteristics, dynamics, and developments. Yet, as with neighborhood organizations, there is a common set of tools, resources, and organizing approaches neighborhood-development practitioners can use in developing the community and promoting its full economic potential, the range of which can be seen in the following examples of approaches designed to assist the elderly:

Greater Southwest Development Corporation in Chicago has responded to a growing housing problem among the neighborhood's elderly homeowners. The houses in which they have lived for years are in need of upgrading, regular maintenance and constant small repairs, but they cannot afford all the costs involved, and they are increasingly limited in the amount of sweat equity they can invest personally in their homes. Greater Southwest established a Senior Citizen/Handicapped Home Repair Service which uses grant money and other resources to address this need. The corporation is also initiating the development of a senior-citizen apartment complex.

Broadway Development Corporation in Cleveland is developing a $2.5 million renovation of a vacant, dilapidated commercial building to create a new mini-mall for the neighborhood. They are also assisting a family-owned grocery store in an expansion project which will double the size of the store and expand the food services available to the community. Lastly, they are working on the renovation of an unused theater building which will create low-cost apartments in the heart of the commercial corridor of the neighborhood.

The Lawrenceville Development Corporation in Pittsburgh is a new neighborhood-development corporation established to provide a vehicle through which the neighborhood can undertake specific housing, commercial and industrial development ventures. One of its major goals is to revitalize the commercial corridor by attracting new businesses and assisting others.

The Liberty Communities Development Corporation of Baltimore has advocated and participated in the early planning of a multi-purpose center which will include senior-citizen services as one-third of its activities. The services will include crafts and other social activities, health services, transportation to and from the center, "meals on wheels," and lunches at the center. The organization has worked also with a local food-store owner who runs a shuttle bus between the shopping center where his store is located and several local elderly apartment complexes.

These examples indicate the variety of levels through which development corporations can assist a community. The Greater Southwest Development Corporation example shows how a development corporation can be very directly involved in the lives of the elderly through such things as home-maintenance services. The Liberty Communities Development Corporation example demonstrates the potential role of development corporations as advocates, planners, and/or coalition builders in the expansion or creation of services. The Broadway Development Corporation indicates how a neighborhood corporation can indirectly better the quality of life for Americans by strengthening the neighborhood's commercial corridor and ultimately keeping the flow of goods and services where residents can get at them. Some neighborhood organizations specialize in social and medical services that are not usually available locally nor adequately provided by external professional service providers. Social workers in cooperation with neighborhood organizations are bridging the gap between client and the professional service providers.

Neighborhood-Based Social Services

As with other major neighborhood entities, neighborhood service providers generally serve a wide range of age groups within a community. For this reason, they often function as multi-purpose or multi-service centers, offering a variety of activities and programs, including youth services, winterization programs, job training and counseling, child care, recreation and cultural enrichment programs, health services, and senior-citizen programs. In fact, because of their ability to provide a human services "tool box" within a community, the other major neighborhood entities make regular referrals to them, pass out literature about their services, and serve on their boards in order to assure that the "tool box" is being used effectively.

The following examples demonstrate how neighborhood service providers can serve a very positive role for persons in American neighborhoods:

HARBEL, Inc. of Baltimore is a multi-purpose neighborhood center on the city's northeast side. It provides a range of services and has an ongoing committee structure in youth counseling and services, neighborhood operations, crime prevention, mental health, community information, and housing assistance. Those programs which help the elderly include mental-health outreach services, home-sharing service, winterization programs, the senior committee, advocacy for and among elderly member groups, and work to further develop the neighborhood's natural helping networks.

The North Ward Educational and Cultural Center serves a large Italian community in Newark. Begun in 1971, it offers a variety of programs and services, including early childhood development, youth enrichment, senior-citizen services, recreation activities, education, vocational training, interaction, health services, cultural-awareness programs and building-restoration assistance. The senior-citizen services have a staff of their own and reach out to more than 2,000 Italian-American elderly. The services provided these elderly include medical transportation, shopping and recreational transportation, outreach, nutrition, information and referral, educational activities, employment, cultural awareness, health screenings and youth escorts.

Employment support group networks in such cities as Chicago and Washington provide the elderly and other unemployed individuals the opportunity to work together for a common goal—employment. The Employment Support Center in Washington offers a variety of employment services to its member self-help groups, including job leads, career counseling, guest speakers, and referrals.

In the older industrial cities, poverty remains high among the elderly. According to Representative Augustus Hawkins and the National Council of Senior Citizens, 25 percent of the elderly live below the poverty level and only 12 percent are employed. Only 21 percent of displaced older workers have found new jobs. An employment "tool box" such as those supplied through employment-support networks may be an important way to address these problems.

In addition to employment-related services, it is clear that neighborhood centers such as HARBEL, Inc. and the North Ward Educational and Cultural Center are effective because they provide elderly services as part of a more comprehensive approach to the overall needs of the neighborhood. They serve a networking, information-sharing, and cohesion-building function as much as they serve a service-delivery function. Their relationship to churches, neighborhood groups, and other neighborhood entities makes them a natural focal point for helping networks in the neighborhood.

Our experiences with and analysis of elderly ethnic Americans suggest that their lack of representation on hospital boards, United Way planning boards, and in the direction of health-planning boards, as well as their absence from the executive suites of major corporations and foundations, has minimized their influence in shaping the nation's care system. The reshaping of accountable and responsive health care is an ideal intergovernmental organizing issue that ethnic leaders should explore.

Local Health Care Campaigns

The ethnic elderly in urban neighborhoods are especially affected by disparities in the health-care system. Among other factors, rising costs, inadequate or absent insurance coverage, and the reduction of public and non-profit hospitals in cities have strained everyone and have especially hurt the elderly. Ethnic elderly may be especially strained not only because they live in cities and because they are elderly, but also because they do not have designated minority status and therefore may not qualify for certain kinds of assistance. Cultural and language barriers may also keep the ethnic elderly from seeking the service they deserve. Rather than organizing to gain minority status, the neighborhoods and communities in which ethnic-American elderly live should organize around convergent issues that the American health-care system has produced and that affect all of the residents.

Local health care campaigns can be effective ways of winning discounts for the elderly from local businesses, hospitals, and doctors, of securing waivers for home and community-based long-term care, of providing transportation services, of utilizing alternative providers, and of getting and using good generic drug laws. Effective health care organizing strategies may grow out of community and neighborhood organizations, concerned parishes, neighborhood residents, and coalitions between and among any or all of these and other neighborhood entities.

The Villar Foundation (1984) published a comprehensive health care organizing manual, which outlines some of the following campaigns:

Hospitals

A hospital campaign is based on focusing upon one hospital to urge its physicians with admitting privileges to accept assignment and provide other Medicare discounts. Hospitals that need to fill up their beds may be willing partners in this campaign based on the prospect that an agreement with the hospital and the doctors who use it will result in increased Medicare utilization. Successful assignment campaigns are based on the perception that enough new patients can be delivered to the targeted provider(s) to make the contract economically worth their while. This can begin on a small scale; the campaign will attract seniors because of its obvious economic advantages.

Doctors

A few years ago, a campaign to convince doctors to accept assignment and provide other discounts for Medicare patients would have had a 50-50 chance of success, at best. But times are changing and physicians now are more amenable than in the past. The success of a physician campaign depends on two approaches. (1) Competition: physicians in over-doctored areas may quickly understand the economic benefits of more patients and free publicity (programs provide enrollees with a list of doctors who have signed on). (2) Guilt and Social Responsibility: as seniors make their plight over medical costs better known, doctors are put in an awkward position. It is heartless for Dr. Greed, who makes $200,000 a year, to charge so much that poor Mrs. Smith with an income of $5,000 a year can not afford to see him.

Transportation Services

The availability of all the medical services in the world is useless if one cannot get to them. Large numbers of the elderly and disabled cannot get health care because they lack transportation to get there. Federal Medicaid regulations issued in 1969 (42 Code of Federal Regulations (CFR) 431.53) require that state Medicaid plans specify that the Medicaid agency will assure necessary transportation for recipients to and from providers, and describe the methods that will be used to meet this requirement. Besides Medicaid, there are other sources of funding for the "transportation disadvantaged." These include Title III of the Older Americans Act, Section 16 (b) (2) of the Urban Mass Transportation Act and Section 18 of the Surface Transportation Assistance Act. Unfortunately, there is little coordination between these various programs, and state transportation plans often either exist only on paper or adopt such strict limits on reimbursable transportation services that few, if any, recipients actually receive help.

Alternative Providers

One way both to increase access and to reduce the cost of care is through the use of alternative providers: nurse practitioners, physician assistants, nurse-midwives, birth centers, and women's clinics. Alternative providers reduce the cost of health care because of their low-technology approach and reasonable charges. They improve access because they practice in underserved areas. They can provide high-quality preventive and primary care. The use of alternative providers has special implications for improved care for the elderly. Alternative providers spend more time with their patients, a crucial ingredient for dealing with the chronically ill. Despite proven benefits of alternative providers, many states limit their practice through licensure procedures. Physicians' strong combat of any attempt to liberalize these laws requires difficult, time-consuming campaigns. A variety of different campaigns can be waged to increase the utilization of alternative providers. Some campaigns have tried to influence hospitals to grant these providers admitting privileges, to get third party payers to reimburse their services, or to protect them through anti-trust legislation. Other campaigns have been aimed successfully at changing state licensure laws.

Generic Drug Laws

Generic-drug-law campaigns seek to increase the role of the patient and, to some extent, the pharmacist in the decision-making process when a patient takes a prescription to the pharmacy. Too often the pharmacist looks at the prescription and dispenses exactly what the prescription says, charging the going rate for brand names. One approach is to require the pharmacist to lay the choice before the customer and allow the customer to make the final decision. Another approach is to demand that the state agency which regulates pharmacies conduct spot checks with undercover inspectors. Still another option is to work for a law requiring that the prices of the best-selling drugs be posted; however, even when this is enacted, many generics don't appear on the top 50 best-selling lists. Generally the best approach is to pay special attention to ways to get the responsible state agency to monitor and enforce the provisions of the law, to get generic drug prices posted along with brand-name prices, and to obtain stiff penalties for violations.

The Ethnic Factor—Again

The legacy and lens of Monsignor Baroni reflects that the civil rights movement and the neighborhood movements should not be decoupled and that mere racialism must broaden to include ethnicity and true pluralism. We think that this reflects substantive justice found in the Catholic perspective on enculturation as well as the procedural justice that appreciates the value of coupling issues rather than decoupling them. Cardinal Bernardin's "seamless garment" analogy (McBrien 2008), which coupled abortion, euthanasia, the death penalty, war, poverty, and human rights, is a classic contemporary example. This, in one more way, highlights that the Catholic perspective on neighborhood revitalization is symphonic and complex as opposed to the Georgist "one note" Single Tax on Land. On one hand, George (1962: Book X, chapter 2) seemed to have had a pluralistic and generous view of culture that reflected a view of "race" that in his time had not yet become rigidified into a mere black/white polarity. On the other hand, he seems to suggest that keeping up "cultural" identity ("maintenance" as he describes it) wastes "mental power" that might otherwise be devoted to progress (George 1962: Book X, chapter 3). Catholicism has obviously seen it differently. To paraphrase Baroni, the "ethnic traditions" are a source of both roots and wings.

The contemporary disarray of the U.S. Civil Rights Commission and the flagging impulses of the civil rights movement can be traced to failures of insight and strategy that separated the civil rights and neighborhood movements. A review of this unfortunate cleavage indicates that it is time to put new wine into the skins of a public agency and a newly inspired citizens' movement. The experiences and disillusionment of the last decade require a new vision of the American reality—not an impossible dream, but a practical community-based approach to urban life for a pluralistic and diverse urban society composed of thousands of neighborhoods.

On one level, the civil rights movement of the 1960s addressed universal human concerns; but on another level it was an attempt to solve a regional problem. The movement embodied an understanding of problems and applied a set of approaches that derived largely from the experience in the South. The slavery experience and its consequences had seared the American conscience in the 19th century. The destruction of its ancient vestiges seared the nation again in our time, once more burning its grief and anger beyond the South.

There were indeed serious social, economic, and civil injustices in the Southwest, Midwest, and North. Poor, powerless, and excluded ethnic Americans had suffered crippling disabilities as a result of discrimination. Yet, it is not at all true, as some asserted, that racism was as deep and as intractable in these regions as it was in the South. The apparent intractability of racism in the industrial cities of the Northeast and Midwest, for example, was a result of faulty analysis and inappropriate approaches to the tasks of justice. Attempts to change patterns and practices that had not been born out of racism (or the desire to discriminate) were optimistically initiated throughout these regions, as well as the entire nation. These attempts gained political momentum; their desire for liberty, justice, and freedom invigorated the spirit of at least one generation.

Because the social reality and common dynamics of a divided nation with unique regional and local characteristics were more complicated and complex, however, the struggle against racism yielded uneven and unanticipated results. Such results grew, at least in part, out of an inability to recognize the importance of, as well as the lack of support for, community-based institutions. The influence of local economic and social-justice institutions on individuals and communities was painfully slow and inefficient for the nationalizing and modernizing thrust of self-confident legal activists and universalist technocrats. Thus, their national efforts tended to devalue all such institutions and their critique of racism and the Southern experience was expanded to a critique of all localism.

Without challenging their critique of racism in the South, it is nonetheless clear and certain that the Southern experience, for the most part, was unlike the urban neighborhood reality of the Northeast and Midwest. In fact, the entire experience of racism in America is overlaid with an array of other experiences and realities. The factors of pluralism, class, ownership, diversity, unionism, education, and coalition politics addressed by political organizations are particularly salient for understanding why the pursuit of civil liberties presented an entirely different challenge to the communities of the Northeast and Midwest.

To focus merely upon racism in the struggle for justice revealed a poverty of analysis that neglected to calculate other intrinsic elements and factors of life there and in other regions. It neglected the importance of community cohesion and non-governmentally negotiated approaches to resolving social and economic inequity, as well as the often modest but usually lasting results brought about by indigenous organization and self-help community-based techniques. To ignore and neglect these complex and sophisticated factors illustrates an inability to understand pluralism, diversity, and the social texture from which citizenship emerged in America. Public therapy cannot be based on an inaccurate analysis of the social reality it intends to cure. A similar misdiagnosis may exist today.

Advocates of social justice may have lost their base of support; various public entitlements are threatened and the civil rights movement is divided and conquered by "the opposition." We are, in fact, at a moment in public affairs when advocates for the public good may succeed, like Pogo, in doing themselves in. By the mid 1980s the stridency of single-issue groups, the rhetoric of racism and bigotry, ethnocentric and religious righteousness, and anti-immigrant hysteria all have strained the coalition-building process. Social and economic analysis designed to measure and remedy illegal discrimination have become twisted debates. Divisive contentions about the reality or relative intensity of racial, ethnic, religious, and sexual inequality have become cost-benefit calculations. The claims of the elderly and handi-capped have fragmented even further the original thrust for liberty and justice. Contradictory findings from many social sciences are used to buttress these conflicting claims for remedies and results. Allowing ourselves to be goaded into such a morass of narrow and special pleas demeans all claims for social and civil justice.

Moreover, it is time to acknowledge that civil rights can hardly be guaranteed if their protection is dependent solely on efforts of a concerned government agency. The civil rights establishment must address the urgent task of enabling persons concerned with civil rights to take the lead once again in designing a new agenda.

It is time for new directions that transcend both the politics of regional approaches to national needs and the politics of designated special status and inter-ethnic manipulation in America. To renew the civil rights movement we need a long-range politics of human devel-opment that transcends region and ethnicity but does not ignore it, which improves economic well-being based on work and need and transcends the politics of unionism and designated special status but does not ignore the dynamics of influence, access, advantage, and mobility, which recognizes that America is, as Father Hesburgh, a former member of the U.S. Commission on Civil Rights, said, "a nation that promised hope, promised dignity and promised freedom for people." These are the political promises we must learn to keep! Finally, though a national effort in civil rights is needed, it is time to recall the words of John Hannah, another former member of the Commission, "If my years of experience here taught me one thing it is that the problem of civil rights may be solved not by national programs, but by local programs; not by federal action, but by community action" (personal recollection).

In the 1960s in America the civil rights movement agreed on the need for national action in search of justice. In the 1980s Americans began to challenge the efficacy of national institutions, with campaign rhetoric appealing to voter dissatisfaction with government and public regulations. This same impulse, however, has provoked another sort of social force, which has coalesced in the neighborhood movement. Rather than endorsing the critique of bankrupt policy by electing anti-government candidates, which simply yields questions of public order to private power, the neighborhood movement calls for the recovery of citizenship through the empowerment of government in support of community-based institutions. The challenge of the 1980s was to secure civil rights in communities and to discover how community-based power can be leveraged beyond a locality and region. The National Neighborhood Coalition argued that it was time for governments to listen to their neighborhoods and thereby to balance the influences of organized interests and private power in America (Hollman 1982).

A reenergized Commission on Civil Rights (CCR) could become the champion of the American neighborhoods and bring their story to government. A renewed CCR could also shape a civil rights agenda designed to understand, to protect, and to encourage community-based institutions. Community-based institutions can create a sense of human scale, individual efficacy, and common citizenship. There is abundant evidence in many countries that community-based institutions have brought about wholesome and helpful bonds between individuals, as well as between people and large-scale institutions. In fact, community-based institutions may create the bonds of social solidarity needed to assure fairness from the government, corporations, the communications industries, and organized interests that dominate the riot of resourcing and litigation that many modern national governments have become.

A society of unconnected and autonomous persons in perpetual litigation, engaged in never-ending struggles for limited resources, hardly engenders the virtues and goals sought through civil rights laws. On the contrary, such strains in times of emergency could well lead to political disintegration and require extraordinary and tyrannical corporate and military remedies. In the face of such a future, the importance of non-governmental institutions as the seedbed of human dignity and civil rights in this society should not be ignored.

Advocacy for enforcement of civil rights laws is no longer sufficient. It is time to refocus the vision of justice, which guides people by reconstituting the bonds of solidarity at the neighborhood level. Discussions regarding the creation or recreation of the CCR provides an appropriate public moment for a renewal of the civil rights movement and the recovery of social solidarity and civility. Such renewal and recovery of certain basic elements of a national tradition can begin because the vast majority of citizens of all ethnic, religious, and cultural traditions believe in liberty and justice for all.

The civil rights movement has demonstrated that society can be changed by political speech and penetrated by legal power. Yet 30 years of progress and growth have shifted public attitudes in a variety of ways. Measured levels of trust in large-scale institutions have plummeted. Many have grown increasingly distrustful of activities supported by large-scale corporations, the national government, and even national service and religious institutions. Confidence is waning in sophisticated systems designed to assure defense and safety. The ability of these institutions to meet national needs is uncertain. We appear to be facing a crisis of confidence and trust. The movement towards liberty and justice for all seems derailed.

It is the moment to explore neighborliness as a certain and basic social and moral feature of the national reality. At minimum, cognizance of the neighborhood in the national equation should enable us to limit the exacerbation of our problems and perhaps enable us to prevent the further erosion into irrelevance of the civil rights movement.

Understanding and governing with civility a neighborhood is a task of uneven difficulty. Therefore, it is important to appreciate the sometimes messy attempts to understand contingency and complexity in human affairs. *A priori* recognition of complexity, not the pretense of righteousness and moral superiority, are essential pre-conditions for the peaceful resolution of conflict, the equitable distribution of resources, and the building of coalitions. Preaching simple answers to a neighborhood or a nation is not an adequate substitute for understanding the dynamics of power and order in an industrial, multi-class, multi-cultural, and multi-ethnic urban world. In fact, it is precisely the analytical and rhetorical failures and the resulting political inability to maintain the necessary coalitions to resolve conflicts that provoked the deterioration of public affairs and undermined the covenant of consent that "inspirited" national promises. Ironically, the legal struggle for rights and the passion of religious language in politics often eroded the bonds of community in which both were rooted. The legal-religious approach was fueled by an unspoken belief that great words produced lasting institutional change and assumed that guilt was a primary moral sentiment.

Given the current focus on economic solutions for human difficulties, the importance of reenergizing the civil rights movement is particularly acute. It is time to recall that, at the deepest level, civility and civil rights are not merely the products of inspired speech and law. They spring from the best and most generous impulses in human society and culture and by most are created, experienced, and learned through and in living communities. For all of their weaknesses and supposed closed character, the structures of society that bring people together, at the human face-to-face level of existence, remain the most lasting and effective guarantee of personhood and civil well-being. Czeslaw Milosz (1980), in his Nobel Award lecture, points toward the enormity of the loss that must be overcome when these little worlds of learning, meaning, and social solidarity are destroyed:

> Perhaps our most precious gift . . . is respect and gratitude for certain things which protect us from internal disintegration and from yielding to tyranny. Precisely for that reason, some ways of life, some institutions become a target for the fury of evil forces—above all, the bonds between people that exist organically, as if by themselves, sustained by family, religion, neighborhood, common heritage. In other words, in many countries traditional bonds of civitas have been subject to a gradual erosion and their inhabitants become disinherited without realizing it.

The poor, powerless, and ignored ethnic and excluded racial groups are signs of unfulfilled promises, but the profound disintegration of the generous and open spirit that made these promises is a stunning irony. It is time to remember national promises of dignity, liberty, and justice for all. To rebuild community in America on an understanding of its complexity, its pluralism and the importance of small-scale community-based institutions is the agenda for the renewal and recovery of solidarity in the pursuit of justice.

Such an enterprise should be grounded in an understanding of the experiences of American neighborhoods, an appreciation of their diversity, and particularly the ethnic elderly who have been ignored and neglected. The preceding discussion of neighborhood definition and operations as well as the examples of approaches used by neighborhood organizations indicate elements of the effort needed to recover and to renew the capacity of community-based institutions. They also suggest the task of reshaping public policy in ways that would not impede and may support the efforts of neighborhood organizations—people helping people equitably to distribute the public and private resources that large-scale modern bureaucratic institutions have used to disenfranchise them and make them a dependent element of public and private domination.

Conclusions and Recommendations

Neighborhoods are a strong determinant of the quality of American life: families live and rear their children in a neighborhood setting, youth are affected by the opportunities and influences they find in their neighborhoods, and older people treasure their neighborhood and look to it for the support they need for independent living. Persons of all ages, income groups, races, and ethnicities want to live in neighborhoods that are safe and clean, contain decent, affordable housing and suitable community facilities, and offer opportunities for civic participation and self-determination.

A variety of neighborhood entities contribute to achieving better communities, including parishes, community newspapers, neighborhood organizations, neighborhood development corporations, neighborhood service providers, and fraternal associations. They should be carefully targeted and thoughtfully assisted in a manner that fosters active and productive partnerships between public agencies, private institutions, and neighborhood-based organizations. Residents should be fully involved in the planning, implementation, monitoring, and evaluation of all public and private programs affecting their neighborhood.

The public and private sectors can make significant contributions to neighborhood life. It is particularly important that sufficient capital flows to lower-income neighborhoods to permit home ownership, housing rehabilitation, development of new enterprises, and support of existing ones. This should be facilitated through a combination of regulations assuring fair treatment of all neighborhoods and selective tax measures offering extra incentives to invest in neighborhoods with the greatest needs. If the land tax can actually be part of ensuring that process, then the data must be prepared to show it so that citizens can support it and elected officials can enact it.

Neighborhood residents need the organizational capacity and sufficient resources to initiate self-help activities and participate as full partners with the public and private sectors. The experience of the past 20 years has shown that small amounts of federal, foundation, and private funds have served as fruitful catalysts in helping various neighborhood entities carry out programs and activities in response to unmet needs. Within their program spheres, these sources of funding and capital should see that the appropriate resources and technical assistance are available for neighborhood-based activities, including community development, housing, youth employment, job training, education, economic development, crime prevention, and health and human services. That a comprehensive approach to neighborhood stabilization and revitalization is required is the legacy the neighborhood movement, as part of the longstanding tradition of Catholic social justice, put into actual successful action.

References

Adreassi, A. (2000). "Fighting Ed McGlynn." *Commonweal*, September 22.
Boyte, H. C. (1984). *Community Is Possible*. New York: Harper & Row.
Broden, T., R. Kirkwood, L. J. Roos, and T. Swartz. (1979). *Neighborhood Identification Handbook*. Washington, DC: United States Department of Housing and Urban Development.
———. (1983). "Neighborhood Definitions: A Bibliography." In *Strengthening Volunteers Initiatives*, 2nd edition. Washington, DC: National Council of Urban Education Associations.
Canon Law Society of America (1999). *Code of Canon Law, Latin-English Edition, New English Translation*. Washington, DC. Available at: http://www.intratext.com/IXT/ENG0017/

Central Housing Advisory Committee (1944). *Design of Dwellings.* London: HMSO.

Committee for the Bicentennial (1975). *Liberty and Justice for All: A Discussion Guide.* Washington, DC: National Conference of Catholic Bishops.

Committee for the Call to Action Plan (1978). *Final Committee Evaluations of the Call to Action Recommendations.* Washington, DC: National Conference of Catholic Bishops.

Cunningham, J. V., and M. Kotler. (1983). *Building Neighborhood Organizations.* South Bend, IN: University of Notre Dame Press.

Fox, T. (1978). "Made in Detroit." *Commonweath,* November 19: 746.

George, H. (1962). *Progress and Poverty.* New York: Robert Schalkenbach Foundation.

Greeley, A. (1975). "Catholic Social Activism: Real or Rad/Chic?" *National Catholic Reporter,* February 7.

Hollman, H. W. (1982). *A Declaration of Neighborhood Roles, Rights and Responsibilities.* Washington, DC: Neighborhood Coalition.

———. (1984). *Neighborhoods: Their Place in Urban Life.* Beverly Hills: Sage Publications.

John Paul II (1991). *Centesimus Annus.* Available at: http://www.vatican.va/edocs/ENG0214/_INDEX.HTM.

Kromkowski, J. A., A. Naparstek, and G. Baroni. (1976). "Neighborhood Revitalization: Neighborhood Policy for a Pluralistic Urban Society." Presented at the White House Conference on Ethnicity and Neighborhood, May 5.

McBrien, R. P. (2008). "Cardinal Bernardin's Seamless Garment." *National Catholic Reporter,* December 26. Available at: http://ncronline.org/node/2926.

Milosz, C. (1980). *Nobel Award Lecture.* New York: Farrar Strauss Giroux.

O'Rourke, L. (1991). "GENO: The Life and Mission of Geno Baroni." Mahwah, NJ: Paulist Press.

Paul VI (1967). *Populorum progression.* Available at: http://www.vatican.va/holy_father/paul_vi/encyclicals/documents/hf_p-vi_enc_26031967_populorum_en.html.

———. (1971). *Octogesima adveniens.* Available at: http://www.vatican.va/holy_father/paul_vi/apost_letters/documents/hf_p-vi_apl_19710514_octogesima-adveniens_en.html.

Roos, L. J., and T. Swartz. (1972). *Workable Program for Community Development.* South Bend, IN: City of South Bend and United States Department of Housing and Urban Development.

United States Catholic Bishops (1986). *Economic Justice for All: Pastoral Letter on Catholic Social Teaching and the U.S. Economy.* Washington, DC: National Conference of Catholic Bishops. Available at: http://www.usccb.org/upload/economic_justice_for_all.pdf.

United States National Conference of Catholic Bishops (1978). *To Do the Work of Justice: A Plan of Action for the Catholic Community in the U.S.* Available at: http://www.justpeace.org/NCCB541978.htm.

Varacalli, J. (1980). *The American Catholic Call for Liberty and Justice for All: An Analysis in the Sociology of Knowledge*, Ph.D. dissertation. New Brunswick: Rutgers, the State University of New Jersey.

Villar Foundation (1984). *The Best Medicine: Organizing Local Health Care Campaigns*. Washington, DC: Villar Foundation.

Weiss, M. (1989). *The Clustering of America*. New York: Harper Collins.

World Synod of Catholic Bishops (1971). *Justitia in mundo*. Available at: http://catholicsocialservices.org.au/Catholic_Social_Teaching/Justitia_in_ Mundo.

Index

for